LEADERSHIP FOR AMERICA

REBUILDING THE PUBLIC SERVICE

LEADERSHIP FOR AMERICA

REBUILDING THE PUBLIC SERVICE

THE REPORT OF
THE NATIONAL COMMISSION
ON THE PUBLIC SERVICE
AND THE TASK FORCE REPORTS
TO THE NATIONAL COMMISSION
ON THE PUBLIC SERVICE

Paul A. Volcker, *Chairman*

Washington : 1989

Lexington Books
D.C. Heath and Company / Lexington, Massachusetts / Toronto

Library of Congress Cataloging-in-Publication Data

National Commission on the Public Service (U.S.)
 Leadership for America : rebuilding the public service / the
report of the National Commission on the Public Service, Paul A.
Volcker, chairman.
        p.   cm.
 Includes bibliographical references.
 ISBN 0-669-21844-8 (alk. paper). — ISBN 0-669-21843-X (pbk. : alk. paper)
 1. Civil service—United States. 2. Civil service—United States—
Personnel management. 3. Government productivity—United States.
4. United States—Officials and employees—Salaries, etc.
I. Volcker, Paul A. II. Title.
JK643.C87 1989
353.006—dc20   89–13243
                                                         CIP

Published simultaneously in Canada
Printed in the United States of America
Casebound International Standard Book Number: 0-669-21844-8
Paperbound International Standard Book Number: 0-669-21843-X
Library of Congress Catalog Card Number: 89-13243

The paper used in this publication meets the minimum requirements of
American National Standard for Information Sciences—Permanence of
Paper for Printed Library Materials, ANSI Z39.48–1984. ∞™

Year and number of this printing:

89 90 91 10 9 8 7 6 5 4 3 2 1

THE NATIONAL COMMISSION ON THE PUBLIC SERVICE

Paul A. Volcker, *Chairman*

STAFF

L. Bruce Laingen, *Executive Director*

Paul C. Light, *Senior Advisor*

Joseph Laitin, *Public Relations Consultant*

Diane Dziwura Yendrey, *Executive Assistant*

Marjorie C. Jones, *Graduate Assistant*

Joseph Foote, *Editor*

TASK FORCE CHAIRMEN AND PROJECT DIRECTORS

Task Force on Public Perceptions of the Public Service

Leonard H. Marks and J. Robert Schaetzel, *Co-Chairmen*

Thomas W. Kell, *Project Director*

Task Force on Recruitment and Retention

Rocco C. Siciliano, *Chairman*

Patricia W. Ingraham, *Project Director*

Task Force on Education and Training

Derek Bok, *Chairman*

Peter Zimmerman, *Project Director*

Task Force on Relations Between Political Appointees and Career Executives

Elliot L. Richardson, *Chairman*

James P. Pfiffner, *Project Director*

Task Force on Pay and Compensation

James L. Ferguson, *Chairman*

Lyn M. Holley, *Project Director*

IN MEMORIAM

Dr. Charles H. Levine, Distinguished Professor of Government and Public Administration at The American University, served as Deputy Director of the Commission staff until his death on September 23, 1988, at age 49. His own wish was that this report, to which he contributed so heavily, might reflect something of his sense of commitment to the need for a strong and dedicated public service, a commitment best expressed in his own words:

" I believe that in many ways public service is the highest service. And that is because it is the hardest and most necessary for our nation's future. . . . [The] linkage between public service and nation-building is an old and enduring one in the American context. It is this relationship and the high ideals of our democracy that ought to make public service—and creating conditions under which it survives—a high priority for everyone. . . . "

C O N T E N T S

THE REPORT OF
THE NATIONAL COMMISSION
ON THE PUBLIC SERVICE

Preface

The National Commission on the Public Service was formed in 1987 following a major symposium in Washington, D.C., on "A National Public Service for the Year 2000." The symposium, jointly sponsored by the Brookings Institution and the American Enterprise Institute, concluded that a private, nonprofit organization should be assembled to prepare action recommendations to the President and the Congress on what the symposium saw as a "quiet crisis" in government.

Simply put, too many of the best of the nation's senior executives are ready to leave government, and not enough of its most talented young people are willing to join. This erosion in the attractiveness of public service at all levels—most specifically in the federal civil service—undermines the ability of government to respond effectively to the needs and aspirations of the American people, and ultimately damages the democratic process itself.

It was this perception that brought together, in the summer and fall of 1987, 36 members of the Commission under the chairmanship of Paul A. Volcker, former Federal Reserve Board chairman. The Commission includes men and women with broad experience in government and private life, as President and Vice President, Senators, Representatives, cabinet level officers and Ambassadors, corporate executives, university presidents and leaders of national nonprofit organizations.

Individually they reflect a broad spectrum of political views and differ on many questions of public policy. Collectively, however, the Commission members share a conviction that rebuilding an effective, principled, and energetic public service must rank high on the nation's agenda. They also agree on the main elements of action proposed in this report to strengthen the effectiveness of government, although there may be differences in emphasis or detail.

Although the "quiet crisis" affects all levels of government, the Commission has been particularly concerned about quality and performance at the senior administrative and professional levels of the federal government. That is where America looks for leadership and where the standards of government service may have their widest influence. For that reason, as well as because of practical limitations in time and resources, the report that follows focuses primarily on these senior federal positions.

The Commission believes, however, that a number of its broad recommendations are also relevant for other parts and levels of government. The Commission hopes that this report, as well as the Commission's task force reports that are being published separately, will become a catalyst for further efforts by state and local governments, as well as by the federal government, to develop detailed proposals for change.

Acknowledgments

The Commission was aware from the outset of its work that it would need the broadest possible base of understanding of public attitudes, as well as access to the wide range of individuals and organizations with expert and working knowledge of the issues involved. The Commission therefore held public hearings in Washington, D.C., Los Angeles, New York City, Atlanta, Boston, Ann Arbor, and Austin. It conducted its own surveys of the views of current cabinet members, recent college honor graduates, and Presidential Management Interns to determine the extent of interest in public careers. It also relied on research by the General Accounting Office, the Office of Personnel Management, and the Merit Systems Protection Board, as well as by individual scholars and practitioners across the nation, all of whom readily responded when requested to open their files to the Commission.

To develop specific recommendations for action, the Commission divided into five Task Forces. Their reports to the Commission form the basis for much of this report, and have been published separately for those wishing to analyze the issues further.

The Commission also benefited from input by the National Academy of Public Administration, the American Society for Public Administration, the National Association of Schools of Public Affairs and Administration, the Harvard University Public/Private Careers Project, the Center for Excellence in Government, the Public Employees Roundtable, and the Senior Executives Association. Hundreds of concerned citizens, college students, and public servants contacted the Commission on their own initiative. A number of scholars and practitioners commented on earlier stages of the Commission's work during a two-day seminar at Princeton University's Woodrow Wilson School. The Commission owes a debt of gratitude to these groups and individuals.

The Commission's work would not have been possible without the generous financial support of the following foundations and business corporations, members of some of whose boards and staffs also contributed ideas and suggestions as the work progressed:

American International Group Inc.
American Telephone and Telegraph Company
Carnegie Corporation of New York
The Dillon Fund
The Equitable Life Assurance Society of the United States
The Ford Foundation
Hallmark Cards, Inc.
William and Flora Hewlett Foundation
International Business Machines Corporation
John D. and Catherine T. MacArthur Foundation
McKnight Foundation
RJR Nabisco
National Westminster Bank USA
Rockefeller Foundation
Alfred P. Sloan Foundation

Finally the Commission wishes to record its deep appreciation for the dedicated work of the staff of the Commission, including not least the interns from several colleges and universities: Andrew Brownstein, University of Virginia; Ronald L. Coleman, University of Southern California; Sharon Gleason, Johns Hopkins University; John P. Knight, George Washington University; Bruce Meier, American University; Lynn J. Olsen, Syracuse University; Erich Vaden, Georgetown University; and Howard Wilson, Howard University. They not only gave of their energy and enthusiasm for public service, but also reminded all of us that the recommendations of this Commission matter most of all to those they represent—a younger generation that is being called upon to carry forward the great enterprise of American citizenship and the essential work of government.

Introduction

ORIGINS AND PURPOSE

In the 1970s and 1980s there were warning signs that the public service needed renewal. Two antigovernment presidential campaigns added to the skepticism engendered by Vietnam and Watergate and encouraged the public to blame the ills of the country on Washington and its "bureaucrats." Many presidential appointees came to office expecting the bureaucracy to undermine their efforts. In response, morale throughout the government slipped, with a majority of senior executives unwilling to recommend public service as a career for their own children. The best and brightest graduates of the nation's premier universities did not see the public service as a challenging outlet for their talents. Pay at higher levels eroded by 35 percent between 1969 and 1989, and at lower levels it lagged behind the private sector.

This discouraging situation reflected a failure of leadership. Citizens did not recognize the connection between the services provided by government and the need to pay for them. This attitude was exploited by some politicians who were willing to reap short-term electoral benefits by capitalizing on antigovernment sentiment among voters. Internal government management systems often discouraged leadership by too much centralization. Any reversal of these trends would require leadership at all levels of American society.

The authors would like to acknowledge the helpful comments on earlier drafts of this introduction of Peri Arnold, Lyn Holley, Marjorie Jones, Rossyln Kleeman, Bruce Laingen, and Michael Hansen.

A small number of leaders in government and business, concerned that the federal public service was being dangerously eroded, convened a conference in 1986 entitled "A National Public Service for the Year 2000," which was sponsored by the Brookings Institution and the American Enterprise Institute. The conference confirmed that there was indeed a "quiet crisis" in the public service and that action to reverse the negative trends was necessary.[1] Former Federal Reserve Board chairman Paul Volcker gave an inspiring keynote address to the conference on the value of the public service, and afterward a small group of conference organizers set out to recruit him to chair a proposed commission on the public service. Volcker agreed, and because of his active and committed leadership, the National Commission on the Public Service will probably be remembered as the Volcker Commission (following Taft, Brownlow, and Hoover). The Commission offered a vision of what the public service might be and proposed concrete steps for implementing that vision.

Chairman Volcker, Executive Director Bruce Laingen (a retired Foreign Service Officer and Chargé D'Affaires in Iran during the hostage crisis), and Deputy Director Charles Levine (a leading public administration scholar) then worked with the Commission's organizers to invite thirty-six Americans distinguished in public service, politics, education, business, and labor to become members of the Commission. After the untimely death of Charles Levine, political scientist Paul Light joined the Commission staff to draft the final report. The diversity of Commission membership reflected a widespread concern about the health of the public service and its importance to the strength of the nation, as well as a recognition that the case for strengthening the public service had to be made credibly to citizens and their political leaders. The Commission was privately funded by a number of foundations and corporations.

After finishing a preliminary analysis, Commission members saw three main threats to the health of the public service: public attitudes, political leadership, and internal management systems. These threats were seen as eroding the ability of the government to function effectively at the same time that demands on government were growing.

The major environmental factor underlying almost all the problems confronted by the Commission was a skepticism, bordering on hostility, toward government which is deeply embedded in the political culture of the United States. The ambivalence of Americans toward government stems from the nation's revolutionary heritage and a distrust of concentrated power. This distrust and suspicion toward the central government have recently taken the form of denigration of the federal government and those who work for it.

---

[1]The term was used in a paper by Charles Levine and Rosslyn Kleeman prepared for the conference entitled "The Quiet Crisis: The Federal Workforce in the Year 2000."

Although distrust of politicians and government power are peren-
nial features of American culture, attacks on the federal government and
"bureaucrat bashing" became particularly virulent after Vietnam and Watergate, and were led by presidential candidates in 1976 and 1980 as well as
by candidates for other offices. Attacks by political leaders were echoed
in the distrust shown toward career civil servants by newly recruited political
executives appointed by recent presidents. Many were convinced that career public employees would not respond to legitimate political leadership.

The third problem facing the public service was internal to the
management systems of the government. The purchasing power of federal salaries had eroded significantly, making it difficult to attract first-rate
political appointees and to retain the best of the career executives. Compounding the pay problem were rigidities in the personnel systems which
made recruitment of entry-level professionals difficult and cumbersome.

To approach these problems, the Commission divided itself into five
task forces. The intent, nevertheless, was to produce one report that would
express the consensus of the Commission. The task force reports were to
be reports *to* the Commission rather than *of* the Commission. Composed
of Commission members and other prominent Americans, each task force
was staffed by one senior professional from the academic public administration community or on loan from a federal agency.

The five task forces undertook to examine the major issues the Commission proposed to address. One task force would focus on the most fundamental and intractable problem: the negative perception of the public
service by American citizens. Managerial issues were responsible for many
of the frustrations and inefficiencies of government management; these
issues were addressed by the recruitment and retention task force. Any
solution to the long-range problems had to involve education, both of public
servants and of the general public, and so education became the focus of
a third task force. Translating policy mandates into programs is crucial
to any democratic government; thus the fourth task force focused on the
relationship between political appointees and career public executives. The
fifth task force addressed the most politically volatile issue, that of pay for
government officials. The Final Commission Report integrated much of
the analysis and many of the recommendations of the individual task forces,
but it also presented a coherent vision for rebuilding the public service.

CONTINUITIES AND CHALLENGES

Throughout this century of profound changes in the scope and complexity of the federal government, a number of major commissions have
addressed issues of public management and governmental structure. The
Taft Commission (Commission on Economy and Efficiency, 1912) proposed
the creation of an executive budget, which was finally done in 1921. The

Brownlow Committee (President's Committee on Administrative Management, 1937) established the intellectual basis for strengthening presidential management of the government and reorganizing the executive branch. The two Hoover Commissions (Commissions on Organization of the Executive Branch of the Government, 1949, 1955) addressed a wide range of issues covering management, structure, and presidential control of the executive branch.

In contrast with these other commissions, the National Commission on the Public Service was not created or appointed by the President or Congress, nor was it supported with public funds. Its staff resources, in comparison with the other commissions, were minimal, with three to five full-time professionals, and the work of members of the Commission was *pro bono* and part-time.

The Volcker Commission revisited some of the same issues addressed by previous commissions. Concerns about the personnel issues of pay, recruitment, and retention had also been addressed by the Brownlow and Hoover recommendations. But the National Commission on the Public Service, unlike its predecessors, also confronted the behavioral problems of declining work-force morale, the relationship between career and political executives, and public attitudes toward the career services. It did not, however, explicitly address executive branch organization, governmental structure, or presidential control of the government, issues that were of primary concern to Brownlow and Hoover. After some discussion, the Volcker Commission also decided to focus primarily on the federal public service, though the Commission's members were concerned about public service at all levels of government.

Among the issues confronted by the Volcker Commission, that of pay for government employees had been a matter of public dispute since the beginning of the Republic. In the twentieth century both the Brownlow Committee and the two Hoover Commissions dealt with the pay issue. The Brownlow Committee wanted to "increase the salaries of key posts throughout the service so that the Government may attract and hold in a career service men and women of the highest ability and character."[2] The first Hoover Commission argued that "salaries, pitifully low in the higher levels. . . must be substantially increased to attract and retain employees with first-rate abilities."[3] The second Hoover Commission also recommended significantly higher pay levels for government executives.

[2]*Report of the President's Committee on Administrative Management*, reprinted in Frederick C. Mosher, ed., *Basic Documents of American Public Administration, 1776–1950* (New York: Holmes & Meier, 1976), p. 135.
[3]*Concluding Report of the Commission on Organization of the Executive Branch of the Government, 1949.* In Mosher, *Basic Documents*, p. 212.

The pay of top-level executive branch officials is now tied to congressional salaries, and since Congress has been unwilling to raise its own pay, increasing executive branch salaries has been impossible. The most visible issue the Volcker Commission addressed was in its recommendation to raise pay significantly for federal executives. The Commission report was scheduled to come out immediately after congressional action on the Report of the Quadrennial Commission on Judicial, Legislative, and Executive Salaries. The "Quad Com" had recommended a 50 percent pay raise for members of Congress to restore purchasing power lost since 1969.

Public reaction, however, was so negative (over 80 percent in most public opinion polls were against the raise) that the proposal was rejected by Congress. Nevertheless, the Volcker Commission stuck by its recommendation, though it proposed phasing in the raises, and further proposed that if pay raises should continue to be politically impossible for members of Congress to enact, then the link between congressional and executive pay ought to be broken. Because of its political visibility, the pay issue tended to overshadow the many other issues addressed by the Commission, and press coverage usually focused on the controversial nature of the pay recommendations.

Other personnel issues taken up by the Commission had also been addressed before. The first Hoover Commission declared, "The centralization of personnel transactions. . . has resulted in unjustifiable delays in handling personnel problems. Recruitment machinery has been slow, impersonal, and cumbersome. . . . The system is not constituted so as to attract and retain sufficient qualified people for the Government's tasks."[4] Nearly four decades later, these same personnel problems were still troubling the public service. The delegation of broad recruitment authority from the Office of Personnel Management to departments and agencies which had begun with the passage of the 1978 Civil Service Reform Act was recentralized in the early 1980s. The Volcker Commission proposed a number of measures to improve the hiring process, to help recruit the best college graduates, and to retain them for a full career in the public service. Proposed improvements included decentralizing hiring authority and using more aggressive recruitment tactics.

The quality of the career service and its relationship with presidential appointees has been of major concern since the creation of the merit system by the Pendleton Act in 1883. The Brownlow Committee proposed in 1936 to "extend the merit system upward, outward, and downward to cover all nonpolicy-determining posts." The Committee believed that its proposals would eliminate "the evils of the patronage system" and open "our civil service more fully and completely as a sound career service, permanent, nonpartisan, competent, fairly compensated, and affording

---

[4]Ibid., p. 211.

promotion to posts of eminence."[5] The first Hoover Commission declared in 1949 that "all positions in the service with the exception of top level policy jobs should be filled by merit system methods."[6] The second Hoover Commission proposed the creation of more political positions so that career civil servants would "be relieved by the noncareer executives of responsibilities for advocacy or defense of policies and programs."[7]

After the increase in the number of political appointees in the 1970s and 1980s, the Volcker Commission concluded that, because of span-of-control and communication problems, responsiveness to the President was actually being undermined rather than enhanced. In addition, career executives were not being fully used, and their career prospects were being cut short. The Commission recommended reversing the trend by reducing the number of political appointees from about three thousand to about two thousand.

The major conviction that the Volcker Commission shared with previous commissions was that presidential leadership was crucial to the executive branch and to the U.S. government. Indeed, the major concern of the Taft, Brownlow, and Hoover Commissions was to give the President the necessary staff, structure, and administrative tools to enable him to exercise his constitutional authority. The Volcker Commission saw no need to enhance the President's power; rather, its proposals were intended to enable the executive branch to work more effectively in carrying out presidential initiatives and implementing the law. Its recommendations, however, were based on the conviction that presidential leadership was necessary in order for most of the Commissions's recommendations to be implemented. This was particularly true in the case of changing the public perception of the career services. Presidential candidates had been a powerful force in creating this negative perception, and presidential leadership would be essential for remedying the situation.

Although there were some major substantive continuities between the Volcker Commission and the earlier major commissions, there were also some differences, particularly in the tactics used to gain public support. For example, the Volcker Commission Report, like that of the Brownlow Committee, was not an attack on "big government"; by contrast, both Hoover Commissions were in part critical of "big government." The Citizens Committee for the Hoover Report was particularly emphatic in citing "horror stories" in order to drum up support for its proposals. And the second

[5]*Report of the President's Committee on Administrative Management, 1937.* In Mosher, *Basic Documents,* pp. 135–36.
[6]*Concluding Report of the Commission on Organization of the Executive Branch of the Government, 1949.* In Mosher, *Basic Documents,* p. 212.
[7]Quoted in Ronald C. Moe, *The Hoover Commissions Revisited* (Boulder, Colo.: Westview Press, 1982), p. 91.

Hoover Commission was seen by some as a direct attack on "big government."[8]

The Volcker Commission Report, like Brownlow but unlike the two Hoover Reports, eschewed any exaggerated claims about saving billions of dollars through its recommendations. The Brownlow Report stated, "We have made no estimate of the amount of money that will be saved by such a rearrangement."[9] However, the proponents of the Hoover Reports, especially the Citizens Committees, claimed that major savings could be achieved if their proposals were adopted. Realistically, the Volcker Commission acknowledged the large cost of increased pay for government employees but argued that the investment was crucial to the future of the nation, that high quality is worth paying for and is necessary for a government to be effective as well as responsive to the people. The Commission tried to minimize the impact by arguing that better management would lead to more efficient operations and that agency budgets should absorb most of the increased personnel costs.

Attacking big government and claiming major dollar savings are ways of gaining public support for management reforms (the private Grace Commission in the early 1980s made extravagant claims for cost savings); criticizing the excesses of bureaucratic processes is certainly another. In its campaign to build public support for the Civil Service Reform Act of 1978, the Carter Administration emphasized poor performance and the need to be able to fire civil servants more easily, rather than the Act's provisions for rewarding excellent performance. But *Leadership for America* self-consciously accentuated the positive aspects of the public service and the need to recognize excellence.

On a number of issues the Volcker Commission had to walk a fine line between cries of alarm (in order to get serious attention for reform) and overstating deficiencies, thus aggravating the very problems it meant to alleviate. If the case were made too convincingly that the public service was suffering from low pay, plummeting morale, recruitment rigidities, and attenuated career prospects, the best and brightest potential recruits might be discouraged from joining the public service. If, on the other hand, the problems were understated, how could enough political support be generated to ensure the adoption of reforms? The Commission also had to strike the right balance between seeming to promote the public service for its own sake and stating the members' conviction that a strong public service was essential for the well-being and security of the nation.

---

[8]See particularly Neil MacNeil and Harold Metz, *The Hoover Report, 1953–1955* (New York: Macmillan, 1956), and the analysis by Moe in *The Hoover Commissions.*
[9]*Report of the President's Committee on Administrative Management.* In Mosher, *Basic Documents,* p. 135.

PROSPECTS

The Final Report of the National Commission on the Public Service and its Task Force Reports performed a number of functions for those concerned about the federal government and public administration. First, the documents provided an authoritative statement of major problems that management of the federal government faced at the end of the twentieth century. Second, the analysis was credible because of the prominence and experience of Commission members and because of the Commission's bipartisan nature. And finally, the report provided a coherent program of reform that, if adopted, would lead in the direction of solving those problems.

The report exhorted political officials to value the career services and articulated to the general public the ideals of public service. For those working in the government it provided a boost to morale and inspiration regarding the importance of their calling. The task force reports assembled the data and provided the rigorous analysis and sound scholarship to support the conclusions of the final report.

But although the report enjoyed broad support in the public administration community when it was released, the question of how to evaluate its "success" remains. One way to gauge the success of a commission is to count the number of proposals that are enacted into statute or adopted in administrative policies and regulations. By this criterion, however, the Brownlow Committee would not be considered a success since most of its proposals were rejected by Congress in 1937.

Some signs pointed toward the success of the Volcker report. First, the 1988 presidential campaign provided relief from the bashing of the government and the public service which had marked other recent presidential campaigns. Both candidates refrained from taking cheap shots at the federal government and made positive statements about the value of public service. After the election, President Bush issued a statement praising the career service, and the first group he addressed outside the White House after his inauguration was a meeting of career senior executives in Washington. He also said that he would seriously consider career executives for presidential appointments. The Final Report of the National Commission on the Public Service was personally presented to President Bush by Paul Volcker in a special White House meeting on March 29, 1989. The President accepted the spirit of the Report, if not all of its individual recommendations.

Some actions proposed by the Volcker Commission were already under way at the time the report was released. The Office of Personnel Management had begun moving in the direction of improving recruitment methods and delegating hiring authority to agencies. The Office of Presidential Personnel had established orientation programs for new presidential appointees and had allowed significant leeway in the selection of subcabinet appointments by cabinet secretaries. Furthermore, President Bush recommended pay increases for political and career executives as well as for federal judges.

The Report was also well received in a series of hearings in Congress, and legislation to implement recommendations was drafted. In addition, the report received praise from several key presidential appointees who would have much to say about the implementation of the recommendations: Chase Untermeyer, Director of the Office of Presidential Personnel; Constance Newman, Director of the Office of Personnel Management; and Frank Hodsoll, Executive Associate Director of the Office of Management and Budget. On the other hand, the political viability of some of the major recommendations was always questionable—for example, a large pay increase, cutting the number of political appointees, and major hiring flexibilities.

When the Commission completed its work during the summer of 1989, it established the Public Service Liaison Committee to coordinate implementation efforts for the following year. Paul Volcker stayed on as Honorary Chairman, and almost all the Commission members agreed to continue their activities to support implementation efforts.[10] The Liaison Committee was not comparable to the Citizens Committee for the Hoover Commission Reports, which had significant funds and launched major public relations campaigns. The Volcker Liaison Committee was designed to act as facilitator, coordinator, convener, and clearinghouse for efforts to implement the recommendations. It intended to work with other public interest organizations to share information, monitor public service issues, and facilitate legislative efforts.

So, several immediate steps were taken to implement the recommendations of the Commission through legislation as well as through administrative policy and regulations. But the most important goal of the Commission and the one most difficult to implement was that of changing the public's perception of the public service. This was most important because the President and Congress are very sensitive to public opinion. Even if they are convinced of the value of administrative reform, they will hesitate to implement it in the face of public opposition, as was vividly demonstrated by the pay raise fiasco that occurred in the spring of 1989. Ultimately, the quality of the public service depends on its ability to recruit first-rate personnel, and if the public does not value the providers of government services, recruitment will be severely hampered.

---

[10]Two new members joined the committee in the summer of 1989: former secretary of defense Frank Carlucci, and former ambassador to Norway and CEO of Quaker Oats, Robert D. Stuart, Jr.

But the criterion of success to be applied to a major commission ought not to be the immediate passage of legislation, as important as that might be. By that criterion the first Hoover Commission was a great success. That success, however, was made possible only by the groundwork laid by the Brownlow Committee in 1937. The impact of the Brownlow Report was not immediately felt, since its recommendations were for the most part rejected by Congress. But in the longer run its impact was great, and it made possible the concrete reforms of the first Hoover Commission. In the words of one scholar, the Brownlow Report was "probably the most important constitutional document of our time."[11] Its greatest contribution was in setting the agenda and providing the context for strengthening the President's managerial capacity over the next several decades.

It is in this context that the impact of the work of the National Commission on the Public Service should be judged. Of course, this means that its success can only be determined retrospectively, from decades hence. If the Commission is then seen to have contributed significantly to an improved attitude toward the public service and a renewed vigor in the management of the government, its most important objective will have been achieved, whether or not any proposals were immediately enacted into legislation. Ultimately, changing attitudes and beliefs and setting agendas for change are of greater far-reaching significance than immediate legislative or administrative reforms.

Elliot L. Richardson
James P. Pfiffner

---

[11]Rowland Egger, "The Period of Crisis: 1933 to 1945," in Frederick C. Mosher, ed., *American Public Administration: Past, Present, Future* (University of Alabama: University of Alabama Press, 1975), p. 71.

Summary and Main Conclusions

The central message of this report of the Commission on the Public Service is both simple and profound, both urgent and timeless. In essence, we call for a renewed sense of commitment by all Americans to the highest traditions of the public service—to a public service responsive to the political will of the people and also protective of our constitutional values; to a public service able to cope with complexity and conflict and also able to maintain the highest ethical standards; to a public service attractive to the young and talented from all parts of our society and also capable of earning the respect of all our citizens.

A great nation must demand no less. The multiple challenges thrust upon the Government of the United States as we approach the 21st Century can only reinforce the point. Yet, there is evidence on all sides of an erosion of performance and morale across government in America. Too many of our most talented public servants—those with the skills and dedication that are the hallmarks of an effective career service—are ready to leave. Too few of our brightest young people—those with the imagination and energy that are essential for the future—are willing to join.

Meanwhile, the need for a strong public service is growing, not lessening. Americans have always expected their national government to guarantee their basic freedoms and provide for the common defense. We continue to expect our government to keep the peace with other nations, resolve differences among our own people, pay the bills for needed services, and honor the people's trust by providing the highest levels of integrity and performance.

At the same time, Americans now live in a stronger, more populous nation, a nation with unprecedented opportunity. But they also live in a world of enormous complexity and awesome risks. Our economy is infinitely more open to international competition, our currency floats in a worldwide market, and we live with complex technologies beyond the understanding of any single human mind. Our diplomacy is much more complicated, and the wise use of our unparalleled military power more difficult. And for all our scientific achievements, we are assaulted daily by new social, environmental, and health issues almost incomprehensible in scope and impact—issues like drugs, AIDS, and global warming.

Faced with these challenges, the simple idea that Americans must draw upon talented and dedicated individuals to serve us in government is uncontestable. America must have a public service that can both value the lessons of experience and appreciate the requirements for change; a public service that both responds to political leadership and respects the law; a public service with the professional skills and the ethical sensitivity America deserves.

" H ow well the tasks of government are done affects the quality of the lives of all our people. Moreover, the success of any political leadership in implementing its policies and objectives depends heavily upon the expertise, quality, and commitment of the professional career employees of government. "

PRESIDENT GEORGE BUSH, 1989

Surely, there can be no doubt that moral challenge and personal excitement are inherent in the great enterprise of democratic government. There is work to be done of enormous importance. Individuals can make a difference.

But unfortunately there is growing evidence that these basic truths have been clouded by a sense of frustration inside government and a lack of public trust outside. The resulting erosion in the quality of America's public service is difficult to measure; there are still many examples of excellence among those who carry out the nation's business at home and abroad. Nevertheless, it is evident that public service is neither as attractive as it once was nor as effective in meeting perceived needs. No doubt, opposition to specific policies of government has contributed to a lack of respect for the public servants who struggle to make the policies work. This drives away much of our best talent which can only make the situation worse.

One need not search far to see grounds for concern. Crippled nuclear weapons plants, defense procurement scandals, leaking hazardous waste dumps, near-misses in air traffic control, and the costly collapse of so many savings and loans have multiple causes. But each such story carries some similar refrains about government's inability to recruit and retain a talented work force: the Department of Defense is losing its top procurement specialists to contractors who can pay much more; the Federal Aviation Administration is unable to hold skilled traffic controllers because of stress and working conditions; the Environmental Protection Agency is unable to fill key engineering jobs because the brightest students simply are not interested; the Federal Savings and Loan Insurance Corporation (FSLIC) simply cannot hire and pay able executives.

"Is 'ok' enough for those who direct the next shuttle mission? After Three-Mile-Island and Chernobyl, what level of competence do we want inspecting our nuclear plants? The next time you take an air flight, do you tell your family not to worry, the controllers aren't the best but they are ok?"

WALTER MONDALE, 1987

This erosion has been gradual, almost imperceptible, year by year. But it has occurred nonetheless. Consider the following evidence compiled by the Commission's five task forces on the growing recruitment problem:

- Only 13 percent of the senior executives recently interviewed by the General Accounting Office would recommend that young people start their careers in government, while several recent surveys show that less than half the senior career civil servants would recommend a job in government to their own children.

- Of the 610 engineering students who received bachelors, masters, and doctoral degrees at the Massachusetts Institute of Technology and Stanford University in 1986, and the 600 who graduated from Rensselaer Polytechnic Institute in 1987, only 29 took jobs in government at any level.

- Half the respondents to a recent survey of federal personnel officers said recruitment of quality personnel had become more difficult over the past five years.

- Three-quarters of the respondents to the Commission's survey of recent Presidential Management Interns—a prestigious program for recruiting the top graduates of America's schools of public affairs—said they would leave government within 10 years.

If these trends continue, America will soon be left with a government of the mediocre, locked into careers of last resort or waiting for a chance to move on to other jobs.

But this need not and should not be. By the choices we make today, we can enter the 21st century with a public service fully equipped to meet the challenges of intense competition abroad and growing complexity at home. The strongest wish of the Commission is that this report can be a step in that process, pointing toward necessary changes, while serving as a catalyst for national debate and further efforts at all levels of government.

" *F* or all the glories of Adam Smith, somebody has to set the rules and adjudicate disputes. Somebody has to defend the country and to explore space. Somebody has to keep the air clean and the environment safe for the next generation. Somebody has to respond to those more mundane, but nonetheless sometimes quite challenging, assignments of keeping government working effectively and efficiently if self government is to work at all. "

PAUL A. VOLCKER, 1986

America should and can act now to restore the leadership, talent, and performance essential to the strong public service the future demands. To those ends, the Commission believes:

- First, the President and Congress must provide the essential environment for effective leadership and public support.

• Second, educational institutions and the agencies of government must work to enlarge the base of talent available for, and committed to, public service.

• Third, the American people should demand first-class performance and the highest ethical standards, and, by the same token, must be willing to provide what is necessary to attract and retain needed talent.

These three themes—**leadership, talent** and **performance**—shape this report. They are both wide-ranging and interrelated. They also provide a framework for a concrete agenda for action, directed toward a series of basic goals discussed in further detail in the report that follows. Specifically, to strengthen executive **leadership**, we call upon the President and Congress to:

• Take action now by word and deed to rebuild public trust in government;

• Clear away obstacles to the ability of the President to attract talented appointees from all parts of society;

• Make more room at senior levels of departments and agencies for career executives;

• Provide a framework within which those federal departments and agencies can exercise greater flexibility in managing programs and personnel; and

• Encourage a stronger partnership between presidential appointees and career executives.

To broaden the government's **talent base**, we call upon educational institutions and government to:

• Develop more student awareness of, and educational training for, the challenges of government and public service;

• Develop new channels for spreading the word about government jobs and the rewards of public service;

• Enhance the efforts to recruit top college graduates and those with specific professional skills for government jobs;

• Simplify the hiring process; and

- Increase the representation of minorities in public careers.

To place a greater emphasis on quality and **performance** throughout government, we ask for the public and its leaders to:

- Build a pay system that is both fair and competitive;

- Rebuild the government's chief personnel agency to give it the strength and mandate it needs;

- Set higher goals for government performance and productivity;

- Provide more effective training and executive development; and

- Improve government working conditions.

To further these basic goals, the Commission makes a series of specific recommendations throughout the report (see Appendix I). Twelve key proposals deserve mention here:

> *First*, **Presidents, their chief lieutenants, and Congress must articulate early and often the necessary and honorable role that public servants play in the democratic process, at the same time making clear they will demand the highest standards of ethics and performance possible from those who hold the public trust. Members of Congress and their staffs should be covered by similar standards. Codes of conduct to convey such standards should be simple and straightforward, and should focus on the affirmative values that must guide public servants in the exercise of their responsibilities.**

> *Second*, **within program guidelines from the President, cabinet officers and agency heads should be given greater flexibility to administer their organizations, including greater freedom to hire and fire personnel, provided there are appropriate review procedures within the Administration and oversight from Congress.**

> *Third*, **the President should highlight the important role of the Office of Personnel Management (OPM) by establishing and maintaining contact with its Director and by ensuring participation by the Director in cabinet level discussions on human resource management issues. The Commission further recommends decentralization of a portion of OPM's operating responsibilities to maximize its role of personnel policy guidance to federal departments and agencies.**

Fourth, **the growth in recent years in the number of presidential appointees, whether those subject to Senate confirmation, noncareer senior executives, or personal and confidential assistants, should be curtailed. Although a reduction in the total number of presidential appointees must be based on a position-by-position assessment, the Commission is confident that a substantial cut is possible, and believes a cut from the current 3,000 to no more than 2,000 is a reasonable target.** Every President must have politically and philosophically compatible officials to implement his Administration's program. At the same time, however, experience suggests that excessive numbers of political appointees serving relatively brief periods may undermine the President's ability to govern, insulating the Administration from needed dispassionate advice and institutional memory. The mere size of the political turnover almost guarantees management gaps and discontinuities, while the best of the career professionals will leave government if they do not have challenging opportunities at the sub-cabinet level.

Fifth, **the President and Congress must ensure that federal managers receive the added training they will need to perform effectively.** The education of public servants must not end upon appointment to the civil service. Government must invest more in its executive development programs and develop stronger partnerships with America's colleges and universities.

Sixth, **the nation should recognize the importance of civic education as a part of social studies and history in the nation's primary and secondary school curricula.** Starting with a comprehensive review of current programs, the nation's educators and parents should work toward new curricula and livelier textbooks designed to enhance student understanding of America's civic institutions, relate formal learning about those institutions to the problems students care about, and link classroom learning to extracurricular practice.

Seventh, **America should take advantage of the natural idealism of its youth by expanding and encouraging national volunteer service,** whether through existing programs like ACTION, the Peace Corps, and VISTA, or experiments with initiatives like President Bush's Youth Engaged in Service (YES), and some of the ideas contained in the Democratic Leadership Council's citizen corps proposal.

Eighth, **the President and Congress should establish a Presidential Public Service Scholarship Program targeted to 1,000 college or col-**

lege-bound students each year, with careful attention to the recruitment of minority students. Admission to the program might be modeled on appointment to the military service academies—that is, through nomination by members of Congress—and should include tuition and other costs, in return for a commitment to a determined number of years of government service.

Ninth, **the President should work with Congress to give high priority to restoring the depleted purchasing power of executive, judicial, and legislative salaries by the beginning of a new Congress in 1991, starting with an immediate increase of 25 percent. At the same time, the Commission recommends that Congress enact legislation eliminating speaking honoraria and other income related to their public responsibilities.**

Tenth, **if Congress is unable to act on its own salaries, the Commission recommends that the President make separate recommendations for judges and top level executives and that the Congress promptly act upon them.** Needed pay raises for presidential appointees, senior career executives, and judges should no longer be dependent on the ability of Congress to raise its own pay.

Eleventh, **the President and Congress should give a higher budget priority to civil service pay in the General Schedule pay system.** In determining the appropriate increase, the Commission concludes that the current goal of national comparability between public and private pay is simplistic and unworkable, and is neither fair to the civil service nor to the public it serves. **The Commission therefore recommends a new civil service pay-setting process that recognizes the objective fact that pay differs by occupation and by localities characterized by widely different living costs and labor market pressures.**

Twelfth, **the President and Congress should establish a permanent independent advisory council, composed of members from the public and private sector, both to monitor the ongoing state of the public service and to make such recommendations for improvements as they think desireable.** The Commission applauds President Bush's pledge of leadership of the public service. Indeed, his recent statements reflect the spirit and concerns that led to the creation of the Commission. However, the problems that make up this "quiet crisis" are many and complex, and have been long in the making. Corrective action will not only require presidential leadership and congressional support, but must be part of a coherent and sustained long term strategy. The proposed independent advisory council is designed to ensure that the state of the public service remains high on the national agenda.

This report speaks directly to a number of audiences: to the *American people* about the importance to their civic institutions of talented men and women; to *young people* about the challenges and satisfactions they can find in serving their government; to *candidates for elective office* about the long-term costs of "bureaucrat bashing;" to the *media* about the need not only to hold public servants to high standards but also to recognize those who serve successfully; to *university schools of public affairs* about developing curricula for the training of a new generation of government managers; and to *business leaders* about the importance of quality government support to the private sector.

Finally, the report speaks to the *civil service* about its obligations to the highest standards of performance. The Commission fully supports the need for better pay and working conditions in much of government. But **the Commission also recognizes that public support for those improvements is dependent on a commitment by the civil servants themselves to efficiency, responsiveness, and integrity.**

" *L* et the public service be a proud and lively career. And let every man and woman who works in any area of our national government, in any branch, at any level, be able to say with pride and with honor in future years: 'I served the United States government in that hour of our nation's need.' "

PRESIDENT JOHN F. KENNEDY, 1963

CHAPTER I

Leadership for Governance

Measured by assets or employees or financial liabilities, the federal government dwarfs any other business in America. But far more significant than any statistical measures are the intangible purposes of government: to ensure the "life, liberty, and the pursuit of happiness" of our citizens.

We as a people focus enormous responsibility on one person—the President of the United States. And indeed, he or she alone can do much to set the tone of government and with Congress set out the main lines of policy. Presidential leadership is both indispensable and an enormous asset. Moreover, positive Presidential leadership is the *sine qua non* of a strong public service.

" *What I think it all boils down to is leadership. Leadership in the White House and leadership in the United States Congress. Don't blame those that make a lifetime of service to the government; give them the kind of leadership they need, and they'll follow and get the job done.* "

PRESIDENT GEORGE BUSH, 1989

But no President can be effective alone. He or she must rely upon a sizeable number of top officials—leaders in their own right—to ensure the quality and effectiveness of government. These men and women—presidential appointees, senior career executives, and personal and confidential assistants—implement the President's agenda, hire and promote the key staff, draft the budget, enforce the laws, try to anticipate problems and get the facts, and motivate the civil service. In doing so, a President sets a powerful example for a 2.2 million non-postal civilian work force, and for the nation as a whole. To the extent presidential and career executives are committed to the highest levels of integrity and performance, and work in full partnership to secure faithful execution of the laws, public respect will also follow.

Unfortunately, there is growing evidence that the supply of talented managers, political and career, in government is dwindling. Among presidential appointees, who are directly responsible for developing and executing the President's agenda, turnover rates have become a serious problem. From 1964–1984, according to research by the National Academy of Public Administration, 42 percent of cabinet secretaries, 62 percent of deputy secretaries, and 46 percent of under secretaries left their jobs after two years or less. Among career senior executives, who provide the essential reservoir of institutional knowledge and professional skills for implementing the President's program, over half say that if a suitable job outside government became available, they would take it.

Perhaps most important, years of campaign "bureaucrat bashing" by candidates for elective office, reinforced by too many instances of ethical lapse, have eroded the sense of pride that once came with government service. Careers that were once seen as proud and lively are increasingly viewed as modest and dull—even demeaning. Today, sadly, fewer than half the government's most senior and most successful executives are willing to recommend a career in public life to their children.

> " *If I as a CEO were to say that I have loafers, laggards and petty thieves working for me, one could hardly expect my people to perform. Nor would such talk inspire customer confidence; indeed they would wonder about us as a company and about me as a CEO.* "
>
> *FRANK CARLUCCI, Secretary of Defense, 1988*

GOAL ONE:

REBUILD THE PUBLIC'S TRUST

Restoring a sense of pride in public service rests in large measure on the public's willingness to trust their own government. Unfortunately, despite a slight turnaround in recent years, nearly half the American public feel that average people have no say in government, while three of four say that politics and government are too complicated to understand.

Some of this distrust arises from a skepticism toward big government rooted in American history; some from opposition to specific policies. Those concerns are natural, and they are often healthy, in a pluralistic society committed to federalism and free speech.

The Commission's focus lies elsewhere, on public perceptions of corruption, waste, and ineffectiveness in doing what government sets out to do. Some of this distrust comes from scandals like Watergate and Pentagon procurement; some from wasteful government programs; some from past campaign rhetoric. Such distrust, if continued, may undermine the democratic process itself. It most certainly acts as a disincentive to potential recruits who too often associate public life with frustration or breaches of integrity. Two pieces of evidence cited by the Commission's Task Force on Public Perceptions illustrate the potential impact of negative attitudes on recruitment:

- A recent survey by the U.S. General Accounting Office (GAO) found that almost 60 percent of federal personnel officers believed that the poor public image of federal employees was hindering their ability to recruit the people their agencies need.

- A 1987 Merit Systems Protection Board survey of college deans and placement officers at the nation's top colleges and universities found that the image of the federal civil service was a primary reason why their public administration graduates were not attracted to government.

Public trust will not be restored unless and until Americans are reassured that those in charge at the top of government will honor their trust and those in the civil service below will commit themselves to the highest levels of service. Toward those ends, the Commission makes the following recommendations:

First, **Presidents, their chief lieutenants and Congress must articulate early and often the necessary and honorable role that public servants play in the democratic process, while at the same time making clear that they will demand the highest performance from those who hold the public trust.**

Second, Presidents must set the highest standards of ethical conduct for those who hold the public trust, and act quickly and firmly to remove those who violate that trust. Members of Congress and their staffs should be covered by similar standards. Codes of conduct to convey such standards should be simple and straightforward, and should focus on the affirmative values that must guide public servants in the exercise of their responsibilities.

" I t's not really very complicated. It's a question of knowing right from wrong, avoiding conflicts of interest, bending over backwards to see that there's not even a perception of conflict of interest. "

PRESIDENT GEORGE BUSH, 1989

The Commission is encouraged by the early steps President Bush has taken to underscore the critical importance of ethical standards in government, including his appointment of a presidential Commission on Federal Ethics Law Reform. That Commission's recommendations deserve urgent consideration, particularly those dealing with the need for an updated and revised executive order governing ethics in government and for a clear and comprehensive ethics manual issued by the Office of Government Ethics.

Despite this important first step, the Commission notes that the problems of the public service will not yield quickly to even the most thoughtful presidential leadership. It has taken time for the erosion of talent to become a cause of deep concern. It will take a sustained, bipartisan commitment to reverse that erosion. The Commission believes that the condition of the public service must remain high on the national agenda in coming years.

Third, the President and Congress should establish an independent advisory council, composed of members from the public and private sectors, to monitor the ongoing state of the career public service and make a bi-annual report to the President. In turn, the President should forward the report to Congress with his own comments and responses, including any recommendations for change that he may have.

GOAL TWO:

IMPROVE THE PRESIDENTIAL APPOINTMENTS PROCESS

The problems new Presidents face in filling the top jobs in government are daunting. First, even if they start planning their transitions during the presidential campaign—as did Presidents Carter, Reagan, and
Bush—it is difficult to find several thousand well-qualified appointees in
fewer than six months.

Second, even if new Presidents can find the talent, the current system makes it increasingly difficult to bring these candidates into government. Some of the problems are inherent in the process. Men and women
are reluctant to interrupt promising careers and uproot families to move
to one of the most expensive areas in the country. But some of the obstacles are unnecessary. Nominees are exposed to an array of complex and
overlapping disclosure forms, most of which become public. Nominees are
asked to make immediate divestiture, whatever the cost and tax burden,
of any financial holdings that might constitute a conflict of interest. And
they are often given little or no orientation about their new responsibilities, in large measure because those doing the recruiting may know little
about the substantive demands of the jobs.

Third, even after new appointees get past the nomination and confirmation process, far too many leave early. The average length of service
for presidential appointees has dropped by almost half since the 1950s,
unnecessarily complicating a President's task of maintaining the energy
and competence of an Administration.

A more effective approach is needed. Presidents must be able to
bring qualified people into office more quickly, and keep them in office
as long as needed. Toward that end, the Commission commends the
National Academy of Public Administration, the Harvard Public/Private
Careers Project, and the Center for Excellence in Government for both
identifying the particular problems of presidential appointments
and proposing a range of viable solutions. Consistent with these earlier
efforts of other groups, the Commission emphasizes the following
recommendations:

> *First,* **the White House Office of Presidential Personnel should be
> given the resources and mandate to perform as an active recruit-
> ing agency for the President.** The Office should neither confine it-
> self to unsolicited resumes nor restrict its search to those who have
> been politically active in the President's campaign. To assist in this
> process, the President should direct the Office to build on the work
> of the Center for Excellence in Government by developing qualifi-
> cation statements for all positions, and make appointments based
> on those merits.

Second, **the financial disclosure process, while a key protection against conflicts of interest, should be streamlined to ease the burdens on potential appointees.** Here, the Commission endorses recommendations by the National Academy of Public Administration and Harvard University's Public/Private Careers Project to simplify the government's financial disclosure form by compressing the current income and property reporting categories. Further, as recommended by the Administrative Conference of the United States, **the Commission encourages Congress to consider legislation to limit the tax penalties of divestiture for those who accept presidential appointments.**

Third, **at the end of their service, presidential appointees should be granted up to three months of severance pay with full benefits as a bridge to outside employment.** Severance pay would act to discourage appointee job-hunting during the last months in office.

GOAL THREE:

MAKE MORE ROOM NEAR THE TOP FOR CAREER EXECUTIVES

From George Washington to the present, Presidents have appointed party leaders, political allies, and compatible personalities to their cabinets and to sub-cabinet jobs in government. That is as it should be. Not only do presidential appointees bring fresh ideas and important experience from the private sector into an Administration; they also help ensure that government is responsive to changing needs. Indeed, many members of the Commission entered government precisely because they wished to support a particular Administration, and because a President asked them to join.

" All public bureaucracies are politicized to some extent—political control of administration is fundamental to a democratic society. The question is, how much politicization is enough— and how should it be brought to bear? "

Task Force on the Senior Executive Service,
Governor Charles Robb, chairman, 1987

There is growing evidence, however, that excessive numbers of presidential appointees may actually undermine effective presidential control of the executive branch. Presidents today are further away from the top career layers of government with 3,000 appointees—approximately 573 presidential appointees subject to Senate confirmation, 670 non-career members of the Senior Executive Service, 110 presidential appointees not subject to Senate confirmation, and approximately 1,700 personal and confidential assistants (Schedule C)—than was Franklin Roosevelt 50 years ago with barely 200. The national agenda is undoubtedly more complex now, and there has been an expansion in the number of federal departments and agencies. But it is also true that federal civilian employment has held remarkably steady over the past three decades, even as the number of presidential appointees has doubled, then doubled again.

From 1933 to 1965, during a period of profound expansion in government responsibilities, the number of cabinet and sub-cabinet officers appointed by the President and confirmed by the Senate doubled from 73 to 152. From 1965 to the present, a span when total employment and programs were more stable, that number more than tripled to 573.

Typically, the increase in presidential appointments has been justified as a way to prod or control reluctant bureaucrats, and to speed implementation of the President's agenda. Thus the operative question is not whether the current number of appointees is large or small, in absolute terms or compared to the total number of civilian employees. The real question is whether the proliferation has in fact made government more effective and more responsive to presidential leadership. The Commission concludes that the answer is "no."

"*B ut a White House personnel assistant sees the position of deputy assistant secretary as a fourth-echelon slot. In his eyes that makes it an ideal reward for a fourth-echelon political type—a campaign advance man, or a regional political organizer. For a senior civil servant, it's irksome to see a position one has spent 20 or 30 years preparing for preempted by an outsider who doesn't know the difference between an audit exception and an authorizing bill.*"

ELLIOT L. RICHARDSON, 1987

First, large numbers of presidential appointees that are beyond the ability of any President or White House to directly oversee, many with plausible claims to their own political constituencies, may actually dilute the President's ability to develop and enforce a coherent, coordinated program and to hold cabinet secretaries accountable. This is particularly true if subordinate appointees are imposed on a department head.

Second, short-term appointees, several ranks deep, can also distance the President and his principal officials from those with the most relevant experience. Career bureaucracies need to be leavened with fresh ideas from outside and need to be responsive to presidential leadership. But they can also be a vast resource of knowledge and impartial judgement. A large number of political positions also takes more time to fill, creating unnecessary delays in the critical first months of an Administration and other unnecessary distractions thereafter.

Finally, layers of temporary presidential appointees between the President and the career professionals who deliver government services year after year inevitably discourage talented men and women from remaining in the career service, or entering in the first place. The ultimate risk is reduced competence among careerists and political appointees alike.

In recommending a reduction in the total number of presidential appointees, the Commission notes that new governments in Britain, France, or Germany operate with fewer than 100 new appointees, yet often implement more sweeping policy changes than in the United States. The United States does not have a parliamentary system, and has many more built-in checks and balances. However, the Commission concludes that a substantial reduction in presidential appointees would be entirely consistent with the President's ability to lead the executive branch, and that indeed a stronger career service would over time enhance his or her effectiveness. Thus, the Commission makes the following recommendations for change in the number and mix of top appointments:

> *First,* **the growth in recent years in the number of presidential appointees, whether those subject to Senate confirmation, noncareer senior executives, or personal and confidential assistants, should be curtailed.** Although a reduction in the total number of presidential appointees must be based on a position-by-position assessment, the Commission is confident that a substantial cut is possible, and believes that a cut from the current 3,000 to no more than 2,000 is a reasonable target.
>
> *Second,* **the President should more frequently consider career officials for sub-cabinet appointments, taking advantage of a prime source of professionalism and experience to his or her Adminis-**

tration. These executives must nonetheless bring unquestioned loyalty to the purposes and agenda of the Administration they serve.

Third, **the President and Congress should set a lower limit on the number of noncareer senior executives allowed within a particular department or agency.** Current law permits up to 25 percent of an agency's senior executives to be noncareer appointees, thereby crowding out opportunities for career officers.

GOAL FOUR:

DECENTRALIZE GOVERNMENT MANAGEMENT

Just as Presidents must be able to appoint philosophically and politically compatible individuals to the top jobs in government, Presidents must also develop adequate mechanisms for overseeing decisionmaking and for implementation of those decisions. Given the complexity of the federal budget and the potential for cross-cutting issues, jurisdictional overlap and disputes among departments and agencies in policy development are inevitable and often constructive. But a President, with the help of the White House staff, needs to control the agenda and to set the basic policy direction.

Once presidential choices are made, however, the decisions should be implemented in the federal departments and agencies where the President's own appointees and government's top career managers must have both authority and responsibility. The jobs will be done well or poorly depending on their competence, morale, and commitment, not on the rules and reporting requirements imposed by the White House staff, Office of Management and Budget (OMB), and Office of Personnel Management (OPM).

Pressure to centralize the key policy choices, understandable as it is, is too easily extended to many administrative decisions once made at the Cabinet and sub-cabinet level. Not only does centralization rob federal departments and agencies of the flexibility and initiative they need to implement the President's agenda, but it often slows the administrative process, creating even greater pressure for centralization. Essential management and regulatory decisions, for example, are now engulfed in red-tape and paperwork to the point that the process often drives the decisions, not vice versa.

The desire to impose close political control and avoid mistakes often forces decisions upward through a seemingly endless chain of command, stifling the very initiative the President needs for successful implementation of policy. Demands for administrative consistency, in the name of equity or White House control, have made it virtually impossible to adapt flexibly to changing circumstances.

A new balance must be created—a balance that returns administrative authority to the federal departments and agencies while retaining necessary elements of oversight with the President and Congress. Toward that end, the Commission makes the following recommendations for decentralizing administrative responsibility to the managers:

First, **provided they receive appropriate program guidance from the President and oversight from Congress, cabinet officers and agency heads should be given greater flexibility to administer their organizations, including greater freedom to hire and fire personnel.** The Commission sees great opportunity for experimentation in this regard, including the kind of flexibilities in pay-setting attempted at the China Lake Naval Weapons Center in California.

Second, **in decentralizing administrative authority and flexibility, the President and Congress must ensure that senior managers receive the executive training to exercise their responsibilities effectively.** The Commission notes the need to strengthen executive development programs at the nation's colleges and universities as one way to provide the broader knowledge and management and professional skills required for greater executive responsibility. (This need for expanded training and greater leadership by OPM is addressed in more detail later in this report.)

GOAL FIVE:

STRENGTHEN THE PRESIDENTIAL/CAREER PARTNERSHIP

Presidential and career executives are partners in the business of government and must work from a relationship of trust. That necessary partnership is too often clouded by mutual suspicion, particularly at the start of a new Administration. Moreover, there is disconcerting evidence that dissatisfaction with presidential appointees has become a major reason why senior career executives leave government. This may be one reason

" The career Senior Executive Service is the institutional memory; it knows how to grease the wheels of government and make them turn. "

SENATOR JOHN GLENN, 1987

why, according to a survey by the National Academy of Public Administration, the number of presidential appointees who rate their career employees competent and responsive dropped roughly 15 points from 1964 to 1984. The drop may be small, but it has been steady from one administration to the next.

At the same time, it is encouraging that the Commission's own survey of recent cabinet officers shows that confidence in the career-service tends to build in the course of an Administration. Career executives want strong presidential leadership—they are demoralized by vacancies, policy vacuums, and a lack of direction. At the same time, the good presidential appointees want strong career support—careerists who know how their institutions work and know how to work their institutions.

The Commission believes that a strong presidential/career partnership involves give-and-take from both. If presidential appointees want the full confidence and support of career officers, they must be willing to listen and invite them into policy discussions. By the same token, once policy choices are made, career executives must be willing to follow and to do so without prolonging public debate. They must be willing to implement the laws faithfully and with full energy. That commitment must be part of the ethic of service for all government executives, career or political.

> "*One of the great mistakes people make in coming in is developing a we/they attitude toward their own staff. . . . Big mistake. There are a lot of potential teammates out there, and you have to find them. And the faster you do, the better.*"
>
> *JOHN GARDNER*

The Commission believes its earlier recommendations regarding the number and mix of senior executives will strengthen this key partnership by making more room for career executives to participate. In addition it makes the following recommendations:

First, **all presidential appointees must receive adequate orientation to office.** Such orientation should be provided during the hiatus between nomination and confirmation, focusing on the substantive policy and administrative responsibilities each appointee faces, the ethical conduct expected of a public official, and the positive role that career officers can play.

Second, Cabinet secretaries and agency heads should be given greater opportunity to participate in the choice of their sub-cabinet officers, particularly where the Office of Presidential Personnel and a cabinet secretary disagree on a specific appointee. Forcing unwanted staff onto a reluctant secretary not only creates potential tension among presidential executives within an agency, but engenders confusion among career executives who simply do not know whom to follow.

> " *I* had always felt that government people were not motivated, because in industry you have various incentives where you can motivate people, and that perhaps government people didn't work so hard because they weren't so highly motivated. Well, I was dead wrong. I find that in this department there are a tremendous cadre of professionals, highly motivated not by financial rewards but to serve their country. It's as simple as that. "
>
> C. WILLIAM VERITY, JR.,
> *Secretary of Commerce, 1989*

CHAPTER II

Enriching the Talent Pool

T he supply of future career federal executives in large measure
depends on the ability of government to build interest in public
life among the nation's most talented young people. Although
recent trends suggest there will be greater mid-career movement in and
out of government, the greatest competition is likely to be at the entry level.
Gone are the days when the brightest students would line up for a chance
at a government job. Gone, too, is the buyer's market that came with the
huge baby boom generation.

> *" F or years, many Federal agencies have been able to hire and
> retain highly educated, highly skilled work forces, even though
> their wages, incentives, and working conditions have not been
> fully competitive with those offered by private employers. But
> as labor markets become tighter during the early 1990s,
> hiring qualified workers will become much more difficult. "*
>
> CIVIL SERVICE 2000,
> *The Hudson Institute, 1988*

The competition for talented young people will continue far into
the future. As the growth in the labor force declines to barely 1 percent

a year in the 1990s and early 2000s, government will have to draw from a much smaller talent pool. Government will also have a much stronger incentive to recruit women and minorities. Indeed, two-thirds of new government workers between now and the year 2000 will be women. These new demographic realities will demand a recruiting strategy more heavily directed toward two-earner couples, minorities, and single mothers. The pressure for flex-time, day-care, and more creative strategies for tapping the minority talent pool will only increase.

GOAL SIX:

REBUILD STUDENT INTEREST

Young Americans have always been a source of creative energy for government. Their natural enthusiasm and willingness to question the status quo are important counterweights to the inertia that can set in as an agency and its work force ages.

Although government still has some advantages in attracting young people—the most significant of which is the exhilaration of working on big issues—it also faces an erosion of student interest in public life. The evidence compiled by the Commission's Task Forces on Education and Training and on Recruitment and Retention suggests hard times ahead for government recruiters in attracting students into public careers:

- According to surveys by the University of California at Los Angeles and the American Council on Education, the percentage of college freshmen who said that it is "important to be well-off financially" rose from 41 percent in 1966 to 76 percent in 1987, while the number who said that the most important reason to go to college was to "make more money" jumped from 50 percent in 1971 to 71 percent in 1987.

- The average starting salary for careers in private-sector consulting and research has gone up 15 percent in real terms over the past decade, while pay for careers in banking, finance, and insurance has jumped 18 percent. During the same period, the real average starting salary for a career in the federal government has fallen 20 percent, and now trails the private sector on average by almost $6,000.

- President Derek Bok of Harvard, in a commencement address in 1988, noted that only 7 percent of Harvard's seniors had expressed an interest in government and that far fewer would actually make a career in government.

Not all the news is bad, however. The number of college freshmen who see helping others as an essential or very important objective in life has remained steady at almost 60 percent over the past 20 years, while the recent increase in campus volunteerism suggests a growing commitment to community service. That flame is a hopeful sign for the future.

> " *There is a debt of service due from every man to his country, proportioned to the bounty which nature and fortune have measured to him.* "
>
> *THOMAS JEFFERSON*

Yet, surveys also show that many students simply do not know enough about government to be interested in careers in government. Even those who take social studies or history courses may not learn the right lessons about how they can make a difference. A majority of a sample of recent high-school graduates could not explain the importance of *Brown v. Topeka Board of Education*, and two-thirds of a sample of college freshmen in 1987 could not describe the freedoms guaranteed by the Bill of Rights.

The Commission believes that an informed citizenry is essential to America's political system, and that a broad sense of civic duty among America's young people is a necessary precursor to a strong public service. The Commission therefore makes the following recommendations designed to rebuild student interest in public life:

First, **the nation must elevate the importance of civic education as a part of social studies and history in the nation's primary and secondary school curricula.** Starting with a comprehensive review of current programs, the nation's educators and parents should work toward new civics curricula designed to enliven textbooks, enhance student understanding of America's civic institutions, relate formal learning about those institutions to the problems students care about, and link classroom learning to extracurricular practice.

Second, **America's communities should increase the opportunity for young people to practice their citizenship skills.** As budget realities have forced many public schools to eliminate extracurricular activities that once served as a training ground for future citizens, the need for alternative sponsors has grown. The Commission urges

local businesses, nonprofit organizations, civic groups, and governments to work together in sponsoring more of the citizenship
activities that students deserve.

***Third*, America should take advantage of the natural idealism of
young people by expanding and encouraging national volunteer service**, whether through existing programs like ACTION, the Peace
Corps, and VISTA, or experiments with initiatives like President
Bush's Youth Engaged in Service (YES) and some of the ideas contained in the Democratic Leadership Council's citizen corps
proposal.

GOAL SEVEN:

RECRUIT THE VERY BEST GRADUATES

Government faces an enormous challenge in recruiting America's
top college graduates. On the one hand, outstanding graduates doubt that
the public sector can fulfill their dreams of meaningful, challenging careers.
On the other, they find that the complexity of entry makes public sector
jobs among the toughest to get.

The Commission's own survey of top graduates in the class of 1988
illustrates the problem. According to the Commission's sample of honor
society students, the public service is not perceived as a place where talented
people can get ahead. Few of the top graduates feel the federal government can offer good pay and recognition for performance. Fewer still say
a federal job can be challenging and intellectually stimulating. Public service
is too often seen as a career of last resort. Consider the following results
from the survey:

- More than 70 percent said the federal government does not offer
  a good chance for responsibility early on in one's career.

- Eighty-six percent said a federal job would not allow them to use
  their abilities to the fullest.

- Roughly half said that most federal jobs are routine and monotonous.

- Eighty percent said federal civil servants do not have the power and
  opportunity to influence government outcomes.

- Fewer than 3 percent said that a person with ability who joins the
  federal civil service has a high probability of ending up in one of
  the top government jobs.

Many of the recommendations presented elsewhere in this report are designed to change these attitudes by setting higher standards for performance and creating more challenging jobs. Government must send a strong signal to America's youth that it is interested in the very best. Toward that end, the Commission makes the following additional recommendations:

> *First*, **the President and Congress should establish a Presidential Public Service Scholarship Program targeted to 1,000 college or college-bound students each year.** Admission to the program should parallel appointment to the military service academies—that is, through nomination by members of Congress—and include tuition and other costs, in return for a commitment to a determined number of years of government service.

> *Second*, **the President and Congress should expand and strengthen the government's current programs for recruiting college graduates into public careers.** Specifically, the Presidential Management Internship program should be expanded from 400 positions per year to 1,000.

GOAL EIGHT:

OPEN NEW CHANNELS OF COMMUNICATION

That there is a growing competition for talented students is clear. However, while American corporations visit the campuses, provide high-paying summer jobs, advertise their positions in accessible publications, and make it easy for students to accept job offers, most government departments and agencies wait until the last minute to make their first contacts.

> *" When I talk with students, I tell them that what you do in government at any given level matters more than what business people at a comparable level do. What they do is good for the management and the stockholders, and sometimes, if they're lucky, for all the customers as well. What you do affects the well-being, the survival even, of millions. "*
>
> *ELLIOT L. RICHARDSON, 1987*

With several notable exceptions, such as the General Accounting Office, the Office of Management and Budget, and the Central Intelligence Agency, most federal agencies have little experience with on-campus recruiting. Nor do most recognize their role in educating young Americans about the value of public life and the intrinsic rewards of government service. Students are left to work their way through the federal hiring process on their own.

If the public sector is to compete effectively for a new generation of video-conscious, computer-literate students, it must also become more adept at communication. The Commission welcomes recent efforts by the Office of Personnel Management (OPM) to bring federal advertising into the 1980s with a positive message on public careers and accessible brochures describing "Career America." More must be done. The Commission makes the following recommendations:

> *First,* **the government's executives, both senior and mid-level, po-litical and career, should serve as ambassadors of the public serv-ice on America's college campuses.** These leaders must be willing to spend more time with America's young people on college cam-puses both before and after the key recruiting periods. In this re-gard, the Commission applauds the effort by the Center for Excel-lence in Government to inform students of the rewards of public careers by co-sponsoring, with The Ford Foundation and selected colleges, visits to campuses by persons from the private sector who have previously served in government.

> *Second,* **to describe and celebrate public careers, government should open new channels of communication with America's college students—at job fairs, and through electronic bulletin boards, com-puter software, and/or video cassettes.**

> *Third,* **OPM should establish a unified federal job bank to help stu-dents find openings in the public sector,** accessible for student "browsing" through 800-line personal computer hook-ups.

GOAL NINE:

SIMPLIFY THE RECRUITING PROCESS

Even when the public sector finds outstanding candidates, the com-plexity of the hiring process often drives all but the most dedicated away. Perceptions of public service as a lackluster career are compounded by the belief among potential candidates that getting a government job is an exercise in frustration. For example, only a third of the honor students surveyed by the Commission said they would know how to obtain a government job even if they wanted one, and only 3 percent actively sought federal employment.

The Commission itself received dozens of unsolicited letters from young people asking how they might go about applying for a government position, and even more describing the disheartening process of months and months of waiting for a call following a job application or for a final decision. For the most talented students, of course, those waits provide ample opportunity to consider private-sector employment.

> " *T* *he current system is slow; it is legally trammelled and intellectually confused; it is impossible to explain to potential candidates. It is almost certainly not fulfilling the spirit of our mandate to hire the most meritorious candidates.* "
>
> CONSTANCE HORNER
> *Director, Office of Personnel Management, 1988*

In moving toward a more effective hiring system, the Commission welcomes recent efforts by OPM to remove some of the obstacles in the process. The Commission makes the following recommendations to further enhance OPM's agenda for change:

First, **OPM should continue to deregulate the hiring process by giving departments and agencies broad, but conditional, authority to set their own rules, as well as through aggressive use and expansion of existing authority to experiment and continued use of advisory and clearing-house mechanisms to share information across government.**

Second, **OPM should experiment with a variety of new recruitment incentives for hard-to-recruit professions—for example, more flexible compensation systems that address the costs of starting a new job.**

Third, **OPM should continue its experiments with on-the-spot hiring of both undergraduate and graduate students to minimize paperwork and delay.**

GOAL TEN:

INCREASE THE REPRESENTATION OF MINORITIES

If the public sector is to reach the nation's talented students, it must become more effective in recruiting minorities. As *Civil Service 2000* envisages, blacks will make up 17 percent of the growth in the labor force between 1988 and the year 2000, while Hispanics will account for an even greater share at 29 percent.

Despite this opportunity for greater minority representation in the public sector, the prospects for placement are mixed. According to a recent Ford Foundation study, the problem appears to be much more one of raising the number of those from minority groups ready to enter the public service than it is one of finding the needed jobs.

If the number of minority students who graduate from high school and college stays constant, the public, private, and nonprofit sectors will continue to compete for a painfully small pool of graduates. Thus, the goal must be to encourage more from minority groups capable of and interested in entering the public policy profession. Toward that end, the Commission makes the following recommendations:

First, **America's educators and community leaders must help more minority students stay in school through high school and college to help build the talent pool.** Without an increase in graduation rates, there will not be enough minorities to fill the available jobs. Although specific recommendations in this respect are beyond the scope of this report, the Commission believes that the current figures are unacceptable if minorities are to play an increasing and important role in the public sector. If graduation rates do not increase, **the Commission recommends that government provide needed training, including high school course work, for blacks and Hispanics upon entry into their government careers.**

Second, **America's graduate schools of public affairs should reach across traditional academic boundaries to interest minority students in public life through cooperative relationships with historically black and Hispanic colleges and universities.** The cooperation must involve (1) a strengthening of the public affairs/public policy/political science curricula at the undergraduate schools to challenge students for graduate training, (2) greater efforts at minority recruitment into schools of public affairs, and (3) an enrichment of the curricula at the graduate schools to create a greater understanding of issues of race in public policy and administration.

The Commission believes these efforts will have a positive impact on minority representation in public life, particularly when coupled with the strengthened civics curricula, scholarship programs, and more effective hiring processes recommended elsewhere in this report. Because of the importance of minorities to the future effectiveness of government, the Commission also recommends that a specific number of Presidential Public Service Scholarships recommended elsewhere in this report be targeted for minorities.

Without a visible commitment at the highest levels of government, however, minority interest in public careers will remain low. From the White House to the state house, the nation's leaders must make a sustained effort to bring blacks, Hispanics, and other minorities into the top positions of government, not solely to reflect the diversity of the American people, but also as role models and mentors for the next generation of public leaders.

CHAPTER III

A Culture of Performance

The desire to perform at full potential is the most important asset any employee can offer. In the private sector, this commitment to performance creates profits. In the government, it creates public value. Although the commitment to excellence is surely necessary in both sectors, it is the very least civil servants must provide to the people they serve.

"We know the human talent is there. We need to find good people, pay them competitive salaries, hold them accountable, and let them produce. Given leadership and motivation, they will do the job."

CHARLES BOWSHER
Comptroller General of the United States, 1988

The commitment to performance cannot long survive, however, unless the government provides adequate pay, recognition for jobs done well, accessible training, and decent working conditions. Quality service must be recognized, rewarded, and constantly reinforced. It is not enough to exhort the work force to do better—government must provide tangible signals that performance matters.

GOAL ELEVEN:
PROVIDE COMPETITIVE PAY AND
DEMAND COMPETITIVE PERFORMANCE

The federal government will never be able to pay its employees more than the private sector, nor should it try. However, if government is to recruit from among outstanding college graduates, and build a high-performance workforce, it must be willing to pay reasonably competitive salaries. Government does not have to match private pay dollar-for-dollar in every position, particularly at the higher levels. But if it is to remain a credible career choice, government simply cannot permit the purchasing power of federal pay to decline year after year and the gap between public and private pay for comparable jobs to widen.

"Over the last decade, [the National Institutes of Health] have not been able to recruit a single senior research scientist from the private or academic sectors to engage in the independent conduct of a clinical or basic biomedical research program."

DR. ANTHONY FAUCI
Director, National Institute of Allergy and Infectious Diseases, 1988

The impact of lost purchasing power and the widening pay gap is clear. Consider the evidence compiled by the Commission's Task Force on Pay and Compensation:

- Half the federal government's personnel officers say that inadequate compensation has become a significant hindrance in attracting the people they need.

- Almost 40 percent of the senior federal executives who left government service in 1985 said their frustrations with proposed and actual changes in compensation were of great or very great importance in their decisions.

- Only 17 percent of the honor society graduates surveyed by the Commission felt the federal government could compete in salary with the private sector.

• The Director of Placement at the Massachusetts Institute of Technology said there could be little doubt why so few of MIT's students take government jobs, noting that for bachelor degree students in engineering, the discrepancy in starting salaries between government and the private sector is as much as $6,000.

Senior public servants have customarily been willing to moderate their salary expectations—a kind of "public service differential"—in return for challenging work, job security, and the opportunity to make a difference. However, according to the most recent salary data, the gap between what government and the private sector pays has grown far beyond the point where government can hope to recruit and retain qualified staff, even as the federal benefits package has become less attractive.

PAY AT THE TOP

Political appointees, judges, and members of Congress have never been paid as much as those in the private sector with comparable responsibilities, and most accept financial sacrifice as part of their public responsibility. Yet, even starting from these relatively lower levels, the senior positions in government continue to lose ground to inflation. Between 1969, when a special effort was made to bring top government salaries into a reasonable relationship with the private sector, and 1988, the purchasing power of executive, judicial, and legislative salaries fell by 35 percent.

> 66 *[T]he current salary levels of our government threaten our ability to generate and attract the most talented, creative, and able individuals of our citizenry to governmental service. We must not continue to rely on a system that attracts to public service those who by family sacrifice or preexisting wealth harken to the call to contribute to the democratic good. We of course must have the idealistic, but we also need the experienced, the able, and the wise.* 99
>
> *GRIFFIN BELL*
> *Former U.S. Attorney General, 1988*

The Commission believes the case for restoring this lost purchasing power is strong, particularly if linked to a reduction in the total number of political appointees in the executive branch and a renewed commitment to the highest standards of integrity and performance. **The Commission recommends action to raise executive, judicial, and legislative salaries to 1969 levels of purchasing power.**

The Commission recognizes that while such an increase may be relatively small in total dollars—$300 million in a budget of $1.16 trillion—it will still be perceived by the American people as excessive, especially if Congress does not act to prohibit such outside income as speaking honoraria. Not only does such income create lingering doubts about the need for an across-the-board increase, but it also undermines public trust in national institutions.

Therefore, just as judges and political appointees have fixed incomes, governed by strict rules against outside earnings, **the Commission recommends that Congress adopt a clearly enforceable ban on speaking honoraria and other income related to their public responsibilities.** If executive, judicial, and legislative salaries are to rise together or not at all, all three branches should be covered by the same rules on outside income and honoraria.

" *F ailure to raise the pay of members of Congress, the Judiciary and senior Administration officials is irresponsible. We will lose good members in Congress—the young members trying to raise a family, educate their kids and maintain two residences. We will lose good judges. We will lose good people who administer programs affecting the lives of millions of people. The quality of work performed by all three branches of government will suffer because we don't have the guts to say what we're worth.* "

REP. DAN ROSTENKOWSKI, 1989

The current pay-setting process for these salaries (the Quadrennial Commission) provides for pay adjustments only once every four years. This being the case, even catching up with inflation is seen as excessive by the public, particularly at a time of budget difficulties. For this reason, **the Commission recommends that the needed restoration of purchasing power in**

senior salaries be extended more evenly over time; e.g., 25 percent now and the balance by the beginning of a new Congress in 1991. Once purchasing power is restored to 1969 levels, the Commission recommends development of a process that will trigger needed increases in a more timely fashion.

These changes should help members of Congress explain the case for pay increases to their constituents. However, if Congress remains unable to act on its own salaries, even with limits on honoraria and a phased-in approach to compensation increases, **the Commission recommends that the President make separate recommendations for judges and top-level senior executives along the lines proposed and that Congress promptly act upon these recommendations.**

PAY IN THE SENIOR EXECUTIVE SERVICE

Failure to increase the top salaries in government also undermines the government's ability to recruit and retain the scientists, cancer researchers, computer engineers, and other senior career executives who manage the essential services of government. These men and women simply should not be asked to absorb further cuts from inflation. They have families to support, children to educate, and mortgages to meet—and, like political appointees and judges, are prohibited from earning outside income or speaking fees related to their employment. They, too, are on fixed incomes, capped by the salaries of political appointees just above.

Given the critical importance of these positions, the urgency of salary increases at the senior career level may be even more pressing than at the political level. Consequently, **if for some reason there is delay in implementing salary increases at the political level, the Commission recommends prompt action by the President and Congress to raise the cap on the Senior Executive Service, even if this means that their pay in some instances could exceed that being received by the political appointees above them.**

PAY IN THE GENERAL SCHEDULE

The case for a "public service differential" becomes increasingly weak further down into the civil service. Among the white-collar, nonpostal members of the civil service covered by the General Schedule pay system, financial sacrifice as a price of a government job is both difficult to absorb and to justify. More important, if government is to fill these key civil service jobs—whether at air traffic control, Social Security processing centers, or cancer research labs—with qualified employees, it must stay at or close to at least average levels of pay offered by other employers.

Unfortunately, after a decade of budget cuts and pay freezes, salaries of most federal employees are clearly lagging behind the private sector.

According to the most recent survey conducted by the Bureau of Labor Statistics, the gap, on average, nationwide is 22 percent. Whether or not that figure accurately captures the differential for particular jobs and areas, there is no doubt that the pay gap has become a disincentive in both recruiting and retaining a high-performance work force. Many young Americans feel they can no longer afford to take a government job, while many civil servants can no longer ignore the call of private pay. If this trend continues, the result could be mediocrity in carrying out the essential tasks of government.

The Commission believes the President and Congress must give a higher budget priority to civil service pay. It is important to recognize, however, that it is no longer appropriate or workable to use a national average to establish an appropriate level of pay. The world of work has changed too much to use such a broad approach. The pay rate for a government secretary working in Phoenix, for example, is much closer to that of the private sector than is the pay of a physician at the National Institutes of Health or an engineer at the Marshall Space Flight Center. Indeed, some wage surveys show that geographic differences can exceed 30 percent for similar jobs.

These locality and occupational differences seriously undermine the fairness of the current civil service pay process, especially when all federal employees receive the same pay whether they work in low-cost areas such as Kansas City or Norfolk, Virginia, or high-cost areas such as San Francisco or Boston. Thus, even if the President and Congress found the $13 billion needed to provide an immediate 22 percent raise across the board, many would still lag behind their counterparts in the private sector, while some would actually be ahead. That is neither fair to the civil service of government nor to the public it serves.

The Commission concludes that the current goal of national pay comparability is unworkable. It recommends instead a pay-setting system that recognizes the fact that public employees live and work in localities characterized by widely different living costs and labor market pressures, and adjusts compensation upward accordingly. Under such a system, federal employees would continue to receive the same base pay for the same job, but in large areas of the country many would also receive an allowance designed to compensate for higher living costs and labor competition. In addition, **the Commission believes that the present ability to pay special pay rates for occupations where there are shortages or strong competitive pressure from the private sector should be extended and broadened.**

MEETING THE COST OF PAY

The Commission recognizes that with the nonpostal, civilian federal payroll at $71 billion per year, any meaningful pay reforms will unavoidably involve substantial sums. However, we believe the proposed approach is more efficient and equitable than an immediate across-the-board increase to close the gap based on a nationwide average. This is also why the Commission supports some phasing-in of the cost. The fundamental need is to begin building a more competitive pay system at all levels of government, and to act now to recognize the disparity in the current pay-setting process.

The Commission is of the view that these changes, including a substantial and prompt narrowing of the gap between public and private pay on a locality-by-locality basis, will create the opportunity for higher performance and productivity within the civil service. Thus, while urging that civil service pay be given a higher budget priority, **the Commission believes that a substantial portion of the cost can and should be absorbed through existing personnel accounts, whether through targeted reductions in employment or the elimination of programs that no longer serve essential public need.**

Agencies with increasing workloads and essential missions cannot be expected to absorb all of the cost. They must be protected from across-the-board cuts that might undermine vital missions, but all can improve productivity. Toward this end, **the Commission encourages the President and Congress to use their respective budget and oversight authorities to monitor closely progress toward improving standards of employee performance, while eliminating duplication of services and unnecessary layers of government through restructuring both within and across departments and agencies.** Not only would such restructuring create significant budgetary savings, but it would also produce more challenging jobs for the future.

GOAL TWELVE:

STRENGTHEN THE GOVERNMENT'S PERSONNEL AGENCY

Building a culture of performance involves day-to-day leadership and guidance from the government's chief personnel agency. Just as the President must articulate the important role that civil servants play in government, the Office of Personnel Management must translate the broad message into specific policies for successful human resource management.

Unfortunately, there has been a sense that OPM may have become more of an obstacle to effective personnel management than a leader. When the government's 1,300 department and agency personnel officers were recently asked by GAO what barriers greatly hindered their agency's ability to hire the people it needed in a reasonable amount of time, over 40 percent said they were frustrated by OPM's lack of a clear recruiting strategy for attracting talented potential employees, half pointed to OPM's cumbersome rules and regulations, and two-thirds cited the length of time required to complete the application process.

The OPM is undoubtedly often blamed for problems beyond its control. Its mission would stretch the capabilities of the strongest agency. Its clientele is huge, and its staff and funding limited. Most important, it continues to be encumbered by operating responsibilities that limit its ability to set policy; not only does OPM operate an extensive federal training program, but it must also approve countless personnel decisions that could easily be decentralized to the departments and agencies.

Moreover, turnover at the top of the agency has been excessive, budget cuts have been deep, and career morale has fallen. Indeed, according to a 1988 GAO survey of OPM's own senior staff, 44 percent said morale in their unit was low or very low, two-thirds said turnover of experienced staff had affected their unit's ability to accomplish its goals, and a significant number indicated problems communicating with the presidential appointees at the top of the agency.

The OPM was created in 1978 to provide efficient, responsive personnel leadership on behalf of the President. Although OPM has never fully realized this potential, the need for such an agency remains. The Commission is encouraged by steps taken by the most recent Director to strengthen its effectiveness. The Commission believes that the President and Congress should take additional steps to restructure OPM, first by strengthening its technical expertise, then by decentralizing unnecessary operating responsibilities and revitalizing its staff. Toward this end, the Commission makes the following recommendations:

> *First,* **the President should highlight the important role of OPM by sustained contact with its Director and by ensuring participation by the Director in cabinet-level discussions on human resource management issues. The Commission further recommends that OPM's current operating responsibilities—e.g., specialized training and approval of routine personnel decisions—should be decentralized to the federal departments and agencies,** thereby allowing it to concentrate on five major duties: (1) providing policy guidance on personnel standards and practices, (2) overseeing implementation of those standards and practices by departments and agencies, (3) providing technical support for departments and agencies that need help, (4) undertaking research on ways to enhance government productivity and performance, and (5) anticipating future trends in the government work force.

> *Second,* **the number of politically appointed managers inside OPM should be significantly reduced.** By its example, OPM would send

a powerful signal to other agencies about the need for partnership between presidential and career executives, and on the importance of room at the top for both.

GOAL THIRTEEN:

INCREASE GOVERNMENT PRODUCTIVITY

Federal productivity can and must improve. Because the federal work force is unlikely to grow in coming years, as the budget pressure remains intense, the federal government will have to do even more with less.

If productivity is to rise—and the American public deserves no less—two obstacles must be addressed. First, as noted by the Commission's Task Force on Recruitment and Retention, the performance appraisal process itself must be strengthened. Seventy percent of the senior executives at the Internal Revenue Service recently said their bonus system did not provide an incentive to meet job objectives, 69 percent said the system is not administered fairly, and 76 percent said there was no direct linkage between their performance and the likelihood of receiving a bonus. Similar perceptions appear to exist across government.

> *" The lack of measurable goals and objectives makes it difficult to know whether important programs and initiatives are succeeding. Lack of a consensus on how to judge success tends to exacerbate political differences. Rather than focusing on ways to improve the situation, too much effort is spent defining, defending, or attacking positions. "*
>
> GENERAL ACCOUNTING OFFICE,
> *The Public Service, a*
> *Report to Congress, 1988*

Second, there must be greater technical support and guidance from OPM. Some of the current performance appraisal systems are so complicated and time-consuming that federal departments and agencies simply cannot comply with their requirements. Indeed, 57 percent of the federal personnel officers interviewed by GAO in 1987 said they have trouble developing clear, measurable, and objective performance standards, while 54 percent say the process is too cumbersome and time-consuming.

What appears to be needed most for motivating higher productivity is a consistent, understandable performance recognition system, and technical support from the government's chief personnel agency. Toward these ends, the Commission makes the following recommendations:

> *First,* in conjunction with the pay increases recommended above, the number of senior executives currently eligible for annual bonuses should be reduced by half to ensure that performance bonuses are only used as bonuses, not as hidden salary increases, and to concentrate scarce budget resources on the highest performers. It is critical to remember that both the bonus system and adequate pay must send the same message—that performance matters.

> *Second,* OPM must take a stronger leadership role in providing assistance to departments and agencies on performance appraisal and productivity improvement. There is ample evidence that agencies want the help. Such measures would improve both presidential and congressional oversight by creating meaningful targets for government performance.

> *Third,* OPM should continue past experiments with "gain-sharing" in agencies. Such experiments allow agencies, employees, and the taxpayer to split the savings that accrue from higher performance and productivity. In continuing these experiments, labor and management must work together to develop a fair public test of this private-sector concept.

This effort to increase government productivity can be extended through further government experiments in collective bargaining. The Commission believes that such experiments can be designed to harness a spirit of cooperation between labor and management in improving government performance, thereby avoiding the confrontational practices which have characterized some private-sector union-management relationships.

GOAL FOURTEEN:

PROVIDE THE TRAINING TO SUCCEED

In any given year, roughly 60,000 to 70,000 white-collar employees join the federal civil service. What is most surprising, according to the Commission's Task Force on Education and Training, is how few of these employees had specific training to be government executives. Most were hired because of specific skills, not because they were generalist managers. Only

808, or 2.7 percent, of the new professional employees hired in 1987 had degrees in public administration or political science, while 23 percent had degrees in engineering and 24 percent in business and accounting.

Not only will most of these new employees need training if they are to move into management positions, but even the relatively small number who enter with appropriate preparation must be given the skills to keep up with a rapidly changing world. As such, training is best viewed as a long-run investment in effective government.

Yet, most federal training is short-term in its focus, duration, and effects. Consider the following conclusions presented by the Commission's Task Force on Education and Training:

- The recent increase in training activity in government appears to have been achieved by reducing the length of programs, eliminating most long-term courses, and spreading the limited dollars so thinly that the effects are of limited value.

- The government spends about three-quarters of 1 percent of its payroll dollars on civilian training, compared with 3 to 5 percent in the most effective private firms.

- With a few exceptions, most federal training is voluntary, individually focused, and job-specific and bears little discernible relation to major agency objectives and missions. Nor is training tied to any performance goals, leaving agencies unable to justify costs in an era of tight budgets.

In addition, according to the Commission's Task Force on Recruitment and Retention, federal training is suffering from an identity crisis. Agencies are not sure what they should train for (short-term or long-term), who should get the lion's share of resources (entry level or senior level), when employees need additional education (once a year or more often), and whether mid-career education is of value.

Although the federal government does a reasonably good job of dealing with specific training needs, such as helping employees learn how to use personal computers, its executive development programs are weak. Career paths are poorly designed, executive succession is accidental and unplanned, and real-time training for pressured managers is virtually nonexistent. At both the career and presidential level, training is all-too-often ad hoc and self-initiated.

The Commission believes that training must receive a higher priority in coming years, both to ensure that talented public servants are allowed to grow and to address the changing public agenda. This means an aggressive training program aimed at all levels of the work force. In pursuit of this goal, the Commission makes the following recommendations:

First, **OPM and the nation's schools of public affairs should work together to define the skills needed by today's public executives.** If the public sector is to continue its movement toward "third-party government," for example, where public managers are increasingly contract managers using private or nonprofit delivery mechanisms, training regimens for senior executives must change. **In addition, to recognize the importance of management as a distinctive skill, the President should create a separate track within the Senior Executive Service for generalist managers.**

Second, **OPM should help departments and agencies design clear career paths for advancement to senior executive positions, and provide guidance on the kinds of executive development curricula and succession planning appropriate to future success.** Unlike the private sector, where managers are groomed for succession upward through careful advancement and education, career public servants often become managers more by fiat and automatic promotion than by experience and skills. In addition, OPM should encourage management training for government specialists—for example, scientists and engineers—before they enter supervisory or executive positions.

Third, **as part of the overall decentralization of responsibility recommended by the Commission, OPM should encourage departments and agencies to develop their own programs, to contract for training with other comparable government agencies, or to look outside government for the training needed for their specialized missions.** In short, OPM should get out of the specialized training business, allowing departments and agencies to take more responsibility for their own training programs.

Fourth, **schools of public affairs should enrich their teaching through a greater appreciation of the role of practical experience. Toward this end, the National Association of Schools of Public Affairs and Administration and its representatives should work toward the establishment of a Public Service Fellows Program, modeled on the prestigious White House, Congressional, and Judicial Fellows programs,** designed to bring teachers of public affairs into government for a year of hands-on experience at the federal and state levels.

GOAL FIFTEEN:

IMPROVE THE GOVERNMENT WORK PLACE

Few things detract more from an employee's desire to achieve than coming to work in a cramped office in a dangerous building in an unsafe neighborhood. Yet this is what happens when government devotes only passing attention to violations of safety regulations that would not be tolerated in the private sector.

Few things undercut motivation more than coming to work in an organization that tolerates sexual harassment. Yet according to a 1988 Merit Systems Protection Board survey, this is what 42 percent of women employees say they faced at work last year, at a cost of $130 million a year in sick leave, absenteeism, and turnover.

Few things reduce commitment more than yet another struggle with the suffocating bureaucracy within an agency. Yet this is precisely what happens when the nation's workers are engulfed in the mass of red-tape that government imposes on itself. No one wants to reduce bureaucracy more than America's public servants themselves.

> " *We need a renewed commitment to provide Federal workers with the tools to accomplish their tasks. . . . Further, we need to provide workers with modern, quality facilities that are located convenient to mass transportation. The work place should be comfortable, include amenities such as access to child development facilities and gyms, and generally compare favorably with first-class office space provided by private-sector employers.* "
>
> *TERENCE GOLDEN*
> *Director, General Services Administration, 1988*

Finally, few things undermine dedication more than seeing fraud, waste, or abuse, and being scared to report it. In the most recent Merit Systems Protection Board survey on the issue, of the 25 percent of federal employees who saw an instance of such abuse in their agencies, 7 out of 10 did not report it.

The Commission believes that changes in government working conditions can be as important for recruitment and retention as a challenging job and decent pay. Therefore, the Commission encourages the President and Congress to consider ways of improving government working conditions, including initiatives on the growing problems of "electronic sweat-shops," on further government-wide campaigns to eliminate sexual harassment in the work place, and on ways to protect those who "blow the whistle" on fraud, waste, and abuse in government. Improving the conditions of work is essential to improving service to the public.

Government must also become more user-friendly. All too often, the public dreads the thought of making contact with government. Images of dreary buildings, endless lines, hassled officials, and strictly enforced office hours even haunt public servants themselves.

If government is to be for the people, it must go where the people are. Government must go to the shopping malls and the branch libraries, even if that means occasionally contracting out to "franchisees" who deliver services. Instead of making the people fit government schedules and government locales, government must fit the people's schedule and needs. Government must abandon the old notion of a Monday to Friday government and 9 to 5 business hours. That is part of improving the conditions of government work for all Americans, government employees as well as the public they serve.

Looking Ahead

If government is to be both responsive to the people's will, and capable of meeting the challenges of the twenty-first century, it must have a public service of talent, of commitment, of dedication to the highest ethical standards. A strong cadre of skilled and committed men and women, working in a partnership of trust with able political leaders, must provide the essential underpinning for the great American venture of self government.

> " *The government of the United States is the largest and most difficult task undertaken by the American people, and at the same time the most important and the noblest. Our Government does more for more men, women, and children than any other institution; it employs more persons in work than any other employer. It covers a wider range of aims and activities than any other enterprise; it sustains the frame of our national and our community life, our economic system, our individual rights and liberties.* "
>
> *The President's Committee on*
> *Administrative Management*
> *(The Brownlow Committee), 1937*

This report is dedicated to that purpose. It sets out a broad agenda for action. It includes specific proposals to encourage the strong leadership, the able talent, and the high performance required to meet the needs of the future. The nation should demand no less.

At the same time, the members of the Commission are convinced that this report, or any report, can be no more than a beginning—a step in a process. What we need—and need urgently—is both national debate and concrete steps.

We are convinced that sustained attention by the President and the Congress will be required.

We will call upon the nation's educational and other public institutions to support the needed effort.

And, not least, we remind the public servants themselves that public trust and support will, in the end, depend upon their own ability to perform and maintain high standards.

TASK FORCE REPORTS

TO THE

NATIONAL COMMISSION ON THE PUBLIC SERVICE

CHAIRMAN

Paul A. Volcker

TASK FORCES

Public Perceptions of the Public Service

Recruitment and Retention

Education and Training

Relations Between Political Appointees and Career Executives

Pay and Compensation

WASHINGTON 1989

Preface to the Task Force Reports

This section of Task Force reports contains the major portion of information, analysis, ideas, and recommendations that underlie the report of the National Commission on the Public Service. As such, this volume represents for policymakers and the public, as it did for the Commission, an essential resource, one that should prove useful in the national debate on the future of the Civil Service.

Concern for the future of the Civil Service—concern that the federal workforce may be ill-prepared to serve the nation in the 21st century—led a group of private citizens, many with previous experience in government, to form the National Commission in the fall of 1987. The group drew its membership from a broad, bipartisan spectrum of men and women who brought many points of view to the task at hand, but who shared a common belief that a strong federal civilian workforce is a prerequisite to efficient and effective federal government in coming decades. The Commission established itself as a privately financed, nonprofit, tax-exempt entity dedicated to placing high on the national agenda the need to strengthen the effectiveness of the career services in government.

At its first meeting, held on October 29, 1987, the Commission formed five Task Forces with Commission members as chairs. Chairpersons were encouraged to recruit as Task Force members as broad and diverse a membership as practicable from within and without the Commission.

The Commission did not ask the Task Forces to undertake any original indepth research, but rather to draw on existing sources—the Civil Service is intensely studied in the academic community, Congress, and the government itself—and to focus on policy issues and long-range objectives.

The Task Forces each met three times, on average, and held many more meetings of smaller groups of members. Task forces freely exchanged information among each other because, as the reader of this volume will soon learn, issues constantly overlap. The Task forces forwarded draft recommendations to the Commission at its meeting of April 26, 1988, and final drafts of their reports with recommendations to the Commission at its meeting of October 19, 1988.

In its report to the public, published as *Leadership for America: Rebuilding the Public Service*, and reproduced as the first section of this book, the Commission drew heavily on the work and recommendations of the Task Forces as well as on other materials and on the views of its own members. In addition, the Commission relied on the Task Force reports to provide the factual support for many statements made in the final report; information on sources for the task force work can be found in the endnotes to each task force report.

The Commission expresses its thanks to the chairpersons and members of the task forces, who gave willingly and generously of their time and energies to attend meetings, discuss issues, review draft materials, and otherwise lend their support to the Commission's work. The Commission also thanks the staff and volunteers who, as described in greater detail in the prefaces to the individual task force reports, worked so diligently to prepare background papers and draft report materials. Without the overall leadership of Ambassador L. Bruce Laingen, who coordinated task force efforts, this volume would not be a reality. We thank, too, Diane D. Yendrey, Executive Assistant, who performed the role of managing editor of this volume. The Commission acknowledges the assistance of Joseph Foote in editing this volume for publication.

Paul A. Volcker
Chairman
National Commission on the
 Public Service

Washington, D.C.
April 1989

CREATING AND PROJECTING A NEW SPIRIT OF PUBLIC SERVICE

The Report of the

Task Force on Public Perceptions of the Public Service

to the

National Commission on the Public Service

TASK FORCE

J. Robert Schaetzel, *Cochairman*

Leonard H. Marks, *Cochairman*

John Brademas

Douglas A. Fraser

John W. Gardner

Andrew J. Goodpaster

Nancy M. Neuman

Norman J. Ornstein

Charles S. Robb

WASHINGTON 1989

THE TASK FORCE ON
PUBLIC PERCEPTIONS OF THE PUBLIC SERVICE

COCHAIRMEN

J. Robert Schaetzel
Former U.S. Ambassador to the European Economic Community

Leonard H. Marks
Former Director, United States Information Agency

MEMBERS

John Brademas
President, New York University

Douglas A. Fraser
Former President, United Auto Workers of America, AFL-CIO

John W. Gardner
Former Secretary of Health, Education, and Welfare

Andrew J. Goodpaster
*General, United States Army (retired), and
Chairman of the Atlantic Council*

Nancy M. Neuman
President, League of Women Voters

Norman J. Ornstein
Resident Scholar, American Enterprise Institute

Charles S. Robb
United States Senator from Virginia

PROJECT DIRECTOR
Thomas Kell
*Senior Staff
National Commission on the Public Service*

WRITER/EDITOR
Elaine Orr

PROJECT ASSISTANT
Sharon Gleason

CONTENTS

PREFACE

T he mission of the Task Force on Public Perceptions of the Public Service has been to draw together general information and data that promised to shed light on American opinion on the nation's government, bureaucracy, and, in particular, the public service. The Task Force drew up recommendations designed to create a more positive image in the eyes of the public and, in so doing, to encourage the support essential to the revival of the quality and morale of the nation's public service.

The Task Force commissioned two basic studies. The paper by Dr. Gregory Foster and Sharon Koval Snyder of the University of Southern California (Annex I) summarizes their exhaustive examination of available polling data as well as the extensive body of research work that has been done in this area. The paper by Dr. Donald F. Kettl of the University of Virginia (Annex II) offers further insight into another critical aspect of public attitudes.

Annex III lists proposals volunteered to the Commission that deserve careful consideration as the government program is launched to revitalize the public service.

In addition to these studies, the Task Force gathered information from a wide range of sources. Here we refer especially to the research of Dr. Charles Goodsell of the Virginia Polytechnic Institute and State University and to papers developed by new federal managers attending sessions at the Federal Executive Seminar Centers in Oak Ridge, Tennessee, and Kings Point, New York. The Task Force also benefited from participation in the Commission's regional conferences held in Los Angeles, Washington, Austin, Atlanta, Boston, New York, and Ann Arbor. Over the months, a series of meetings were held at the Commission's headquarters with academic, public, and private experts in the field and, of special value to the Task Force, with many former public servants.

A team of advisers (Annex IV) was organized to review the observations and recommendations that flowed into the Commission. The analyses of this team of volunteers materially assisted the Task Force as it prepared its report.

Ms. Elaine Orr edited the initial draft of the report, which was reviewed in early October 1988, at a special workshop organized by the Woodrow Wilson School at Princeton University. Drawing on this discussion, a semi-final version of the report was prepared and presented to the full National Commission at its meeting on October 19, 1988.

Thomas Kell served as Project Director through the courtesy of the U.S. Office of Personnel Management. The Task Force expresses its thanks and appreciation to its editor, Elaine Orr, for her efforts in preparing a succinct final draft of this report from the abundance of materials developed for our consideration.

We also very much appreciate the efforts of Gregory Foster and Sharon Koval Snyder for their research and preparation of "Public Attitudes Toward Government" (Annex I), and to Donald F. Kettl for "The Image of the Public Service" (Annex II), two documents central to the efforts of the Task Force.

The Task Force is grateful as well to the numerous individuals who shared their views with the Commission and the Task Force by contacting us directly at our Washington, D.C., office or by appearing at one of the several Commission-sponsored regional dialogues. So many different people helped this Task Force, in so many different ways, it is impossible to thank you all.

J. Robert Schaetzel, Cochairman
Leonard H. Marks, Cochairman
Thomas Kell, Project Director

Washington, D.C.
April 1989

EXECUTIVE SUMMARY

A merican citizens' perceptions of their government and of their public service are paradoxical. This paradox is rooted in American history and culture, resting in good part on an inherent suspicion of government and a romantic dream of frontier days. The attitudes of Americans, it should be noted, differ in this respect from those of European citizens towards their governments and public service. These latent American sentiments of distrust have been nurtured, especially over the past dozen years, by the anti-government rhetoric of the past two Presidents.

Yet, unaware of the contradiction, this same public takes pride in its democratic traditions and institutions, and demands and expects a host of services that only the government can provide. Furthermore, poll after poll finds that a substantial majority of Americans are more than satisfied with the service they receive from individual civil servants, whether it be over income tax questions or a lost Social Security check.

This paradox is also evident in the attitudes of college graduates toward government service. Although increasing numbers of secondary and college students are drawn to community service and the Peace Corps, far fewer students these days show interest in government compared with careers in business. One recurrent objection is that the government bureaucracy is far too big and the individual has little chance to make a difference.

Public perception contains an abundance of myth and only a modicum of reality. The public believes, for example, that the government servant is less productive and enjoys more benefits than his or her counterpart in business. Government Accounting Office (GAO) studies find that the reverse is true: productivity of the civil servant is marginally greater than that of comparable, private-sector employees, and the benefits, other than pay, are about the same for both sectors.

Public opinion is not all mythology. As in the private sector, the government does not always provide efficient or courteous service. Ethical standards are occasionally ignored, there are agencies that could be better managed, and programs could be administered with greater efficiency. Again a paradox. These problems will continue and worsen if the government cannot recruit and hold public servants of the highest quality.

Negative stereotypes of the civil servant, reflexive hostility toward government, and absent-minded "bureaucrat-bashing," from whatever quarter, create an environment favorable to worsening of the "quiet crisis" that now afflicts public service. Polls consistently indicate that senior career executives put at the top of the list of complaints not inadequate compensation, but low morale and declining self-respect. A hemorrhage of the most experienced public servants is occurring, of those with the institutional memory indispensable to effective government.

Basic and peculiarly American cultural traits cannot be substantially altered. A more positive and constructive view of government and the public service, however, must and can be generated. President Bush has struck this note. Support for government and interest in public service were strong, for example, in the Administrations of Franklin D. Roosevelt, Dwight D. Eisenhower, and John F. Kennedy. If this essential change is to come about, a collective effort must be mounted—one led by the President and supported by the Congress and by many sectors of society. Secondary schools, colleges, and universities must take the lead in educating their students about government, the importance of careers in government, and the satisfaction derived from such service.

A skilled government workforce, one competent to handle the complex relationship between the public sector and the business world, is of critical and growing importance to the business community. At the heart of the democratic process are public interest groups concerned with basic national problems—environmental issues, consumer protection, education, and child care. Their concerns must encompass not merely the making of laws and regulations, but also assurance that there is in place a cadre of trained and dedicated civil servants to administer these programs.

Finally, the work of this Task Force has proven beyond any doubt that there is no quick and easy solution to the basic problem of public perception of the public service. A sustained effort, drawing on the support, resources, and cooperative efforts of the executive branch, the Congress, the business community, the media, universities, and the many interest groups will be required.

RECOMMENDATIONS

To deal with the problems identified in its study, the Task Force offers five recommendations:

RECOMMENDATION 1

The President, in close cooperation with members of the Congress, cabinet officials, and heads of agencies, must lead efforts to create a work environment that will attract top people to public service careers and encourage them to remain in the public sector.

RECOMMENDATION 2

The goal of government must be to achieve excellence in all of its programs. Achieving this goal is primarily, although not exclusively, the responsibility of government managers. It is also important that the management systems with which they work support, rather than hamper, program delivery.

RECOMMENDATION 3

Government leaders and managers must work together to ensure that the concept of "service" is a central principal of government, and that those who perform this service have the opportunity to develop fully the talents to perform it well.

RECOMMENDATION 4

The executive branch should emphasize, through its public information structure, positive aspects of government and the people who serve it.

RECOMMENDATION 5

These reforms require sustained commitment and effort. To this end, an independent tripartite council on public service should monitor implementation of the foregoing activities.

CREATING AND PROJECTING
A NEW SPIRIT OF PUBLIC SERVICE

Often preceded by the word "faceless," the word "bureaucrat" connotes more than its literal definition of a person who works in a large, highly structured organization. Public perception assigns a pejorative meaning that reflects the view that "bureaucracy" is unresponsive, slow, and out of touch. Indeed, the *Random House Dictionary of the English Language* defines bureaucrat as an official in a bureaucracy or "an official who works by fixed routine without exercising intelligent judgment."

Yet, that same public is justly proud of the American form of government, with its democratic traditions vested in an elected President and Congress and in a strong judiciary as arbiter of constitutional questions. They cite with pride such federal organizations as the Office of the Surgeon General, the Beltsville Agricultural Laboratory, and the Food and Drug Administration.

Why then the pronounced contradiction between the public's benign perception of its system of government and its negative view of the people responsible for its day-to-day activities? And why is government service less valued here than in other Western cultures, such as in France and the United Kingdom?

These are among the questions that the Commission's Task Force on Public Perceptions of the Public Service addressed. Through a series of interviews with current and former public officials, an extensive review of public opinion surveys, and consultation with advisory groups, the Task Force developed a composite picture of how the public sees its government and public service, the reasons for these perceptions, the impact such negative images have, and efforts that have been made to correct these misconceptions. The Task Force then forwarded five recommendations to the Commission.

WHAT PEOPLE REALLY THINK IN PEORIA

In part, mistrust of government stems from the American political heritage. Born in revolution, founded on the precept that people have the right to choose their own form of government, and having built a nation from a wilderness, America embodies individualism and self-achievement. Politicians assert that they "pulled themselves up by their bootstraps," and school children learn that rewards come from winning first prize in the science fair or spelling contest. In contrast, integration, teamwork, consensus—qualities that a bureaucracy requires—are less valued cultural components here than they are, for example, in Japan. Exceptions to this anti-government bias historically arise in times of crisis, and the public can be moved by leaders. Americans rallied around President Franklin D. Roosevelt and thought of themselves as "working with the government" during the Great Depression and World War II.

What do the people really think? The answer seems to be: opinions are ambiguous and contradictory. Professor Charles Goodsell found that citizens tend to condemn government in polls that asked abstract questions about "bureaucracy," but they usually report satisfaction when they are asked about their personal experiences with public agencies.[1] The

University of Michigan's Survey Research Center, in a survey segment that focused on citizen encounters with bureaucracy, asked people who had sought help from a government agency what they thought about the offices and individuals they encountered. On overall satisfaction with the way the office handled their problems, 43 percent responded "very satisfied" and 26 percent "fairly well satisfied." With respect to the effort government employees made to help, 16 percent answered "more than they had to" and 57 percent said "about right." On the perceived efficiency of the office, 43 percent replied, "very efficient" and 31 percent "fairly efficient." More than three-fourths of the respondents declared that they had been treated "fairly" by the office.[2]

Citizens appear to fear government intruding into their lives—reflecting another historically based attitude. A 1983 Lou Harris poll asked whether it was possible that a government in Washington would use confidential information to intimidate individuals or groups that it believes are its enemies. Eighty-seven percent said such abuse was possible, and of those, 70 percent said it was likely.

A 1987 Gallup Organization poll of 4,000 adults underscored the high level of public expectations of government and a widespread degree of frustration, alienation, and powerlessness. At the most basic level, 57 percent agreed that government was really run for the benefit of all the people. Seventy-one percent believed it was the responsibility of government to care for people who cannot care for themselves; 62 percent thought government should guarantee every citizen enough to eat and a place to sleep; and 53 percent thought government should help more needy people, even if it meant going more deeply into debt.

Conversely, 73 percent said that, generally speaking, elected officials in Washington lose touch with the people fairly quickly; 63 percent said that something run by the government is usually inefficient and wasteful; and 58 percent said that dealing with a federal agency often is not worth the trouble. Yet 78 percent believed that voting gives people some say about how the government runs things.[3]

In contrast with the relatively poor esteem in which the public holds the federal government is the public perception of state government. Scholarly and journalistic assessments of state government performance judge it much improved over two or three decades ago. It is enhanced by more active, professionally staffed legislatures, longer terms for governors and broadened government activities.[4] Some observers attribute the improved perception of state governments to their recruitment of professional public servants and their comparative fiscal good health—in times of large federal budget deficits, many states (often by statute) must balance their books.

WHAT FUELS THE ANTI-GOVERNMENT FIRE?

It has been traditional in American politics to run on a "throw-the-rascals-out" platform. Recent Administrations, particularly the Carter and Reagan Administrations, have embellished this old plank by running campaigns that not only strongly criticized Washington but also attacked the people who work for the government.

The rhetoric was sometimes extreme. President Reagan remarked, "When you are up to your eyeballs in alligators, it's sometimes hard to remember that you came here to drain the swamp." President Carter said, "The Civil Service system has become a bureaucratic maze which rejects merit, tolerates poor performance, permits abuse of legitimate employee rights, and mires every personnel action in red tape, delay and confusion." For a public instinctively suspicious of government, these judgments from its elected leaders could not have been more damaging.

Added to the politicians' anti-government rhetoric is the basic public confusion over the role of government in society. Most citizens want safe neighborhoods, income security, good schools, and cures for illness, but they are suspicious of the bureaucracy that provides these services. They fail to recognize that the federal government is efficient enough to send out 63 million Social Security and Medicare payments, on time, each month. While wanting the government to win the war on cancer and lead the urgent search for a cure for acquired immune deficiency syndrome (AIDS), the public fails to appreciate why the government should finance scientific conferences or pay salaries necessary to attract the best talent to carry out this essential research.

Not all negative public perceptions are wrong or baseless. People can encounter inefficiencies and even rudeness at service agencies. The government has purchased hammers and coffee makers for outrageous prices. Unlike a private business, which can correct problems out of the spotlight, government fraud and waste are the stuff of headlines and can reinforce established public perceptions.

Ironically, government attempts to reform itself have occasionally had the perverse effect of highlighting its problems. For example, in trying to convince the Congress and the public that Civil Service reform was needed, the Carter Administration transformed the initial image of its bill from a measure to improve government and protect whistleblowers into a proposal to make it easier to fire incompetent civil servants. The Office of Management and Budget illustrated this point with a 21-foot chart, showing the steps required to fire a clerk-typist believed to be incompetent. The chart had an irresistible appeal to cartoonists and to feature and editorial writers. This effort clearly worked: the bill passed.

Too often, it is overlooked that government's self-policing mechanisms identify inefficiencies. Administrative systems created and managed by public officials result in millions of cost-effective purchases. Positive images of public service are not the stuff of TV's nightly news. The media and its audience are attracted to the visual and the negative.[5] (See Annex III.)

Contributing to the public's negative image of government is the succession of ethics scandals, evidence of corruption in military procurement, and questionable or at least unpalatable political fund-raising and special-interest activities. Citizens have come to feel that access to the political process is available only to organized and well-heeled lobbyists and that high elected office is available only to the wealthy or the well-funded. The resulting sense of alienation ricochets against public servants.

RISK OF PERCEPTIONS BECOMING REALITY

Unjust negative public perceptions of the public service drive highly qualified, experienced people out of government and discourage the most qualified from joining it. Thus, the danger is real that perceptions will become reality.

It appears that the constant derogation of public service is taking its toll. Overall, the 1980s have seen declining enrollments in many public service education programs, with fewer graduates entering employment in federal, state, or local governments.

In a June 9, 1988, commencement address, Harvard president Derek Bok noted that only 7 percent of the seniors at his university "say that they are interested in government and far fewer will actually make a career in public service."[6]

One of the more damaging results of public disparagement of the bureaucracy has been its impact on the morale of those now in the federal civil service. Surveys over the past seven years show that an increasing majority of the upper ranks of public service—Senior Executive Service members and those at the GS-15 level—say they will not recommend that their own children emulate their careers. In its recent survey, *Government Executive* magazine found that 57 percent of the 3,900 respondents would not recommend a government career to young people.[7]

Several groups of mid-level managers who participated in 1988 seminars at federal Executive Development Centers summarized for the Task Force their understanding of the public's perception of civil servants and their own interpretations and beliefs. Their summaries are revealing and disquieting. They are concerned that recent "bureaucrat-bashing" is taking its toll on the federal workforce and its ability to recruit talent. They are frustrated at being unable to meet their own standards of productivity and efficiency because so many essential factors are beyond their control—shrinking budgets, procurement restrictions, and so forth. In many cases, what the public views as red tape often involves producing the audit trail necessary to ensure accountability and equity in public spending.

This evidence does not mean that the nation is condemned to live with a second-class public service, but it should warn the public of the danger that future Presidents, governors, and mayors may face this reality. The warning is present in the dramatic increase in student selection of business administration over public administration, humanities, or education, fields that have been traditional choices for those who later enter government service.

Fortunately, counter-forces are at work, seeking to ensure that the public is aware of the good work done in federal, state and local government. Further, efforts are under way to enhance the quality of government service to the public, which will contribute to changes in attitudes.

EFFORTS TO MITIGATE NEGATIVISM AND BUILD QUALITY

What is being done to change this pattern of negative perception and generate pride in public service? President Carter began and President Reagan expanded (after initially trying to end) the Presidential Management Intern (PMI) Program, designed to bring many of the best of graduates with masters in public administration (MPA) degrees into government. After the early efforts of Donald J. Devine, as the first Director of the Office of Personnel Management (OPM), to cut back the Civil Service and to decrease recruiting as part of an overall strategy, his successor, OPM Director Constance Horner, subsequently worked to revitalize federal efforts to recruit good candidates; she regularly cited examples of effective public managers.

Several private organizations promote public awareness of good government, often while concurrently recognizing individual achievements. The American Society for Public Administration and the National Academy of Public Administration jointly present the annual National Public Service Awards. The Public Employees Roundtable annually heralds "unsung heroes" through its Public Service Excellence Awards, presented to federal, state, and local organizations. The annual Flemming awards as well as those of the Federal Executive Institute Alumni Association and the Senior Executive Association also call attention to outstanding public servants.

At all levels of government and in the private and nonprofit sectors, there are some organizations whose purpose it is to enhance the quality of governments' work. The President's Council on Management Improvement (PCMI) has created a management partnership among federal agencies that, since 1984, has launched more than 80 initiatives in financial and human resource management, communications, and the organization and structure of government. In 1988, the PCMI ran the first government-wide conference on quality and productivity, and it maintains a speakers' bureau and an extensive publications program. With the Public Employees Roundtable, PCMI sponsors Pride in Public Service Recognition Week to celebrate quality services provided by federal employees and agencies.

The Federal Quality Institute, established through OPM, trains federal managers in quality awareness, advises agencies on how to implement the "total quality management" concept, and maintains a productivity resource information center for federal managers. Also under way at OPM is the Organizational Excellence Project, designed to select examples of agency excellence, develop background information on how such agencies achieve excellence, and disseminate this information to federal managers and the public.

The General Accounting Office (GAO) designed a framework for examining the quality (defining quality to include employee capabilities and the degree to which they match job requirements) of the federal workforce. Prepared at the request of the House Post Office and Civil Service Committee, the GAO document is one of the many indications of Congressional interest in federal management improvement.[8]

At the state and local levels, organizations such as the National Governors' Association and the International City Management Association have management improvement projects under way and operate information dissemination efforts to share results. In fact, so many groups are interested in intergovernmental management that there now exists the Coalition to Improve Management in State and Local Government, whose 21 cooperating organizations work together to help states, counties, and cities to develop executive capabilities to cope with rapid economic and social change, fiscal shortfalls resulting from reduced federal grant funds, and increased demands for service.

Just when the tide seemed to be turning against government-bashing, it has been discouraging to hear tired cliches such as that the most feared words are, "We're from the government and we're here to help," or charges that State Department officers are more concerned about foreign interests than those of their own country. Fortunately, the 1988 Presidential campaign evidenced little of such rhetoric.

What can the government itself do to enhance the image of the public service, and thus encourage talented people to seek public-sector careers? Who should lead this effort?

ACCEPTING THE CHALLENGE

Major responsibility for elevating the public perception of the public service, and the self esteem of the civil servants, lies with the President and the Congress of the United States.

The President alone has the position and authority to influence and lead all levels of public service, the nation's education system, and the general public. In addition, through their continuing public visibility, legislative activity, and constituent services, members of Congress are in a unique position to work with the President and influence citizen perception of government. Conversely, when the President and members of Congress denigrate the federal workforce, they reinforce the public's inherent distrust of it. As Donald F. Kettl notes in Appendix III, "The public's image of the public service can be improved only if the President takes the lead."

But even a strong public commitment by the President will not bring about a major transformation of public attitude. Efforts must be consistent and sustained. The President must ensure that his philosophy is shared and executed by his cabinet officers. The executive branch must join forces with the Congress to influence crucial segments of society: youth, the academic community, business leaders, and specific public interest groups.

The first two annexes to this Task Force report provide detailed data and information on public attitudes toward government and the public service and on the role of the media. Annex III lists proposals volunteered to the Commission that deserve careful consideration as the government program is launched to revitalize the public service.

With these factors and information in mind, the Task Force offers five recommendations to improve the public's perception of the public service and the quality of service provided to the public.

RECOMMENDATION 1

The President, in close cooperation with members of the Congress, cabinet officials, and heads of agencies, must lead efforts to create a work environment that will attract top people to public service careers and encourage them to remain in the public sector.

This leadership responsibility should begin with Presidential transition planning and be reflected in the orientation of designees to cabinet-level positions, transition team leaders, and all who speak on behalf of the President, as suggested in other task force reports in this volume. The President must fix in the minds of these key players that to be on the team is to work with the career service, not against it. Only the President can make clear that negativism and bureaucrat-bashing will not be tolerated. The Congress has an equally important role, especially early in a Presidential term, because it holds confirmation hearings and sets the agenda that controls public service legislation.

In terms of more direct action, the President can demonstrate his commitment through a range of symbolic and substantive actions, such as: expanding the Presidential Rank Awards Program, perhaps adding categories for entry and mid-level staff; increasing the percentage of Foreign Service Officers named ambassadors; meeting regularly with the Director of the Office of Personnel Management on issues related to the federal workforce; citing in speeches, including the State of the Union address, exemplary programs and the employees who manage them.

It is also crucial that the President and Congress concert their efforts to rejuvenate the career service. If essential statutory changes are to be brought about, Congressional views must be sought early in the process.

RECOMMENDATION 2

The goal of government must be to achieve excellence in all of its programs. Achieving this goal is primarily, although not exclusively, the responsibility of government managers. It is also important that the management systems with which they work support, rather than hamper, program delivery.

Positive public images of government are created through effective delivery of public services. As the President establishes the framework for a positive work environment, it is the responsibility of senior and mid-level federal managers to ensure that each agency has a workforce of the highest quality, one that recognizes the critical importance of service to the public.

The Task Force on Public Perceptions recognizes that effective delivery of services can only be produced within a management structure that insists upon efficient operations and that rewards innovation. Currently, layered levels of regulations and procedures often combine with a rigid federal personnel system to inhibit quick response and employee initiative.

RECOMMENDATION 3

Government leaders and managers must work together to ensure that "service" to the public is a central goal of government, and that those who perform this service must in turn have the opportunity to develop fully the talents to perform it well.

The Task Force believes that the President, Governors, and mayors set the tone for workforce expectations and morale, and that they should emphasize that those who work in the public sector are there to serve the American public. At the same time, senior managers—political and career—play an important role in ensuring that staff have the right skills and opportunities to use those skills, with the goal of providing effective service. Existing agency training and executive development programs meet some of these needs, but more can be done. Personnel development and improvement efforts should be keyed to the organization's mission, as clearly stated by its senior leaders.

Department programs designed to recognize excellence require: sustained leadership from a central point within the organization; ample opportunity for grassroots employee contributions and participation; and close ties to the employee awards systems. Drawing on current governmental efforts and on private-sector experience, the Task Force believes that a government agency—at any level of government—can establish such a program. At the federal level, it could be coordinated through an organization such as the PCMI or OPM.[9,10]

RECOMMENDATION 4

The executive branch should emphasize, by making use of the various department and agency public information officers, the positive aspects of government and the people who serve it.

Public information efforts within departments and agencies are focused, as they should be, on the substantive work and accomplishments of their organizations. They focus on this work primarily in the context of working with and informing their constituencies, the media, and the authorization, appropriation, and oversight committees of the Congress.

Missing in the current approach is a strong effort to remind the nation that the range of government products are being delivered by people, not "faceless bureaucrats." When young people are considering careers, they should not be left with rosy abstractions but informed by specific flesh-and-blood examples that the individual public servant can and does make a difference. The message remains the product: the quality of programs and the manner in which they are provided.

The Task Force recommends that a central management agency such as the Office of Management and Budget (OMB) ensure that examples of effective programs are collected and disseminated within and outside government. The Task Force believes that responsibility for actual dissemination should rest with the public information offices throughout government because of their knowledge of successful agency programs.

RECOMMENDATION 5

These reforms require sustained commitment and effort. To this end, an independent tripartite council on public service should monitor implementation of the foregoing activities.

If the process of reform is to succeed, a small, prestigious, non-partisan advisory group, aware of problems that have led to the current crisis and the remedial action required, will be essential. To that end, an independent tripartite council on public service should be formed. While many of these issues will preoccupy the Directors of the OPM and the OMB, the basic function of this body should be support and oversight.

Such an independent council would be responsible on behalf of the President and Congress to focus attention on the public service. It would anticipate problems, recognizing that governments by their nature are preoccupied by the immediate. One of the tasks of an advisory group would be to ensure that government agencies, private bodies, and interest groups concerned with public service concert their efforts on a long-term program of reform and reconstruction.

Finally, as has been amply demonstrated over the years, Presidents need not be bound by the advice of this or indeed any other advisory group, but they do need and deserve the opportunity to hear the advice and recommendations of disinterested experts.

ENDNOTES

1. Charles T. Goodsell, *The Case for Bureaucracy—a Public Administration Polemic* (Chatham, N.J.: Chatham House Publishers, Inc., 1985).
2. Daniel Katz et. al., *Bureaucratic Encounters* (Ann Arbor: University of Michigan Institute for Social Research, 1975).
3. Gregory D. Foster and Sharon Koval Snyder, "Public Attitudes Toward Government: Contradiction, Ambivalence, and the Dilemmas of Response," a report submitted to the Task Force on Public Perceptions of the National Commission of the Public Service (February 1988).
4. Neal R. Peirce, "Public Service in the States," in *The State of American Public Service,* a report of a symposium of the National Academy of Public Administration (November 1985).
5. Donald F. Kettl, "The Image of the Public Service in the Media," a report submitted to the Task Force on Public Perceptions of the National Commission of the Public Service (March 1988).
6. The shift in career preferences of college students away from the public to the private sectors is discussed in detail by James K. Conant in "Universities and the Future of the

Public Service," *Public Administration Quarterly*, Vol. 13, No. 2 (Summer 1989).

7. Timothy B. Clark and Marjorie Wachtel, "The Quiet Crisis Goes Public," *Government Executive* (June 1988).

8. U.S. General Accounting Office, *Federal Workforce: A Framework for Studying Its Quality over Time*, GAO/PEMD-88-27 (August 1988).

9. Emilie G. Heller, "Design for Organizational Excellence Project," a project design paper for the Office of Executive Personnel, Office of Personnel Management (November 1988).

10. The need for renewed emphasis on high standards of service delivery by government organizations is discussed by James K. Conant in "The Growing Importance of State Government," *Handbook of Public Administration*, April 1989, and "Can Government Organizations Be Excellent Too?," *State and Local Government Review*, Vol. 19, No. 2 (Spring 1987).

ANNEX I

PUBLIC ATTITUDES TOWARD GOVERNMENT: CONTRADICTION, AMBIVALENCE, AND THE DILEMMAS OF RESPONSE

A Report Submitted to the

Task Force on Public Perceptions

of the

National Commission on the Public Service

by

Gregory D. Foster   Sharon Koval Snyder

FEBRUARY 1988

CONTENTS

INTRODUCTION

O n September 16–17, 1986, the Brookings Institution and the American Enterprise Institute convened a conference, A National Public Service for the Year 2000, which assessed how well the federal public service is prepared to meet current and future responsibilities. Participants believed that changing public attitudes toward and expectations of the federal government, combined with economic and social trends, are raising basic questions about the meaning of "public service."

One disturbing trend discussed was that the public continues to have negative attitudes toward "the mess in Washington" in general, and "the bureaucracy" in particular. Participants believed several factors contributed to the diminished attractiveness of the federal public service: a general decline in popular interest in "service" as such, including the failure of political leaders to stress the importance of public service; relatively low pay; complex conflict of interest and disclosure requirements; and a belief on the part of some people that public service does not require the "best and the brightest."[1]

From the conference emerged the recommendation to create what would become the National Commission on the Public Service, formed to examine changing concepts of the "public" and analyze ways in which the needs of various "publics" are or could be addressed. It is not enough, however, to ascertain public attitudes, we must also determine whether they are grounded in a mature appreciation of how government works, or whether they reflect a bias that is a by-product of our socialization process.

Walter Lippmann went to the heart of the matter:

> The subtlest and most pervasive of influences are those which create and maintain the repertory of stereotypes. We are told about the world before we see it. We imagine most things before we experience them. And those preconceptions, unless education has made us acutely aware, govern deeply the whole process of perception.

This paper, prepared at the request of the Public Perceptions Task Force of the National Commission on the Public Service (NCPS), seeks to determine public attitudes toward government and the basis for them. Presumably, if attitudes can be identified, action can be taken in response to them or attempts can be made to influence them in constructive directions. To the extent that public attitudes can be differentiated by factors such as age, sex, education level, occupation and the like, contemplated actions can be targeted at appropriate segments of the population.

The authors reviewed public responses to more than 1,200 survey questions posed to the U.S. public between 1971 and 1987 by 39 major survey organizations or teams. Although there is a wealth of relevant data in the public domain, one quickly learns that answers to a broader range of questions must be sought. For example:

> Does the public believe that government performs essential functions in their lives?

Does the public think that government performs as well as it should?

Are public attitudes toward government directed principally toward the federal government, toward government at other levels (state, local), or toward government in general?

Are public attitudes toward the federal government directed principally toward the executive branch or toward the congressional and judicial branches as well?

Are public attitudes toward federal bureaucrats directed principally toward career civil servants or toward political appointees?

Are public attitudes toward federal careerists directed principally at more senior or more junior bureaucrats?

Do public attitudes toward government derive principally from: personal experiences with government, news stories, statements by public officials, personal acquaintance with government workers, some combination of these factors, or other factors?

What is there about federal workers that most influences how the public views them—technical competence, accountability and ethical behavior, dedication, demeanor, social standing, compensation, the nature of their jobs, some combination of these factors or some other factors?

Does the public really know very much about government workers and the work they do?

Answers to many of these questions remain frustratingly elusive. Nonetheless, the insights that can be drawn from the data evaluated here provide a more reasoned basis to define the nature and intensity of public attitudes and to deal with the their origins and effects.

PRINCIPAL FINDINGS

Public attitudes toward government are complex, inconsistent and none too stable over time. If one attempts to discern how the public feels about public service and public servants (or more specifically, civil servants), the picture is even murkier.

Nonetheless, three things do stand out. First, we know little about the nature or origins of public attitudes. Second, the picture probably is not nearly as bleak as we tend to think it is. Finally, Americans really want to believe in government—to reaffirm the wisdom of the country's founders—even if our culture makes it difficult for them to do so.

Government as an Issue

Compared to more provocative issues such as the deficit, inflation, or war and peace, government performance has been of relatively little concern to the U.S. public for the past two decades. Rarely have more than one to three percent of those queried said dissatisfaction with, or lack of trust in, government is one of the most important problems facing the United States.

The rare exceptions to this rule have been flamed by the events of the day. For example, in October 1971, when people were dissatisfied over the Vietnam war, nine percent of those questioned by the Gallup Organization identified government as the issue that bothered or angered them most (compared to 14 percent who identified the war and 12 percent who identified crime and lawlessness).

In late 1973, five percent of those queried by Gallup identified dissatisfaction with government as the most important problem facing the country, while another seven percent were split among corruption in government, lack of trust in government, and Watergate itself. This compared to 50 percent who were most concerned about the high cost of living, taxes and high prices, and 14 percent who focused on high food prices.

Finally, in the period leading up to the 1980 presidential election, when dissatisfaction with President Carter was high, the proportion of respondents who identified lack of government leadership or dissatisfaction with government as a main issue facing the country reached six to eight percent in several polls. However, as typified in an October 1980 Yankelovich, Skelly and White poll, this compared to 64 percent who mentioned inflation and 17 percent who mentioned unemployment as the foremost national problem.

The Need for Government

The extent of the public's reliance on government is a source of intense and complex feelings.

Characterized as "the most exhaustive study of the American electorate ever undertaken," a 1987 nationwide survey of over 4,000 adults by the Gallup Organization for Times Mirror underscored the high level of public expectations of government and widespread degree of frustration, alienation, and powerlessness. Fifty-seven percent agreed that government really is run for the benefit of all the people. Seventy-one percent believed government should take care of people who can't take care of themselves, and 53 percent think government should help more needy people, even if it means going deeper into debt. Seventy-eight percent believe that voting gives people some say about how the government runs things.

Conversely, 73 percent said that, generally speaking, elected officials in Washington lose touch with the people pretty quickly; 63 percent said that when something is run by the government it is usually inefficient and wasteful; and 52 percent said that average people don't have any say about what the government does.

A 1985 National Opinion Research Center survey found large percentages of the U.S. public who believed it probably or definitely should be government's responsibility to: keep prices under control (73 percent); provide a decent standard of living for the old (86 percent); provide health care for the sick (81 percent); and provide industry with the help it needs to grow (59 percent). Conversely, respondents believed it probably or definitely should not be government's responsibility to: provide a job for everyone who wants one (62 percent); and reduce income differences between rich and poor (56 percent).

Numerous other surveys over the past six years have found sizable percentages of the public supporting a major role for government in such areas as funding and setting priorities for energy development (Opinion Research Corporation, 1984, 1985); seeing that the poor are taken care of, that no one goes hungry and that every person achieves at least a minimum standard of living (Lou Harris, 1981); providing services such as medical care and legal advice to those who cannot afford to pay for them (NBC News/Associated Press, 1981); ensuring that we have adequate future supplies of domestic oil and natural gas (Opinion Research Corporation, 1984); promoting equal rights and opportunities for blacks, other minorities, and women (Gordon Black/*USA Today*, 1984); providing health care for the homeless (Kane, Parsons and Associates, 1986); creating jobs for the unemployed (Opinion Research Corporation, 1982); and dealing with abuse of children, wives, the elderly and the handicapped (Lou Harris, 1981).

Despite the broad range of services the public expects government to provide and the range of issues on which it is to take the lead, the public is ambivalent about its reliance on government. In a 1981 Roper survey, respondents were asked whether government should, in general, work through local voluntary groups to provide services even when those services could be more cheaply provided directly by government agencies. Forty-seven percent said yes, while 45 percent said no. When the question was reworded, so that respondents were asked to assume that the level of support was the same for both organizations, respondents preferred voluntary organizations by 49 to 34 percent.

Three *Los Angeles Times* polls reflect something of the public's ambivalence between the recognition of government's roles and the deeply ingrained societal values of individualism and the work ethic. When asked whether government is responsible for the well-being of its citizens or whether the people are responsible for taking care of themselves, respondents replied:

	Government	People	Not sure/refrained
September 1983	43%	49%	9%
January 1985	39	55	6
April 1985	24	67	9

The ultimate irony arises when the public is asked whether they would favor reducing the federal workforce. Consistently since 1971, polls conducted by the Opinion Research Corporation, NBC News/Associated Press, Gallup, Roper, and ABC News/*Washington Post* have shown sizable majorities who favor such reduction. A February 1981 ABC News/*Washington Post* survey found 71 percent favored President Reagan's proposal to cut the number of federal workers in non-defense jobs by five percent over the ensuing two years. Roper polls in 1979 and 1980 showed that over 60 percent favored a constitutional amendment to limit the number of government employees.

Government Power

Although there is plenty of evidence to support the perception that the public considers government too powerful, the reviews are mixed. For example, National Opinion Research Center and Roper polls in early 1985 found 52 to 55 percent of respondents believed government has too much power, compared to 33 to 38 percent who believed it had the right amount. In contrast, a July 1986 *Los Angeles Times* poll found that only 38 percent felt government had too much power, versus 50 percent who felt it has the right amount. Results of polls conducted for the Advisory Commission on Intergovernmental Relations show a trend, since 1978, in favor of more vigorous use of power by the federal government.

The 1987 Gallup/Times Mirror poll cited earlier provides a sense of where the public stands on intergovernmental affairs. Forty-seven percent feel that the federal government should not be able to overrule individual states on important matters, and 75 percent believe the federal government should run only those things that cannot be run at the local level. In 1981, the Roper Organization found that 55 percent of respondents thought that the balance of responsibility had tipped too far toward the federal level. By contrast, a 1987 CBS News/*New York Times* poll found only 39 percent thought the federal government has too much power compared to 47 percent who believed the federal-state balance to be about right.

The most consistency in this respect is in *Los Angeles Times* polls in 1981, 1982, 1983 and 1985. Each asked, "Do you approve of President Reagan's proposal to give more power to state and local governments?" Affirmative responses averaged 79.5 percent.

Generally, people believe state governments operate more efficiently than the federal government. In a 1981 Gallup poll, 67 percent said the state government is more likely to administer social programs more efficiently. Fifty-one percent of those polled by ABC News/*Washington Post* in 1982 said the same thing.

Much of the fear of government reflects "Big Brother" concerns. A 1984 Roper poll asked the public whether they thought that confidential individual information in data banks being made available to government agencies and private organizations currently represented a serious threat to the citizenry. Seventy-two percent said yes. A 1983 Lou Harris poll asked whether it is possible that a government in Washington will use confidential information to intimidate individuals or groups it feels are its enemies. Eighty-seven percent said it is possible, and of those, 70 percent said it is likely.

Government seems to be viewed as more intrusive than the news media. A 1982 ABC News poll asked whether respondents believed that television news organizations invade people's privacy more than government agencies do. Forty-one percent said yes, while 44 percent said no.

Government Performance

Public assessments of government performance are decidedly mixed. A January 1987 Opinion Research Corporation survey asked respondents how they would rate the quality of government in Washington. Fifteen percent said above average or excellent, 39 percent said average, and 45 percent said below average or poor. Conversely, 66 percent of those queried by an August 1986 Roper poll indicated that they were more or less satisfied or very satisfied with the way the federal government is run.

A January 1985 survey by the Analysis Group asked how effectively the federal government was performing certain functions. Table 1 shows the range of responses.

Law enforcement is one area in which more people feel positively than negatively about federal performance. A 1984 Gordon Black survey for *USA Today* found 86 percent of those questioned said the FBI was somewhat or very effective. A 1981 Harris survey showed that more people felt positively than negatively about federal law enforcement performance, although neither side represented a majority.

Public opinion seems to vary by level of government. When asked by the Roper Organization in 1981 whether the phrase "efficient and well run" characterizes the federal government, 74 percent said no. Only 49 percent said no when asked about local governments. A 1979 Roper survey found that 27 percent of those questioned rated the management of federal agencies good or excellent, while 51 percent rated state agencies that way with 59 percent for local government.

Table 1
Federal Effectiveness at Different Functions
Question: How effective is the federal government at _____?

	Very Effective	Effective	Ineffective	Not Effective At All	Don't Know
Maintaining military defenses	19%	69%	8%	1%	2%
Cleaning up toxic and hazardous wastes	5	38	48	6	3
Regulating doctors' fees and hospital costs	3	21	56	15	4
Providing social security for retirement	10	65	20	4	2
Providing welfare for the poor	8	61	26	2	3
Providing retraining programs for workers in declining industries	4	33	44	8	11
Providing special reading, math, and computer programs for young black children	5	27	41	6	22
Providing farm price supports to protect the income of farmers	11	41	33	6	9
Helping out American banks that have bad loans in Africa and Latin America	6	32	25	4	33
Supporting research and development in high-technology areas	12	59	15	2	11

Source: Analysis Group

Roper polls conducted during 1976–1978 reflected that the public differentiates among the performance of different branches of government, and again within different levels. Among those deemed to be doing not very much or very little to solve the nation's problems were Congress (identified by 55 percent of respondents), the president (49 percent), administration officials (55 percent), state governors (41 percent), state legislatures (44 percent) and local city officials (49 percent).

Seventy two percent of those queried in a 1978 Opinion Research Corporation poll thought the best way to cut government spending was through more efficient government operations rather than cutting programs. Yet, when asked what effect they thought cutting waste and inefficiency in government agencies and departments would have on the deficit, 11 percent said it would make hardly any difference, 36 percent said it would bring the deficit down a little, 41 percent said it would bring the deficit down a lot, and seven percent said it would just about eliminate the deficit.

Presidential Influence

Time and again, the public has looked to fresh presidential leadership as the impetus for improved government efficiency. In early 1976, 88 percent of the respondents to a Lou Harris poll indicated that restoring confidence in government should be a major concern and priority for the next president. Following Jimmy Carter's election, the Roper Organization asked whether the public expected him to reorganize government agencies and departments to improve efficiency. Seventy-three percent said yes. Moreover, 63 percent said it was very important and another 29 percent moderately important that he do so. When Roper asked, in December 1979, whether the president had succeeded in this regard, 50 percent of those questioned said no, 33 percent said yes, and 17 percent said they didn't know. Comparable results were provided by CBS/*New York Times* polls conducted at various points throughout President Carter's term.

Even as the public expressed its disappointment with President Carter's ability to rein in big government, it again reflected high expectations that the next president would do better. Sixty-two percent of the respondents to a November 1980 ABC News/Lou Harris poll felt that Ronald Reagan would restore public confidence in government. The same month, the Opinion Research Corporation asked the public how likely it was that Reagan would increase the efficiency of government operations and reduce the size of government. Seventy percent thought it somewhat or very likely that he would increase efficiency and 66 percent somewhat or very likely that he would reduce government's size.

Four years later, 61 percent thought Reagan had done only fair or poor in improving efficiency and 65 percent that he had done only fair or poor in reducing the size of government. When asked how likely it was that Reagan would achieve these two goals during his second term, 61 percent said it was somewhat or very likely that he would increase government efficiency, while 50 percent deemed it somewhat or very likely that he would reduce the size of government.

Overall Trust and Confidence

Elevated public expectations are reflected nowhere more clearly than in the public's response to questions about their level of trust and confidence in government. The faith most Americans have in the structure of the nation's political system is reflected in a 1981 Roper poll in which 67 percent of respondents said that the political system is basically sound—although eight out of 10 who said this also thought the system needed some improvement.

The federal executive branch enjoys more public esteem than organized labor, Congress and, in recent years, the press and television. However, it consistently ranks below organized religion, education, medicine, the Supreme Court, the military, the scientific community and finance and big business. National Opinion Research Center data from 1973 through 1987 shows that of the "four estates"—the executive branch, Congress, the Supreme Court and the press—only the Supreme Court has a larger proportion of the public who have a "great deal" or "only some" confidence in it.

A February 1987 *Los Angeles Times* poll asked the public to identify those institutions in which they had lost the most confidence. Twenty four percent of respondents mentioned the federal executive branch, making it the most often mentioned. A 1986 Market Opinion Research survey in support of the President's Blue Ribbon Commission on Defense Management found that although 69 percent had only some or hardly any confidence in the federal government, 78 percent felt this way about Congress and 75 percent felt this way about major companies.

A question regularly asked by many polling organizations is, "How much of the time do you think you can trust the government in Washington to do what is right—just about always, most of the time, or only some of the time?" Polls conducted by CBS News/*New York Times* between 1976 and 1987 suggest a pattern of increased confidence at the outset of a new presidential administration, followed by a gradual diminution of confidence over time. The results coincide with those of other surveys during the same time by the Roper Organization, ABC News/*Washington Post*, the Gallup Organization, and others.

Compared to other levels of government, the federal executive branch holds its own fairly well in the public's eyes. Asked how much confidence they had in the various levels of government, 19 percent of the respondents in a 1985 Lou Harris poll said they had a great deal of confidence in the federal government, compared with 16 percent who expressed the same level of trust in state government, and 18 percent in local government. The same question, posed eight years earlier, had shown 23 percent of respondents with a great deal of confidence in federal government, 19 percent in state government and 21 percent in local government.

Other polls are not as consistent. Gallup surveys in May 1980 and July 1981 show that confidence in local and state government exceeded that in federal government in May 1980 and was just the opposite the following year.

The Advisory Commission on Intergovernmental Relations (ACIR) regularly asks, "From which level of government do you feel you get the most for your money—federal, state or local?" Trend data for the period 1973—1986 show the public considered the federal government best ten times during the 14 year period, including one tie with local government. It finished second to the local level three times; and it lost to state and local together only once (1984).

When asked about their confidence in specific departments and agencies, the public responds relatively more positively. In Roper Organization surveys conducted in each April and August in 1983 and 1985, over half of the respondents expressed favorable opinions of most federal departments and agencies (considered in the aggregate). August 1985 data showed 59 percent so inclined. Some of the respondents' percentages of favorable opinions of particular agencies were as follows: Veterans Administration (85 percent), National Park Service (79 percent), Food and Drug Administration (74 percent), Federal Bureau of Investigation (72 percent), National Highway Traffic Safety Administration (70 percent), Consumer Product Safety Commission (69 percent), Occupational Safety and Health Administration (63 percent), Environmental Protection Agency (58 percent), Central Intelligence Agency (53 percent) and the Internal Revenue Service (48 percent).

Such findings provide reassurance that, once beyond the level of generalities about government, the public displays confidence in federal institutions. There is little ground for firm conclusions. Clearly, service organizations seem to inspire relatively more trust and confidence than policy organizations. But the basis upon which the public differentiates among organizations remains shrouded in mystery.

Honesty and Integrity

While trust and confidence are undoubtedly influenced by government performance, it is safe to assume that the honesty and integrity of public servants (however we choose to define them) also contributes to public perceptions.

U.S. citizens rated federal government officials well below most other key occupations in terms of their ethical practices. Between July 1973 and June 1983, Opinion Research Corporation asked how the public rated ethical and moral practices of "average workers" and occupational groups such as physicians (consistently ranked highest among the specific occupations), bankers, scientists, and government officials at various levels. Only labor union leaders consistently rank below federal officials. Interestingly, average workers, who were always near the top of the public's preferences, took the lead for the last survey.

Prior to the Iran-Contra and Pentagon procurement scandals (the effects of which have yet to be assessed), there were signs that public sentiment was becoming more favorable. In a February 1987 Roper Organization survey, 53 percent of respondents said they thought people in government were taking payoffs in return for favors. As high as this figure may seem, it represents a steady drop from the 66 percent who said the same thing in March 1976.

Judging from the results of an April 1986 *New York Times* poll, people seem to feel better about the ethical standards of the federal government than they do about those of business. By a margin of 35 percent to 24 percent, respondents indicated their belief that the federal government's moral and ethical standards were higher, while 15 percent thought federal government and big corporation standards were essentially equal. Twenty six percent had no opinion. This compares with 1980 *Los Angeles Times* poll figures which found 31 percent of respondents picking labor, 24 percent business and 17 percent government as the institution having the highest standards of honest and integrity. Another 25 percent either were not sure or felt none of these three institutions had the highest standards.

There is some evidence that the public's opinion of public officials is largely a reflection of what they think of politicians, in particular. Sixty-one percent of those interviewed by ABC News/*Washington Post* in May 1987 thought the level of ethics and honesty of politicians was not good, or was poor. Seventy-four percent of those responding to an earlier 1987 poll by Yankelovich, Clancy, and Shulman felt that a lack of example set by political leaders contributes to lower moral standards in the United States.

Hardly anyone thinks the moral climate of politics has improved over time. Only 11 percent of those asked by the May 1987 ABC News/*Washington Post* poll thought the overall level of ethics and honesty in politics had improved over the past ten years. Forty-eight percent felt it had fallen and 40 percent thought it had stayed the same. These results are consistent with those of a 1973 Lou Harris and Associates poll, in which 50 percent said that politics was more corrupt than it had been previously, 42 percent said the situation was not much different, and only four percent were convinced that politics had become less corrupt.

There are conflicting signals from the public concerning its willingness to tolerate lying by government officials. Sixty-three percent of those by the *Los Angeles Times* in December 1986 (just after the Iran-Contra scandal became public) said the U.S. government is never justified in lying to the public. But when the *Times* repeated the question in July 1987 (immediately following Lieutenant Colonel Oliver North's televised testimony before the Iran-Contra Committee), 49 percent said the government is sometimes justified in telling such lies; 44 percent said it is not.

Because government officials periodically deny the truth of reports that appear on network television news program, ABC News asked in June 1984 whom the public thought was more likely, under such circumstances, to be telling the truth—the government officials or the network news programs. Sixty-five percent chose the news media, while only 14 percent picked government officials. Another 12 percent said that neither side is truthful or it depends on the situation.

When dealing with specifics, public opinion is less harsh. Asked, in 1984 by Yankelovich, Skelly and White, whether they felt IRS employees are honest and could never be bribed, 54 percent indicated modest to strong agreement. Fifty-nine percent were confident that the IRS would never try to take more money from them than it should.

There seems to be fairly strong belief that laws to govern ethical conduct of public officials are appropriate and necessary. Fifty-two percent of respondents to a 1981 Lou Harris poll disagreed with the idea that the laws passed after Watergate to guard against conflicts of interest in public life and to require financial disclosure by those appointed to high office went too far. Forty three percent thought they did. Fifty percent opposed cutting back some of those laws, while 45 percent favored such cutbacks.

Appraising the Public Servant

Surveys virtually never ask how people feel about civil servants, per se. An October 1982 Roper poll showed that 41 percent of those queried had a fairly good or high opinion and 49 percent a not-too-good or poor opinion of "federal agency and department officials." By comparison, an April 1981 *Los Angeles Times* survey showed a 55 percent favorable rating and a 38 percent unfavorable rating for "government workers." Are the differences due to the timing of the surveys, the samples selected, an actual improvement in attitudes, a distinction the public makes between "officials" and "workers," or to some less obvious factor? The answer is not clear.

In a 1981 Gallup survey, the one instance in which the public was asked about its confidence in civil servants, 55 percent said they had quite a lot or a great deal of confidence, while 43 percent said not very much or none at all. Similarly, although the term "bureaucrat" has been invested with a great deal of semantic baggage, the results of one survey suggest that the public is reasonably discerning in distinguishing the label from those who wear it. Forty-one percent of those responding to a 1986 Roper poll indicated that the term "bureaucrat" carried a negative connotation; 37 percent said the term was just descriptive.

The public is divided on what motivates public servants, but much more consistent in its perceptions of how hard public servants work. Forty-five percent of those in a 1981 Roper poll said government officials tend to act more from self-interest, while 44 percent said they act in the public interest. However, 60 percent of those asked by Roper in November 1981 said government workers are less industrious than private sector counterparts; 30 percent said they worked just as hard. This coincides with a 1972 Lou Harris poll in which only 11 percent said that government employees have above average productivity, compared to 40 percent who said average and 39 percent who said below average.

Government workers consistently fare poorly when compared to business. A 1978 Roper survey found 58 percent said business attracts the best people, 71 percent said business is run more efficiently, 52 percent said business attracts the best middle and lower level employees, and 42 percent said that business contributes more to making people's lives better. Twenty-three percent said the two sectors are equal in the last respect, and 25 percent thought the federal agencies contribute more.

The public does appear to differentiate between politicians and other public officials. A November 1980 Roper poll showed that 24 percent had a fairly good or high opinion and 71 percent a not-too-good or poor opinion of politicians. Comparable figures for federal agency and department officials were 36 and 51 percent.

Government workers are seen to receive better pay and benefits than their private sector counterparts. Nearly 70 percent of those questioned in an April 1982 ABC News/*Washington Post* survey said that government pay and benefits are better. In a November 1981 poll, 38 percent said that government employees are fairly paid, compared to 44 percent who said they are overpaid.

The public remains ambivalent about cutting federal pay. When a January 1985 *Los Angeles Times* poll asked whether respondents favored a five percent pay cut for federal civilian workers or some other way of cutting government expenses, 52 percent favored the latter; 42 percent favored the pay cuts. Much depends on what the "other" is. Lou Harris polls conducted six months apart in 1984 and 1985 found that by relatively narrow margins (10 percent), the public preferred cutting federal pay to cutting defense spending.

Contributing to this ambivalence is how the questions are framed. When asked whether they would favor cutting federal pay by five percent to reduce the federal deficit, 48 percent of 1985 Harris poll respondents favored the idea, while 47 percent opposed it. In a CBS News/*New York Times* poll conducted two weeks later, 38 percent said cutting federal salaries (an unspecified amount) would be a good way to cut the federal deficit, 50 percent said it was a bad idea. The Harris poll also asked whether respondents, as a member of Congress voting to reduce the annual deficit by more than half, would vote for or against cutting federal pay by five percent. Fifty-five percent said yes; 25 percent said no.

While public attitudes toward government workers appear to be impressionistic and based on infrequent contact, data is somewhat skimpy. Results of a 1976 Roper poll offer some insight. Asked to identify individuals in different occupations with whom they had a speaking acquaintance, respondents put teachers and sales people at the top of the list (named by 70 percent), city employees fourth (54 percent), state employees ninth (38 percent), and elected federal officials seventeenth (eight percent). While the poll did not ask about non-elected federal workers, it seems unlikely they would have ranked much higher than elected officials.

Government as a Calling

Despite the limited interaction with federal workers, the public seems positively disposed toward the federal service as a career choice. Fully 80 percent of those queried by a February 1985 CBS News/*New York Times* poll responded favorably when asked how they would feel about a young person choosing to become a federal employee. Yet, when Roper asked adults in 1973 what field they would most like to see their son or daughter enter, only 4 percent named federal service. The same question drew similar responses in a Roper survey three years later. When respondents were asked, in a 1977 Roper poll, how, if at all, their choice would change if all occupations were paid the same, civil service became the career choice of only six percent queried. Concern about government service can be traced, in part, to concerns about the potential for advancement. An October 1986 Roper poll showed that 45 percent said the government offers good to excellent opportunities, while 50 percent said fair to poor.

Table 2

**Question: "In the next 20 years, where do you think a young person who
_____ would do better—in business, government, in a profession
such as law or medicine, or teaching?"**

	Business	Govt.	Profession	Teaching	None/ Not Sure
Is a go-getter	56%	19%	13%	4%	8%
Wants to make money	47	14	31	2	6
Is well-organized and efficient	41	20	20	11	8
Gets along with people	31	20	15	25	9
Wants to lead a well-ordered life	27	14	28	20	11
Has a first-rate mind	25	20	32	13	10
Is highly creative	24	8	28	30	10
Likes to have a good time	23	18	20	13	26
Wants security	22	26	34	9	9
Has good leadership qualities	21	53	9	11	6
Is idealistic	18	19	20	29	14
Dislikes pressures	10	16	19	21	34

Source: ABC News/Louis Harris Associates

The desirability of government as a career choice seems to reflect the public's stereo-typed notions of government workers. A January 1979 ABC News/Lou Harris survey of adults, reflected in Table 2, shows the public considers leadership qualities very important to government service, but is cynical about government's ability to use and reward such attributes as creativity, intelligence and initiative.

Judged in their entirety, these findings are cause for encouragement and concern. While there are modest indications that there is some public affinity for the federal service as a career choice, there is also a tendency for people to rely on stereotypes in making such judgments. The need to reconcile these and other seemingly incongruent perspectives creates a clear imperative for further investigation of the questions posed in this study.

WHO IS SAYING THESE THINGS?

There is a tendency to treat the public's opinions as "The Public Opinion"—as if the views of the many can be converted into an undifferentiable whole. This leads us to overlook the real differences that underlie the apparent sameness or, conversely, to overlook the commonalities among the differences.

The findings presented in this study provide a needed empirical foundation that permits us to transform our intuitive sense of the public's attitudes toward government into something more substantive and defensible than impression alone. To really diagnose the reasons for public mood or to formulate effective responses, we need a deeper level of analysis.

One step toward this is to investigate the demographic bases for the opinions dealt with in this inquiry. This chapter will focus, whenever possible, on differentiable characteristics such as respondents' age, gender and education level. A word of caution: demographic variables are not leading indicators of the public's attitudes toward government. If anything, the picture presented in this chapter is full of complexity and contradictions, and may heighten our uncertainty.

Age

On the whole, the older segments of the population are relatively more favorable toward government than younger groups. Nonetheless, the younger age group (18–24 in most surveys, 18–29 in others) usually runs a close second, depending on the question. Both run well ahead of the middle age groups, who regularly express the most negative attitudes toward government.

A 1987 Gallup/Times Mirror survey brings clearly into focus the complexities age brings to issues about alienation. In response to the statement, "People like me don't have any say about what the government does," the 60-and-over age group expressed the most agreement, and the 50–59 group the least. In response to the statement, "Elected officials in Washington lose touch with the people," the 40–49 age group expressed the most agreement and the 18–24 age group the least. Somewhat in contrast, though, the 18–24 group agreed least and the 60-and-over group agreed most with the statement, "Most public officials care what people like me think." Presented with the statement, "Voting gives people like me some say about how the government runs things," those in the 25–29 age group showed the greatest level of agreement, while the next higher age group, 30–39, showed the least.

Those in the 60-and-over group uniformly, and by sizable margins, register the strongest approval of government performance in: treating people with dignity, providing quality services, providing services efficiently, giving fair treatment, and preventing fraud and abuse. But, in the recent Gallup/Times Mirror survey, this age group also showed the strongest agreement with the statements, "When something is run by government, it is usually inefficient and wasteful," and "Dealing with a federal government agency is often not worth the trouble."

Young adults, under age 30, regularly reflect the highest degrees of trust and confidence in the federal government and the most confidence in the federal government's ethical standards. The 60-and-over group hold high opinions of the federal departments and agencies.

Uniformly, it is the older groups (especially those 60 and over) who most strongly agree that federal workers are better paid than their private sector counterparts and that federal pay should therefore be cut. However, these age groups also register the most favorable impressions of government workers, and they are most optimistic about the chances of getting ahead in government. Young adults occasionally exceed the 60-and-over group in favorable views of government workers. For example, a 1981 Gallup poll, which oversampled 18-24 year olds, showed that 62 percent of them had a great deal or quite a lot of confidence in the civil service.

One of the least explicable findings resulted from a 1985 CBS News/*New York Times* poll which asked respondents how they would feel about a young person choosing federal service as a career. Eighty-four percent of those in the 45-59 age group (usually one of the most negative toward government) responded favorably, compared to 82 percent in the 18-29 group, 81 percent in the 30-44 group (also typically negative), and 74 percent in the 60-and-over age group.

Gender

Women are generally more favorably disposed than men toward the federal government, but results can be mixed. Women tend to expect more from government and men tend to be more cynical and alienated from it. Men believe that government—especially the federal government—has too much power and that it should be reduced.

Women view federal government performance more favorably across a range of services. Somewhat in contradiction, men uniformly give more favorable responses than women when asked how much trust and confidence they have in the federal government. Men are also more inclined to give the federal government the benefit of the doubt on honesty and integrity.

Women are more likely to say that federal government workers are better paid than others, but men favor federal pay cuts more strongly. Women express more favorable impressions of government workers, but are only moderately more positive than men in assessing opportunities for getting ahead in government. Eighty percent of men and women recommended the federal government as a career option for a young person in a 1985 CBS News/*New York Times* poll.

Race

Respondents' race can be a predictor of attitudes toward government, but it also has internal contradictions. For example, non-whites seem to be more cynical toward and alienated from government than whites, and they are more likely to expect government to bear more responsibility than individuals for citizens' well-being. However, non-whites also feel more strongly that the federal government has too much power, which should be curtailed. Non-whites tend to respond more favorably on government performance, although the margins are frequently small and, in some cases (e.g., giving fair treatment) government gets higher marks from whites.

Results are more mixed on trust and confidence. In the 1987 Gallup poll for ACIR, a larger proportion of non-whites than whites indicated that they had more confidence and trust in the people running the federal government than they had in those running state and local governments. In the same poll, though, whites had more trust and confidence than non-whites in the federal government's ability to carry out its responsibilities.

ABC News/*Washington Post* and National Opinion Research Center polls conducted in 1987 indicated whites also were much more likely than non-whites to say that government in Washington can be trusted to do what is right most of the time. A 1987 *Los Angeles Times* poll also showed whites are less likely to have lost confidence in the federal executive branch as a societal institution. However, in a 1985 Roper poll, non-whites expressed more favorable opinions toward federal departments and agencies.

Whites are more likely than non-whites to think that federal workers are better paid than their private sector counterparts, and to support federal pay cuts. In contrast, non-whites tend, with occasional exceptions, to have more favorable impressions of government workers. They also view opportunities for getting ahead in government more favorably than whites, and are more supportive of a young person choosing federal employment as a career.

Income

Respondents' income level is an especially unstable predictor, although it sometimes produces findings that would be intuitively expected. For example, the lowest income group (less than $10,000 annually) is regularly more cynical and alienated than all other income groups.

A 1985 *Los Angeles Times* poll suggests that middle-income groups ($20,000–$50,000 annually) are more likely than lower-income groups and appreciably more likely than higher-income groups to expect government, rather than individuals, to be responsible for personal well-being. Those in the middle-income bands are most inclined to say that the federal government has too much power, while those at the lower income levels (especially below $10,000) are most likely to name government as the institution that should have its power cut back for the good of the country.

A 1987 Gallup/Times Mirror survey showed low-income respondents are most favorable toward government performance. This coincides generally with responses to two questions from a 1982 Yankelovich, Skelly, and White survey about how well the public thought government was doing in providing efficient services and preventing fraud and abuse. However, in three other areas from that survey—treating people with dignity, providing quality services, and giving fair treatment—moderate income groups (up to $30,000) tended to give government the highest marks.

Trust and confidence issues reflect more mixed opinions. In the 1987 Gallup poll for ACIR, the lowest income group (less than $15,000) expressed the most trust and confidence in the federal government, over state and local governments. Moderate income groups expressed the greatest trust and confidence in the federal government's ability to carry out its responsibilities. Yet, two 1987 polls—each asking, "How much of the time do you trust government in Washington to do what is right?"—found, in one instance, the most favorable response from those earning over $50,000 and, in the other, from those in the medium salary bands.

Those in the lowest income bracket tend to have the most favorable impressions of government workers; are most convinced that government provides good opportunities to get ahead; and are most supportive of a young person choosing a federal service career. However, they also are more likely to believe that federal workers are better paid than their private-sector counterparts and that federal pay should be cut accordingly.

Education

Respondents' education levels present complexities and contradictions and are frustrating to interpret. Those with less than a high school education tend to be more cynical toward and alienated from government than other groups, but they also seem most convinced that government bears more responsibility than individuals for citizens' well-being. These individuals are less likely than those with moderate education (high school graduates and those with some college), but considerably more likely than the highly educated (college graduates) to think that the federal government has too much power and that it should be curtailed.

College graduates in the 1987 Gallup/Times Mirror survey were least likely to agree with the statement that dealing with a federal government agency often isn't worth the trouble, while those with less than a high school education were least likely to agree that things run by government are usually inefficient and wasteful. In the 1982 Yankelovich, Skelly and

White survey, those with the least education gave the highest ratings to government performance in preventing fraud and abuse; the moderately educated gave the highest marks to
government in providing quality and efficient services; and college graduates' highest marks
went to government performance in giving fair treatment and treating people with dignity.

In the 1987 Gallup survey for ACIR, those without a high school diploma most preferred the people who run the federal government over those who run state and local government, while college graduates expressed higher levels of trust and confidence in the federal
government's ability to carry out its responsibilities. In the 1987 National Opinion Research
Center poll, college graduates gave the most favorable response when asked how much of
the time they thought they could trust government in Washington to do what is right. Asking the same question in 1987, the ABC News/*Washington Post* poll found the moderately
educated were most favorable. In both polls, the least educated respondents expressed the
lowest levels of confidence. Yet, when asked by the *Los Angeles Times* in 1987 to name the
institutions in which they had lost the most confidence lately, those without high school diplo-
mas were least likely to name the federal executive branch.

The moderately educated have the best general opinions of federal departments and
agencies; are most likely to see government as offering good opportunities to get ahead; and
are most supportive of a young person choosing a career in the federal service. The least
educated are the strongest supporters of the federal government's ethical standards, and
tend to have the most favorable impressions of government workers. But they also believe
more than other groups that federal government workers are better paid than others and
that federal pay should be cut.

Political Affiliation

Political affiliation provides the most clear-cut findings, although they are not one-
sided or predictable. Democrats are more cynical toward and alienated from government
than Republicans, and are more committed to the belief that government, rather than the
individual, should bear primary responsibility for citizens' well-being. However, Democrats
also feel that the federal government has too much power and that it should be cut back.

Democrats are far more likely than Republicans to give the federal government high
marks for performance; Republicans give better marks for providing quality services and
giving fair treatment. Democrats place more stock in federal government ethical standards
than do Republicans.

Republicans repeatedly reflect higher levels of trust and confidence in the federal
government, and give slightly more favorable opinions of federal department and agency
officials. Democrats have more favorable impressions of government workers in general.
Republicans are somewhat more supportive of a young person making federal employment
a career choice, but they are also more convinced that federal workers receive better pay
than their private-sector counterparts and that federal pay should be cut accordingly.

Geographic Origin

While it is possible to say that the South and Northeast have slightly more support
for the federal government than the Midwest or West, this is not clear-cut. In fact, midwestern
respondents were more supportive, and those from the South least supportive, that government, rather than the individual, is responsible for citizens' well-being. The South (followed

by the West) reflects the strongest beliefs that the federal government has too much power and that it should be curtailed.

The South leads other regions in support of the federal government's ethical standards; and, with minor exceptions, the South and Northeast reflect the greatest levels of trust and confidence in it. The Northeast gives the federal government slightly higher marks on performance, while the South has the strongest beliefs that government offers opportunities to get ahead. The Northeast is the most favorable and the South least so about a young person choosing the federal service as a career. The two regions hold equally favorable views of federal department and agency officials. The West has the most favorable impressions of government workers in general, with more affinity for state and local government.

TWO POINTS OF REFERENCE

How do the findings in this analysis compare with other attempts to understand public attitudes toward government? This chapter presents two major investigations—one by the Brookings Institution and the other by the Institute for Social Research —for comparison. Both of these focus on the tendency of the American people to be guided by negative stereotypes of government and government workers.

The Brookings Study

The Brookings Institution study was based on more than 5,000 interviews with federal employees and nonfederal populations (the general employed public, students, educators, and business groups) between April 1960 and February 1961. It focused on the so-called "federal personnel problem," defined as attracting top-quality people to the federal government. The study assessed: 1) the patterns of occupational values among a wide variety of key groups in U.S. society; and 2) the images those groups have of the U.S. government as an employer and of federal public servants in their occupational roles.[2]

The study found that four-fifths or more of respondents in all groups were willing to generalize about—stereotype—federal civil servants, although respondents at higher education and occupational levels proved a little less willing than others. From one-fifth to two-fifths gave essentially ambiguous (as opposed to favorable, unfavorable, or ambivalent) descriptions of civil servants, a finding which suggested that substantial numbers of people are relatively "neutral" about federal employees.

In the general employed public, favorable descriptions of federal civil servants heavily outnumbered unfavorable ones; among higher level nonfederal groups, favorable descriptions decreased. Federal employees were more favorable than comparable nonfederal groups. However, federal executives and upper level federal groups gave fewer favorable responses than did those lower in the federal hierarchy.

Members of the general employed public most often attributed to the civil servant characteristics such as good personal character, capability for doing the work because of training and ability, being a good worker, and having an agreeable personality. Among many of the elite groups outside the federal service, references to such favorable qualities declined, and the number of people increased who described the civil service as security-conscious, lacking in ambition, adaptable to routine, a poor worker, and noncreative and dull. Members of the general federal populations were more likely to mention favorable characteristics of civil servants, while less likely to make critical comments. People in the elite federal groups made more positive and more negative statements.

In most groups, federal employees were rated high on honesty. They were rated lower on their interest in serving the public, level of ability, amount of respect they received, and drive to get ahead. Top level civil servants were rated higher than top level business executives on honesty and interest in serving the public. However, they tended to be ranked below their business counterparts on their ability and the respect they were accorded, and especially on their drive to get ahead.

All groups of respondents thought security was the most common reason why a person might become a federal civil servant. However, some groups, particularly college teachers and high school and college students, placed considerable emphasis on other motives, such as a desire to be of service.

Groups outside the federal service rated government relatively low on the chance it provides "a young man of ability" with "real success." (Women were uniformly more favorable than men toward government, and apparently their chances for "real success" were not an issue.) Large private businesses gave higher ratings on this factor. The government's comparative position grew worse among high status groups, with special business groups (executives, natural scientists, social scientists, engineers) comparing government most unfavorably with corporations. Nearly all federal populations shared the feeling that private business exceeds the government in opportunities for "real success," but they gave business less of an edge than did comparable people outside government.

In all groups, government compared better with business on chances for getting ahead or for reaching one of the top level jobs than it compared with business on opportunities for real success. Apparently, while people believed opportunities for moving up were as good, they also felt that the top in government provided fewer chances for "real success" than did the top echelons of the business world.

Institute for Social Research

The Institute for Social Research at the University of Michigan based its study on an omnibus survey of 1,500 adults during April–May 1973. The objectives of the study were to: 1) obtain information about the utilization and underutilization of major government services among various sectors of the population; 2) find out how people evaluate government offices which have dealt with their problems; and 3) see how their own experiences with public bureaucracy are related to their more general attitudes toward government.[3]

Approximately 58 percent of respondents report contact with at least one of seven service areas considered: employment service, job training, workmen's compensation, unemployment compensation, public assistance, hospital and medical care, and retirement benefits. This part of the study reported a high degree of satisfaction. Negative stereotypes of bureaucracy tended not to be supported. Overall, approximately three out of five clients stated that their problem had been resolved. Only one in five thought the agency personnel had not exerted enough effort to be helpful. Only one in ten felt that the appropriate bureaucrat had been hard to find, and only one in five thought that the agency had been inefficient. Three out of four respondents felt they had been treated fairly. Forty-seven percent said they had the right to appeal decisions they did not like.

Attitudes toward the overall political system were complex. While 61 percent of respondents agreed that by and large most government offices did a good job, they were less en-thusiastic about such general characteristics as promptness, fairness, considerate treatment, and the like. Yet when specific experiences were compared with such general evaluations, the former were more positive than the latter. For example, 80 percent felt they had received fair treatment in their contact with government agencies, but only 42 percent rated govern-ment offices in general as fair. A closer evaluation of data revealed that a negative experience with an agency lowered a respondent's general evaluation of government, but a positive ex-perience did not raise it.

The study's authors speculated that the general low rating of characteristics of govern-ment service may reflect stereotypes of public bureaucracy. This interpretation coincided with other study findings which compared public bureaucracy with private enterprise. The negative evaluations of government in general seemed inconsistent as well with respondents' preferences for allocating major social tasks. They preferred that government, rather than private enterprise, handle such tasks as: preventing pollution, controlling crime, providing job retraining, and delivering hospital and medical benefits. Within government, respon-dents favored state and federal agencies over local agencies.

Perhaps the most penetrating insight from this study was the authors' proposition that people are characterized by cognitive complexity rather than cognitive consistency. The inconsistencies showed two modes of responses were tapped: one ideological, one pragmat-ic. General evaluations of bureaucracy seemed to tap ideological impulses, while specific evaluations of experiences were based more on pragmatic considerations. Thus, what may have been working was an ideology of stereotypes rather than strong personal values and convictions.

A SEARCH FOR REMEDIES

Where does this leave us? We do know that, relative to other issues of the day, govern-ment is only a blip on the public consciousness. The public expects government to provide an extraordinarily wide range of services, yet it consistently favors federal workforce reductions.

Although the public maintains a continuing wariness of concentrated power, it has mixed views of whether the federal government has too much power. Federal government is seen as not very efficient or well run, but such assessments vary according to the type of service provided and the nature of the function performed. Rather than cut programs to cut the deficit, people prefer more efficient operations. And, while the public invariably expects a new president to improve government operations, these expectations are rarely met.

We also know that the federal executive branch, though not commanding very high levels of public trust and confidence, fares better than state and local governments and looks even better when people are asked to judge particular departments and agencies. The pub-lic does not generally feel good about the honesty and integrity of public officials, but these views seem to be influenced by negative attitudes toward politicians. We know that, while government workers are perceived to work less hard, be less productive, and receive higher pay and benefits than their private sector counterparts, the public is ambivalent about cut-ting federal pay. Finally, we know that the public seems to view federal service rather posi-tively as a career choice, although there is continuing doubt as to whether government offers good opportunities for getting ahead.

We do not know at whom public attitudes toward government are directed; how they were formed; how the public differentiates the federal executive branch from other branches and levels of government; whether they differentiate public officials from politicians, careerists from political appointees, senior workers from junior workers; or what image of government is presented to the public by the news media and senior public officials themselves.

One thing that seems clear is that the public's general impressions of government are based on negative stereotypes inculcated into us all by the socialization process. Can anyone remember the term "bureaucracy" used as anything but an epithet? Precisely because stereotyping is so pervasive and fundamental, any attempt to affect public perceptions of government must confront the phenomenon directly.

Can stereotypes actually be changed? Years of communications research have shown that strongly held beliefs—especially those based on first-hand experience—are highly resistant to change, while weakly held beliefs, based on general impressions, are more malleable. Stereotypes seem less likely to be deeply held beliefs than simply deeply embedded impressions. They seem less a part of our conscious repertory than a subconscious stream of illusions, less derived from a sense of conviction than a set of intuitive premises whose logic has been accepted unquestioningly.

In line with the theory that there is a direct relationship between attitudes and behavior, there is something to be said for improving government performance as a way to improve public attitudes. In reality, the relationship is not so simple; stereotypes intervene. Thus, our deeper concern must be to ensure that when government performance and the behavior of government workers are satisfactory, public attitudes toward both are commensurately favorable.

The authors offer four general approaches for achieving this linkage between government performance and public attitudes.

Emphasize public education as the principal means of counteracting the ignorance and insensitivity that underlies all stereotypes.

Improve the public image of government and government workers by increased compensation and increased recognition.

Play on the public's attraction to big business as an idealized model of managerial excellence by making the government operations seem more businesslike, and government workers more entrepreneurial.

Play on the public's preference for decentralized government by decentralizing more of government's functions, thereby presumably enhancing the image of the federal government by diminishing its role.

These ideas, though attractive in some respects, raise other dilemmas. For example, having public management emulate private management might make the former marginally more efficient—symbolically and actually—but it would undermine the distinctive features of public management that should be heralded. Devolving responsibilities from federal to state governments might be more comforting and less impersonal, but it could produce state-centered parochialism antithetical to emerging global conditions that demand greater centralization at national and even supranational levels.

It will be difficult to determine what population to target in attempting to influence public attitudes. For example, we know that older segments of the population are somewhat more favorable than young segments toward government. We also know that the values and life goals of youth—represented by college freshmen—have shifted in the past 20 years toward those more tied to money, power, and status. Values that have declined most are those tied to altruistic activities and social concerns. Given such factors, the question is whom to target: youth who, though representing the future will have to be convinced; or older age groups who, though having only to be reaffirmed in their beliefs, represent the past?

Another example relates to whether efforts to influence public attitudes should be targeted at higher or lower education and income groups. Individuals with higher levels of education and income are generally more negative toward government than others. They are also, however, opinion leaders. Because they are better informed and more involved, their opinions are well-developed. Should one, therefore, expend time and effort to convert opinion leaders, or circumvent such elites and go directly to the public?

Solutions to these and other dilemmas will not come easily, but the difficulty should not deter affirmative action.

It is almost insultingly easy to excoriate government; to do so is convenient and socially acceptable—perhaps even socially expected. It is difficult to praise government—a truly lonely experience for which there are no social rewards, and may even be penalties. Only when respondents can hide behind the anonymity of a survey are they comfortable in breaking these social fetters. Thus, in a very tentative sense, the findings presented in this study provide some hopeful signs of latent goodwill that warrant further exploration, and perhaps exploitation.

The way to exploit such latent goodwill may lie in a phenomenon we might term "normative sway." If people are told repeatedly that they feel a particular way about something, over time they will conclude that is how they should feel. However, in the absence of external incentives, the reverse does not seem to hold; people who are told they should feel a certain way will not necessarily come to feel that way.

For our purposes, the lesson is this: if the public is told that—contrary to what they have been led to believe—they actually feel good about government, gradually they will come to believe they should feel that way. At that point, a snowballing effect will start to occur. Accordingly, to the extent that stereotypes are inevitable, the prevailing stereotype of government and government workers is more likely under such changing conditions to become positive.

The idea of "normative sway" is, of course, entirely speculative. As such, it can be approached only as a sort of living experiment that may or may not be successful. But that should not dissuade us from trying. The imperative to come to grips with the nature and origins of public attitudes toward government seems eminently clear. Unless we do so, we will have only ourselves to blame if suddenly we awaken to a state of affairs similar to that once ominously, if hyperbolically, described by Rousseau:

> As soon as public service ceases to be the chief business of the citizens, and they would rather serve with their money than with their persons, the State is not far from its fall.

ENDNOTES

1. Documents from a Brookings Institution-American Enterprise Institute for Public Policy Research Project: A National Public Service for the Year 2000, June 1985–November 1986 (Washington, D.C.: The Brookings Institution, Center for Public Policy Education, January 1987).
2. Franklin P. Kilpatrick, Milton C. Cummings, Jr., and J. Kent Jennings, *The Image of the Federal Service* (Washington, D.C.: The Brookings Institution, 1964).
3. Daniel Katz, Barbara A. Gutek, Robert L. Kahn, and Eugenia Barton, *Bureaucratic Encounters: A Pilot Study in the Evaluation of Government Services* (Ann Arbor, MI: University of Michigan, 1975).

Acknowledgments

The authors extend their appreciation to the staff of the Roper Center for Public Opinion Research—especially to Mark G. Maynard of that organization—for assembling the data that made this report possible.

We also want to express our thanks to Ambassador Bruce Laingen, Executive Director of the National Commission on the Public Service, for his unstinting support of the effort, and to Diane Dziwura and Marjorie Jones of the Commission staff for easing our administrative burden immeasurably.

THE IMAGE OF THE PUBLIC SERVICE IN THE MEDIA

Background Paper Prepared for the

Task Force on Public Perceptions

of the

National Commission on the Public Service

by

Donald F. Kettl

MARCH 1988

CONTENTS

EXECUTIVE SUMMARY

The performance of public servants, especially at the federal level, is a sore issue among some members of the media. Columnists complain about "lollygagging employees in federal agency halls" and incompetent employees who cannot be fired. Bureaucrats are natural lightning rods for dissatisfaction about government performance and for conflicts over government programs. By contrast, positive stories about improving performance do not play well on television or in newspapers. The story calculated to make the reader's blood boil attracts the most attention and hence wins the greatest prominence.

There are, however, important rhythms in newspaper coverage. A survey of articles about the public service printed in the *New York Times* from 1975 to 1986 reveals three important trends:

• Newspaper stories increased dramatically after change-of-party elections as new Presidents begin a flurry of activity.

• Stories about perks—public servants' salaries and benefits—peak immediately after elections as new Presidents seek instant leverage on federal spending.

• Stories about performance peak at the President's mid-term as he begins to worry about increasing his control of government programs.

The President thus sets the overall agenda for media coverage of the public service. Stories about the public service, however, tend to mutate from positive to negative images, as two case studies of newspaper coverage illustrate: the Carter Administration's proposal, enacted in 1978, to reform the civil service system; and the Reagan Administration's response, in 1987, to the Quadrennial Commission on Executive, Legislative and Judicial Salaries's proposed pay increase for top government officials.

In civil service reform, the Carter Administration consciously shifted the agenda from enhancing performance and protecting whistleblowers to making it easier to fire incompetent federal employees. In the pay increase debate, Congress's haggling over who would be tarred with increasing congressional pay undermined other proposals for dealing with the pay compression problem of top public servants. In both cases, the President had it within his power to place the public service issue on a higher, more positive plane, and in both cases—for both pragmatic and partisan reasons—he decided not to do so.

The public service thus is typically an issue of little moment in the media, an issue easily transformed and overridden by higher stakes battles. The experience of the last twenty years, however, demonstrates that this need not be so. The timing and content of the public service debate are the President's to decide. The public's image of the public service can be improved only if the President takes the lead.

INTRODUCTION

The performance of public servants, especially at the federal level, is a sore issue among some members of the media. Nick Thimmesch, a columnist for the *Los Angeles Times* syndicate, bluntly complained, "The sight of lollygagging employees in federal agency halls quickens anger."[1] A *Chicago Tribune* columnist, Michael Kilian concluded, "Judging by some of the federal agencies I've dealt with, if the unit in charge of policing incompetence did its job, there'd be no one left for the other unit to manage. . . . Under the present setup, the only grounds for dismissal seem to be violations of war crime statutes, public child molesting during working hours, and the burning of public buildings during months that end in "r.'"[2]

Bureaucrats are natural lightning rods for dissatisfaction about government performance and for conflicts over government programs. For federal level bureaucrats, the problem is even greater. They are both more distant from most people (so the typical citizen does not have first hand knowledge of what they do) and are the largest part of "big government" (so they are the people alienated citizens love to hate). A 1964 study showed that just over half of all those surveyed had a positive image of the public service, a significantly lower percentage than for big business.[3] Since then, Watergate and a succession of bureaucrat-bashing Presidents have undoubtedly worsened that image.

Just as important, the 1964 study showed that two-fifths of those surveyed had *no* opinion on the quality of federal public servants. That finding sharpens a basic paradox that highlights the crucial role of the mass media in shaping the image of the public service: those who have opinions often have strong ones, but apathy is pervasive. Thus, images that the media conveys—words, stories, and pictures—play a critical role in energizing public debate.

Images of the public service are particularly ill-suited to television. Debates over the performance of governmental workers do not translate easily to 90-second "news bites" and rarely do they suggest the lively pictures that network news shows require. The public service is more of a newspaper issue, but even on the printed page editors must find some hook on which to hang the story. Good government issues typically do not make good newspaper stories, and general news stories about the public service tend to settle to the back of newspapers when they run at all. It is the story calculated to make the reader's blood boil that attracts the most attention and hence wins the greatest prominence. The following newspaper editorial cartoons, drawn from the Civil Service reform debate in 1978, illustrate the point. (See Figures 1, 2.)

Thus, the low salience of public service issues, the natural inclination of the media to pitch stories in a way that most stimulates readers' interest, and the obvious lure of tales of abuse conspire to make it difficult to present the public service in a positive light.

Figure 1

© SAN FRANCISCO CHRONICLE, May 8, 1978, p. 51. Reprinted by permission.

Figure 2

"As one sloth to another I think we've taken this as far as it can go . . ."

© SAN FRANCISCO CHRONICLE, September 15, 1978, p. 60. Reprinted by permission.

CYCLES OF NEWS COVERAGE

Over the years, newspaper coverage of the federal public service has been cyclical, and the President has shaped those cycles. The coverage of public service stories in the *New York Times* illustrates these cycles. From 1975 to 1986, the total number of stories—editorials, features, and news items—has varied with presidential elections. The number of stories increased dramatically after change-of-party elections, from President Ford to President Carter, and from President Carter to President Reagan. The *Times's* coverage of the public service between elections, by contrast, has been much less active. (See Figure 3.)

Figure 3
Coverage of the Civil Service
in the New York Times

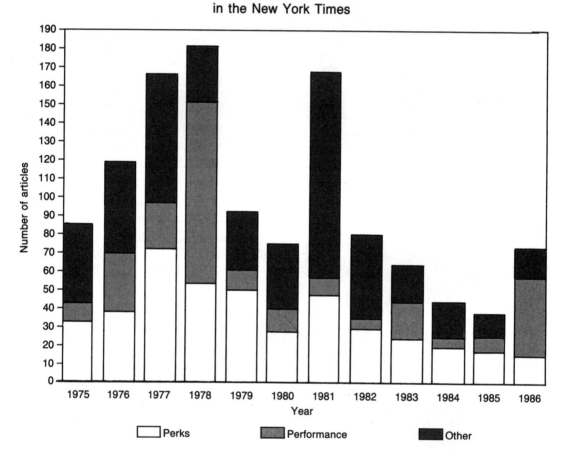

The kind of stories, moreover, has varied with the electoral cycle. The stories can be divided into three groups:

- *Perks*—stories about public servants' salaries, benefits, retirement programs, and other perquisites.

- *Performance*—stories about positive behavior by public servants and, more often, about malfeasance and problems of presidential control.

- *Other*—stories about the wide range of other public service issues, from the right of federal employees to strike to employees' access to dial-a-porn telephone numbers.

Immediately after presidential elections, stories about perks increase. In an era of large budget deficits, new Presidents have sought instant leverage over federal spending, and outlays for salaries have offered the most immediate target of opportunity. Hiring freezes, as well as other strategies for controlling government salaries and benefits, had a natural lure. Thus, in 1977 and 1981, the number of stories about public servants' perks significantly increased and then soon settled back to lower levels.

Stories about public servants' performance increased at mid-term. In 1978, for example, President Carter launched a major effort to reform the civil service system (which will be examined in more depth later in this paper), and the *Times's* coverage of performance issues hit its highest point of the period. During the Reagan Administration, stories about performance increased in 1983 and 1986. The stories in 1983 were a varied lot, but in 1986, the Reagan Administration's drug testing proposal generated substantial ink. Attorney General Edwin Meese worried that drug use might potentially compromise the 1.5 million federal employees who had access to classified materials, and he recommended a testing program to weed out drug users. The strongest finding, however, is that news coverage of performance issues was otherwise remarkably thin, especially after Carter's civil service reform proposals.

Other stories rose and fell less predictably. Conflict of interest stories dominated post-Watergate news coverage, but they dwindled with the Carter Administration. The air traffic controllers' strike dominated news coverage in 1981. Throughout the rest of the period, however, random events triggered occasional reports.

Newspaper coverage of the public service, as measured by the number of stories in the *New York Times*, thus has followed a rhythm based on presidential initiative:

- In general, newspaper coverage has tended to be relatively light. In the absence of presidential activity, there on average was no more than one story per week. In 1985, the frequency dropped to one story every ten days. Thus, the public service does not naturally generate much coverage on its own merit.

- News coverage follows presidential initiatives—whether proposing major reforms in the civil service, instituting a hiring freeze, firing air traffic controllers, or conducting drug tests. News coverage follows the issues as the President defines them.

- Since Watergate, presidential initiatives have followed a rhythm: early attention to spending and hence to public service perks, mid-term attention to management and hence to public service performance.

- Other stories have been less predictable. The President nevertheless has set the agenda even for the offbeat and for the unpredictable.

The President and his key staff are thus responsible for how newspapers cover the public service. It is the President's program that stirs newspaper attention from the typical state of lethargy.

Two case studies illustrate how the content of such stories is shaped. The first is President Carter's 1978 proposal to reform the civil service system, through the Civil Service Reform Act. The second is President Reagan's reaction to the 1986 report of the Quadrennial Commission on Executive, Legislative and Judicial Salaries, which recommended a substantial increase in pay for high government officials. Each case study will examine how eight major newspapers played the issue:[4]

Atlanta Constitution
Chicago Tribune
Los Angeles Times
New Orleans Times-Picayune
New York Times
Wall Street Journal
San Francisco Chronicle
Washington Post

THE CIVIL SERVICE REFORM ACT OF 1978

Jimmy Carter campaigned for the presidency on a platform of restoring citizens' confidence in government. He cited a report that A. Ernest Fitzgerald had been fired as an Air Force efficiency expert because he had blown the whistle about cost overruns on the C-5A, the service's massive transport plane. If elected, he promised to protect federal employees who reported dishonesty by superiors or government contractors.

That promise lay dormant for the first year of the Administration as President Carter struggled to gain control of the budget. In February, 1978, however, "administration spokesman" began preparing the ground for the President's plan by issuing background statements picturing the proposal as a way to protect whistleblowers. An Associated Press (AP) story, which ran in many newspapers around the country, quoted a civil service spokesman as saying that the administration wanted to make it easier for government employees to report wrongdoing.[5]

President Carter announced the proposal on March 2, 1978, with the pledge, "I came to Washington with the promise, and the obligation to help rebuild the faith of the American people in our government." He continued, "We want a government that can be trusted, not feared; that will be efficient, not mired in its own red tape, a government that will respond to the needs of the American people and not be preoccupied with needs of its own." He argued that it was easier to promote and transfer an incompetent federal employee than to dismiss him. That, the former peanut farmer said, was no way to run a farm, a factory, or a government. To fulfill this promise, a four part civil service reform:

• To create a senior executive service, which would provide a permanent cadre of top government managers:

• To streamline disciplinary procedures for federal workers;

• To create an incentive system for middle managers;

• To decentralize federal government hiring by delegating more authority to the agencies.

Just before President Carter announced the plan, *Washington Post* columnist Haynes Johnson wrote, "What the Carter Administration has been trying to achieve is a new system which would do two things: truly protect a merit system for government workers, and at the same time give government service more flexibility, more incentives, better management."[6] Indeed, the first blush of newspaper attention applauded the Administration's approach of better government through better management.

Administration strategists, however, soon determined that "better management" would be a tough issue on which to sell the civil service reform. Opposition was growing from veterans' groups, since veterans would lose their preferential status in the competition for federal jobs, and among some federal unions which distrusted the plan. As Administration official Alan K. "Scotty" Campbell put it, "from the political viewpoint, we have the general public on our side. There is a quiet acceptance of the need for change than can be used to influence Congress to support our concept. But it's a tough issue to rally people around— like trying for support on a local level for a city planning issue."[7]

To build support, they decided to dramatically illustrate how hard it was to fire a civil service employee—and thus how much the system needed fundamental reform. Office of Management and Budget aide Harrison Welford unveiled a 21-foot long chart showing the steps the government took to fire a clerk typist who was, by the Administration's account, incompetent and consistently late for work. The chart illustrated the 21-month process— one foot for each month—of reports, appeals, and the boxes of files required to document and process the charges. In the end, the clerk resigned rather than file yet another appeal, an appeal that would further have lengthened the process.

The chart immediately appealed to feature and editorial writers. An article distributed through the *New York Times* news service described it: "Looking like a diagram of the circuitry for an intercontinental ballistic missile, its 21 feet of boxes, triangles, and zigzagging lines chronicle the memos, warnings, suspensions, and conferences needed to dismiss one lowly federal employee."[8] The problem was so great, the *San Francisco Chronicle* editorialized that "This most obdurate bastion of bureaucracy has withstood the attacks of a progression of Presidents who eventually left the battlefield on their shields, rather than carrying them."[9]

The problem of firing federal workers especially exorcised the editors of the *Chicago Tribune*, who along with their columnists saw it as the penultimate problem of the federal service. Columns complained about "lollygagging" and workers flush with "incompetence."[10] Its editorial writers had a sarcastic solution: "The firing process is so hard we must divide the 2,900,000 Civil Service employees into two groups. One segment of 1,450,000 will be put to work trying to fire the other 1,450,000, who will of course be kept busy filing appeals or trying to mix up the first 1,450,000. It will be a long, verbiage laden process. But at last will come victory. No more Civil Service workers left."[11]

President Carter's proposal drew more even handed editorial support around the country. The *Washington Post* applauded it as "on the whole, an excellent plan."[12] The *New York Times* editorially concluded, "surely Congress recognizes that the public wants better government service. The proposed Civil Service reform can provide it."[13] A *Wall Street Journal* op-ed article praised the plan for trying "to reassert management control over the bureaucracy by clarifying the difference between managers and workers and giving managers greater leeway in handling personnel matters."[14]

Despite such support, however, the 21-foot chart became the symbol of the President's proposal and the irresistible hook for columnists and editorial writers. *New York Times* columnist Anthony Lewis expressed the "everyman" position in a column circulated around the country:

> Government doesn't work. So millions of Americans—perhaps most of us—feel. Anyone who travels around this country and listens knows that people everywhere talk resentfully about the unresponsiveness, the ineptitude of government. Faith in its ability to get things done is at a dismally low ebb. . . .
>
> But most Americans know the shortcomings of government at a level less grand than the development of great new policies. They encounter the government when some personal interest is at stake: in disability benefits or taxes or business regulations. They have to deal with bureaucrats, and the experience is frustrating. Too often they find incompetence, insensitivity, or insolence. . . .
>
> At present it takes as long as twenty one months to fire a stenographer, in a process that costs the government—that is, us—up to $100,000. In fact, the process is so burdensome that practically no one is ever fired.
>
> We were taught in school that one of the great forward steps in American government came when the "spoils system"—political appointment of federal employees—was replaced by the "merit system." But as politics can be corrupt, so a Civil Service without incentive for new ideas and better performance can be stifling. . . .
>
> Government employees, with their booming pay over recent years, have made the Washington area one of the most prosperous in the country—and built up great resistance to any change in their status. If there is to be reform the rest of us will have to speak up.[15]

The Carter Administration struggled to overcome strong opposition, especially by the veterans' groups and employee unions, by sending officials to Capitol Hill to testify. There they told stories of one official who earned a $40,000 salary at the Environmental Protection Agency for "doing next to nothing." Then there was another employee making $50,000 "who hadn't been seen for years." As the AP reported in a dispatch widely reprinted around the country, "They were what one administrator called high level welfare cases—persons who weren't performing their jobs but who were paid anyway because it was too tedious and time consuming to try to fire them."[16]

The *Chicago Tribune*, which consistently displayed outrage over the reports, headlined a page-one feature "Our Civil Service: A Shield for Incompetence." (The inside continuation of the story was headlined, "Carter's Solution: Make It Easier to Fire the Laggards.") The EPA official had "found a pot of gold at the end of the rainbow"; the employee who had not been to work in years had "found the goose the lays golden eggs," the *Tribune* explained. "These two cases differ only in degree from thousands of others in the federal bureaucracy that lend solidity to President Carter's observation that 'the public suspects there are too many government workers, that they are underworked, overpaid, and insulated from the consequences of incompetence.'" One Administration official concluded that "what tends to happen in the system" is that bosses just transfer their inefficient employees "someplace else, and we all of a sudden will get a hall full of people who are doing nothing."[17]

Even Washington's "company town" newspaper, the *Post*, succumbed to the irresistible lure of the story, calling the firing appeal process the "Loch Ness monster of the bureaucracy—a costly, predatory protector and leveler of civil servants whose coils of red tape are more to be feared than all the most dreadfully worthless employee." A feature on the civil service firing process quoted Barry Kefauver, personnel director of the Federal Trade Commission, "The 'high cost of canning' is much greater than [the cost of] shoving the person off in a corner and letting them waste away at $35,000 a year, as far as the public interest is concerned."[18]

The Administration thus stirred up strong newspaper support for the civil service reform plan by playing to citizens'—and editors'—innate post Watergate distrust of government and, especially, its workers. In the process, of course, the Carter Administration risked making its victory Pyrrhic, by denigrating the very system it was trying to strengthen.

At the same time, Administration officials were paradoxically contending that it was too easy to fire whistleblowers. A Tom Wicker column in the *New York Times* cited two cases of employees who had been fired for pointing out wrongdoing—one about a General Service Administration worker dismissed for pointing out shoddy GSA workmanship, another about a Food and Drug Administration worker fired for complaining about FDA's vaccine approval process. "That's what traditionally happens to 'whistleblowers,'" Wicker noted. They "need protection from vengeful superiors or colleagues," he concluded.[19] The irony was rich but unnoted: the Carter Administration was simultaneously arguing that it was nearly impossible to fire incompetent workers, yet it was all to easy to dismiss whistleblowers. No newspaper appeared to catch the paradox.

Nevertheless, the Administration's plan drew enthusiastic editorial endorsement from the nation's newspapers:

• The reorganization would do much to improve the federal bureaucracy's flexibility and efficiency.... The reform plan is reasonable, thoughtful and workable. *Los Angeles Times* [20]

• The stakes in Civil Service reform are high.... Of course, discretionary powers over promotion and tenure can be abused. But the absence of discretionary power guarantees an infinity of laziness, inefficiency, and waste; it is a greater abuse than the propose Civil Service reform could prove to be. *Chicago Tribune* [21]

• When he introduced the proposals in March, the President said they would mean less job security only for incompetent federal employees, while conscientious civil servants would benefit from a change that recognized and rewarded performance. That is a good reason to enact the proposals. A better reason is that they would give the American people more effective and responsive government. *New York Times* [22]

• On Senate approval of the bill in August: "one has to be thankful for this effort to streamline the bureaucratic behemoth: to inject a little life and competitiveness into that deadening miasma that so often permeates government service.... [W]e can only say that civil service reform is very definitely an idea whose time has come." *San Francisco Chronicle* [23]

• President Carter's thorough Civil Service reform package is in large part sensible and well directed. Its goals are to reduce bureaucratic drag by making it easier to get rid of deadbeats and misfits, to beef up the merit system by rewarding good performers and to increase responsiveness by creating a top executive corps for special assignments. *New Orleans Times-Picayune* [24]

After Carter won final passage of the program in October 1978, the newspaper stories characterizing his victory were much different from those describing his initial proposals. The early stories focused on whistleblowing and governmental performance. The stories summing up the bill focused far more on the bill's provisions making it easier to fire civil servants. The AP reported, "The measure is designed to emphasize performance over seniority in determining whether a federal worker gets a raise or a promotion and to make it easier to weed out nonperformers."[25] United Press International's lead more directly attacked the firing issue:

> A civil servant who is the subject of four complaints in one year for being discourteous to the public could wind up looking for another job.
>
> Such conduct—or, more accurately, misconduct—could mean dismissal under terms of the 1978 Civil Service Reform Act that President Carter will sign today at a White House ceremony.
>
> The new law is aimed at producing a "leaner," more efficient federal bureaucracy. The accent is on rewarding good performance, but the law also has provisions making it easier to weed out those who don't measure up.[26]

The *Wall Street Journal* characterized the bill as giving the President "more flexibility in firing incompetent bureaucrats, rewarding superior ones and switching workers around as the government's needs change."[27]

Few Washington observers had given the Carter Administration much of a chance of winning civil service reform. It is typically difficult to attract political support and popular enthusiasm for management issues, so the Administration's victory confounded capital cynics. The Carter Administration beat the odds, in part, by transforming the image of the bill from a good government and whistleblower protection measure to a proposal to make it easier to fire the incompetent civil servants that many newspaper columnists believed were everywhere. The 21-foot chart and congressional testimony about employee no-shows were calculated to build enough political support to overcome the resistance of federal employee unions. (The Administration found it had to surrender on the veterans' preference issue.)

The negative image of the public service that the Administration created played well in the newspapers. It gave an attractive hook for writers and editors who otherwise had a hard time grappling with management issues. At the same time, however, the Administration very consciously transformed the image of its legislative efforts: from the positive management improvement focus to a negative bureaucrat-bashing focus. It painted an aura of incompetence around federal employees to replace the do-good, whistleblowing image with which it first launched its campaign.

THE QUADRENNIAL COMMISSION ON EXECUTIVE, LEGISLATIVE AND JUDICIAL SALARIES (1986–87)

Eight years later the focus was on pay, not performance. The Quadrennial Commission on Executive, Legislative and Judicial Salaries argued in its December, 1986, report that top officials in all three branches of government were woefully underpaid. The Commission, headed by businessman James L. Ferguson, recommended that salaries for cabinet secretaries be increased from $88,000 to $160,000, that members of Congress be raised from $77,400 to $135,000, and that district court judges receive an increase to $130,000. In all, the Commission's recommendations directly affected 3,000 top federal officials who, it argued, had through inflation suffered erosion in their buying power since the last major salary increase in 1969.

While the central focus of the Commission's work was on these 3,000 officials, the recommendations indirectly affected about 7,000 other senior career civil servants. The ceiling on salaries for these civil servants was pegged to the salary of assistant secretaries. Members of the Senior Executive Service (SES) and some other senior careerists suffered from "pay compression:" the inability to receive increases, including cost of living increases, because that would push their salaries above the pay of political appointees. Raising the salaries of political appointees, as the Commission recommended, thus would also have had the indirect effect of raising the ceiling for career officials.

At first, the issue drew relatively little attention except from the *Washington Post*, which editorially supported the Commission's recommendations: "Most federal workers at lower and middle levels receive fair compensation. But at the top, salaries have been compressed. The fire chief of Los Angeles, the city manager of Phoenix and the director of higher education in Georgia all earn more than the secretaries of defense and state." The paper concluded, "Salary increases won't make millionaires of public servants. But they will make it possible for people who are not independently wealthy to serve the country without shortchanging their families."[28] The *Atlanta Constitution* agreed that "salary increases are justified, though not necessarily the 60- to 80 percent increases suggested" by the Commission.[29] The *Los Angeles Times* joined in, editorially arguing, "There will be political flak, but now is the time for the President and Congress to make a bold move and approve the salary schedule as proposed by the Commission. . . . When pay scales become second rate, so will personnel."[30]

Not everyone agreed the full increase was needed. James J. Kilpatrick's syndicated column, for example, contended: "[S]ome raises are needed. The problem is to find the balance between too much and not enough."[31] But syndicated columnist Carl T. Rowan warned of what was to come: "Brace yourself for a bitter battle, some demagoguery and a lot of political cowardice."[32]

Rowan's prediction was on the mark. Two features of the proposed salary increase soon enraged journalists around the country. One was the way in which the quadrennial pay process worked. The Commission reported to the President, who then included in the executive budget his recommendation on what pay increase, if any, these top officials should receive. The pay increase took effect automatically unless both houses of Congress voted to disapprove the increase. The *Atlanta Constitution*, which in general supported a modest increase, found the procedure offensive. "Playing straight with the electorate will go a long way toward demonstrating that congressmen deserve pay raises."[33]

The second feature was the sheer size of the increase, which struck many observers and members of the general public as too large. *Chicago Tribune* columnist William R. Neikirk argued, "they don't deserve a pay raise. In fact, considering what they've earned in recent years, they should have their pay cut by, let's say, five percent. I firmly believe there's more sentiment in the country for a pay cut than a pay raise for these top federal officials."[34] Neikirk challenged the Commission:

> The most naive assumption of the Commission is that higher salaries will at-tract the best and the brightest to the government. But we all know deep in our hearts that this is a fallacy—that boosting pay will not bring any better government. It will merely enrich the incumbents.

To support his point, Neikirk asked his readers to write in with their comments. Within three days, he was swamped with 1,420 replies. Only five readers supported the Commission's re-quest, while another ten readers favored a five- to ten percent increase. Half of his respon-dents favored a pay decrease of five percent, and one-fourth favored a ten percent cut. Among the more lively of the responses were:

> "These people have been living in a dream world too long."

> "I think the federal commission . . . ought to be tarred and feathered, then hung and quartered. . . . If they are to be paid on merit, they all should take a 50 percent cut."

> "I rate most members of Congress about 3 or 4 points below prostitutes and thieves."

> "One cannot buy wisdom in the marketplace."

> "Increasing salaries does not buy an increase in quality of performance in poli-ticians, and this has been demonstrated often."[35]

Lost in the volatile debate over salary increases for members of Congress were the implications for top career officials. Lost, too, was a Reagan Administration proposal to end within grade longevity increases for civil servants and to substitute a merit-pay system. Such raises took effect automatically, in addition to annual cost of living increases, as civil ser-vants advanced a step each year within their grade. The Office of Management and Budget had in late 1986 sought to end these annual increases, to use some of the money to fund a merit-pay plan, and to earmark most of the savings to reduce the deficit. The Office of Personnel Management fought OMB and won; all of the money saved from the proposal was to be used instead for merit pay.

Compared with the wide coverage given the Commission's recommendation, news-paper coverage on the merit-pay proposal was far more limited. Only the *Washington Post* and the *New York Times* (along with their news services) featured news stories about the plan.[36] It won strong editorial support:

> "[T]he federal work force is badly in need of the stimulus that a merit pay plan could provide. . . . Federal employees have not had a happy time of it in recent years. Suc-

cessive presidents have campaigned against them; the bureaucracy has become an easy punching bag, a symbol of discontent against government. As the budget has tightened, new limits have also been put on pay and benefits.... In the long run, merit pay is far more likely to help the federal service—lift its reputation and morale— than hurt it." *Washington Post* [37]

"Government at all levels has been hurt by the practice of giving raises for just showing up and doing a minimally competent job, with no extra money left over to reward initiative and excellence.... This government and this country can no longer afford a practice that rewards the minimal performer at the expense of the high producer." *Chicago Tribune* [38]

President Reagan's fiscal 1988 budget, proposed in January, 1987, took a middle course. He recommended a $89,500 salary for top officials, which would take effect unless both houses of Congress voted to disapprove. He also promised to submit a merit-pay plan to Congress within two months. Meanwhile, the White House announced a week after the fact that the President had signed a New Year's Eve executive order that increased the pay for the 7,000 members of the SES, an action that got lost in the broader and louder debate over pay increases for top officials.

The Commission's Report had created a difficult political problem for the Reagan Administration. The budget struggle revolved around the deficit, and the worst political signal to give, Administration officials feared, was a pay increase for federal officials. Moreover, OMB had lost the merit-pay fight; instead of being a deficit reduction measure, it had become a good government plan. On the other hand, top officials worried that eroding salaries were costing the government strong talent, especially in the federal judiciary. The Administration thus decided to recommend a modest increase—and to pass the hot potato on to Congress. The Democrats who controlled the House and Senate then faced a difficult choice: to do nothing and allow their pay increase to take effect, or to go on record for reducing government costs but to deny themselves an increase that they all thought they deserved.

The *Washington Post* favored the increase: "Pay raises for judges, high level federal executives and members of Congress are a good idea."[39] The *Chicago Tribune*, however, was enraged at the proposal but enormously entertained at the show members of Congress displayed:

The prospect of a pay raise has put members of Congress in a cruel bind: They want the raise but don't want to be seen voting for it. This has spurred Senate and House leaders to find wholly new techniques of buck passing. Not all of them work; by now, in fact, the contestants have gotten themselves into such a complicated jam that a referee will have to figure out how to pull them apart.... Congress was not expecting this. It had invented a seemingly foolproof way to keep itself off this very hook [through the creation of the Commission].[40]

Congress in the end allowed President Reagan's recommendations to take effect. First, the Senate voted to disapprove the increase and passed on to the House the ultimate responsibility. House members wanted the increase but simultaneously wanted to put themselves on record opposing it. They concocted a resolution of disapproval that had no legal effect, and the top officials received the pay increase in February. The merit-pay plan, meanwhile, slipped from the top of the agenda as it lost promise for reducing the deficit. Instead of a major presidential initiative to be sent to Congress by March, it became a low level plan quietly introduced during the summer of 1987.

Thus, over the two months in which the salary recommendations were on center stage, the issue rapidly mutated. The merit-pay plan changed from a deficit reduction measure to a performance enhancing one. At the same time, the Commission's salary recommendations got lost in congressional wrangling.The parliamentary buck passing and maneuvering was not lost on observers around the country, and it swamped the lower stakes issue of dealing with pay compression afflicting top civil servants. The media had generally supported the pay increase, but Congress's tactics eroded that support.

Salary increases for bureaucrats were, in general, not a very big issue. Salary increases for members of Congress, however, were a very big issue. The Commission's recommended increases were too large for any Washington official to take seriously. Moreover, such recommendations from a Commission dominated by private sector executives scarcely strengthened the case. Originally, the Commission was to recommend what government executives would make for doing the same job in the private sector. Since members of the general public were likely to doubt that many private sector executives earned their salaries, the recommendations created little political support to the suggestions.

Presidential-Congressional haggling on pay for members of Congress was inevitably a top level political struggle that energized cynics, both in the media and among the general public, who believed that members of Congress were overpaid. Thus, so long as salaries for public servants remain linked to pay for political appointees—and these salaries stay tied to congressional pay—the low stakes, public service salary issues are likely to be overwhelmed by the huge battles that occur every time Congress considers its own pay.

The central issues of the 1986–87 battle over top level salaries changed during the debate, just as the issues of the 1978 civil service reform campaign had. The positive features of the Quadrennial Commission's proposal—implicit relief of the pay compression problem for top career officials—and of the Administration's merit-pay plan—explicit rewards for high performance—both changed into negative stories. If the civil service reform issue mutated because of tactical decisions by Carter Administration officials, the pay increase issue changed because of a struggle between the houses of Congress over who would be responsible for increasing their own pay. In both cases, the public service was a second order issue swamped by far larger tidal waves of presidential and congressional politics.

CONCLUSION

In general, the media give the public service relatively scant attention. There are few appealing visual images or big time battles to tempt network television, and run of the mill issues of public management—if they find their way into the newspapers at all—are typically relegated to the papers' deep recesses. Coverage of the federal public service by local papers is usually nonexistent; only the largest issues, covered by wire service reports, find their way into local papers—and almost never into local television and radio.

The public service does sometimes, however, rate prominent and sustained attention. That happens at the President's initiative, in putting a story on the news agenda, and often in defining how the story is played. Early in their terms, Presidents have tended to pay special attention to civil servants' perks. In mid-term, they have worried more about performance. And intermittently, they have dealt with a vast array of other issues. Both case studies, moreover, demonstrate that positive stories about good management are hard to promote and, in fact, tend to become transformed into more sensational, negative issues. President Carter and his staff decided to sell civil service reform as a quicker way of firing incompetent federal workers. President Reagan's staff struggled over just what form the merit-pay proposal would take, and then surrendered the turf to Congress's embarrassing fighting. In both cases, the President had it within his power to place the civil service issue on a higher, more positive plane, and in both cases—for both pragmatic and partisan reasons—he decided not to. Moreover, Congress so politicized the pay issue that serious attention to pay compression became impossible. Both cases were an editorial writer's dream.

The public service thus is typically an issue of little moment in the media, an issue easily transformed and overridden by higher stakes battles. The experience of the last twenty years, however, demonstrates that this need not be so. The timing and content of public service issues are the President's to decide. The public's image of the public service can be improved only if the President takes the lead.

ENDNOTES

1. Thimmesch column, *Chicago Tribune*, March 6, 1978, Sec. 4, p. 2.
2. Kilian column, *Chicago Tribune*, March 7, 1978, Sec. 3, p. 2.
3. Franklin P. Kilpatrick, Milton C. Cummings, Jr., and M. Kent Jennings, *The Image of the Federal Service* (Washington, D.C.: The Brookings Institution, 1964), 207–12.
4. These newspapers were chosen for two reasons. First, they represent a geographic cross section of the nation. Second, each one has a detailed index of stories covering the period under investigation.
5. The AP dispatch was carried in, among other newspapers, the *Los Angeles Times*, January 5, 1978, Sec. I, p. 8; and the *New Orleans Times-Picayune*, January 5, 1978, Sec. 1, p. 9.
6. *Washington Post*, January 25, 1978, p. A3.
7. Quoted in *Washington Post*, February 26, 1978, p. K1.
8. The news service article was run, among other newspapers, in the *Chicago Tribune*, March 5, 1978, Sec. 1, p. 6.
9. San Francisco Chronicle, March 6, 1978, p. 38.
10. *Chicago Tribune*, March 6, 1978, Sec. 4, p. 2; March 7, 1978, Sec. 3, p. 2.
11. *Chicago Tribune*, February 27, 1978, Sec. 4, p. 2.
12. *Washington Post*, March 6, 1978, p. A18.
13. *New York Times*, April 21, 1978, p. 26.
14. Robert W. Merry (a member of the Journal's Washington bureau) column, *Wall Street Journal*, April 12, 1978, p. 26.
15. Anthony Lewis, *New York Times*, April 10, 1978, p. 23.
16. *Chicago Tribune*, May 5, 1978, Sec. 1, p. 3; and *San Francisco Chronicle*, May 5, 1978, p. 8.
17. *Chicago Tribune*, May 28, 1978, p. 1.
18. *Washington Post*, September 15, 1978, p. A2.
19. Tom Wicker column, *New York Times*, May 2, 1978, p. 35.
20. *Los Angeles Times*, May 28, 1978, Part VI, p. 4; August 4, 1978, Part II, p. 4.
21. *Chicago Tribune*, June 3, 1978, Sec. 1, p. 8.
22. *New York Times*, May 30, 1978, p. 16.

23. *San Francisco Chronicle*, August 28, 1978, p. 40.

24. *New Orleans Times-Picayune*, August 30, 1978, Part I, p. 16.

25. Reported in *Los Angeles Times*, October 7, 1978, Part I, p. 1.

26. Reported in *San Francisco Chronicle*, October 12, 1978, p. 10.

27. *Wall Street Journal*, October 4, 1978, p. 7.

28. *Washington Post*, December 17, 1986, p. A26.

29. *Atlanta Constitution*, editorial, December 21, 1986, p. D2.

30. *Los Angeles Times*, December 19, 1986, Sec. II, p. 6.

31. James J. Kilpatrick column, *Washington Post*, December 30, 1986, A21. The column also ran, among other places, in the *Atlanta Constitution*, December 28, 1986, p. B3.

32. Carl T. Rowan column, *Washington Post*, December 18, 1986, p. A27. The column ran, among other newspapers, in the *Atlanta Constitution*, December 18, 1986, p. A27.

33. *Atlanta Constitution* editorial, December 21, 1986, p. D2.

34. William R. Neikirk column, *Chicago Tribune*, December 21, 1986, Sec. 7, p. 1.

35. William R. Neikirk column, *Chicago Tribune*, December 28, 1986, Sec. 7, p. 1.

36. *Washington Post*, December 17, 1986, p. A1; and *New York Times*, December 17, 1986, p. 23. The *San Francisco Chronicle* ran the *New York Times* news service dispatch, December 18, 1986, p. 16.

37. *Washington Post* editorial, December 19, 1986, p. A20.

38. *Chicago Tribune* editorial, December 22, 1986, Sec. 1, p. 12.

39. *Washington Post* editorial, January 7, 1987, p. A20.

40. *Chicago Tribune*, February 9, 1987, Sec. 1, p. 12.

ANNEX III

SUGGESTED ACTIONS TO IMPROVE
PUBLIC PERCEPTIONS OF THE PUBLIC SERVICE

Following is a summary of possible actions that might be taken by various individuals or organizations to help counteract negative public perceptions and stereotypes regarding the public service. These suggestions are drawn from the many recommendations volunteered to this Task Force.

The President

• Include the need for vigorous and well qualified public services in Inaugural, State-of-the-Union, and other addresses.

• Visit federal civilian worksites from time to time. Arrange for photo opportunities that link the President and Federal employees with delivery of vital services.

• Annually present a major award or recognition to a civil servant or civil-service organization.

• In cooperation with the Congress establish an independent, tripartite Advisory Council on the Public Service, or an equivalent organization, in support of the civil service.

Independent Advisory Council on the Public Service

• Serve as a "translator" of national economic, demographic, and educational conditions and trends to the public service.

• Encourage establishment of a coordinating council to assist all organizations (federal, state, local, non-profit, employee organization) providing public information about the public service.

• Work with organizations such as the Public Employees Roundtable, American Society for Public Administration, National Academy of Public Administration, Center for Excellence in Government, etc. to maximize the effectiveness of their individual efforts to promote public service.

• Establish, participate in, and promote special "days"/"weeks" and awards to recognize public service.

• Urge public employers to establish and maintain strong public outreach programs: participation in conferences, speakers bureaus, high quality recruiting materials, presentations to community groups supported by high quality publications, films, videotapes, etc.

• Coordinate response to unwarranted attacks on the public service.

• Establish an award for the news media for the most balanced, interesting stories that put public service in perspective.

• Promote establishment of journal and radio/TV series devoted to public service issues.

• Encourage the entertainment industry to include civil servants and public service themes in programming for mass audiences.

• Sponsor development of a series of film and videotape products to inform students of the satisfactions of a public service career upon their graduation from high school or college. Programs would show public employees helping to solve national problems and would also be suitable for community groups.

• Develop, perhaps with the Advertising Council, a public-service, mass-media advertising campaign to supplement public-employers' recruiting efforts. The campaign would have a secondary effect of communicating positive impressions of public service to the public at large.

• Serve as "watchdog" for the President on the state of the career services and prepare periodic reports to the President.

• Encourage "plain English" in Government communications.

Central Management and Personnel Agencies

• Establish a committee or network of public information officers drawn from each federal department and agency and encourage the committee to include the role of civil servants in information releases regarding accomplishments of their organizations. Develop and share with the public information officers government-wide civil-service publicity themes and materials.

• Provide guidance to government agencies (personnel, public information offices) to encourage their publicizing awards and other positive contributions of their employees.

• Develop effective network of internal publications and send them regular items of interest to public employees.

• Promote development of more effective systems for internal communications with federal employees.

• Encourage agencies to develop speakers bureaus to represent their organization and the public service to community groups. Develop and distribute materials to support speakers.

• Provide guidance, themes, research, and assistance to federal agencies and to state, local, and other organizations that request it.

• Maintain information regarding research on questions pertaining to public perceptions of the public service. Collect and report findings of public opinion research groups or university researchers.

• Develop an information campaign that links federal, state, and local civil services with the U.S. Constitution. A Constitution awareness campaign continues through 1991.

• Encourage the establishment of "hotlines" for citizen (1) complaints about and (2) praise for Federal civil servants.

• Ensure development and delivery by all federal agencies of training and incentive programs that promote excellence in performance and delivery of services to the public.

• Promote quality and courtesy by government personnel in all "front-line" services with emphasis on telephone courtesy.

• Develop and distribute to federal agencies and to the public information regarding excellent performance or service delivery by Federal organizations.

• Develop high quality recruiting materials to supplement those developed by agencies.

• Ensure that the federal government is well represented on campuses and at other recruitment sources and that all government recruiters are well supplied with general public-service information as well as with specific recruiting materials.

Federal Departments and Agencies

• Establish an "ombudsman" position in the office of the department or agency head to hear employee concerns; to provide a conduit from the work force to top management.

• Establish and support a community outreach program to represent the agency and its employees to community groups. Techniques such as citizen advisory groups, open houses, internships and personnel exchanges, adopt-a-school programs, and speakers bureaus are examples.

• Develop and submit employee-accomplishment stories to "grassroots" media —hometown newspapers, local cable television programming, alumni and professional society publications, etc.

• Gather information concerning the public's perception of the agency's performance. Communicate these findings internally. Communicate the improvements to the public.

Department of Education

• Assess the current state of education regarding the role and importance of civil services in American government.

- Encourage development of curricula and materials that support better understanding of the public service.

- Encourage programs that enable children to visit nearby federal offices and installations as well as those of state and local governments.

- Support public-service organizations such as Campus Compact, the Public Employees Round Table, etc. that work to advise students of job and internship opportunities in the public sector, provide scholarships, and encourage development of curricula.

Congress

- Help the public see public servants at work: Highlight examples of good programs or effective individual performance in speeches, constituent newsletters, and news releases.

- Create a fund to develop, implement, and maintain a national civil-service outreach and communications program.

- Direct GAO to audit the program and determine at the end of five years whether it should be continued.

- Establish matching-funds grant programs to support public service education and information programs.

- Provide funding for the Congressional Federal Government Service Task Force, which is presently funded by the Senators and Representatives who make up the Task Force.

- Establish a "Gold Star Award," (in opposition to the "Golden Fleece Award") to recognize effective public management.

- Establish a "constituent services unit" staffed with professionals to resolve the problems constituents have with federal or government agencies.

State and local governments

- Develop outreach and education programs to support state and local civil services.

- Establish a coordinating body to support state and local civil-service communications programs and to exchange resources and information among federal, state and local programs.

Non-government organizations

- Develop, implement, and maintain information and education programs to support quality civil service at all levels of government.

- Form a coordinating committee to link non-government organizations that conduct information programs on behalf of the public service* with one another and with the federal, state, and local civil-service communications programs.

*Such organizations include the National Academy of Public Administration, American Society of Public Administration, Public Employees Roundtable, Center for Excellence in Government, National Association of Schools of Public Affairs and Administration, National Association of Government Communicators, and public employee and teachers' unions, associations, and professional associations.

ANNEX IV

PUBLIC PERCEPTIONS TASK FORCE REPORT TEAM

Mr. Norm Chlosta, Deputy Chief, Resource Management and Evaluation Branch, Office of Pesticide Programs, U.S. Environmental Protection Agency.

Dr. James Conant, Professor, Graduate School of Public Administration, New York University.

Mr. Don Dillin, Automation in the Office, Inc., former federal public information officer and past president, National Association of Government Communicators.

Dr. Robert B. Gair, Planning Officer, Bureau of Public Debt, U.S. Department of the Treasury.

Ms. Libby Garvey, Director, Washington Internships Unlimited.

Ms. Emilie G. Heller, Director, Organizational Excellence Project, U.S. Office of Personnel Management.

Mr. Gerald K. Hinch, Director, Office of Equal Opportunity, Veterans Administration.

Ms. Joan Keston, Executive Director, Public Employees Roundtable.

Ms. Ada Kimsey, Writer/Editor, U.S. Merit Systems Protection Board.

Mr. Frank A. Lancione, Management Consulting Services, Coopers & Lybrand.

Dr. Paul Lorentzen, Washington Public Affairs Center, University of Southern California.

Mr. Thomas G. McCarthy, Director, Institute for Public Service, Seattle University.

Mr. James J. McGurrin, Deputy Director, Bureau of Intergovernmental Personnel Programs, U.S. Civil Service Commission (Ret.); Legislative Counsel and Assistant General Counsel, American Federation of Government Employees (Ret.).

Mr. Bruce Moyer, Legislative Counsel, Federal Managers Association.

Mr. Fredric Newman, Director, Civilian Personnel, U.S. Army (Ret.).

Mr. Jack Niles, Director, Membership Department, National Association of Retired Federal Employees.

Ms. Marian O. Norby, Writer/Editor, U.S. Air Force (Ret.).

Mr. Joseph Oglesby, Director, Office of Public Affairs, U.S. Civil Service Commission (Ret.); Director, Public Relations, National Association of Retired Federal Employees (Ret.).

Mr. Bernard Posner, Public Relations Counsel, National Organization on Disability; Executive Director, President's Commission on Employment of the Handicapped (Ret).

Mr. William M. Ragan, Director, Office of Public Affairs, U.S. Civil Service Commission (Ret.).

Ms. Shannon Roberts, Director, Communications Committee, President's Council on Management Improvement.

Dr. O. Glenn Stahl, Director, Bureau of Policies and Standards, U.S. Civil Service Commission (Ret.); Author, *Public Personnel Administration.*

Ms. Mary N. Stone, Director of Research and Citizen Education, League of Women Voters.

Ms. Lee (Treese) Tupman, Writer/Editor, U.S. Civil Service Commission, U.S. Office of Personnel Management, U.S. Department of the Interior (Ret.).

Dr. Gary L. Wamsley, Professor, Center for Public Administration and Policy, Virginia Polytechnic Institute and State University.

Dr. James R. Watson, Executive Director, National Civil Service League (1949–1963); Vice President, Professor Emeritus, Rutgers University (Ret.)

COMMITTING TO EXCELLENCE

Recruiting and Retaining a Quality Public Service

The Report of the

Task Force on Recruitment and Retention

to the

National Commission on the Public Service

TASK FORCE

Rocco C. Siciliano, *Chairman*

Anne Armstrong

Walter A. Haas, Jr.

Herschel Goldberg

Donald Kennedy

Elmer B. Staats

WASHINGTON 1989

THE TASK FORCE ON
RECRUITMENT AND RETENTION

CHAIRMAN

Rocco C. Siciliano
Former Under Secretary U.S. Department of Commerce
Former Special Assistant to the President for Personnel Management

MEMBERS

Anne Armstrong
Former U.S. Ambassador to Great Britain

Walter A. Haas, Jr.
Honorary Chairman of the Board, Levi Strauss & Co.

Herschel Goldberg
Admiral, United States Navy (Ret.)

Donald Kennedy
President, Stanford University

Elmer B. Staats
Former Comptroller General of the United States

PROJECT DIRECTOR

Patricia W. Ingraham
Associate Professor of Political Science
State University of New York at Binghamton

STAFF ADVISER

Ronald P. Sanders

CONTENTS

PREFACE

The Task Force on Recruitment and Retention was charged with determining the dimensions of recruitment and retention problems for the federal government. The Task Force examined proposed solutions to those problems, and in this report recommends specific actions to the President, the Congress, the Director of the Office of Personnel Management, and relevant federal agencies.

To accomplish its objectives, the Task Force undertook study activities from December 1987 to October 1988. These included:

• The entire Task Force and smaller groups of some of its membership met to determine the most important problems to be considered.

• Staff collected and analyzed academic literature and research related to the issues of recruitment and retention. Governmental reports and documents covering the same issues were also analyzed.

• The Chairman and/or the Project Director attended regional hearings of the Commission in Ann Arbor, Austin, Los Angeles, and Portland, Oregon.

• Task Force members and staff held two formal meetings with personnel and human resource directors from major federal agencies in Washington, D.C.

• Task Force members and staff conducted a large number of interviews and information gathering meetings with representatives of the Office of Personnel Management (OPM) and the U.S. General Accounting Office.

• The Task Force submitted formal requests for analyses of agency-specific recruiting and retention problems to agencies—such as the Internal Revenue Service, the National Science Foundation, the U.S. Air Force, and others—that had collected relevant data for internal management purposes and were willing to share it.

• The Task Force held formal meetings for review and comments on early drafts of the report in Washington and in Princeton, New Jersey. In both cases, the Task Force received comments from academic experts as well as career managers and personnel directors.

• Finally, the National Commission authorized two research studies on behalf of the Task Force on Recruitment and Retention. The first supported doctoral research being conducted by Ronald Sanders, "The Best and Brightest: Can the Public Service Compete?", which surveyed members of four national honor societies to determine if, and under what circumstances, recent honor graduates would consider the public service as a career. The second study, prepared by Robert Goldenkoff, a Presidential Management Intern (PMI), surveyed recent PMIs to determine their satisfaction with federal employment and their attitudes toward their experience with the prestigious Presidential Management Intern Program.

In all of these activities, the Task Force benefitted from extensive volunteer assistance. Indeed, the outpouring of interest in and support for the activities of this Task Force sometimes strained our abilities to use all offers fully. That large group includes the personnel directors and other federal managers who served on our advisory groups, the many federal managers who offered informal advice and information, and the many career civil servants across the country who wrote the Task Force about their personal experiences in the public service. Constance Horner, the Director of OPM, and her staff provided important assistance throughout our study and kept us abreast of rapidly changing OPM activities related to recruitment and retention.

Two other persons provided invaluable support and analysis: Rosslyn Kleeman, from the General Accounting Office, and Ronald Sanders, from the U.S. Air Force, were critical to our ability to understand both problem and potential solution at many points in our study. We thank them for sharing their remarkable abilities with us.

We worked closely with the other Task Forces at many points in our analysis. In particular, we appreciate the assistance of James Pfiffner, project director for the Task Force on Political Appointments, and Peter Zimmerman, project director for the Task Force on Education and Training. Under the direction of L. Bruce Laingen, Executive Director, the permanent staff of the Commission, Diane D. Yendrey, Administrative Assistant, and Marjorie Jones, Graduate Assistant, provided superb support throughout the process.

Finally, we are grateful to the late Charles H. Levine for the advice and direction he provided to this Task Force in the months before his death. Working with Charlie was a grand experience and one that we will not forget.

Rocco C. Siciliano, Chairman
Patricia W. Ingraham, Project Director

Washington, D.C.
April 1989

EXECUTIVE SUMMARY

T he federal government today confronts serious problems in recruiting and retaining a quality workforce. The problem is multidimensional and not amenable to easy solution. The increasing need for a highly skilled and technically expert public service requires, however, that solutions be sought. Demographic projections for the next 20 years demonstrate that the problems will only become more severe. Four major components make up the problem. First, inadequate compensation works strongly against the ability of government to recruit in urban areas, in areas with high concentrations of high-tech industry, and in occupations with limited applicant pools. This problem is most severe for engineering, scientific, and research personnel. Federal recruiters do not have the flexible "bag of tools" available to private recruiters in an increasingly competitive environment.

Second, government is not considered an attractive employer by many recent college graduates, including some who are already government employees. Most of these students do not consider government work to be challenging or creative. Furthermore, they perceive their best opportunity for recognition and career satisfaction to be in the private sector.

Third, there is a widespread sense that the overall quality of federal entry level employees is declining. No government-wide data exist, but most agencies and many managers report this perception. The limited efforts at documentation that do exist consistently report declining quality.

Finally, a large number of senior career managers have resigned or retired from government in the past 10 years. There is strong dissatisfaction with the performance evaluation system instituted 10 years ago by civil service reform; managers also report dissatisfaction with opportunities for executive and career development. In some agencies, morale is alarmingly low.

RECOMMENDATIONS

To remedy the problems outlined above, the Task Force recommends the following actions (the complete recommendations appear at the end of the Task Force report):

RECOMMENDATION 1

Make an exemplary public service a national priority.
The President, the Congress, and the Office of Personnel Management must make leadership and support of the public service a top and early priority. Too often in the past, bureaucrat bashing has been the norm. The emphasis should be on respect, trust, and high standards for performance and accountability.

RECOMMENDATION 2

Align accountability and responsibility in the federal personnel system.
Decentralize activity and delegate authority throughout government and executive agencies. Centralization has led to control through ever-increasing numbers of rules and regulations. Modern government is too complex and the problems it faces too severe to continue this trend. Managers must be allowed greater flexibility and accountability. Managerial authority and competence must be emphasized and supported. However, continued decentralization must occur only within the framework of a government-wide statement of goals and priorities for human resource management activities.

Create a series of management demonstration projects whose purpose is to foster and monitor experiments in alternative approaches to maximizing managerial flexibility. Permit innovations in budgeting, staffing, and task definition. Evaluate carefully to determine replicability to broader government settings.

RECOMMENDATION 3

Meet the challenge of recruiting college graduates head-on and aggressively.
Simplify, expand, and clarify federal hiring activities. Advertise positions widely and from a central point. Provide federal recruiters the same flexible bag of tools that private recruiters enjoy. Allow travel and housing assistance, recruitment bonuses for hard-to-hire occupations, guaranteed training and education opportunities, and other positive incentives for choosing a federal career.

Be aggressive in meeting the challenge of recruiting recent college graduates and graduate students. Establish a federal loan forgiveness program. Create a system of grants to colleges and universities willing to commit to recruiting an excellent and diverse group of students for public service education. Create a limited and prestigious Public Service Scholarship program. This program must contain offset provisions that prohibit colleges and universities from reducing other aid by the amount of the scholarship.

Broaden and simplify student employment programs. Employ programs such as Cooperative Education more extensively and more flexibly. Expand the Presidential Management Intern Program; create agency-specific intern programs and the funds to support them. Greater care must be taken to place and direct interns so that maximum long-term benefits accrue to both the intern and the agency. Consider potential career paths for the interns early on, and provide counseling about opportunities and mentoring to obtain them.

RECOMMENDATION 4

Create and support a federal executive development strategy and support and reward executive excellence.

Create a federal executive development strategy that emphasizes leadership training and ability. Emphasize career development and long-term opportunities in federal management. Reward excellent managers, and give them the flexibility they need to manage both employees and other resources.

Create a Government Executive track in the Senior Executive Service (SES). Permit membership only on the basis of outstanding executive experience and leadership. Base awards and incentives for this group on human resource management contributions and innovations.

Model executive development opportunities and training on the military development strategy, which specifies clear stages of growth and development. Inform career managers of available opportunities and resources.

Restructure federal training opportunities so that the options available to agencies and managers are guided by a clear training strategy. Funds expended by OPM for training must support and strengthen that strategy.

Rectify problems with the SES bonus and mid-level manager merit pay systems. Performance evaluation still does not work in many agencies. It is time to make it work and to provide adequate financial bonuses for managers, or to find a new system. At least half of the members of the SES and of the mid-level managerial merit pay group are currently eligible for bonuses. This is too many for the system to function effectively as an incentive.

Symbolic awards as well as financial incentives must be strengthened. Many such opportunities currently exist, but they are not well publicized or are not used to maximum advantage.

The federal benefit system, most notably the health insurance component, must be rectified if it is to be an incentive for federal employment. As lateral entry becomes a more common feature of federal employment (as it must as entry-level recruitment pools shrink), attractive benefits will become a critical part of effective recruiting.

Create retention awards and bonuses that can be used on a selective basis to retain career executives who are critical to the effectiveness of important federal programs and agencies.

COMMITTING TO EXCELLENCE: RECRUITING AND RETAINING A QUALITY PUBLIC SERVICE

There was a time when the call to public service promised honor, respect, and the chance to make a difference. There was a time when the merit system promised that the truly meritorious would be recognized and challenged to give their best to government. There was a time when public service was not synonymous with burdensome and confining procedures and regulations. There was a time when those who chose the public service did not also have to choose limited financial and career opportunities.

For many in the federal service, that time has passed. It has passed in an age that can ill afford its demise. Never have demands on the public service been so complex, so intense, and so difficult of solution. Technological and scientific advances mandate that government and its employees be at the forefront of scientific abilities and understanding. Human resource management confronts the limits of existing skill and theory. Demographic and economic projections for the year 2000 promise that the demands will be even greater in the future. For many, there is a quiet crisis in American government and in the federal public service.

The twin issues of recruiting high-quality employees into the career service and retaining excellent employees who have already entered are at the heart of the quiet crisis. If government is unable either to attract new public servants or to retain critical members of its workforce, the future is bleak. The need to value merit, competence, and accountability, not rules and regulations, is important; the need to restore the challenge and vitality of a public career, and to give government the tools to compete for excellent employees, is profound. At the same time, the need to make a commitment to excellent management, to management that relies on individual accountability and individual responsibility, is a serious challenge. Institutions and managers that value individual employees and their development must be cultivated. For too long these problems have been distorted by simplistic analyses of governmental issues and problems. In these times, it does not make sense to label government the problem or to denigrate its function and its employees. Rather, we must turn to it to solve some of the most vexing problems in U.S. history.

The complexity of the recruitment and retention problem mirrors the diversity of the federal government. That government is not the faceless mass of bureaucrats so often portrayed in the media. Federal employees include engineers, astronauts, marine biologists, research scientists, nurses and Navajo speaking recreation planners. What they do and how they do it are vitally important to every citizen. That they do it well should be an issue constantly before the public. The debate must be about merit, not as it is known now, but as it could be—a term meaning high quality, accountability, pride, and acceptance of challenge.

RECRUITING EXCELLENT PUBLIC SERVANTS: THE DIMENSIONS OF THE PROBLEM

There are 3 million employees in the federal civilian workforce. That is approximately 3 percent of total civilian employment in the United States. Members of this group represent more than 900 different occupations. They are employed by more than 100 different agencies. Their wages and salaries are determined by more than 30 different pay systems.[1] Many enter the federal government each year, and many also choose to leave (Figure 1). The accession and separation rates shown in the figure are not wholly comparable. Government statistics report only outsiders' entries to the career service, but all exits. Conversions from temporary to career status, for example, are not counted in accessions so that total is artificially reduced. Nonetheless, it is clear that significant changes occur in the federal workforce each year. The recruiting task is major and continuing. The retention problem is constant.

Figure 1
New Entrance and Total Exit Rates for Nonpostal Federal Employment
1978–1987

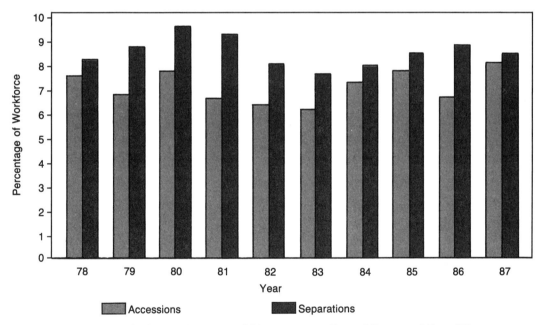

Source: U.S. Office of Personnel Management, Central Personnel Data File.

The numbers in the "excepted authority" category in Figure 2 include approximately 37,000 students who entered through programs such as the Cooperative Education Program, the Stay in School Program, and the Presidential Management Intern Program. Lawyers and most doctors also enter through special excepted authorities. Additional diversity and complexity is demonstrated in a brief analysis of the occupational composition of the federal service. The nonpostal civilian workforce includes professional, administrative, technical, and clerical employees (called PATCO employees) and blue-collar workers. (Postal em-

Figure 2
Method of Entry to Career Federal Service in 1987

Appointment of Outside Candidates 1987

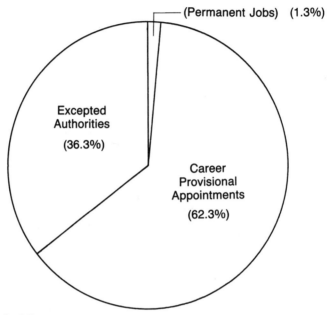

Source: U.S. Office of Personnel Management, Central Personnel Data File.

ployees are in a separate category; they enter the federal service through a separate system.) Even if only professional employees are described, additional diversity is obvious. Of 359,000 in 1987, more than 100,000 were engineers. Another 75,000 were biological scientists, physicists, or mathematicians. Accountants and other financial management specialists constituted another 40,000.[2]

In the past, the recruiting task has been made more complex by the need to ensure diversity in the workforce. Affirmative action and equal opportunity programs have been one means of meeting these objectives. The 1987 Ford Foundation report, "Increasing the Representation of Blacks and Latinos in the Profession of Public Policy," identified another part of the problem:

> Access [of minority students] to postsecondary and graduate studies has been impeded by the combined economic recession and the federal reduction in support for education.... Today, the limited supply of financial aid at colleges and universities is exhausted quickly.

Both federal personnel policies and federal education policies must continue to address the issue of diversity. By the year 2000, however, this problem will have an additional dimension. Projections by the Council on Economic Development and others indicate that in 2000, 85 percent of the recruitment pool will be composed of women, minorities, and recent immigrants. For the managers of the future, the task will be not only ensuring diversity by recruiting; it will be to guarantee to a newly diverse workforce adequate management training and development opportunities. The realities of the recruiting pool must be reflected in organizational authority and power.

To describe recruiting and hiring in the federal government is, therefore, an exercise in simplifying enormous complexity. Prior to 1982, that description most often began with the centralized entrance examinations administered by the Civil Service Commission or, after 1978, by the Office of Personnel Management (OPM). The example provided by one of these exams—the Professional and Administrative Career Examination (PACE)—illustrates the recent federal recruiting experience.

The consistent failure of the PACE, the primary entry-level recruiting process for federal managers, to place a proportionate number of minority applicants on civil service lists led to legal challenges in the 1970s. In 1979, in a case now known as *Luevano v. Devine*, a group of five civil rights groups charged adverse impact, noting that although 42 percent of the white candidates taking the exam passed with a score of 70 percent or higher, only 5 percent of the black candidates and 13 percent of the Hispanic candidates did so. Despite the fact that PACE scores counted in appointments to only 35 percent of entry-level professional or administrative positions in 1978, its centralized nature and concomitant familiarity made it an important recruiting device. In 1982, OPM abolished the PACE examination. No centralized general entrance examination has existed since then.

In 1985, as a partial remedy, the OPM introduced six occupation-specific examinations. These exams covered the occupations in which hiring was most extensive; together, they included about 52 percent of federal hires. In addition to these specialized exams, which are administered and graded by OPM, candidates can enter the federal service through agency-level hiring. The OPM used Schedule B, an excepted authority created in 1910, to delegate noncompetitive hiring authority to the individual agencies. The agencies hiring most extensively—the Department of Defense (DOD), the U.S. Customs Service, the Internal Revenue Service (IRS), the Social Security Administration (SSA)—used this authority most. These agencies had also relied most heavily on the centralized examinations.

The complexity of the recruiting task is further clarified by an examination of how people enter federal government service. Although the federal personnel system is consistently described as a "merit system," considerably more than one-third of the employees who entered in 1987 did so through excepted, or noncompetitive, means (Figure 2).

A much larger number of agencies either did not hire during the early 1980s or were given limited hiring authority by OPM as the need arose. For these agencies, hiring in the future will be especially difficult. Lack of experience—especially in competing for employees—and lack of resources for recruiting and hiring will seriously hinder their efforts. Even for agencies that have been hiring, decentralization—the loss of a central information source—and the virtual absence of monitoring have created problems. Agency recruiters often have trouble finding potential employees; placement officers and students do not know where to look for federal jobs. A high percentage of student honor society members—the best and the brightest—do not know how to get a job with the federal government (Figure 3). Further, when potential hires are found, the time-consuming federal hiring process often loses them.

Constance Horner, Director of the Office of Personnel Management in the Reagan Administration, provided an apt summary of one part of the problem: "The current system is slow; it is legally trammelled and intellectually confused; it is impossible to explain to potential candidates. It is almost certainly not fulfilling the spirit of our mandate to hire the most meritorious candidates."[3] But not all of the problems are with the system. For the past 20

Figure 3
According to the Class of 1988's Top Graduates...

Appointment to the Federal Service is a complex, time-consuming process

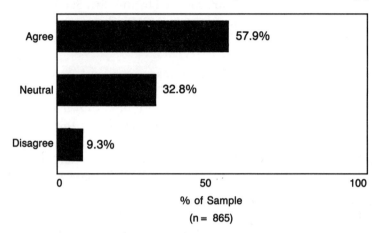

If I wanted a job with the Federal Government, I would know how to go about getting one

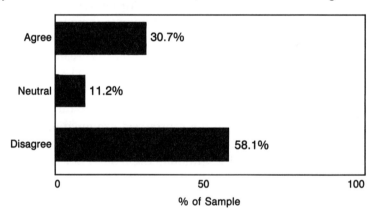

(From Sanders, Ronald P., "The Best and Brightest—Can the Public Service Compete?" 1988)

years, both the institution of the public service and those who serve have been the targets of nearly constant attack by elected officials. There is absolutely no doubt that the negative image of the public service thus created is a serious detriment to efforts to recruit. Overcoming this image will be a test of national and political will.

To understand the complexity of federal recruiting, consider the specific variables involved. Recruiting problems vary by region of the country, by agency and occupation, by level of hire, by quality of hire and by changing demographic conditions. It is useful to consider each of these in turn.

Recruiting Problems by Region

Regional variations in recruiting are closely related to the federal compensation system and the inability to compete with private-sector salaries. The primary problem areas are the Northeast—particularly the New York and Boston metropolitan areas—and California. The demand for skilled labor in those areas makes competition fierce, and low federal salaries severely diminish the government's ability to compete effectively. The private sector recruiter's "bag of tools" in such areas is impressive and diverse: up-front recruiting bonuses, payment of interview and other travel costs, moving expenses, housing assistance for both the house left behind and the house in the new location—such inducements allow private firms to tailor an offer to the needs of the employee being recruited. In addition, the "quality gap" between the fringe benefits offered by the private sector and those offered by the federal government has widened dramatically. Health insurance is the most prominent example.

The Silicon Valley in California illustrates these points. Living costs are high. Although many highly skilled people work there, the intense concentration of high-tech industry creates high demand. Further, private firms generally pay their employees well. The federal installations in the valley compete directly with the high-tech private sector. One federal agency in this area, National Aeronautics and Space Administration's (NASA's) Ames Research Center, reports problems in recruiting procurement specialists. A glance at salary differential alone demonstrates why: the federal entry-level (GS-5) salary is $16,357, barely enough to live on in the area. The average entry-level salary (for comparable non-federal jobs) is $21,779, a differential of 33.2 percent. For a midlevel position, a federal GS-11 contract-procurement specialist earns $29,341. The private-sector counterpart now earns $42,772, a 45.8 percent differential.[4]

The regional problem is equally serious for other agencies. The IRS, for example, reports constant problems in Northeast metropolitan areas. The IRS reported to the Task Force that:

> **Even when it is able to interest potential employees in the federal government, IRS reports that up to 50 percent of those who accept jobs do not report for work because they obtain a better paying job between the time they accept the IRS offer and the time the agency is able to put them on the payroll.**

In many other areas of the country—less urban, less competitive—agencies report that they can hire when they have jobs available and the authority to hire. This element is one part of a complex recruitment mosaic: intense problems exist in some areas of the country, and few problems occur in others.

Recruiting Problems by Agency and by Occupation

Recruiting problems vary by agency because of different levels of hiring activity and because many of the occupations for which it is most difficult to hire cluster within specific agencies or sets of agencies. The DOD, IRS, Customs, and the SSA have encountered problems because they have attempted to hire relatively large numbers of people. Among the agencies hardest hit by occupational recruiting difficulties are those that need large numbers of scientific and research personnel. The Naval Research Laboratory (NRL), which has carefully analyzed recruitment problems for 1981 through 1987, reports: "We have difficulty in recruiting quality candidates in the following areas, finding only a limited number of candidates and none of acceptable quality: physicist (image processing), oceanographer (remote sensing oceanography), electronics engineer, and computer specialist."

The Naval Research Laboratory also notes that, during calendar years 1984 and 1985, the NRL was unable to fill 94 positions for scientists and engineers. Its report concludes: "This inability to hire an adequate number of qualified scientists and engineers...will ultimately result in either putting the Laboratory out of business or in forcing the Laboratory to hire personnel who do not meet the Laboratory's qualification standards."[5]

Similar problems have been reported by all agencies attempting to recruit scientific personnel.

Other occupations have also been difficult for recruiters. The IRS reports serious problems in recruiting accountants; virtually all agencies report difficulties in hiring qualified computer specialists, and NASA notes serious difficulties in hiring skilled technicians. The OPM has permitted agencies to hire directly for some occupations, but has not done so in others that also have limited hiring pools. Although government-wide data on recruiting difficulty are not available, one proxy for the strength of the link between occupation-specific difficulties and agency problems is the number of efforts to bypass the system. In this regard, the federal white-collar "special rate" program tells a dramatic story. In this program, increases above the General Schedule are authorized for positions for which it is especially difficult to recruit and retain staff.

The number of special rate positions rose from about 8,000 in fiscal year 1977, to almost 34,000 in March, 1984, to 37,000 in 1986.[6]

In addition, many agencies are requesting different personnel systems. The DOD, NASA, the National Institute of Standards and Technology, the Veterans Administration, and the National Institutes of Health have requested—or already received—more flexible systems.

Recruiting Problems and the Level of New Hires

Although recruitment problems exist for both entry-level and higher level hires, some differences are worth noting. A Merit Systems Protection Board study concluded that the federal government's ability to hire recent college graduates was limited by three factors: a perception that federal jobs pay less than do comparable jobs in the private sector; a lack of general information on federal career opportunities combined with limited on-campus recruitment efforts; and the negative public image of the federal bureaucracy.[7] That assessment masks some stark numbers: Harvard University President Derek Bok noted in his 1988 Commencement Address that less than 5 percent of the general public is interested in government service as a career. Leading universities such the Massachusetts Institute of Technology, Stanford University, and Rensselaer Polytechnic Institute, which could supply the hard-to-fill engineering positions in government, all report that only 2 to 3 percent of their graduates accept a position in the federal civil service. Even more troubling, some of these universities and colleges report that federal recruiters have given up and no longer visit the campus.

The pervasive negative image of a public service career has had a devastating effect: a national survey of honor society graduates in the liberal arts, business administration, and the sciences and engineering reported that those students consistently ranked federal government as a third or fourth choice (out of six). More importantly, an overwhelming majority of these students believed that most federal jobs were routine and monotonous, that such jobs would not allow them to use their abilities fully and that the civil service offered little opportunity to show initiative or creativity.[8] This image of the public service persists even for many students who chose a public career. A recent survey of students in the Presidential Management Intern Program found that these students, although frequently given the best entry experience government can offer, still believe that in most respects, the private sector is superior (Figure 4).[9]

Figure 4

In What Sector, Public or Private, Are You More Likely to Find the Following Benefits?

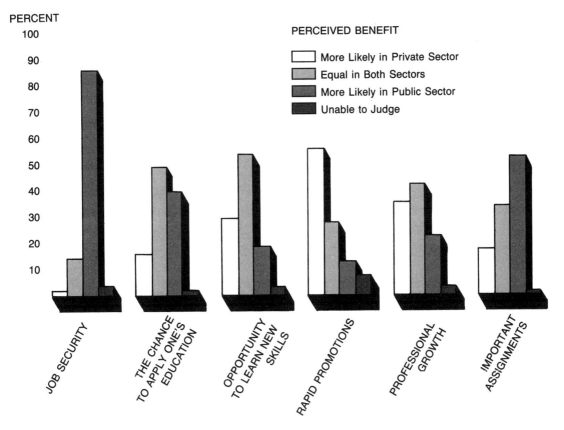

Quite clearly, however, pay and the negative image of the public service have an effect on higher level recruiting as well as entry-level hires—in fact, the effects are exacerbated for mid-and upper level hires. Pay comparability with the private sector decreases as the federal employee's experience and responsibility increases; many private-sector, mid-level staff would have to take a pay cut if they were to accept a federal position. In addition, because job satisfaction and contribution are important to older, more seasoned workers, the endless rounds of bureaucrat bashing and the generally negative work environment they create exact a high toll in recruitment potential. The steady politicization of upper management levels has also affected the recruitment and retention of senior managers. As political appointments increase, senior careerists must report to more levels of less experienced political executives. The placement of appointees in positions that were reserved for career staff aborts the career ladder of senior civil servants and severely limits their opportunities for advancement. In combination, these attributes of the contemporary public service create an extremely uninviting work environment.

An additional problem is the extremely limited nature of lateral entry to mid-level and senior management positions. New ideas and approaches are important to the vitality of federal management. Further, the high exit rate for members of the Senior Executive Service (SES) and other senior managers has created a shallow career cadre in some agencies. Early retirees from the private sector and other private-sector managers could help to fill this gap. The Intergovernmental Personnel Act of 1970 provides one formal means of assistance, but it has been used infrequently in recent years. Furthermore, only a few executive development programs emphasize external hires; many agencies prefer to promote from within. Nonetheless, high retirement rates and changing demographics in the next 10 years mandate new attention to lateral entry.

Recruiting Problems and the Quality of New Hires

This area must be approached cautiously not only because data are limited, but also because reckless analysis can cast an inappropriately negative light on current members of the civil service. Except in its earliest days, the U.S. civil service has been nonelitist. In contrast to the British, French, or West German career services, which have high social status and limited access, the American system has been high quality, but also broad-based and egalitarian. (The U.S. Foreign Service, which until recently fostered an elite image, is an exception to this generalization.) This success has been a long-term source of justifiable pride. In recent years, however, some analysts of the federal personnel system and some federal managers have commented on a perceived decline in the quality of new employees. The General Accounting Office (GAO) provides the following "snapshots":

• The Internal Revenue Service studied the quality of their incoming revenue agents, compared with new staff of accounting firms, by giving a national test of accounting knowledge and found that 84 percent of the comparison group outside government scored higher than the mean of the federal group in each of two years of testing.

• The Merit Systems Protection Board found that 35 to 36 percent of the managers they surveyed believed that, in the years 1982 to 1986, the quality of applicants for professional and administrative jobs at entry, middle, and senior levels had declined.

• The GAO reviewed Environmental Protection Agency Superfund staff and found that 39 percent of the employees had a problem ensuring the quality of their work because of a lack of skilled personnel.[10]

Preliminary government-wide data gathered by the Office of Personnel Management (OPM) demonstrate that the above snapshots are not exceptions, but describe a wider federal experience. In addition, many agencies report that, in the absence of the ability to make external hires, they are promoting staff who have previously been passed over for promotion. Still others report that they are able to make quality hires only by raiding other federal agencies.

A representative of the National Weather Service said: "We deal with recruiting by stealing from other agencies."

Such a practice, of course, generates cycles of new problems as a few excellent employees become constant targets of raiding, while the overall service is not rejuvenated by its new employees.

Quality is an illusive term. Measuring it will always be difficult. The GAO has noted that three kinds of information are needed before assessment of employees' quality can begin: data on essential knowledge, skills, and ability; data on individual attitudes, values, and motivation; and information on the ability to consider the match of individual capacities and job needs. None of this information currently exists in a retrievable form. In addition, in the diverse federal government, it will always be necessary to consider quality agency-by-agency and occupation-by-occupation, in many cases using measures that are agency- or occupation-specific. Despite the absence of conclusive evidence, however, there is a deepening sense that the problem is significant and must be addressed.

The quality problem is, in part, the outcome of past recruiting and hiring constraints. The OPM has observed that such constraints often led to hiring the "best of the desperate," rather than the best and the brightest. This is undoubtedly attributable in some part to the vagaries of the budget cycle, which makes the future availability of funds uncertain or demands that, when funds are available, they be quickly expended. The decline in quality also reflects the widespread sense that a federal career is not an attractive career, however, and is therefore directly linked to a collective failure to value the public service. If good government is a public objective, quality must be emphasized in the public service.

Recruiting Problems and Changing Demographics

Demographic projections from a variety of sources demonstrate that all of the above problems will be intensified in the future. The Department of Labor's *Workforce 2000*[11] and the OPM's *Civil Service 2000*[12] both warn that there will be fewer college graduates, but many more jobs requiring specialized skills and abilities. Competition for the brightest recent graduates will be even more intense than today.

Other components of the recruitment pool will also change. The Committee for Economic Development and others point out that the workforce of the future will necessarily draw much more heavily on recent immigrants and on women.[13] The Committee provides the following summary:

• Workforce growth will slow from 2.9 percent in the 1970s to only 1 percent in the 1990s.

•The number of entry-level workers aged 16 to 24 will decline by some 2 million, or 8 percent.

•Minorities, immigrants, and women will constitute more than 80 percent of workforce entrants between now and the year 2000.

•Minorities will constitute more than 50 percent of the workforce entrants between now and the year 2000.

•More than 30 percent of students in U.S. public school are educationally disadvantaged, many of whom are from minority group families.

•Women will constitute more than 60 percent of workforce entrants between now and the year 2000, and more than 60 percent of all working-age women will be employed.

•The workforce as a whole will grow older as median age rises from 36 to 39 by the year 2000.

Although all the implications of changed recruitment pools are not yet clear, some are obvious. Women entering the workforce for the first time (or reentering after an absence) and recent immigrants may need training or retraining. A larger number of women and of two-career families in the workforce points to the need for new and more flexible benefit and incentive patterns. The availability of high-quality and low-cost day care for children of working parents, for example, will become critical. Additional flexibility in hours and in workplace will assume new importance. In short, it is unlikely that the present package of federal benefits and opportunities will prove adequate in the future. Greater flexibility and innovation as well as additional training or retraining activities will be key to effective recruiting.

RETAINING EXCELLENT CAREER PEOPLE AND SKILLS

Retention is the other facet of the public service in decline. The recruitment problems have constrained federal efforts to bring in new blood, new ideas, and fresh perspectives. Failure to retain senior career managers has created a drain on program and managerial expertise at the other end of the system. These two aspects of decline feed on one another in destructive ways. Constantly decreasing resources, both human and financial, have added to the frustration and dissatisfaction of senior career officials; the high rates at which senior members become disillusioned and leave further decrease the attractiveness of the public service as a career.

The retention problem has many dimensions. Among the most significant are extremely low morale, overburdened management systems, loss of individual authority and prerogatives, and lack of recognition. A theme common to all of these is the pervasive sense that the public service is neither respected nor valued. One letter to the National Commission on the Public Service contained this assessment: "Government-employee bashing and poor pay are slowly, but surely, changing the character of the federal workforce and *not* for the better."

Retention problems may be analyzed in relation to new hires, hard-to-hire occupations, senior managers, and political executives. Each level of the problem is significant; each has somewhat different implications. Although there is not a common solution, there is a common message:

Failure to retain important members of the career service means that the federal government enters a constant and costly cycle of recruiting and training. Because of the severity of recruiting problems, failure to retain means that the cycle is not only costly, but increasingly debilitating.

Retaining New Hires and Hard-to-Hire Occupations

As recruiting difficulties have increased, some agencies have turned to advocating that the federal government be viewed as a training opportunity. Indeed, a "start your career with us" theme is becoming increasingly common in federal recruiting literature. In such a scenario, the new recruit joins a federal agency for a period of two to four years, receives necessary on-the-job training and education, then uses the new skills and abilities to move to a higher paying job in the private sector. Many see this approach as the only possible way to recruit effectively, especially for hard-to-hire occupations and for those agencies that hire large numbers of people. Quite clearly, however, such a strategy incurs significant costs.

The IRS provides an unusual opportunity to examine the costs of failing to retain seasoned employees. Because IRS revenue agents identify and capture funds that would not otherwise flow to the federal government, the cost of attrition in this category can be related to an approximate dollar loss to the government. The IRS provided the following analysis at the Task Force's request:

> During fiscal year 1987, nearly 1,200 revenue agents were separated from IRS. Of that group, about 690 quit government service, meaning they departed for reasons other than retirement, death, or transfers to other government jobs.... Of the 690 revenue agent "quits," over 250 were at the GS 11, 12, 13 and above grade levels. The departure of these 250 trained professionals resulted in a loss of approximately $630 million in annual revenue recovery. [In their place] the Service must hire trainees, usually at the GS-7 level.... The (approximately) $630 million attributable to senior "quits" was replaced by about $174 million, attributable to GS-7 trainees.... The aggregate cost to the government can be as high as a half-billion dollars per year.

In an independent analysis of its problems, the Department of Agriculture reports that its Soil Conservation Service has a 50 percent turnover rate for new hires. "We're getting the rejects from the private sector," said one manager. "They leave us as soon as they get the chance."

The DOD approached the issue from another way. It asked: Are higher aptitude professional and administrative employees more likely than others to leave DOD for private industry? In conjunction with the Educational Testing Service, DOD analyzed the relationship between test scores, satisfaction with federal service, and intent to remain in service. The DOD reported: "College graduates, those with more years of education, those with higher GS grade levels, and those with higher SAT scores are less likely than others to say they expect to remain in DOD or in the Federal Government." Furthermore, "Years of education and college graduate status are both negatively related to job satisfaction and...retention."[14] The answer to DOD's question is, unfortunately, yes. The best often do leave the Department of Defense.

Failure to Retain Senior Managers

There is considerable evidence that senior career managers are finding government service less attractive and, in fairly large numbers, are choosing to leave. The Senior Executive Service (SES), once viewed as the solution to government's management problems, is the focus of most attention in this regard. The Merit Systems Protection Board reported that, by the end of 1985, 52 percent of the charter members of the SES were no longer in government service. The Board noted that there were a number of reasons for the high exit rate, including resigning in the year in which maximum retirement benefits were available and the opportunity for better paying jobs in the private sector.

More recent data indicate, however, that the exit problem continues and that the explanations for it are somewhat more complex than earlier thought. Benda and Levine report exit rates above 11 percent in 1985 and above 10 percent in 1986.[15] Those numbers reflect an increase in the number of decisions to retire early, at the age of 55. Moreover, the reasons for retiring appear to have changed. The General Accounting Office's survey of members of the SES who left in 1985 found that the quality of political management and a deteriorating work environment were major reasons for the decision to leave government. Pay, however, also continued to be a factor.[16]

Pay Compression and Pay for Performance

The critical and overarching issue of compensation is discussed in the report of the Task Force on Pay and Compensation in this volume. In talking about retention, however, it is necessary to focus on one aspect of compensation for senior managers: pay compression. A first-level manager (GS-13, step 1) has a beginning salary of $41,121. The top career management level in the SES begins at just $67,038 (SES-1). Furthermore, although SES salaries technically range about 20 percent from the entry level to a top level of $80,700 (SES-6), the President's Commission on Compensation of Career Federal Executives reported in 1988 that the actual range is closer to 8 per cent. This is dramatically removed from the private-sector experience. It becomes especially debilitating in the public sector because many of those who report to top-level managers continue to advance up the pay scale, thus severely limiting the pay differential between those who manage and those who are managed.

The opportunities provided by pay for performance and the bonus system established by the Civil Service Reform Act of 1978 thus become significant. Just as the SES itself was declared the only game in town by many who joined it in 1979, performance bonuses have become the only way to escape the federal pay trap. This is so despite the fact that the size of the bonus pool is limited by law and the average bonus is not large. In 1987, for example, 2,006 members of the SES received a performance bonus. The average size of the bonus was $5,894. This represents an approximate doubling in the number of recipients from 5 years earlier, when 1,095 awards were made. The average award in 1982 was slightly larger—$6,287. The Presidential Rank Award system makes it possible for a smaller group of senior executives to receive larger bonuses—generally about $20,000. On average, however, only about 2 percent of the SES membership received these awards from 1980 through 1987.[17]

Unfortunately, critical elements of the pay for performance system are not working properly. The most significant problem, and one that occurs across all levels of management and in all agencies, is that bonuses are not perceived to be linked—even tangentially—to performance. This failed link, combined with small awards, leads to attitudes such as those of one manager who noted, "It's an insult, not an incentive."

A 1986 Merit Systems Protection Board survey found that more than seventy percent

of the career executives who responded believed that the SES compensation system did not help in recruiting and retaining highly competent executives. A 1987 study of senior career executives in a major federal agency reported: "Executives approve of the concept of a bonus pay system, but have deep seated concerns about the way the current SES bonus system is administered...78% said that the SES bonus system did not provide an effective incentive for them to meet their job objectives...69% said the SES bonus system is not administered fairly...76% said there is not a direct link between their performance and their likelihood of receiving an SES bonus."[18]

The OPM has proposed legislation that would increase the size of the bonus pool, eliminate the tie to Executive Schedule salaries, and increase the total amounts of rank awards. All of these would begin to remedy current inequities; the problem of performance evaluation remains central, however, and must be addressed.

Morale and Motivation Among Senior Career Managers

Serious morale problems are a tragic and endemic hallmark of the federal service. Communications to the National Commission on the Public Service included these assessments: "I currently have 29 years of civil service employment and today, more than ever, I hate to admit to anyone that I work for the Federal Government. Working conditions and employee morale are at their lowest." A federal employee in the Northwest said: "Based on my 26 years in civil service, I see the lowest morale yet." From Texas, a career manager wrote: "Under no circumstances will I allow my college-educated children to consider a civil service career." These spot assessments reinforce survey findings from the General Accounting Office, the Merit Systems Protection Board, the Federal Executive Institute Alumni Association, and, most recently, *Government Executive* magazine.

Low morale and high dissatisfaction inevitably affect the ability to retain seasoned managers. An important part of public service motivation flows from the knowledge that the employee is performing a valued service in pursuit of an important policy objective. Negative rhetoric such as that directed at the career civil service in the past 15 years has cut that motivational link for many.

Managerial Constraints and Retention of Senior Managers

Despite pay and morale problems, substantial evidence exists that many government managers are still committed to public service and want to be good managers. This evidence was apparent in a 1988 *Government Executive* survey in which nearly 70 percent of the respondents reported morale problems, and 76 percent reported that their jobs were satisfying or exciting and indicated deep commitment to their jobs and their agency and a strong desire to "get on with managing."[19] This strong commitment to the public service is a major resource.

The complexity and red tape of the current system is a substantial obstacle to that resource's being fully tapped. Volumes of rules and regulation govern federal managers— personnel procedures alone have generated nearly 10,000 pages of directives. Add to that financial accounting procedures, information mandates, and the many other central control systems that define the federal management environment, and the frustration of many excellent managers becomes understandable. Further, federal managers must operate within a system that links personnel needs and functions only to the personnel system, separating it from managerial, budgetary and program considerations. In one respect, therefore, the contemporary federal manager operates in an environment of unnecessary regulation and constraint. In another, however, he or she operates in a void: there are few clear managerial prerogatives, and few ways to exercise the judgment that is critical to good management.

To be more effective and to be more likely to remain in the federal service, therefore, federal managers must be freed of the many regulations and constraints that limit both their authority and their accountability. One objective of the Civil Service Reform Act of 1978 was to create "systems that could be used effectively by honest people." As the year 2000 approaches, the need for flexible management systems that value and reward individual initiative and accountability is greater than ever before. A manager who is trusted, respected, and challenged is more likely to stay in the federal service. Only a manager with the authority really to manage can be held accountable for success or failure. More flexible systems are not only in the best interest of the federal manager, but also in the best interest of good government.

The Federal Employee Retirement System and the Retention of Senior Managers

The federal retirement system has long snapped "golden handcuffs" on the wrists of many members of the federal service. After an employee has spent a number of years in civil service, he or she would be reluctant to leave because of the nontransferability of accrued benefits. The new federal employee retirement system (FERS) contains some portable benefits, and although it is difficult to estimate the long-term impact of FERS, one outcome clearly will be increased exit. It also appears likely that those most likely to leave will be those most in demand in the private sector—and thus those most difficult for the government to have hired in the first place. Some argue that increased exit will be beneficial, that government will be reinvigorated by the regular need to hire new staff. This will be true only if the federal government is consistently able to hire high-quality employees and if the budget is able to bear the cost of nearly constant training. The likelihood of the government's becoming a short-term employer, training people for longer term private sector employment, is great. No government-wide data are now available in this area; some means for closely monitoring the situation must be found.

THE ROLE OF THE OFFICE OF PERSONNEL MANAGEMENT

When the Office of Personnel Management was created by the Civil Service Reform Act of 1978 and Reorganization Plan No. 2, it was envisioned as a central human resource planning agency. The Reform Act gave OPM broad powers to delegate responsibility and authority to the agencies, and specified that OPM develop a "monitoring" function to determine that delegated responsibilities were carried out in an appropriate way. The OPM has not met early expectations and remains, in many ways, an agency in search of an identity.

Although OPM operated for a brief time at the end of the Carter Administration, it was President Reagan who really shaped the early character of OPM. Many would argue that it was shaped in primarily negative ways. President Reagan's first appointee as Director of OPM took a political approach to both the position and the agency. During his tenure, the number of political appointees at OPM more than quadrupled, from 8 to more than 32. In 1988, the number of political appointees at OPM was still high.

Equally troubling is the fact that the political appointees to OPM were often actively hostile to the career civil service. The frequent turnover of those appointees created constant turbulence in the agency. More than 60 percent of the political members of the Senior Executive Service at OPM stayed in their positions for less than one year. Budget cuts and reductions-in-force at OPM eliminated entire functions related to planning and evaluation. The morale of those careerists who remained with the agency was low and the organization's effectiveness was severely diminished.

The appointment of Constance Horner as Director in 1985 signalled a new direction for the OPM. The Federal Executive Institute was revitalized and a new director named. The decentralization authority granted by the Civil Service Reform Act was used more extensively to facilitate recruiting and hiring. The SES was given additional support and encouragement. Significantly, in 1987 and 1988 the agency paid serious attention to promoting the public service and to recruiting, preparing, and distributing polished "Career America" recruiting materials. In June 1988, Director Horner introduced a new plan for civil service hiring. Although specific provisions have not been determined, the existing Outstanding Scholar Program will be expanded. In its new form, it will permit agencies recruiting on campuses to hire, on the spot, qualified graduates with a grade point average above a certain level (probably 3.00).

This direct-hire authority will be supplemented by a series of occupationally based exams that will cover some of the positions formerly filled by the PACE exam. The exams will include a component, called the Individual Achievement Record, that OPM expects to "build measures of character directly into the written exams."[20] These examinations are still being developed and their validity must be carefully examined. Although they have been useful in the private sector, their transferability to a public setting must also be closely analyzed. All of these efforts represent efforts to address existing gaps in the system, but it is too early to assess their overall impact.

At the same time that these events are occurring, there is consensus that OPM stands at the crossroads.

A recent survey in *Government Executive* found that federal managers placed OPM among the least successful federal agencies. The Merit Systems Protection Board and the Federal Labor Relations Authority, also created by the Civil Service Reform Act of 1978 and also critical to an effective public service, joined OPM at the bottom of the list.[21]

Horner acknowledges the need for continued growth and change and suggests that OPM should move toward being the "management consultant for the federal government." *Civil Service 2000* recommends that OPM support much-expanded experimentation in personnel and compensation systems. Other options include: leading a major research and development effort and supporting innovation in new and substantive ways; serving as the long-range strategic planner for the federal workforce; and assuming a leadership role in training and development. None of these functions contradicts another; all are important. The OPM is central to the revitalization of the workforce. Is management consultant its correct role? If not, what is?

RECOMMENDATIONS FOR ACTION

To resolve the problems outlined above and to prepare for the demands of the future, the Task Force on Recruitment and Retention recommends that the President and Congress consider the following major initiatives:

RECOMMENDATION 1

Make an exemplary public service a national priority.

A. **Lead the Public Service.** Do not burden the public service and the nation with leaders of modest—or worse, negative—expectations. Guarantee that the Office of Personnel Management (OPM), the Merit Systems Protection Board, and the Federal Labor Relations Authority have leadership of the highest caliber. Charge those leaders with establishing and supporting high expectations for public service performance and productivity. Charge those leaders with achieving national goals and priorities through effective and excellent administration and service delivery.

(1) Reorganize OPM to provide leadership, challenge, and innovation. Transfer routine operating responsibilities, such as retirement, to an agency, such as the Social Security Administration, better equipped to deal with them.

(2) Emphasize research: Create an OPM that asks critical questions about motivation, productivity, and job satisfaction.

(3) Emphasize innovation: Create an OPM that champions change and innovation, communicates its lessons, and stands as an object lesson of its value.

(4) Emphasize using resources better and more productively: direct OPM to make productivity a top priority once again.

B. **Respect the Public Service.** Do not tolerate the bureaucrat bashing and denigration of the public service that have marked the past 15 years. The career civil service is a national resource; its vitality depends on public trust and support. Elected officials, from the President to Members of Congress, must make a committment to positive leadership and to nurturing, not destroying, public trust in the public service.

C. **Challenge the Public Service, Demand that Expectations be Met.** Much of the negative rhetoric has been based on the assumption that career civil servants would not—indeed, could not—respond to change. Assume instead that, with clear direction and support, the public service will work with elected officials to achieve necessary change. Guarantee positive direction and support throughout government. Establish a partnership for good government that clearly includes the public service.

In the context of that partnership and without reverting to punitive intent, hold the public service to high standards of performance and conduct. Career civil servants are deeply committed to good management and good government. Those few who are not do not belong in government. Encourage individual authority and innovation and remove procedural constraints on managerial capacity. Create a system that rewards excellence and commitment, and does not reward only longevity or survival.

D. **Sell the Public Service.** Publicize the federal service. Talk about the things it does well, about the many opportunities it offers, about the enormity of the problems it tries to solve. Honor the public service in public ceremonies and in political events. Acknowledge the contribution that career civil servants—bureaucrats—make to the society's well-being. Direct OPM to be an advocate, an advertiser, and an ardent recruiter of excellent candidates.

RECOMMENDATION 2

Align accountability and responsibility in the federal personnel system.

A. **Decentralize Within a Framework of Government-Wide Objectives and Standards of Accountability.** Create a system that gives managers the authority they need to manage. The current system—or, as some maintain, nonsystem—removes important authority from the career managers who are most responsible for the day to day activities of government. Control through multitudes of regulations and procedures, administered by a central agency removed from service delivery, has created managers with limited power but full responsibility for any problems that occur. Greater congruence between operating responsibility and managerial authority is absolutely necessary.

Significant decentralization activities have already begun to occur. The decentralized recruiting and hiring that occurred under Schedule B, the cooperative agreements between many federal agencies and various colleges and universities, and the recent OPM announcement regarding the expanded use of the Outstanding Scholar Program are important examples. Additional decentralization is necessary, however, to meet the diverse needs of federal agencies. Some occupations are uniform across government, but many remain closely tied to agency mission. The responsibilities of a procurement officer at a NASA Space Flight Center differ from those of a procurement officer in the Department of Agriculture. Computer specialist responsibilities and skills for the Internal Revenue Service, the Soil Conservation Service, the Air Force Systems Command, and the Federal Aeronautics Administration vary dramatically. To match skill—or potential for skill development—with agency needs requires additional decentralization to the agency level.

New activities must become candidates for decentralized administration. Job classification is one example. The need for flexibility and adaptability mitigates strongly against continued centralization. A manager from the Internal Revenue Service said, "[W]e have a great need for new occupations. The existing classification system just does not serve our needs. For example, engineers for our computer systems—how would you grade and classify such people? How can we hire them? One estimate is that there may be a need for 4,000 to 4,500 new occupations a year [government-wide]. . . ." The OPM should examine the implications of eliminating the Classification Act of 1949 and of allowing all classification activity to occur at the agency level.

The OPM must support small demonstration projects in this and other areas. More flexible and innovative classification schemes should be tested in a variety of agency settings and for a variety of occupations. Managerial discretion should be emphasized.

The Commission recommends the creation of management demonstration projects, under the research and demonstration authority granted the OPM by the Civil Service Reform Act of 1978, whose purpose is to create and monitor experiments in pure managerial flexibility. Managers would be selected for the demonstration from the executive (rather than the scientific or technical) ranks of the Senior Executive Service. The staff assigned, as needed for the duration of the project, would have rank-in-person status. The manager would be given a guaranteed budget for the three-year period, objectives, and the freedom to reach those objectives in whatever way he or she determines most feasible, relying on common sense and the managerial expertise for which he or she was selected. Monitoring would be minimal and would focus on implications of increased flexibility for retention of senior managers and on the transferability of lessons learned to other government settings. The experiments would approximate, to the greatest extent possible, the managerial authority and prerogatives enjoyed by private sector executives.

All additional decentralization should occur, however, only in the context of a government-wide personnel management strategy that establishes government-wide objectives and standards of accountability. Further, decentralization must occur with the clear understanding that not all federal agencies are equally able to assume additional tasks and responsibilities. There is a need for central technical assistance and education, as well as for coordinated and timely information dissemination.

B. **Delegate.** Transfer authority and accountability, not just activities. The Civil Service Reform Act of 1978 gave OPM far-reaching authority to delegate personnel functions to agencies. Testing and examining is one such function. The OPM has delegated this authority as needed for direct hires. It is not clear to what extent the testing activities proposed for the new occupation based examinations will be delegated to the agencies. Constant OPM scrutiny is necessary to ensure that agencies have the requisite authority to meet current and future challenges. In addition, agencies must be constantly encouraged and supported in their efforts to delegate internally, so that managerial responsibility matches managerial authority throughout government.

C. **Simplify.** Eliminate the federal personnel red tape jungle. One federal manager wrote, "OPM is its own worst enemy. They create a mountain of standards, most of which are so far behind the curve that they are totally unrealistic." In performance evaluation, in hiring, in classification, and in many other areas, the goal must be to minimize paper and to maximize flexibility. Two examples clarify the need for simplification.

First, the extensive use of background checks for many occupations should be reduced. The process is time-consuming, costly, and of questionable value. The OPM now is running an $11-million deficit because of these investigations. Further, because the investigations are paid for by revolving funds generated by OPM's training unit, their exorbitant cost directly eliminates many potential training opportunities.

The second example involves the system for veteran's preference. Congress has determined that preferential treatment for military service is desirable. The current system is so cumbersome, however, that it can, and sometimes does, work against the veterans it is designed to help.

The long-term objective in simplification must be for OPM to provide broad standards and principles and to retain broad oversight responsibility and capability, but to delegate to the agencies the responsibility to devise simple and fair specific procedures.

RECOMMENDATION 3

Meet the challenge of recruiting college graduates head-on and aggressively.

A. **Establish a Federal Service Loan Forgiveness Program.** Every available demographic projection warns that future competition for fewer college graduates will be intense. A program that would forgive some part of a federal education loan for a set term of federal service is one way to increase government's competitive edge.

B. **Establish a System of Grants to Those Colleges and Universities That Will Recruit**

Students to be Trained for Public Service Careers. Declining resources at many colleges and universities have reduced, or in some cases eliminated, the ability to recruit energetically. To ensure a multicultural workforce, however, the pool of available applicants must be broad-based and diverse. To the extent that the federal government is able to assist colleges and universities to recruit and train a diverse group of students and to channel those students into the public service, the career service will be both broadened and strengthened. This new initiative could well be supported by private foundations with a concern for the long-term well-being of the public service.

    C. **Create a Limited but Prestigious Public Service Scholarship Program.** The need to recruit competitively will be dramatic in the next two decades. The private sector will compete more aggressively and with more money than today. The demand for skills will increase as the pool of college graduates decreases. In 1988, the annual cost of some private colleges approached $20,000. If current rates of increase continue, the annual cost of an undergraduate education will exceed the average American family's annual income within the next 20 years. Many good students will be unable to afford a college education and even those who attend public universities will graduate with large educational debts. New opportunities for financial assistance will be attractive. *Congress should create a well-publicized, highly competitive public scholarship program that will provide significant funding for undergraduate education in return for a fixed period of federal service. Minority students must be a particular target for this program. The program must contain an offset provision that will prohibit colleges and universities from reducing total financial assistance by the amount of the scholarship.*

    Several such proposals have already been advanced. In 1988, Representative Patricia Schroeder introduced the Excellence in Government Management Act, which would have established 1,000 fellowships government-wide. The fellowships were modeled on the Department of Defense's Reserve Officer Training Corps, which provides partial education funding in return for a specified length of service following graduation.

    D. **Advertise Existing Financial Opportunities Widely and from a Central Point.** Opportunities, such as the existing Truman Scholarship Program and the Patricia Harris Fellowships, that now assist students interested in a career in government (although not necessarily at the federal level), could and should be advertised with public service fellowships. Students must have a convenient and central source of information about all public service scholarships and fellowships.

    The harsh reality of the next 20 years is that the recruiter with financial incentives will get the attention of the most students. To level the playing field for government recruiters, the federal government must offer a variety of financial incentives.

    E. **Make It Easier for Student Employees to Become Permanent Employees.** Broaden and simplify existing student employment programs. The Cooperative Education Program, which permits students (called coops) to alternate periods of study with periods of employment and compensation, is one example. Many organizations use it as a means of targeting students in hard-to-hire occupations such as engineering. As early as sophomore year in college, the student is able to mix part-time government employment (and compensation) with continued study. From the agency perspective, the program is valuable because it permits early and agency-specific training, because it provides some financial assistance to the student, and because it permits the agency to assess the student's potential as an employee. The program is also valuable because employees who enter the civil service in this way generally have a higher retention rate than other employees. A study of attrition of procurement officers at NASA's Goddard Space Flight Center, for example, found that, "[R]etention of coops converted to full-time permanent positions was highest at 67 percent, compared to 49 percent for other external hires."[22] Other agencies report similar statistics.

In June 1988, OPM announced a simplification of the coop program that will make it easier to reach agreements with participating colleges and universities and to convert students to full-time employees. The grade at which students became staff had been a problem for many. This was most notably true for people with a master's degree, because they could be appointed only to a GS-7. The new guidelines appear to raise that appointment level to a GS-9. Additional flexibilities are also necessary if more agencies are to recruit and retain coop students. Among these is the need to reanalyze the balance between periods of employment and periods at school. A program calling for a semester at school and a semester away, for example, is disruptive to both student and employer. In addition, more flexible travel reimbursement policies are necessary, so that assistance can be provided to students who must travel to work assignments and reside there for a lengthy period.

F. **Use Student Internship Programs as Aggressive Recruiting Tools.** Expand the use of other internship programs. Internship opportunities, such as the Presidential Management Intern Program, provide high-quality candidates for the career service. Before 1988, 200 interns were selected for the program from a national competition each year; in 1988, the total number of interns was increased to 400. The nature of the selection and the prestige of these internships generally provide bright, capable, and committed students to the agencies in which they are placed. This program's interns are likely to be among the managers of the future if they stay in government service. The number of program applicants however, has decreased by more than half in recent years. Although this is a program with good potential, some changes are necessary.

At present, the Presidential Management Intern Program is aimed at graduate students in schools of public administration and public policy. This is an appropriate target and one that provides well-trained students who are interested in general management. *The federal government, however, generally hires specialists, not future managers. An expanded Presidential Management Intern Program aimed directly at students with technical or engineering skills and an interest in management would provide early exposure to management needs and activities, and would enhance long-term management capabilities for scientific and technical agencies.*

In addition, all government agencies should receive the necessary budgetary support to create their own internship programs. As is the case now in the Department of Defense, these agency efforts should not be driven and limited by existing vacancies, but by careful analysis of future management needs. All internship activities in the federal government should be based on a clear understanding of the need for career development opportunities, of the need for clear career paths, and on the commitment of the agency to the intern as a valued and important employee.

If the intern experience is not a useful one, some of the best and brightest that government is able to recruit will be disenchanted with federal service early on. Both government-wide and agency-specific strategies for the development and retention of Presidential Management Interns and other interns must be developed and promptly implemented.

G. **Make It Easier to Hire Good Graduate Students.** Facilitate on-the-spot hiring of students with graduate degrees. Advanced education will become increasingly important to government employees in the years ahead, but many of the simplified hiring practices now in use apply only to undergraduate students, not to graduate students. For many occupations, graduate students are prime targets for government recruiters. Flexible and fast authorities should be extended to them.

H. **Use Those Who Are Challenged by Public Service to Challenge Others.** Some of government's most effective recruiters rely on senior managers for on-campus recruiting efforts. The General Accounting Office, widely recognized for its recruiting success, sends its most senior people to "sell" the agency. Senior managers understand and are able to communicate the complexity and excitement of a federal career.

I. **Create Innovative Tools for Federal Recruiting Efforts.** Provide flexible incentives that recruiters may choose from to meet the needs of each candidate. Private-sector organizations are able to tailor incentives; public-sector organizations must be able to do the same. Moving expenses, recruitment bonuses, the promise of future educational support, and the assurance of career development and training are all tools that should be available when needed. They will not be necessary for every hire; they will be necessary for critical hires.

This flexibility must be buttressed by the following supports: First, clearly visible information channels are needed from the federal government to college and university placement offices and key faculty members. These must include the specialized schools of public administration and policy, as well as other colleges and universities that are likely to provide a pool of candidates for hard-to-hire occupations. There is a strong need for a central information source and referral point. Such a central function would complement and supplement, not replace, individual agency efforts.

Second, agencies with specialized recruiting needs must develop systematic communication with likely sources—professors and professional groups as well as specific colleges and universities. The Air Force Professor Tour, in which professors in engineering and other technical fields are "toured" through Air Force facilities and equipment, is one example of such a process.

Third, additional broad-based flexibility in advertising job opportunities in the federal government is needed. Newspaper advertising, the use of employment agencies and, in some cases, executive search organizations, will be a necessary part of creating a candidate pool. All these techniques must be strengthened and expanded.

It is necessary to ensure that all of these strategies and tools are used to guarantee a representative workforce that exemplifies not only the excellence, but also the diversity, of the American population.

RECOMMENDATION 4

Create and support a federal executive development strategy; support and reward executive excellence.

A. **Define Who and What a Federal Executive Is.** Federal Management systems suffer from a basic problem: the definition of management is left largely to chance. When the Senior Executive Service was created, for example, eligibility was determined by pay level, not by managerial or executive responsibility. Yet a research scientist who was a GS-16 had different authority and responsibility from that of a GS-16 who managed programs and people. For many purposes, however, and certainly in the SES, the two are lumped together. Recognizing and rewarding executive contributions are made more difficult. *To emphasize the importance of management generally and executive development in particular, a clear government executive track should be created in the SES. Membership can be gained only through previous management or executive experience. Bonuses and other awards will be made on the basis of human resource manage-*

ment capability and contributions, and excellence in staff development and other key human resource functions.

B. Emphasize the Development of Career Paths. Clear career development plans and paths are rare in the federal service. Few agencies have created executive development systems, even for members of the SES. Unlike the private sector, in which managers are groomed for future responsibilities or selected because of specific management skills, career civil servants often automatically become managers when they reach a certain grade.

The military development strategy, with its clear stages of development and growth, is often recommended. The clarity of career development options, the opportunities available to assist in meeting career objectives, and the ability to plan for the longer term are as attractive to those with an interest in a civilian public service career as they are to military personnel. Other models are also available. The General Accounting Office has a well-developed executive development plan for new members of the SES. It familiarizes them with agency-wide operations, as well as with longer term management options. The Internal Revenue Service has developed a comprehensive executive development plan that clearly outlines the steps and talents necessary to achieve executive status in that organization.

Many agencies would be aided in their efforts if a government-wide strategy existed. This is yet another case requiring broad central principles for decentralized application.

C. Define and Train for Leadership. The ability to lead is key. Both individual agencies and the Office of Personnel Management must make a strong committment to developing the executive leaders of the future. That means that a clear training strategy must exist and resources must be available to all agencies. The OPM is the largest vendor of federal training contracts; currently, no significant strategy guides their dissemination. Although federal training centers exist, they are not tied to an overall strategy. The Federal Executive Institute, which could serve as a kind of graduate school for executive and leadership development, needs a basic level of common training to draw on. That common base does not now exist.

The creation and support of leadership development strategies are not only appropriate foci for federal training funds, but also speak to a critical government-wide need. The OPM must exercise aggressive leadership in this effort. Leadership development activities have been ignored for too long.

Individual agencies must identify the employees for whom training and development would be most beneficial. Agencies must take the development of their own people seriously. The frequently stated sentiment that "there's not much future in the federal government" is directly related to the failure to create an organizational family, to recognize and reward individual contributions, and to create common organizational purpose. Good leaders do all of those things. Their development and support is crucial to future effectiveness.

In these, as in all federal training efforts, special emphasis must be placed on women and minorities, and on incorporating them into the federal management structure. As they assume a majority role in the workforce population, their leadership skills must be recognized and developed.

D. Structure an Adequate and Appropriate Incentive System. Little is known about what motivates public-sector employees and why. Much thinking in this regard is based on a simple transfer of private sector techniques. When the SES was created in 1978, for example, it contained a financial incentive system. Members of the SES compete with other members in their agencies for various financial bonuses and awards. Prior to its government-wide adoption, the incentive system had never been tested or evaluated in a federal setting.

The Civil Service Reform Act also created a merit pay system for mid-level managers (grades GM-13 to GM-15). Both the SES and the merit pay systems rely on performance evaluation to determine "winners"; *at both management levels, there is a pervasive belief that existing performance appraisal mechanisms do not work.* For both merit pay and the SES bonus systems, it is time to *make* the system work and to make the rewards worthwhile, or to find an alternative.

The performance evaluation process must be simplified; at present it is viewed as a paper exercise unrelated to any positive outcome. Managers at all levels, including the political executives who rate senior career managers, should be trained in using performance evaluation techniques in an equitable and effective way. The issue of who is eligible for the awards must be addressed. Our earlier recommendation for a government executive track in the SES would specify that the bonuses awarded to that group would reward only good management—other bonuses could be set aside for unusual scientific, research, or public service contributions. This would greatly clarify both the purpose of the award and the composition of the group within which each manager competes for recognition.

Eligibility is also related to the question of how far into the organization the individual award system should be driven. Currently, half of each organization's SES membership is eligible for an annual bonus. Well over half of merit pay managers in most agencies qualify for a bonus. In our view, this is too many. The current system encourages using the bonus system as a supplement to an inadequate salary, rather than as a reward for outstanding performance. First, federal managers' salaries must be made more comparable with their private sector counterparts salaries; then, and only then, the bonus and award system must be refocused, both to reward fewer managers and to reward truly outstanding performers.

The usefulness of nonfinancial rewards for excellent public service must also be recognized and expanded. Symbolic recognition that rewards outstanding contributions and that explicitly reinforces the larger purpose of the public service—to serve the public—can be powerful. Many nonfinancial awards and methods of recognition exist, but have not been fully employed or publicized. At one time, the National Civil Service League provided an important set of visible rewards for exemplary public service. New honors and awards, based on that model, should be created and emphasized in the future.

E. **Examine the Role of Mobility in Career Development.** Many organizations consider the ability to move an employee from office to office and from region to region basic to his or her career advancement. The Senior Executive Service contains a provision that its members could be moved both within and among agencies. The underlying assumption in both of these cases deserves new analysis. Is mobility good? Are there cases in which mobility is bad? For what positions and what purposes is mobility desirable? Are there cases, in this era of two-income families, in which the benefits of mobility to the organization are outweighed by the costs to the individual employee? The recent reports *Workforce 2000* and *Civil Service 2000* both emphasize that more women and more two-income families will characterize the workforce of the future. If mobility is essential for executive development, should there be a bonus for the willingness to move? All of these questions and many more are relevant to the contemporary public manager. They will become even more relevant in the future as more women assume managerial roles. They should be addressed now.

F. **Rectify the Federal Benefit System.** The federal benefit system is complicated and burdensome. It is already clear that the new federal retirement system will create additional demands for portability of other benefits and for new lateral-entry incentives. At present, the federal benefit system is a detriment to effective recruiting.

The most obvious example is health insurance. The costs are rising each year and more federal employees are carrying lower levels of coverage than they need to avoid consistently increasing costs. These costs are attributable in large part to the plethora of plans available to federal employees and the concomitant failure to pool risk. By failing to adhere to basic principles of health insurance, the current system guarantees that costs will continue to rise while benefits remain level or decline.

Action by Congress is necessary to change the rules of the federal benefit system. This change should be a high priority for the President and for Congress, as well as for the Office of Personnel Management. Change will occur only gradually in this area, but the questions and their implications should be considered now. Good benefits are an important part of an attractive career choice. The quality of federal benefits has already eroded; further erosion will be seriously detrimental to effectively recruiting and retaining valued employees.

G. **Create Retention Awards and Bonuses.** In the past 10 years, the number of senior managers who chose to retire at age 55 increased substantially. With their departures, the federal government lost valuable resources that will take years to replace. The *Government Executive* survey cited earlier indicated that many of those people would have stayed longer had even a modest bonus plan been in place. Of course, not all managers should be coaxed to stay. For those in critical positions, however, and especially for those in hard-to-hire or sensitive occupations, the validity and value of a serious effort to keep them is clear. The use of a retention bonus must be *highly* selective, but it should be an option for federal executives.

CONCLUSION

The problems faced by the career civil service today will only become more profound. They will involve not only recruiting from different pools, but also retraining existing employees for new tasks and occupations. The gargantuan tasks facing federal personnel systems demand intense commitment and superb skill—problem-solving strategies, not piecemeal, reactive attempts to cope. Selling the public service as a challenging and valued career must assume a high priority. It must be accompanied by a new emphasis on professional and ethical public service, for political as well as career members of the public service. Elected and appointed officials must not only establish and support high standards and expectations for career performance, but also create an environment in which career civil servants can work with appointees with trust and respect. Elected officials and the public must understand and value both the institution of the public service and its individual members.

The public service, in turn, must understand that its duty to serve the public can never be compromised. Excellent and honorable government must be the standard for all.

ENDNOTES

1. Congressional Research Service, "Characteristics of the Federal Workforce" (Washington, D.C., October 1987).
2. Data are from the Central Personnel Data File, U.S. Office of Personnel Management, Washington, D.C. Entrance data exclude transfers from one position to another and returns to the workforce after leaves of absence. Exit data exclude intragovernmental

transfers and leaves of absence.

3. Constance Horner, speech Before the Career Entry Recruitment Conference, Washington, D.C., June 23, 1988.

4. U.S. Merit Systems Protection Board, "Attracting Quality Graduates to the Federal Government" (Washington, D.C., May 1988).

5. U.S. Department of Defense, Naval Research Laboratory, "Data on Problems Recruiting and Retaining Scientists and Engineers" (Washington, D.C., January 1986).

6. Charles Levine and Rosslyn Kleeman, "The Quiet Crisis: The Federal Workforce in the Year 2000" paper prepared for the Brookings Institution-American Enterprise Institute Conference on the Public Service in the Year 2000, Washington, D.C., September 1986.

7. U.S. Merit Systems Protection Board, "Attracting Quality Graduates to the Federal Government" (Washington, D.C., May 1988).

8. Ronald Sanders, "The Best and the Brightest: Can the Public Service Compete?" Paper prepared for the National Commission on the Public Service, Washington, D.C., October 1988.

9. Robert Goldenkoff, "That the Best May Serve: Methods of Recruiting and Retaining Federal Entry Level Personnel" paper prepared for the National Commission on the Public Service, Washington, D.C., September 1988.

10. U.S. General Accounting Office, "Federal Workforce: A Framework for Studying Its Quality Over Time" (Washington, D.C., August 1988).

11. *Workforce 2000: Work and Workers For The 21st Century* (Indianapolis, Indiana: The Hudson Institute, June 1987).

12. *Civil Service 2000* (U.S. Office of Personnel Management, June 1988).

13. Committee for Economic Development, "The American Population: Trends and Issues" (Washington, D.C., April 1988).

14. U.S. Department of Defense, Defense Manpower Data Center, "Civilian Personnel and Administrative Employees in the Department of Defense: Baseline Data on the Incoming Cohort" (Washington, D.C., October 1987).

15. Peter Benda and Charles Levine, "Reagan and the Bureaucracy: The Bequest, the Promise and the Legacy" *in* Charles O. Jones, ed., *The Reagan Presidency: Promise and Performance* (Chatham House, Chatham, N.J., 1988).

16. U.S. General Accounting Office, "The Senior Executive Service: Executive's Perspectives on Their Federal Service" (Washington, D.C.: July 1988).

17. Data from the Executive Personnel Data File, U.S. Office of Personnel Management.

18. U.S. Merit Systems Protection Board, "Federal Personnel Policies and Practices—Perspective From the Workplace" (Washington, D.C.: December 1987); and U.S. Department of Treasury, Internal Revenue Service, "The Treatment of IRS Executives" (Washington, D.C.: April 1987).

19. Timothy B. Clarke and Marjorie Wachtel. "The Quiet Crisis Goes Public" *Government Executive* (June 1988): 14–29.

20. Constance Horner, *supra* note 3.

21. Clarke and Wachtel, *supra* note 17.

22. Gail S. Williams. *A Study of Attrition Among Goddard Space Flight Center Contract Specialists,* unpublished master's degree paper, the Maxwell School of Citizenship and Public Affairs (Syracuse University, Syracuse, N.Y.: May 1988).

ANNEX I

THE "BEST AND BRIGHTEST": CAN THE PUBLIC SERVICE COMPETE?

Executive Summary of a

Research Project Sponsored by

The National Commission on the Public Service

by

Ronald P. Sanders

INTRODUCTION

Much has been said and written of the public service's apparent inability to attract quality human resources to its ranks. This difficulty—often characterized as a crisis—seems especially acute among top college graduates, and it stands to worsen as these graduates enter a "sellers" labor market in the 1990s. However, evidence of such a crisis is inconclusive, establishing a *prima facie* case at best. For example, the General Accounting Office has observed that support for such claims consists almost entirely of "individual anecdotes, unsystematic sampling of (current) employee or supervisory opinions, or . . . inferences from other data such as comparisons of Federal and non-Federal employees' pay and benefits." To be sure, these are viscerally persuasive, but there remains an empirical burden of proof.

In an effort to meet this burden, the National Commission on the Public Service sponsored the research project detailed in the attached report. It is specifically designed to assess the standing of the public service (and the Federal civil service in particular) as a prospective employer of the nation's top college graduates. As a means of gaining access to this select group, we surveyed 865 new members of four major collegiate academic honor societies: Phi Beta Kappa, for liberal arts students; Beta Gamma Sigma, for students of business administration; Sigma Xi, for students in the sciences and engineering; and Pi Alpha Alpha, for students of public administration. We asked members of this sample group two principal questions:

First, what do you want most in a job? In this regard, we asked respondents to rate and then rank 11 possible job outcomes in terms of importance: advancement opportunities, autonomy on the job, financial reward, personal growth and development, prestige in the community, professional recognition, job security, service to society, cooperative and congenial social relations, pleasant working conditions, and challenging work.

Secondly, given these possible outcomes, do you believe that the public service, among other employment alternatives, can provide those that are most important to you? In this regard, we asked respondents to rate the "likelihood" of realizing important job outcomes in the Federal civil service, state and local government, large private corporations, small businesses or professional firms, academic institutions, and the military.

Our respondents are arguably the "best and brightest" of the Class of 1988. Representing a dozen academic disciplines from more than 200 colleges and universities, over 92 percent of our sample have a Grade Point Average (GPA) of 3.5 or better, on a 4.0 scale; their overall average GPA is 3.72. More than half have completed graduate school, with the remainder receiving undergraduate degrees, and all have entered the very labor markets that the public service must tap. Thus, their views have important implications for government. These views and the recommendations that derive from them are briefly summarized below.

SUMMARY OF RESULTS

The results of our research may be simply stated. In looking for work, the top graduates of the Class of '88 are motivated primarily by intangible rewards, such as challenging work and the opportunity for personal growth, rather than pay and promotion. There is good news for the public service in this. Our results suggest that it need not attempt to compete for the best and brightest on a politically prohibitive "dollar-for-dollar" basis; however, the bad news is that top graduates do not see the public service as providing those intangible rewards that are most important to them. It is contribution, not compensation, that seems to drive the market for top college graduates, and the public service fares poorly in this regard.

In relative terms, pay and promotion are among the least important job outcomes of our sample group. Of the 11 outcomes rated by that group, opportunity for advancement and financial reward ranked ninth and tenth overall (prestige was last); business graduates ranked promotion and pay fifth and eighth respectively. Men placed greater importance on financial reward than women; however, overall, almost 84 percent of those responding said that "making a lot of money" was not a measure of real success, and over 62 percent felt that they would be satisfied with "earning enough money for a comfortable standard of living."

In sharp contrast, the best and brightest in all disciplines ranked challenging work and the opportunity for personal growth as their two most desired job outcomes, by wide margins. Over 72 percent said that challenge was "essential" in a job, while 64 percent said the same about personal growth.

Interestingly, service, characterized as "work that is intrinsically worthwhile to society," also emerged as one of the more important outcomes to our sample overall—only business majors ranked it low. About half of all respondents felt that such work was "the main thing that matters about a job." Autonomy was also ranked among the most important requirements. These requirements, ranked by relative importance, are summarized in Figure 1.

By themselves, these results are somewhat encouraging. They suggest that the public service need not engage in a "bidding war" with its competitors for the best and brightest—*if* it can offer the intrinsic rewards that are most important to them. Unfortunately, our sample sees little chance of that in today's public service. According to our data, top college graduates see such service as intrinsically "barren," where, almost by definition, it should be just the opposite.

Our sample ranked the Federal service, state and local government, and military fourth, fifth, and sixth, respectively (out of the six possible employment alternatives posed in our survey) in terms of providing challenging work and the opportunity for personal growth, although women tended to give the Federal government somewhat better marks in this area. Public administration students rated opportunities for personal growth in government service no better than did those in other academic disciplines—"just as likely as unlikely." Our respondents found challenge and opportunity for personal growth to be much more likely in academic institutions, small businesses and professional firms, and large corporations.

Only about six percent of our sample strongly felt that government work was "challenging and intellectually stimulating," while more than 70 percent did not believe that it offers a good chance for responsibility early on in one's career. Almost 86 percent did not think that a government job would allow them to use their abilities to the fullest, and about half stated that most civil service jobs were routine and monotonous. Graduates in business administration, the sciences, and engineering were especially critical of government in this respect.

As might be expected, only in providing job security does the public service rank ahead of all other employment alternatives. However, security is of only moderate importance to

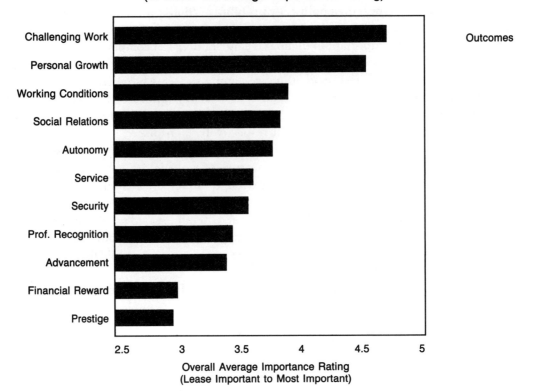

Figure 1
Outcome Importance
(In Order of Average Importance Rating)

Overall Average Importance Rating
(Lease Important to Most Important)

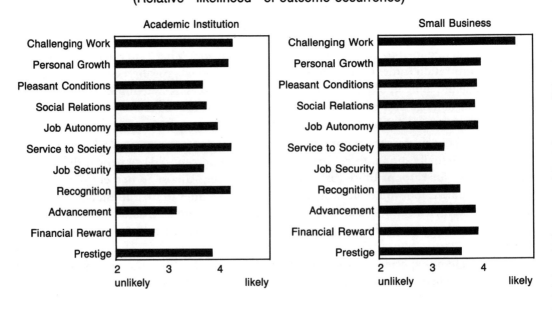

Figure 2
Profiles of Employment Alternatives
(Relative "likelihood" of outcome occurrence)

Figure 2 (continued)

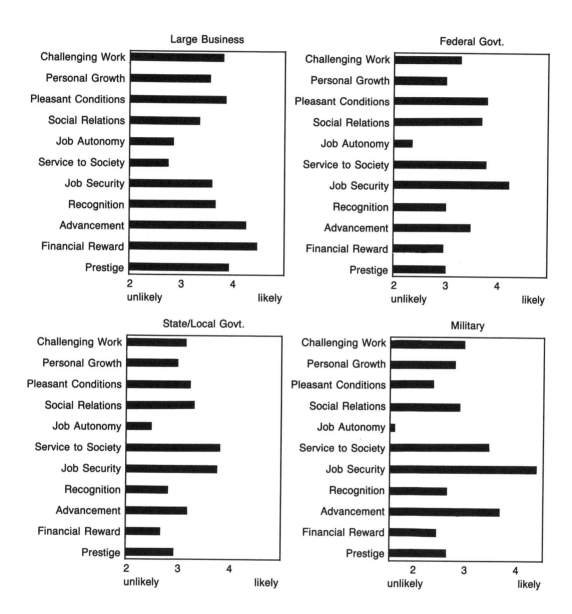

our sample; while 75 percent indicated that the government provides a great deal of security, only 25 percent stated that security was more important than opportunity. Female respondents placed somewhat more importance in job security.

Profiles of each employment alternative are provided in Figure 2. These show graphically the comparative "likelihood" of realizing important job outcomes in each such alternative, according to our respondents. Outcomes are listed in overall order of importance. Similarly, employment alternatives are listed in order of their overall "likelihood" of providing those requirements, with academic institutions and small businesses and professional firms emerging as our sample's "employers of choice."

According to the results outlined above, government faces considerable difficulty in competing for top college graduates. This difficulty is compounded by our respondents' belief that entry into the Federal service is complex and time consuming; 56 percent (over 64 percent of our female respondents) characterized the appointment process in this manner, while only about 30 percent overall stated that if they wanted a job with the Federal government, they would know how to go about getting one. Only public administration students expressed relative confidence in obtaining such a job. Overall, academic institutions were rated as the most difficult to enter, with the Federal service and state and local government seen as only slightly less difficult (the military was perceived to be the easiest to enter).

The public service thus seems to be doubly damned, both unattractive and impermeable to the best and brightest. This is confirmed by the fact that only a very few of our respondents have either sought or accepted government employ. 86 percent of our sample have never applied for entry into the Federal service, and over 92 percent have never had an employment interview with a Federal agency. Of the 403 respondents in our sample who have already accepted employment, only 16 have entered the Federal civil service, with 29 going to work for state and local governments and 2 entered military service; however, about half of those entering government service have an academic background in public administration or a related field. Almost 38 percent of those who have accepted employment now work for large private corporations, with 21 percent employed by academic institutions. The employment choices of this part of our sample group are portrayed in Figure 3.

Figure 3
Respondents' Organizational Choices
(n = 403)

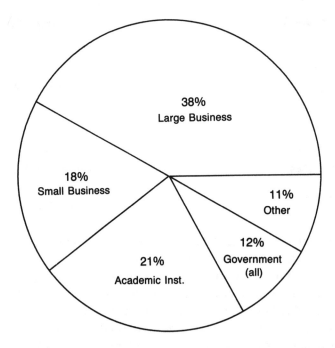

Per Cent of Respondents Who Have Already Accepted Employment

RECOMMENDATIONS

As disturbing as these results may be, we have argued that they contain some cause for optimism. They suggest that the public service can compete for the best and brightest by emphasizing the intangible rewards that should be inherent in its work. Our sample of top college graduates does not believe that public service is likely to provide these intangibles, but this may be more myth than reality. As many of us know from first-hand experience, government service can be intrinsically rewarding—the potential exists in many, if not most government positions, and if the public service can "add value" to its jobs and its organizations in this regard, it *can* compete. We recommend four interrelated strategies for doing so:

First, leadership must set the stage. The inherent rewards of public service must be forcefully articulated and reinforced by our nation's political leaders and others who shape public opinion; their explicit acceptance of the civil service as an essential part of governance, and their portrayal of the civil servant as a respected actor in that process, can serve as a powerful magnet for the best and brightest.

Secondly, government must also establish human resource management policies that materially enhance the intrinsic value of its jobs and the quality of "working life" in its component organizations. Job enrichment and organization development techniques have been accepted in theory and proven in practice, and these should also become an explicit and integral part of public personnel policy. To date, they have not been.

Third, government service must also become less impermeable to potential applicants. The entry process must become more streamlined and understandable, with provision for "on the spot" appointment for talented candidates; in the Federal service, the Office of Personnel Management has made excellent progress in this area, with much of the impetus provided by civil rights litigation. At the same time, public organizations need to employ more sophisticated and flexible recruiting strategies, including a recruiting "bag of tools" that allows employment offers to be tailored to the needs of individual candidates. The relative attraction of women to government service, and their expected emergence as a powerful force in the labor market of the 1990s, would seem to underscore the advantages of tailoring terms and conditions of employment to the needs of particular labor market segments.

Finally, government must market itself as an employer, persuading the labor markets of the virtues and rewards of public service. This is not new: Dow Chemical ("Dow lets you do great things") and our armed forces ("A great place to start"), among others, have become very sophisticated in this regard. In many respects, our research resembles a market survey, and it offers a credible start towards such a marketing campaign by identifying what the best and brightest (and various segments thereof) want most in a job.

In summary, it is clear that a crisis exists. As it now stands, the public service cannot compete for top college graduates, for those graduates believe that it cannot provide the rewards that they value most. However, in large part, this view of public service is a fiction. Such service can be challenging and fulfilling; the opportunity to contribute to matters of public policy, even in some small way, can compensate for many things. If these intangibles are reflected in the reality of public service, government will be able to attract the best and brightest to its ranks.

INVESTMENT FOR LEADERSHIP

Education and Training for the Public Service

The Report of the

Task Force on Education and Training

to the

National Commission on the Public Service

TASK FORCE

Derek Bok, *Chairman*

John Brademas

Donald Kennedy

Donna E. Shalala

Carolyn Warner

WASHINGTON 1989

THE TASK FORCE ON EDUCATION AND TRAINING

CHAIRMAN

Derek Bok
President, Harvard University

MEMBERS

John Brademas
President, New York University

Donald Kennedy
President, Stanford University

Donna E. Shalala
Chancellor, University of Wisconsin

Carolyn Warner
Former State Superintendent of Public Instruction, Arizona

PROJECT DIRECTOR

Peter Zimmerman
Associate Dean, Kennedy School of Government
Harvard University

RESEARCH ASSISTANT

Anne Stone

CONTENTS

PREFACE

The National Commission on the Public Service asked the Task Force on Education and Training to examine the role of the educational system in strengthening the education and training of those aspiring to careers in government and strengthening the skills of those already in government.

The Task Force held several meetings as a group and there was considerable informal communication among members and staff.

In its initial inquiries, the Task Force planned to focus primarily on the education and training of those who enter government and the training of those already in government jobs. However, our initial inquiries and discussions led the Task Force to focus on a much broader question, i.e., how the educational system itself conditions people to consider the possibility of a career in public service.

This consideration led to a series of inquiries into questions such as the quality and character of social studies education at the secondary level, what kinds of community service/ public service programs exist at the secondary and undergraduate level, and what effect they appear to have on students' professional orientation. The Task Force did not have the resources to examine these questions as thoroughly as it would like. However, our inquiries were sufficient to acquaint the Task Force with the issues in this area and to persuade us that there is an important interaction between the teaching of social studies and extracurricular community service activities on the one hand, with the question of public attitudes toward government and government careers on the other.

Project staff examined a wide range of research and reports in areas such as training and recruitment. With the assistance of the Office of Personnel Management (OPM), recent hiring patterns at the federal level were analyzed. Staff met with several groups of federal officials, including members of the Interagency Advisory Group and its Committee on Development and Training. Informal meetings were held with other groups of federal officials, including representatives of employee groups. Focus group conversations were held with undergraduate students to ascertain their interest and perceptions of public service, which supplemented extensive examination of polling data provided by the Roper Organization. To better understand the factors affecting student career choice, the Task Force examined extensive polling of college freshmen done by Alexander Astin of the University of California at Los Angeles, conducted its own poll of 40 college placement offices, and interviewed representatives from a wide range of campus service organizations. In addition, the staff participated in several small meetings with faculty from public policy and public administration programs to discuss emerging hypotheses and tentative conclusions.

The Task Force chairman presented the preliminary conclusions of the report to a group of academics and practitioners at a commission-sponsored meeting at Princeton, New Jersey.

The Task Force wants to acknowledge in particular the efforts of Peter Zimmerman of Harvard University, who served as project director, and the diligent research work of Anne Stone. The Task force is grateful for the contributions of many current and past government officials. Particular thanks goes to Dr. Philip Schneider at OPM's Workforce Information Bureau, to Rosslyn Kleeman of the General Accounting Office, to Mary Broad of the Defense Communication Agency, to Terry Newell of the Department of Education and to Ann Brassier, formerly OPM's Assistant Director for Training. A number of other officials preferred not to be acknowledged by name.

Derek Bok, Chairman
Peter Zimmerman, Project Director

Cambridge, Massachusetts
April 1989

EXECUTIVE SUMMARY

Government is one of the principal vehicles through which we, as Americans, strive to realize our collective goals and aspirations, whether they are to defend our shores against potential enemies, to prevent the illegal import of drugs, to protect the environment, or to educate our children. Every citizen has a vital stake in the quality and capacity of our governmental institutions. While we often disagree on specific goals or particular means, no one's interest is served by mediocrity in public service.

Those in the educational arena must do more to strengthen the quality of public service. We believe that the nation's education system, including secondary schools and community colleges as well as four-year colleges and universities, can make a material contribution to expand public knowledge, awareness, and understanding of government; to enhance the inclination of young people to pursue public sector careers; and to help the government renew and strengthen its performance through better employee training and development.

To begin with, the nation's secondary schools and community colleges can contribute to more effective government by doing a better job of preparing young people to be active participants in our democratic process. The nation must find ways to improve the teaching of social studies, civics, and U.S. history and government in our schools and colleges. This leads to our first two recommendations:

We must undertake a comprehensive review of social studies education in our high schools, asking how we can do a more effective job of preparing young people for citizenship.

Community colleges and undergraduate institutions must also examine their contribution to the development of informed citizens.

The recent awakening of student interest in community service activities presents a real opportunity for government. There is much to be said for expanding existing service programs, such as VISTA, Action, and the Peace Corps, and for recent Congressional proposals to offer support toward the costs of college in exchange for community service. Yet little has been done by government agencies or educational institutions to link this growing interest in community problems to the possibility of a government career.

This consideration leads us to further recommendations:

Government agencies must increase their visibility on college and university campuses and make vivid the challenge and opportunity associated with federal employment.

Congress should adopt a program that will subsidize the college education of a stipulated number of outstanding students in return for public service. President Bush's YES program and the proposed Excellence in Government Act offer two interesting possibilities that should be explored.

Universities must give greater visibility to the opportunities for government service.

Our remaining recommendations address the need to improve the preparation and in-service training of those committed to careers in government service. Today, there are significant shortcomings in federal government human resource policies. Government agencies spend far too little on training of all kinds and concentrate their efforts on meeting narrow, short-term needs. The area of greatest concern is the plainly inadequate attention paid to the development of management and executive leadership in the civil service.

These observations lead to further recommendations.

Federal agencies should actively recruit and hire more graduates from professional schools of public policy and public administration as a source of potential executive talent. Programs such as the Presidential Management Intern program should be expanded.

Much greater attention and resources must be devoted to the strategic management of human resources within the federal government. Particular effort must be focused on the training and development of managerial and executive leadership.

Federal agencies should modify their training policies to utilize the potential contributions of the educational community.

At the same time, schools and faculties of public affairs should respond by vigorous efforts to build effective midcareer programs.

The American experiment in self-government faces a momentous challenge as we move into the last decade of the twentieth century. The complexity of the problems confronting our society is unprecedented. The range and scope of government responsibilities has never been greater. At the same time, the political and governmental institutions on which we depend are fragmented, held in low esteem, and widely distrusted by the American people.

Today, we have the opportunity and obligation to do more to prepare young people to meet the challenges of government, both as active citizens and committed public officials. We have the opportunity and obligation to capture the imagination of young people who would help build a more just, safer, and caring society through careers in public life. We have the opportunity and obligation to harness the imagination and capabilities of our educational system to help strengthen our governmental institutions. The nation has the opportunity and obligation to strengthen the managerial and professional capacity of the federal career service. We must not fail to meet these obligations and seize these opportunities.

INVESTMENT FOR LEADERSHIP: EDUCATION AND TRAINING FOR THE PUBLIC SERVICE

The Task Force on Education and Training has examined how government agencies and the educational system (particularly colleges and universities) can improve the quality of people attracted to public service and to enhance their performance as public servants. Our inquiry addresses three areas of concern:

• How can the educational system—from secondary school through college and graduate school—increase interest in, and understanding of, the opportunities for a career in public service?

• How do people prepare for government service? Who chooses these careers, and what qualifications and training do they possess? What contribution can universities make through programs designed to train people for such careers?

• How effective are government training programs in enhancing the knowledge and skills of public servants, and what contribution can universities make to improve such training?

The discussion that follows is primarily concerned with the federal government. In a report of this size, it is simply not possible to do justice to the varying problems and practices of 50 state governments and their local and municipal subdivisions. Nevertheless, the information we have gathered leads us to believe that most observations and recommendations in this report apply generally to many state and local governments.

The Importance of Good Government

It would be difficult to exaggerate the importance of increasing the quality and effectiveness of government in the United States. Government has grown in size and importance to affect almost every aspect of Americans' lives—their health, the quality of their environment, the vitality of their economy, their security from foreign attack, their well-being in old age. Little reason exists to believe that the significance of the public sector will diminish in the foreseeable future. Even during the past eight years, under a national Administration noted for its distaste for big government, the size of the federal workforce did not decline but actually grew by 5 percent.

Not only are the issues facing government important to all Americans; they are at least as complex and difficult as those confronting other institutions, and probably more so. The huge size of government is itself a complicating factor. The federal government is by far the nation's largest employer, with assets and annual expenditures that dwarf even very large private organizations such as IBM, Exxon, or General Electric. Federal employment includes some 3 million civilians and an additional 2 million men and women in the armed forces. Annual federal expenditures now exceed $1 trillion. By comparison, General Motors, the world's largest industrial corporation, employs about 800,000 people and has annual sales approaching $100 billion.

Yet it is not just size that makes the federal environment so complex and challenging.

Other factors add complicating dimensions to public service. First, the nature of government work differs significantly from that of the private sector. It is far more difficult to reach agreement about appropriate goals, how they will be assessed, and what level of resources will support them. In a federal system, differences of opinion arise over the proper level of government needed to perform particular functions. Division of responsibility among three separate branches of government makes the task of policy formation and implementation much more difficult and cumbersome than it is in a unitary, hierarchical organization.

Second, federal agencies themselves produce few of the government's goods and services.[1] For example, the mechanisms of environmental protection, although the subject of federal law and regulatory action, are produced through the activities of many private firms. The technology for national defense and much of the research for public health are products of private institutions. Federal programs for social services, housing, unemployment insurance, and job training are administered through the states. It requires great administrative skill, extensive institutional knowledge, and political subtlety to achieve federal goals through states, cities, and private organizations whose own goals, incentive systems, and values often diverge from those of the federal government.

Third, standards of democratic accountability complicate the tasks of government and add to the challenge facing federal officials. Most people believe that government employees are (and should be) held to especially high standards in justifying their decisions and in accounting for the use of public resources. As a consequence, important differences exist in procedure and standards between the federal government and other institutions. Many inefficiencies result. Elaborate strictures and checks and balances are coupled with intricate requirements for documentation and unyielding demands for protection against any who might appear to benefit improperly from public programs or policies. These safeguards confound and complicate the task of the government employee.[2]

Fourth, although the federal government annually hires nearly 100,000 people, from blue-collar and clerical workers to scientists and engineers, fewer than 1 percent have been trained in programs specifically devoted to government, public policy, public administration, or public affairs. The others often have little knowledge of the special nature and characteristics of the government they serve. For some, deep within the federal bureaucracy and buffered from contact with the public, legislators, or service providers, the failure to understand the differences between government and business may be of limited consequence. As officials move up into supervisory and managerial positions and interact with the public and other recipients of government goods and services, however, they must master new skills and knowledge to be effective.

Fifth, like other institutions in American society, the public sector faces shifts in the character of the national workforce that will further complicate the task of government. Two recent studies, *Workforce 2000 and Civil Service 2000*, describe the changes ahead. Although the federal workforce is likely to remain stable in size, it is changing dramatically in composition. By the turn of the century, only 20 percent of new entrants to the federal workforce will be white males, the group that now predominates in policy making and management positions.[3] This demographic trend alone suggests subtle alterations in the culture and values of the workplace. Changes in skill requirements will challenge federal managers further. On the one hand, many more positions will require special qualifications, such as computer skills, engineering, or health and environmental science backgrounds. On the other hand, many potential entrants competing for federal jobs are likely to have low skills, come from economically and educationally disadvantaged groups, and require extensive training.

The urgent task for government and the educational community is to attract young people of quality and character to public service, prepare them well for the challenges they face, renew periodically their skills and commitment, and ensure a stream of well-trained, experienced executives to help government adapt to the many demands of a complex, rapidly evolving world.

ATTRACTING ABLE YOUNG PEOPLE TO PUBLIC CAREERS

Is the government able to attract young women and men of high calibre to government careers? Has there been a perceptible decline in the quality of young people seeking public service careers? If there is such a problem, what are the underlying causes and what might be done about them?

I have sat through hour after hour of testimony on the deterioration of the career civil service. Managers, employee representatives, and academics have said the best employees are leaving, good college and graduate students no longer consider a public service career, and government cannot hire the people it needs in high technology and scarcity occupations.[4]

> U.S. Representative Patricia Schroeder
> Chair, House Subcommittee on the Civil Service

It is the perception of many top government executives that the quality of federal personnel is declining. Seventy-three percent of respondents to a 1988 *Government Executive* survey said that their agency is experiencing a "brain drain." In the same survey, 59 percent of respondents said that the quality of new hires at their agencies was "marginally worse" or "much worse than in prior years."[5] According to a recent Merit Systems Protection Board study, most respondents felt that the quality of applicants for their work groups had declined in the past four years.[6] Although it must be kept in mind that these are the impressions of veteran employees who may exaggerate the virtues of the "good old days," the prevalence of such reports is disturbing.

Other data from various agencies suggest that people currently being hired and retained by the government are not always the highest achievers:

• The Internal Revenue Service hires accountants whose average score on the Certified Public Accountants (CPA) exam is in the 54th percentile; those hired by the Big Eight accounting firms score on average in the 86th percentile.[7]

• The Office of Personnel Management (OPM) reports that new hires in the late 1970s scored in the mid-90 percentile range on the Professional and Administrative Career Exam (PACE). The PACE exam is no longer used; however, in areas that have job-specific entrance exams designed to replace PACE, new hires have scores that average only in the mid-80s.[8]

• Concern is widespread that the federal government is no longer able to recruit successfully for engineering and technical talent at the nation's top engineering schools.[9]

• Student interest in government jobs in areas such as social work and public school teaching (the latter constituting one-fifth of public sector employment) has fallen sharply over the past two decades.

• A survey of top honors graduates, conducted for the Commission's Task Force on Recruitment and Retention, found that these students do not associate federal government careers with challenging work or the opportunity for personal growth and development. These findings may explain the fact that, although 10 percent of all college graduates have achieved a 3.5 grade point average, only 2 percent of college graduates entering the federal service have a 3.5 average, suggesting that federal agencies are not attracting a proportional share of top students on college campuses.[10]

Student Attitudes

As reports from the workplace suggest that government is not attracting the best students, so does evidence from the nation's campuses indicate that student interest in government careers is low. For example, a survey of 40 college placement officers found that only 7.5 percent of graduating students indicated interest in any form of government career (including federal, state, local, or military service). Because government jobs constitute nearly one-fifth of the labor force and employ a larger share of college graduates than the economy as a whole, the current level of interest in government careers suggests slim pickings for government recruiters.

In explaining low student interest in government careers today compared with 20 years ago, one university official wrote:

> There are students interested in public sector positions, but many are afraid they will get stuck in uninteresting jobs. Government is not so much a place where one would "sell out" to the establishment (as in 1967) as a place where one would be bored.[11]

The evidence from campuses and the workplace tends to bear out this observation. The consequences seem likely to grow more severe as one considers projected changes in the governmental workplace. The June 1988 OPM report, *Civil Service 2000,* suggests that technological advances will continue to increase the complexity of many jobs; that the professional and technical categories will grow while the number of clerical workers declines; and that the biggest areas of growth will be in the most highly skilled fields. At the same time, the new portable federal retirement system may increase turnover by removing financial disincentives to leaving the government in mid-career.

Here, then, is the basic problem. The federal workplace is evolving in a way that will require stronger professional and technical skills in the future. At the same time, student interest in government careers is disproportionately low; and, evidence suggests that government is not able to attract its share of the nation's most talented and promising young people.

Our investigation led us to conclude that defining the problem solely in terms of recruitment may miss a larger and more important phenomenon. Low student interest in government careers appears to reflect a more general pattern of changing attitudes among young people. Student knowledge and interest in public affairs has deteriorated significantly over the past generation or so. This decline may contribute to problems in recruitment as much as do specific government recruitment practices. Moreover, government institutions cannot hope to flourish where public attitudes reflect ignorance and apathy toward public affairs.

To examine student attitudes, this Task Force surveyed existing literature on the subject, interviewed students, and surveyed career counselors. The following findings emerged.

Students appear to hold a favorable view of the government in the abstract. In national polls, young people (aged 18 to 29) invariably respond more positively than their parents to questions such as, "Overall, how much trust and confidence do you have in the federal government to do a good job in carrying out its responsibilities?"[12]

Enthusiasm for government seems to wane, however, at the prospect of actually working there. Although 73 percent of young people responded that they have "trust and confidence" in the government to do a good job, only 45 percent of that age group considered "opportunities to get ahead in government" to be "excellent" or "good."[13]

Career interests of students—reflected in their choice of a college major, the extracurricular activities they pursue, and the jobs they choose upon graduation—are decidedly centered in the for-profit arena. Over the past 20 years, business has risen to be the most popular choice, attracting about 25 percent of college students as a major field, and more than 50 percent of college graduates for a first job. Other professional areas—engineering and law, for example—have also made gains in popularity. Interest in government and public service-related jobs, on the other hand, has dropped significantly from already low levels during the same period.[14]

Why are careers in business so much more popular? Many social, political, and economic factors contribute. One factor stands out in many analyses. Students today exhibit increased concern for financial security and well-being as a top priority. The percentage of freshmen who said that it is "important to be well-off financially" rose from 41 percent in 1966 to 76 percent in 1987. Similarly, in 1985, 72 percent of students agreed with the statement that "the chief benefit of a college education is to increase one's earning power" (up from 56 percent in 1967).[15]

For students concerned with financial reward, the widening gap in starting salaries between the public and private sectors can only discourage interest in public sector careers. As recently as 1977, starting salaries for banking, consulting, and the federal government were quite close (Table 1). In the past decade, however, government salaries have not kept up with inflation, and a gap of more than 35 percent now exists between entry-level salaries for banking and consulting organizations and those offered by federal agencies.

Table 1
Starting Salaries for College Graduates by Employer
1972–1987

Employer	(In Constant 1982 Dollars)				% Change
	1972	1977	1982	1987	
Consulting and research organizations	19,652	17,467	19,678	22,613	+15%
Banking, finance, and insurance	18,118	16,487	18,458	21,300	+18
Federal government	19,469	17,122	15,722	15,624	−20
Public school teachers	15,185	13,670	12,769	14,894	−2

Analysis by Martha Leape, Director of Career Services, Harvard College.
Sources: College Placement Council, Office of Personnel Management; and National Education Association.

Evidence likewise suggests that students feel little sense of obligation toward the society in which they live and little personal stake in the democratic system. When high school seniors in 1980 were asked to rate the importance of various life goals, those most consistently chosen were "being successful in my work" and "finding the right person to marry"; lowest in popularity were "working to correct social and economic inequalities" and "being a leader in my community."[16]

Some of these observations appear to support the common perception of today's students as self-centered, overly preoccupied with financial security, and uninterested in social issues. And yet, despite these financial concerns, student interest in community service seems to be increasing. High school and college participation in community service has grown substantially over the past several years, a trend that seems to have occurred independently on many different campuses. A *Newsweek-on-Campus* poll in 1988 reported that 35 percent of students polled said that they participate in some kind of social service activity. At Harvard, where the career office conducts an exit poll returned by more than 90 percent of graduating seniors, the percentage of students who said they had given time to community service during college increased from 35 percent in 1983 to 57 percent in 1987. At Tulane, the number of students volunteering through its campus public service organization has doubled in the past two years, making community service the most popular extracurricular activity. And representatives from the Campus Outreach Opportunity League, a student-founded, student-run organization that helps develop college public service programs, report that the number of participating campuses has grown from 30 in 1984 to 461 in 1988, and that they are inundated with new requests for help.[17] The Commission's own survey of honors graduates found that for many top students, the opportunity to be of service to society is an important factor in career choice.[18]

The picture that emerges is complex. The past two decades have witnessed real shifts in student attitudes. The importance of financial success has increased, while interest in political affairs has declined; yet involvement in community service appears to be surging on many campuses. Student interest in being of service to others and contributing to the community seems widespread and sincere. Moreover, students are not hostile to government; they simply fail to see it as an outlet for their public service impulses.

Civic Education

These observations led the task force to focus on the state of civic education—to ask what kind of job schools are doing in preparing young people to play the role of active, informed citizens. A well-informed citizenry is not only important to the health of a democratic society but also a necessary base for a vital public service. Yet many indicators, from declining respect for public officials to steady slippage in voter turnout (from 62.8 percent in 1960 to 50 percent in 1988), have led commentators to express concern for the state of civic education.[19]

Abundant evidence suggests that students graduating from high school lack both the knowledge and the values to be active, informed citizens. The National Assessment of Educational Progress conducts frequent tests of elementary and secondary school students' knowledge of American history and government. The results are consistently poor. Not only do students lack knowledge; they often graduate with little understanding of or concern for social issues. Only about one-third of college freshmen in 1987 said they could "describe the freedoms guaranteed by the Bill of Rights." Worse yet, almost half of those who could not describe those freedoms said they had "no interest" in learning about them.[20] The number of college freshmen who considered "keeping up with political affairs" important dropped from 58 percent in 1966 to 38 percent in 1985.[21] Small wonder that when federal employees were asked "if our high schools and colleges adequately teach students about government," 92 percent answered no.[22]

In recent times, civic education has been considered to be the responsibility of elementary and secondary social studies curricula. But there is much concern among social studies educators today that schools are not performing well in providing citizenship education. The biggest problem, according to many, is the lack of a clearly articulated rationale for social studies education. As one commentator writes:

> Educators agree that the overarching goal of education is to develop informed, thinking citizens, capable of participating both in domestic and world affairs. . . . [Educators do not, however,] make explicit what the meaning of citizenship is or should be, what explicit roles public citizens (as distinguished from private persons) should play in social and political life. I do not find much clue as to what our "informed, thinking citizen" should be informed or think about in his or her role as citizen. I find no hint as to what kind of society or government it is that this citizen is being prepared to participate in.[23]

The lack of an adequate rationale is manifest in all aspects of social studies education. Textbooks are widely considered to be of poor quality, dull, and uninspiring. Yet according to a recent study, ". . . most teachers questioned . . . seemed content to see to it that students knew the textbook and could discuss current events in light of the assigned reading."[24] In addition, curricula are often diluted. Most of today's social studies curricula are based to some degree on the recommendations of the 1916 Commission on Reorganization of Secondary Education—Committee on Social Studies. The Committee proposed a curriculum that contained three essential components: civics, U.S. history, and European history, taught in two three-year cycles beginning in the seventh grade. Although the framework of these cycles remains in place today, the curriculum has been expanded to offer elective alternatives from among such disparate fields as psychology, anthropology, and philosophy. Although these are worthy subjects, their inclusion in a program of study originally designed to teach citizenship must necessarily obscure that goal.

If young people are going to learn about their government and the responsibilities of citizenship, it is important that social studies curricula place a higher priority on civic education. But progress has been hampered by serious differences of opinion over the goals of civic education. As society itself has become more divided over questions of value, educators have become wary of anything that sounds like indoctrination or inculcation of beliefs. All these difficulties, unfortunately, have helped to produce many young people who have little knowledge of or interest in the fundamental precepts of American government and society and have no strong feelings about the roles they will play in society beyond providing for their own well-being.

An active, involved, and informed citizenry is the essential foundation of the American democratic political system and a necessary precondition to a strong public service. The evidence cited above leads us to urge a major review of secondary social studies education. Specifically, such a review should examine how the nation can enhance student understanding of American political and governmental institutions and the values that underlie the

American system of government. It is important that such a review be comprehensive and that it link learning about institutions, values, and procedures to issues of concern to students in their schools and communities.

Once students have graduated from high school, their civic education becomes a matter of choice rather than a prescribed part of their curriculum. Available data suggest that undergraduates are unlikely to acquire further knowledge of any sort about their country. Sixty-one percent of college seniors polled by the Educational Testing Service, for example, had not taken a college course in any aspect of U.S. history.[25] In the great majority of colleges, moreover, students need not take a basic course in American government. For most undergraduates, contact with government and public service is primarily made through extracurricular activities, summer jobs, and career offices.

School-Based Initiatives in Community Service

Despite the deficiencies in their curricula, educational institutions have acted in recent years to encourage voluntary public service among young people. Across the country, youth service organizations and conservation corps are involving high school and college students in efforts to conserve government lands, tutor inner-city children, or work in homeless shelters and soup kitchens. Volunteer activities on college campuses are gaining momentum as students and administrators spread the spirit of public service. Innovative internships and awards are being designed and implemented to interest students in community work.

These efforts are clearly making an impact; no doubt young people who participate in public service activity change their perspectives in a significant and positive way, both enriching themselves and becoming more responsible and active citizens. In California, for example, the Constitutional Rights Foundation, a nonprofit youth service organization, devotes itself to initiating volunteer activities in high schools. The goal is to develop student leadership skills and self-esteem while building a commitment to public service.

Students, parents, teachers, and members of the communities served by the programs attest to the positive effects of student participation in public service activity. Parents and teachers report better attitudes toward school, self, and others through involvement in Foundation-sponsored programs. When asked how important they thought it was for students to participate in community service, parents overall rated the importance to be 4.6 on a scale of 1 to 5. Even more significantly, students themselves testify to the effects of service:

> Many things bring joy, but there is no feeling like the one I get when an elderly person smiles and says thank you for caring, or a child beams when he beats you at musical chairs. I'll continue my community work long after high school.

> When the teachers started to tell us that we could change the world to make it better, I couldn't see it. But I think now that maybe we can make the world better. . . . [Y]ou need to start someplace, even if it's just cleaning the street and the gang stuff [graffiti].[26]

Although extensive evaluations have not been made of most college programs, campus officials as well as students affirm their importance. Predictably, leadership is important in expanding these opportunities. Campus Compact, a consortium of more than 100 college and university presidents dedicated to encouraging public service on their campuses, surveyed its members to assess the degree of existing public service activity. Among the conclusions of the final report was the observation that "the best incentive for public service seems to be a commitment to service on the part of the institution from the president on down. . . . Strong institutional support for public service results in increased levels of student participation in service."[27]

Congressional Proposals for Community Service

The growing interest in community service has reached the highest levels of government. Indeed, several proposals before the 100th Congress attempted to encourage involvement in public service and to increase citizenship awareness:

• A youth service bill, sponsored by Representative Leon E. Panetta, would provide federally sponsored youth service programs in both conservation and social service areas. These programs would target underprivileged youth (aged 16 to 24) and pay them (approximately) minimum wage salaries plus educational scholarships in compensation for their work. Although employment of underprivileged youth is clearly an important rationale for the proposal, emphasis is given also to the importance of facilitating public service opportunities for the young in general. As Representative Panetta put it, "A national voluntary youth service and conservation program, especially one with an education component such as is included in our amendment, could go a long way toward encouraging college students to do public service work, during and after their formal education."[28]

• A mandatory service bill, sponsored by Representative Robert Torricelli, would require all young people to perform one year of some kind of national service, to be completed between the ages of 18 and 25. The program would be run by a national service agency though jobs would be provided and supervised at the state and local level. Students would be able to choose between military and civilian service; for the latter, a wide variety of options, serving health, social, or educational needs, would be available.

Two other proposals offer different versions of the idea of financial assistance for education in exchange for public service:

• A proposal by Senator Claiborne Pell would require two years of community service before college at modest pay ($600 per month) in exchange for two years of financial aid for college, paid by the government to a maximum of $7,200 each year.

• The Democratic Leadership Council has proposed creation of a Citizens Corps in which civilian or military service would be compensated with subsistence wages plus "national service vouchers." These vouchers would be redeemable for one of three purposes: to defray the cost of college, to fund vocational or job training, or to make a down payment on a home. Under this proposal, existing federal educational loans and grants would be phased out and replaced by national service, although especially needy students would be able to supplement their vouchers with loans. The voucher system would be able to offer more aid to students than existing federal grants and loans. The Democratic Leadership Council's intent is to "make federal aid a magnet for broad participation in the Citizens Corps."

The proliferation of these legislative proposals illustrates how awareness of the public service problem has grown. Each of the proposals has merit in that it would encourage valuable forms of community service. The proposals also have the laudable aims of increasing citizenship awareness and fostering an interest in making a difference through public service. We have not attempted to evaluate the details of each of these proposals. Nevertheless, we offer a word of caution regarding the notion of mandatory public service, found both in the mandatory service bill proposal and in the requirement of the Democratic Leadership Council that students engage in public service in order to qualify for educational grants. Such proposals would not encourage, but instead would require, participation in public service. The risk is that requirements of this kind will produce a community service corps too large to be administered effectively while arousing resentment in a substantial fraction of the participants. Such resentment may be communicated to others in ways that poison the attitudes of all participants and thus do far more harm than the current lack of civic awareness.

From Community Service to Careers in Government

Students who participate in community service activities do not automatically think more seriously about a government career. Community service may increase one's desire to help others and expand one's awareness of social problems, but more must be done if students are to pursue their civic interests by seeking to work for the government. Schools can help make this connection by use of television programs on government activities, by field trips, and by active encouragement of student government. Colleges can do their part by strengthening their curricular offerings and by organizing a variety of extracurricular activities that acquaint their students with the opportunities government provides to address important social problems. Speeches by public figures, opportunities to participate in meaningful student government, and internships in federal agencies and in legislative offices can all play a useful role. Finally, the federal government can assist these efforts by expanding student employment, particularly in hard-to-reach disciplines such as computer science and by providing more internships, especially through the Presidential Management Internship Program.

An example of the type of initiative made possible by strong campus leadership is the effort made at Stanford University in recent years following a report that demonstrated a low rate of student participation in public service activities. Stanford took a number of steps not only to increase student involvement in community service but also to stimulate interest in government as well. For example, the university created a program that established a mini-campus, in Washington, D.C., where students spend a semester simultaneously taking government policy-oriented seminars with resident faculty and participating in government internships. Stanford also inaugurated the John Gardner Fellowship, a postgraduate award that supports several students for a year's internship with a prominent civil servant who acts as mentor.

Concrete results have only just begun to emerge from these initiatives, but early returns are promising. Stanford reports that 70 graduates, or approximately 5 percent of the class of 1988, are currently working for the federal government, compared with an average of roughly 2 percent reported by respondents of other colleges in our survey.[29]

To attract students to government careers, however, will require much more vigorous efforts not only by universities but also by the federal government. We turn, therefore, to a brief review of current recruiting practices on the part of federal agencies.

Government Recruitment Efforts

It was the unanimous opinion of college career counselors whom we surveyed that the federal government is falling far short of the private sector in its on-campus recruiting. Respondents stressed the low visibility of government opportunities, poor recruiting materials, unenthusiastic representatives, and long waiting periods for hiring that characterize government recruitment. The following comments suggest current perceptions on campus:

Application forms and procedures...are currently so illogically burdensome that even local agency representatives try to find ways around the system.... Many students are dissuaded by this image of needless bureaucracy.

Students are often frustrated by the fact that the on-campus recruiter usually does not have the power to make hiring decisions.

The materials describing government jobs are a disaster! All they talk about is job security, pay, and obligations.... [They must] tell what is attractive about a job, why someone would enjoy it, what future opportunities would be possible.[30]

As far as volume of recruiting is concerned, a comparison between governmental and private recruiting activity at Harvard, the Massachusets Institute of Technology (MIT), and the University of Wisconsin reveals the degrees to which the government is out-recruited at these schools. At Harvard, the 244 organizations—public and private—that recruited in 1987 held a total of 3,386 interviews with undergraduates. Of those interviews, government agencies held only 20 (compared with 1,388 by investment banks).[31] More than 400 public and private organizations recruited at MIT in that year, of which only 19 were government agencies—despite a widespread and much-discussed shortage of scientists in the federal government.[32] Similarly, 112 organizations recruited at Wisconsin, of which 15 were government, social service, or community organizations.[33]

Our questionnaire, which asked respondents to list the government agencies that recruit at their campuses, revealed that only a few agencies visit a large number of schools—most notably the Central Intelligence Agency (CIA), followed by the Peace Corps. Although a large number of agencies recruit somewhere, very few had been to more than a quarter of the 40 schools surveyed.[34]

When asked how they thought the government could improve its recruitment of students, career counselors made a wide variety of recommendations, that fall into three basic categories.

First, government needs to improve the quality of its recruiting and visibility on campus and act to use more creative advertising; send more professional and more enthusiastic representatives to campuses; participate more in prerecruiting efforts, such as career days or campus visits to talk with faculty; encourage more direct contact with career center directors; and make informational campus visits to discuss public service possibilities in lectures or seminars.

Second, government agencies should have the authority to offer a variety of financial incentives that could provide more paid summer jobs and internships; offer tuition reimbursement for college graduates; and offer scholarship incentives for eventual hires.

Third, government agencies must work to increase access to existing jobs with efforts to centralize and disseminate information about job openings; hasten and simplify application procedures; and allow on-the-spot job offers to be made.

When asked about recruiting initiatives at their agencies, several personnel directors said that they had begun to combat the problem of maintaining quality with new recruiting strategies. One agency has started to offer "faculty tours" of its scientific facilities to encourage professors to interest their students in the agency's work. Others do targeted recruiting to reach minorities, remote areas of the country, or students still in high school. Some agencies report they are making greater use of line managers in recruiting, particularly in technical fields. Line managers may better convey the excitement and possibilities of government work and excite student interest. Every agency that reported conducting aggressive, creative recruiting campaigns also reported success in attracting what they judged to be higher quality employees.

The Office of Personnel Management has launched initiatives to address two of the most serious recruitment obstacles: the lack of visibility and accessibility of most government agencies to college students, and the slow, bureaucratic hiring process. The newly developed "Career America" brochure offers an upbeat description of various government jobs (from engineering to arts and information), information about whom to contact for each job type, and a forecast of employment prospects. The accessible prose, attractive layout, and positive quotations from current employees are clearly designed to attract the attention of college students and to counter the poor image of government bureaucracy and ineffectiveness.

In addition, OPM is taking steps to decentralize and speed up the hiring process. A new proposal would allow recruiters to make on-the-spot job offers to candidates with high college grade point averages. The OPM also intends to accelerate or waive exam-taking for certain jobs, allowing speedier offers to be made in many fields, and to delegate examining authority in certain situations.

In addition, Representative Patricia Schroeder has introduced a proposal that addresses directly the problem of recruiting able young people to federal service. The draft Excellence in Government Act would create a fellowship program for aspiring civil servants modeled after the military Reserve Officer's Training Corps (ROTC). The merit-based fellowship would provide tuition, books and study supplies, and a monthly stipend for college and graduate students in exchange for government service in the summers and upon graduation. The 1,000 fellowship recipients each year would be selected to fill specific needs of the federal government and would be placed in federal jobs upon graduation, where they would be required to serve for at least twice the period for which they received the fellowship. The program would be administered by OPM.

Implementation of such a program will require close cooperation between OPM and participating agencies to match student backgrounds with agency needs. But the proposal has merit and deserves support.

With these new proposals, the federal government is beginning to respond realistically to current recruiting and hiring problems. Further possibilities exist to open new lines of communication with students through the use of free video cassettes portraying opportunities in government service, state and local job banks, electronic bulletin boards posting job openings, and the like. The OPM's own assessment of the need eloquently sums up our findings:

> Increasingly, the people we need are not shopping. They are being pursued by aggressive employers. . . . Federal employers will increasingly need to actively seek effective people, not passively wait for them to apply to a central hiring hall to be examined and referred.[35]

Although the initiatives and proposals sketched above are encouraging, most are in the proposal stage and none has been fully implemented. It will require a steadfast commitment to see them through. Too often in recent years, recruiting initiatives have been deferred on grounds of political transition or budgetary retrenchment. The nation must not further delay an aggressive and imaginative assault on the problem.

EDUCATION AND TRAINING FOR FEDERAL GOVERNMENT CAREERS

In a typical year, 60,000 to 70,000 permanent white-collar employees join the federal civil service.[36] About half are professional and administrative employees, most with college degrees and many with advanced training in the natural and social sciences, engineering, law, medicine and other fields. (The remaining entrants are in the technical support and clerical ranks.)

Data on the occupational fields and educational level of entrants to the professional and administrative ranks of the federal government make clear that this segment of the federal work force is highly educated (Table 2). More than 75 percent of entrants to the federal professional and administrative ranks have college degrees. And 31 percent of all federal employees have college degrees, compared with 23 percent of the overall U.S. workforce.[37]

Selected data indicate the academic backgrounds of those permanent, full-time professional and administrative staff hired in 1987 who had college or advanced degrees (Table 3).[38] What may seem surprising at first glance is how few of these employees have had specific training for government, that is, majored in fields such as public administration, government, or political science. Only 302 of the new employees hired in 1987 had degrees in public administration, and only 506 had degrees in political science or government. Together, 2.7 percent of new entrants had degrees in these fields, while 23.9 percent of the entrants had studied business administration or accounting.

The figures in Tables 2 and 3 reflect the specialized focus of much of the federal workforce. In particular, large numbers of engineers and scientists are required for agencies such as the Departments of Defense, Energy, and Health and Human Services as well as for agencies such as the National Aeronautics and Space Administration, the National Institute of Standards and Technology, the National Oceanographic and Atmospheric Administration, and the Environmental Protection Agency. In most instances, the federal government recruits people for specific slots in specific agencies. The suitability of candidates is most often judged by the requirements of a specific job, for example, by the training needed to be a missile flight control electronics engineer or a personnel classification specialist. In short, the federal government is a government of specialists, most of whom remain with a single agency for the bulk of their careers.[39]

This orientation persists even though it is well documented that top management jobs

Table 2
Occupational Field of New Professional and Administrative Entrants to Federal Service (1987)

Occupational Field	Professional Positions Highest Academic Degree				Administrative Positions Highest Academic Degree			
	# of New Entrants	BA	MA	Ph.D.	# of New Entrants	BA	MA	Ph.D.
Social Science	811	21%	49%	24%	658	52%	18%	2%
General Administration and Clerical	–	–	–	–	3,528	50%	20%	1%
Biological Science + Health Science	5,027	56%	13%	4%	62	40%	40%	5%
Accounting + Budget	4,041	77%	8%	–	1,257	81%	11%	–
Engineering	7,206	82%	13%	2%	41	51%	15%	–
Law	1,584	82%	13%	3%	280	7%	11%	1%
Business + Industry	–	–	–	–	2,247	62%	12%	1%
Physical Science	978	48%	26%	23%	14	71%	7%	–
Education	1,168	43%	51%	4%	543	21%	19%	3%
Investigations	–	–	–	–	2,643	67%	9%	–
Transportation	–	–	–	–	2,612	29%	2%	–
All other Fields	1,107	64%	26%	6%	2,647	–	–	–
All Hires	21,922	70%	17%	4%	16,532	51%	12%	1%

Source: Dr. Philip Schneider and Ralph Nenni, U.S. Office of Personnel Management, Workforce Information Branch. Communications to Task Force dated September 23, 1988.

in the federal government have a high degree of functional similarity.[40] And, although there is little doubt that management in government is quite different from management in the private sector,41 the federal personnel system seems to take little note of this, recruiting far more graduates from business programs than from programs in public administration or government.

The result is a federal workforce that may be well trained to perform specific tasks but is often untutored in the most basic structural, procedural, and institutional knowledge of government. Because many federal careers are relatively narrow, it is possible for officials to rise to senior executive levels without acquiring any real understanding about how key institutions such as Congress, the White House, or central overhead agencies (the Office of Management and Budget, the General Services Administration, and OPM) actually operate. The lack of sophisticated appreciation for public management and the nature of government often contributes to misunderstandings, friction, and waste when career officials encounter political appointees, Congressional staff, and other interests in the policy arena. Too often, career officials become disillusioned or cynical, attributing crass motives to individuals and institutions they do not understand.[42] Such disillusionment can have serious consequences for the productivity and commitment of these officials and may undermine the morale of their organizations as well.

This deficiency might be remedied by recruiting larger numbers of workers who have specialized in the study of government or public administration. Alternatively, one might look to the training and development of specialists in government who are preparing to move into supervisory and managerial roles. It is to these two topics that we now turn.

Table 3
Selected Academic Backgrounds of New Entrants to Federal Professional and Administrative Positions (1987)

Academic Field	With College or Advanced Degrees	% of Those with Degrees
Library Science	102	0.3%
Architecture	148	0.5%
Fine Arts	157	0.5%
Home Economics	160	0.5%
Public Administration	302	1.0%
Communications	332	1.1%
Literature/Letters	363	1.2%
Mathematics and Statistics	467	1.6%
Political Science and Government	506	1.7%
Psychology	578	1.9%
Computer and Information Science	731	2.4%
Biological Sciences	879	2.9%
Physical Sciences	1,080	3.6%
Health Professions	2,665	8.9%
Engineering	6,801	22.7%
Business and Accounting	7,154	23.9%

Source: Dr. Philip Schneider and Ralph Nenni, Office of Personnel Management, Workforce Information Branch. Communications to Task Force dated September 23, 1988.

University Training in Public Affairs

More than 200 programs in institutions of higher learning teach public administration and policy analysis to prepare young and mid-level professionals for careers in public service. Many of these programs are designed to educate successful executives and leaders of the government's career service. What role do they actually play in preparing people for government careers?

Undergraduate Programs in Public Affairs

Fewer than one-third of the 200 academic programs in public affairs and administration offer instruction at the undergraduate level. These programs enroll just over 5,000 undergraduates in four-year colleges and universities around the country. Of these students, it is estimated that fewer than 5 percent go on to careers in the federal government. One survey estimates that the top three outlets for graduates of these programs are business (23 percent), graduate study (19 percent), and local or municipal government (19 percent).[43]

There appear to be several different kinds of undergraduate programs for public service. One group, characterized by Princeton's Woodrow Wilson School and Duke's Institute for Policy Sciences, offers courses rooted in traditional academic disciplines such as economics, history, and political science, but with a strong public policy or public affairs orientation. Many have an interdisciplinary focus and supplement discipline-based work with special projects, seminars, and internships to provide integration and practical experience.

Other schools, such as the University of Southern California or Indiana University, offer a full concentration in public administration. After two years of liberal arts studies, students take traditional courses in budgeting, personnel, planning, and the like, often coupled with a focus on a particular policy area, such as the environment, criminal justice, or social services. These programs are found where there are strong schools or departments of public administration—virtually all with graduate programs—for which the undergraduate programs are important adjuncts and sources of potential students.

Other programs form a part of undergraduate political science majors. In these programs students mix public administration courses with traditional political science offerings in a liberal arts context.

A fourth group of programs, often the most vocationally oriented, is found in schools of business or management. A number of these combine offerings in business and public administration. Their curricula emphasize professional skills such as accounting, finance, personnel, and organizational behavior and management.

Most of the undergraduate programs in public affairs begin from a liberal arts base.[44] We endorse such an orientation. Further, we believe it important that programs educating young people for public affairs address the structure, institutions, history, and underlying political philosophy of American government. The previously noted weaknesses in civic education and the lack of specific preparation for government on the part of so many public employees make it all the more important that public affairs programs ensure that their graduates are well versed in the American political system.

The government and our society will also benefit if public officials have a broad acquaintance with different fields, ideas, and disciplines. Young people who would be administrators in public agencies need familiarity with history, arts and literature, politics, and science and technology as well as a knowledge of the techniques of budgeting or personnel administration. A sound undergraduate base in the liberal arts is a widely acknowledged method of developing the habits of mind, conceptual ability, and beginnings of judgment necessary for success in a professional career.

A second point deserves mention. In view of current hiring practices, at least at the federal level, there may be an important secondary mission for those undergraduate public administration programs with a strong base in American history, government and politics. More than 60 percent of new federal employees join the government with a B.A. or a B.S. degrees. As the data in Tables 2 and 3 suggest, coursework in undergraduate public affairs programs could make a material contribution to the education of students majoring in engineering, science, or business programs who plan public sector careers. Public administration educators should consider whether they might offer a minor in public affairs for students in other departments. Federal officials should look with favor on applicants who have demonstrated mastery of a special field coupled with the study of public affairs. Indeed, because many arenas in society interact with and are influenced by government action, a minor in public affairs could be useful to students planning careers in fields such as law, business, science, and education.

Graduate Training in Public Affairs

Graduate training in public affairs is a relatively recent addition to professional education in the United States. Although medical schools were founded in the 18th century, law schools in the 19th century, and business schools early in the 20th century, a mere handful of graduate schools in public affairs were in operation at the end of World War II. Indeed, as recently as 1960, only about a dozen such programs existed. Since then, the number of programs has grown rapidly, particularly during the 1960s and 1970s, following the expansion of government at all levels.

Today, there are over 200 graduate programs in public policy, public administration, and public affairs. Most of them offer master's degrees to young people seeking careers in public service. A brief account of enrollment trends reveals that, after a period of dramatic growth, numbers have fallen off somewhat in recent years (Table 4).

Public affairs programs exist in a variety of institutional settings. About one-third of them are housed in academic departments of political science; another one-third are separate departments of public administration or public affairs within larger faculties, for example, in a college of arts and sciences; about 15 percent of the programs exist as separate professional schools; and the remainder are combined with programs in business, management, or other fields.

Table 4
Recent Trends in Public Affairs Education*

	1973	1975	1979	1981	1985	1987
Number of Graduate Programs	101	138	185	192	193	208
Enrollment/Master's Program	10,975	20,254	28,191	24,419	22,872	23,311
% Full-time Students	NA	NA	37%	35%	37%	37%
% Pre-Service	NA	NA	26%	31%	30%	25%
Master's Degrees Granted	2,403	4,545	5,644	6,736	6,300	6,428
% Placed in Federal, State or Local Government	NA	NA	73%	66%	55%	61%
(Federal Placements)	NA	NA	(19)	(17)	(16)	(21)

*National Association of Schools of Public Affairs and Administration 1988 Annual Report

Despite their different institutional homes, what unites these programs is their focus on professional education with a master's degree in public administration (in some schools the degree is in public affairs or public policy) as the principal product. The National Association of Public Affairs Schools states that "the purpose of the professional master's degree in public affairs and administration is to prepare individuals for positions of leadership in public service."[45]

Something of a split in the field exists between programs that serve different target audiences. The first group educates predominantly full-time, pre-career students, most of whom complete their degrees. The second group of schools trains largely part-time, in-service professionals, a smaller fraction of whom obtain their degrees. In the latter category are many professionals, in fields such as social service and criminal justice, who take graduate coursework in public administration to help them qualify for promotion or higher pay.

There is also a distinction between the newer public policy programs and the more traditional public administration programs. Public policy programs emerged in the late 1960s and early 1970s. These programs focused their initial training on the "science" of policy choice, emphasizing criteria of efficiency and utility. Their intellectual roots were mainly in economics, and their inspiration owes much to the operations research work of the RAND Corporation and then Secretary of Defense Robert McNamara's emphasis on systems analysis as a tool to aid public decisionmaking.

Many of the traditional public administration programs trace their mission back to Woodrow Wilson's call for a science of administration. Early leadership and initial inspiration came from the diverse group of great scholar-practitioners of the 1930s such as Louis Brownlow, Leonard White, Charles Merriam, and Luther Gulick. Many of these programs began as offshoots of political science departments and mix political science courses with training in the traditional skills of administration, such as planning, organizing, budgeting, and personnel.

In the past decade, the distinction between the policy schools and public administration has begun to blur; many public administration programs have incorporated courses in policy analysis, and many public policy programs include training in administration and management. Graduates of both kinds of programs find jobs in federal, state, and local government, business, and nonprofit institutions. The government portion of the market may have diminished somewhat since a long period of growth in government employment ended in the late 1970s. More recently, tax reductions, faltering local economies, and federal cutbacks in domestic spending have all contributed to some tightness in the government job market.

Only a few hundred of the graduates of these programs take career positions in the federal civil service. Others find employment in Congressional staff positions, as assistants to political appointees, and with the military. Larger numbers of graduates take initial jobs in state and local government and, as Table 3 suggests, a significant fraction of those receiving degrees are already in government service.[46]

The field of public affairs has grown dramatically in the past 25 years. It is only beginning to stand securely alongside law, medicine, and business. Its schools and programs still face a number of important issues.

First, public administration and public policy are relatively new career options for prospective students. Many deans and admissions directors say that the real challenge lies in persuading students to seek public affairs education instead of graduate study in business or law. Indeed, business and law enrollments grew at a faster rate than public affairs during the early 1980s (although growth in applications to schools of law and business also seem to have slowed in the past few years).

Second, public administration and public policy programs must establish close working relationships with professionals in government, business, and the nonprofit sector. Such relationships are particularly important because the field of public affairs stands in need of much work on both empirical and theoretical dimensions of public affairs. Close relationships with public agencies can facilitate faculty research and development, as well as ensure that government officials are familiar with the benefits of public affairs training.

Third, a number of programs need strong support on their campuses. Many are relatively small (with fewer than 10 faculty) and of recent vintage. Such programs are vulnerable to modest shifts in enrollments and student interest. Moreover, they may find it hard to compete successfully for the time, resources, and attention of university leadership.

Fourth, many of the programs in their teaching and research are remote from the hurly-burly of practice, particularly at the higher levels of government, where elected and appointed political officials hold sway. Because politicians and political appointees come from a wide variety of backgrounds, they hold no particular brief for schools of public affairs. Conversely, few schools have embraced the issues facing political leaders as a focal point for research or teaching. Such institutions may not appear to be meeting perceived needs or concerns of top governmental officials, and support for these schools may consequently be lacking.

Important issues relating to graduate education in public affairs also arise for government. First, dozens of vigorous programs are completed by able young people who can and should aspire to federal careers. Government needs to take advantage of the dramatic change in the quality and quantity of students who are completing such programs and seeking careers in public service.

Second, as already suggested, the federal personnel system seems to offer relatively few opportunities for graduates of public affairs programs. Of some 822,000 professional and administrative employees in the federal civil service, only 7,699 (0.9 percent) have public administration academic backgrounds.[47] A total of 272 members (4 percent) of the Senior Executive Service hold public administration degrees. In a real sense, the federal government is not showing an interest in the general analytic and administrative skills these programs teach. (The principal exception is the Presidential Management Intern [PMI] program, initiated when a former dean of public administration headed OPM).[48]

Third, government has not sought to take advantage of the new capacity represented by public affairs programs to extend and support research on government operations, management, and policymaking. Despite the high cost of government operations and the enormous stakes involved in many decisions, federal agencies have taken relatively few initiatives to promote research about their own activities.

These concerns may simply reflect the relative immaturity of the field. After all, the dramatic growth in government's size and role has come only since World War II. Only a dozen public administration programs were in being as recently as 1960. Many of the most vital programs are of even more recent vintage. Growing pains are not unique to programs of public policy and administration. It took perhaps a half-century for the concept of general management[49] in business to become fully recognized and accepted in practice and in the teaching of business schools.[50] Even today, only 30 percent of the chief executive officers of U.S. corporations hold a master's degree in business administration, although the proportion is rising steadily.[51]

The business example should be instructive for public affairs schools. Over the past two decades, business faculties have witnessed a steady growth in demand for their training. An important ingredient in building the market for business training has been the success of short executive education programs for top corporate leaders. These programs strengthen the managerial skills of corporate executives while showcasing business school faculty and curricula. They have helped to establish credibility for graduate business training and to build relationships between corporations and business schools.

We believe the business experience with executive education should be closely examined by schools of public affairs. Of course, the success of any ventures in executive training for public officials will depend importantly on government training policies. It is to the question of government training that we now turn.

GOVERNMENT TRAINING AND DEVELOPMENT

If few employees have received any formal training or preparation for working in the distinctive arena of public service, what efforts does the government make to equip its personnel to discharge their duties with efficiency and dispatch? What can one say about the quality and quantity of government programs for the training and development of its own employees?

Interviews with federal training officials suggest that many agencies and their leadership lack clarity about the purposes, costs, and benefits of training and development for their employees.[52] We suggest that at least the following three purposes might usefully be kept in mind:

Proficiency on the Job

Most early training takes place on the job, as the new employee begins to learn from practical experience about organizational structure, policies, procedures, personalities, products, and so on. In most jobs, however, formal training is also provided at the outset to equip employees with basic skills and knowledge too complicated to learn at work. In other cases, such early training can accelerate learning and adaptation to changing policies, procedures, and technology while providing an opportunity to reinforce professional norms and values and to reflect and improve upon current habits and practices.[53]

Training for Renewal

Studies of productivity invariably reach the conclusion that worker commitment is the single most important ingredient in the productive functioning of complex organizations.[54] This insight has led many progressive organizations to participate in educational programs that do not seem to relate directly to the business or tasks at hand. In the 1920s, for example, noted executive and scholar Chester Barnard, then in the Bell system, developed a special course in the humanities at the University of Pennsylvania for promising young telephone executives.[55] Some organizations, such as IBM, require that employees participate annually in some form of continuing education, whether it be an Outward Bound adventure or a humanities seminar. The object is to stimulate and broaden the employee in the expectation that he or she will return to work with renewed vigor and new insights.

Recent years have also seen a dramatic expansion in corporate programs in more practical areas of personal concern such as employee health promotion and disease prevention, personal finance, stress management, and so on. Such programs recognize that improvements in employee physical, emotional, and financial well-being pay long-run dividends in worker productivity and commitment.

Training for Growth and Executive Development

In all organizations, there is a continuing need to prepare promising specialists to step into managerial and executive leadership roles. The task of developing executives has received particular emphasis in large corporations, which have long believed that the development of managerial and executive talent is a vital organizational task.[56] Special attention is paid to the recruitment, training, and assignment of future managers and corporate leaders. Programs to develop such potential managers emphasize a balance between formal training and on-the-job experience, headquarters and field assignments, and staff and line positions as well as opportunities for service and visibility with top corporate officers.

The armed services take a similar approach to the development of officers. Frequent job rotations provide future military leaders with broad perspective on the service and its operations. Challenging command assignments are interspersed with formal opportunities for training and reflection. In both corporate and military settings, the development of executive talent is the product of systematic career management programs that produce a stream of highly qualified candidates for top jobs.

Training in the Civil Service

Training in the federal Civil Service runs the gamut from remedial development of basic clerical and office skills to advanced programs for senior executives. Most federal agencies have written training policies, and all operate or support some training activities for their employees. Although OPM sets overall policy and provides general guidance, agencies are free to develop their own plans, design their own programs, and allocate resources as necessary to meet their perceived needs. There are only a few common points in the careers of government employees where most agencies provide for regular training:

- The OPM requires that all agencies "consider" the training needs of employees newly assigned to supervisory roles. Most agencies follow OPM guidelines and provide newly appointed supervisors with 80 hours of supervisory training.[57] In some instances the supervisory training is provided through OPM programs; in other instances agencies conduct their own in-house programs using agency employees or contracted instructors.

- The OPM requires that virtually all candidates for senior executive service positions complete a two-week OPM executive development course, or an acceptable substitute. These mandated programs have become a staple offering of OPM's three executive seminar centers. In addition, candidates for and incumbent members of the Senior Executive Service may participate in one of the residential programs of the Federal Executive Institute (FEI), located in Charlottesville, Virginia. The FEI program is perhaps the only experience that bonds senior members of the civil service, providing them with some measure of unity and common experience.

The most recent published estimates report that total expenditures on federal training are about $550 million for 2.2 million federal civilian workers (excluding the U.S. Postal Service). This sum amounts to approximately 0.8 percent of the amount spent on federal payroll. In contrast, one estimate for all Fortune 500 firms places training expenditures at 3.3 percent of payroll, and many progressive and successful firms spend 5 to 10 percent of payroll on employee training and development.

The OPM regularly reports government-wide training statistics for federal agencies; its figures for fiscal year 1985 were taken to represent a typical year (Table 5). Clearly, only about half of all government employees have any training at all in a typical year. Those who participate average approximately two instances of training apiece, spending six to seven days altogether. The OPM estimates that the cost per instance of training is about $325. Averages, however, mask significant variation among agencies. For example, the Internal Revenue Service (IRS) has relatively extensive training and development activities. Although the rest of the federal civilian workforce averages about three-quarters of a training instance per person per year, the IRS average is three times greater. The IRS estimates that it spends about 8 percent of payroll on training, a rate 10 times higher than the rest of the federal government. The IRS requires all of its professional employees to receive at least 40 hours of continuing professional education each year.[58] At the other end of the spectrum is the tiny U.S. Arms Control and Disarmament Agency, which reports that it spent a total of $26,000 (about 0.01 percent of the agency budget) on training in fiscal year 1987.

Table 5
FY 1985 Federal Training*

	Instances of Training	Hours per Instance	Employees Trained	Total Employees in Pool	% of Employees Trained in FY '85
Executives (SES or Equivalent)	7,033	29	3,695	8,446	44%
Managers/ Supervisors	237,380	30	152,365	263,755	58%
Nonsupervisory Personnel	1,449,094	30	755,087	1,830,100	41%

*U.S. Office of Personnel Management

Several developments are worthy of note:

• A number of agencies, such as the Federal Aviation Administration, the IRS, the Foreign Service Institute, CIA, and the Naval Air Systems Command, have developed in-house training programs that prepare their employees for the special challenges and complexities associated with their particular mission.

• The past few years have also seen efforts to collaborate across bureaus and departments to improve opportunities for training. For example, the Treasury Executive Institute (TEI) conducts short training programs for constituent agencies of the department to address issues of common concern that cross agency boundaries. Such programs unquestionably contribute to building stronger departmental identity. The Army has recently launched a management staff college, attempting to emulate for its civilians the kind of service-wide training that is routinely available to the uniformed military.

• Some agencies have made training a requirement, as they see its connection to maintaining the capacity of their professional workforce. For example, the Comptroller General has mandated that all government audit staff must complete 80 hours of continuing education in each two-year period.[60]

- Finally, the Federal Executive Institute (FEI), which opened in 1968, continues to offer programs for senior civil service managers and members of the Senior Executive Service. The FEI has come through a turbulent period and has recently acquired new leadership and revised its programs. Currently it enrolls 800 to 900 federal managers at the GS-15 and Senior Executive Service (SES) levels each year.

Although one can point to some signs of progress in federal training and development, an undercurrent of dissatisfaction with these efforts remains. The following criticisms occur most frequently:

- With a handful of exceptions, federal training is short-term in its focus, duration, and effects. Although training "instances" doubled between fiscal year 1975 and fiscal year 1985, this growth was accomplished without increasing the real dollars spent on training. The apparent gains, therefore, have only been achieved by reducing the length of training, eliminating most long-term programs, and spreading the limited dollars so thin that they are likely to generate limited value.

- Federal expenditures on training are absurdly low, if training is understood to be an element of investment for growth and productivity.[61] The federal government spends about three-quarters of 1 percent of its payroll dollars on training. In contrast, many of the top-rated companies spend as much as 10 percent of payroll for this purpose, while the military devotes as much as 15 to 20 percent of its payroll dollars to this goal. In our interviews, federal training directors attributed the low investment in training and development to the lack of strategic planning by agency leaders (both political and career) and to the parochial perspectives of many top careerists, who are themselves the product of narrow career paths.

- In most instances, agencies lack strategic plans for employee development and training. With a few exceptions, such as IRS and EPA, federal training is voluntary, individually focused, and job-specific and bears little discernible relation to major agency objectives and mission.[62]

Apart from these deficiencies in training, the whole federal approach to management development is weak in several respects:

- First, employees are largely recruited as specialists; there is little recruiting on broad measures of ability, particularly aptitude (and interest) in management.

- Second, career paths are narrow, "tunneled through narrow organizational tubes"[63] so that civil servants have little opportunity to gain breadth or managerial perspective.

- Third, promotions—even to top executive positions—are largely based on programmatic or policy expertise, rather than on general management ability or leadership potential. It is particularly noteworthy that only about one in five individuals appointed to SES jobs has participated in agency SES candidate development programs.[64]

- Fourth, few of those joining government and pursuing government careers have any formal training in government, political science, or public administration.

• Finally, federal agencies have not had great success in developing and promoting women and minorities into senior executive positions, despite their ample numbers in the federal workforce. The excellent performance of a few institutions, such as the U.S. Army, provides a standard to judge the results of other federal agencies.[65]

In view of these well-documented aspects of the federal personnel system, coupled with the unique and frustrating environment of federal management, one might expect to see an aggressive and ambitious program of training and management development. In fact, a number of agencies do have solid programs for executive development, including the Forest Service, EPA, IRS, and others. But too many agencies act as if a few weeks at a seminar is all that is needed to turn a career specialist into a federal executive.

The federal government does a reasonably good job of dealing with specific workplace issues, such as the introduction of new technology or the implementation of new legislation or regulations. This conclusion is consistent with the results of our interviews with many federal training officials, who say that they orient most of their training toward "immediate, short-term, on-the-job returns." As the focus of training moves from specific, narrowly defined job skills, however, toward developing the subtler skills and behaviors of management and leadership, evaluations become less flattering. About 5 percent of federal training expenditures are devoted to managerial and executive training. In contrast, the uniformed military and many large businesses combine a budget for formal executive training that is several times larger, with extensive programs of rotation and successively more responsible assignments aimed at developing qualified groups of candidates for top management and leadership positions.

Marver Bernstein, a wise and thoughtful observer of federal affairs for more than four decades, put these problems in a broader perspective:

> Training of government employees tends to flourish best in a climate of respect for careers in public service. Several factors serve to encourage a commitment to training. They include a patent understanding that payoffs in training are long-term, not short-term; a willingness to stimulate and sustain linkages to universities devoting major resources to education for the public service; a conscious recognition that most specialists in technical and professional fields are more likely to become effective managers if they undergo training for managerial responsibilities; and a lively expectation, underlined dramatically by our recent history, that new technology and scientific discoveries as well as transforming changes in the nation's economy, work force, and population mix place a premium on training to overcome obsolescence and to anticipate the immediate future. When these conditions are markedly absent, as they have been in the 1980s, the commitment to training becomes marginal at best.[66]

Although the weaknesses of federal training are real, the opportunities for improvement are obvious. A substantial investment in training, a conscious effort to broaden assignments, and a focus on building managerial capacity could all make a positive contribution to the capacity of future federal executives to work more effectively in a challenging environment.

The University Role in Mid-Career Education

The federal government has not moved to take advantage of the dramatic growth in higher education programs devoted to public administration and public affairs. Just the opposite is true. Several years ago, OPM abolished its university relations office, eliminated most university research on personnel and management issues, and terminated the Education for Public Management Program, the only government-wide, long-term, university-based training program. Such actions have been openly hostile to the university community at a time when their potential contribution to government training and management is substantial and growing.

Historically, something of a mismatch has also existed between federal policies and programs for mid-career and executive education and those of most universities and schools of public affairs. The reasons are worth restating.

First, federal law, regulations, and tradition all discourage reliance on the private sector (including the university community) for training and education.[67] In most other policy areas, the federal presumption is that the private sector can and should supply federal needs for goods and services. A decision not to rely on the private sector calls for justification and review. In contrast, federal training policy presumes a reliance on government trainers and facilities. This attitude has made it difficult for even the best university programs to find a federal market.

Second, despite its reliance on in-house resources for training, the federal government does not invest to improve the quality of its programs. There are no major federal institutes with permanent staffs, ongoing research programs, and sustained curriculum development efforts. If the federal government devoted a fraction of 1 percent of its annual budget to management research and curriculum development, universities would flock to Washington with proposals, initiatives, and creative approaches. But the government provides few opportunities for universities to contribute.

Third, government training policies emphasize brief, job-focused training programs to achieve near-term results.[68] Long-term training—which has the character of investment in human capital—has been eliminated from most agencies' budgets. Most universities are skeptical of the intellectual quality of the typical three-day government seminar and are unwilling to get involved. Hence, to the extent that government agencies look outside for assistance, consultants and professional trainers dominate the market.

A recent survey of many public affairs schools found that few of them engage in non-degree mid-level or executive training.[69] Of more than 100 schools surveyed, only a handful had even a single program of at least a week's duration. A number of universities, such as the University of Texas, the University of Washington, Duke University, the University of Colorado, and Carnegie-Mellon University conduct at least one such program. Only one school (Harvard University) appears to have made large-scale mid-career, and executive training for government officials an integral element of its institutional strategy. Harvard's offerings include intensive programs for newly elected members of Congress, newly elected mayors, members of the SES, national security officials, state and local officials, school superintendents, and more.[70]

Universities will need to consider significant issues before initiating mid-career or executive programs for government officials:

• Because they have not established systematic links with the professional community, many schools lack sufficient knowledge about the government marketplace;

• Teaching experienced professional audiences poses a major challenge for many faculty. Seasoned public officials can be demanding and impatient with dull lectures or abstract, theoretical presentations. As a result, schools will have to work with their faculty to improve classroom performance if they are to succeed; and

• Experienced professional audiences bring different expectations and needs to college campuses. Serving a professional audience requires different administrative standards and levels of service, and may require different facilities (classrooms, housing) as well.

Notwithstanding these problems, mid-career and executive programs have the benefit of bringing faculty into regular contact with experienced professionals who may challenge both the faculty's teaching approach and class content. Relationships that evolve from such programs can yield research and professional development opportunities for faculty, and may lead to internships and regular jobs for pre-career students. Most important, such programs are both a crucible for testing faculty ideas and a vehicle for influencing the character and quality of professional practice in government. As a result, both the universities and the government have much to gain from collaborating more actively in the development of these programs.

CONCLUSION AND RECOMMENDATIONS

Government is one of the principal vehicles through which we, as Americans, strive to realize our collective goals and aspirations, whether they are to defend the nation's shores against potential enemies, to prevent the illegal import of drugs, to protect the environment, or to educate our children. In the American system of government, achieving such goals depends on the successful actions of many individuals and institutions in both the public and the private sectors.

As the last decade of the 20th century approaches, there can be little doubt that government needs to attract, develop, and retain professionals of the highest caliber. There are weaknesses, however, in many of government's policies, programs, and procedures that stand in the way of recruiting and retaining the high quality personnel needed by the federal system. It also appears that the nation's political leadership does not fully appreciate the hazards of failing to address the "quiet crisis" in government.

Those in the educational arena can also do more to strengthen the quality of public service. We believe that the nation's education system, including secondary schools and community colleges as well as four-year colleges and universities, can make a material contribution to expand public knowledge, awareness, and understanding of government, to enhance the inclination of young people to pursue public sector careers, and to help the government renew and strengthen its performance through better employee training and development.

To begin with, the nation's secondary schools and community colleges can contribute to a more effective government by doing a better job of preparing young people to be active participants in our democratic process. The nation must find ways to improve the teaching of social studies, civics, and U.S. history and government in schools and colleges. At present, few schools are doing the job they must if young people are to be given a reasonable appreciation of the problems, challenges, opportunities, and responsibilities that come with citizenship in our democratic system. In planning their curricula, colleges and junior colleges do not take sufficient account of these inadequacies in the prior background of their students. If schools and colleges moved to remedy these deficiencies, the nation could expect more of its young people to consider public service in planning their careers.

These considerations lead to our first two recommendations:

RECOMMENDATION 1

The nation must undertake a comprehensive review of social studies education in high schools, asking how a more effective job of preparing young people for citizenship can be done.

Such a review should examine how schools can enhance student understanding of American political and governmental institutions and the framework for democratic government. The goal should be to relate formal learning about institutions, values, and procedures to problems that students care about, and to link activities in the classroom with extracurricular activities of a civic nature, including community service programs, field trips, and student government activities, in order to help students connect classroom learning to their personal interests and experience.

RECOMMENDATION 2

Community colleges and undergraduate institutions must also examine their contribution to the development of informed citizens.

Here the problem is more subtle, but several constructive steps are possible. Many students wish to direct their studies toward vocational ends, and only a minority will elect formal instruction in government. Yet many fields of study encounter issues of public interest which, if properly treated, can spur greater understanding and appreciation of government. Colleges can also assess the knowledge their entering students have of American history, the political system, and institutions of government and try to adjust their curricula to take account of serious gaps and inadequacies. In addition, encouraging students to participate in community service programs can strengthen the sense of civic responsibility and awaken concern for the needs of others.

There is a paradox in the attitudes of American youth toward careers in government. On the one hand, young people today are clearly more concerned with financial security and "getting ahead" professionally than were their predecessors a generation ago. At the same time, there is marked growth of interest in community service among young people all over the country. The problem is that students do not associate government with their impulses to help people and contribute to their community. For too many young people, government seems big, bureaucratic, and boring.

The dramatic awakening of student interest in community service activities presents a real opportunity for the federal government. There is much to be said for expanding existing service programs, such as VISTA, Action, and the Peace Corps, and for recent Congressional proposals to offer support toward the costs of college in exchange for community work. Yet little has been done by government agencies or by educational institutions to link this growing interest in community problems to the possibility of a government career. This conclusion leads us to make a further set of recommendations:

RECOMMENDATION 3

Government agencies must increase their visibility on college and university campuses.

Public officials should visit colleges more frequently. Federal agencies should expand internships (particularly the Presidential Management Internship Program), cooperative programs, and other opportunities to give young people a first-hand look at the possibilities of a government career.

RECOMMENDATION 4

Government agencies must make vivid the challenge and opportunity associated with federal employment.

They should recruit much more extensively, using line managers who can excite student interest in government jobs and careers. They must improve quality of career information.

Federal hiring procedures must be made competitive with the private sector, permitting speedy, responsive decisions rather than long, frustrating delays. To communicate more effectively with students, government officials should experiment with electronic bulletin boards, state and local job banks, free video cassettes on opportunities in public service, and software on how to find jobs in government. Finally, federal agencies must develop active systems of career management to back up promises made on campus and provide opportunities for rapid advancement to those of exceptional ability.

RECOMMENDATION 5

Congress should adopt some form of program modelled on the experience of the Reserve Officers Training Corps to subsidize the college education of a stipulated number of outstanding students in return for federal service.

The Youth Engaged in Service (YES) proposal of President Bush and Representative Schroeder's proposed Excellence in Government Act offer promising examples of this approach.

RECOMMENDATION 6

Universities must give greater visibility to the opportunities for government service.

By offering courses, public events, speeches by public figures, government internships, and the like, schools and programs in public administration and public policy should become magnets for students in all fields of study who have an interest in public affairs. Career placement and counseling offices throughout the university should take the initiative in attracting government recruiters and ensuring that students have access to full information about government careers.

Our remaining recommendations address the need to improve the preparation of those committed to careers of government service. And, we must strengthen the overall management of human resources within the federal government. Today there are significant shortcomings in government training programs. Government agencies spend far too little on training of all kinds and concentrate their efforts too much on meeting immediate, short-term needs. The area of greatest concern is the plainly inadequate attention paid to the development of management and executive leadership in the civil service. Unlike corporations or the armed service, the federal civil service hires specialists almost exclusively. It does not seek able people of broad background and education who are well suited to the integrative tasks of leadership and management, and it does little to prepare promising civil servants for these roles. Employees are promoted largely on the basis of their specialized training or knowledge; a decade of programs to develop candidates for the Senior Executive Service has failed to improve upon this record. These observations lead to our final recommendations:

RECOMMENDATION 7

Colleges should seek to offer more breadth to undergraduates in specialized majors who plan careers of government service.

Many specialized undergraduate programs graduate substantial numbers of students who seek employment in government. These programs should be broadened to require some work on U.S. politics, government institutions, and political philosophy as well as the specialized skills and knowledge needed for particular jobs.

Undergraduate programs and schools of public administration should develop joint courses with such programs and consider offering minors to students specializing in these fields as a way of enlarging their knowledge about government.

RECOMMENDATION 8

Federal agencies should actively recruit and hire graduates from professional schools of public policy and public administration as a source of potential executive talent.

The skills provided by these programs are of considerable value to government agencies. In turn, these schools should establish closer contacts with the government to ensure that their curricula and teaching methods are properly attuned to the long-term career needs of federal officials.

RECOMMENDATION 9

Much greater attention and resources should be devoted to strategic management of human resources with particular emphasis on in-service training and executive development.

Federal training policies should reflect an appropriate balance between short- and long-term needs of government agencies and personnel by developing programs that do not merely concentrate on immediate skill and information requirements, but also provide opportunities to develop the broader knowledge and basic management skills required for positions of greater executive responsibility.

The OPM should adopt a policy requiring regular training for all professional employees. At a minimum, the Comptroller General's standard for government audit employees, which requires 80 hours of continuing professional education every 2 years, could be extended to all civil service professionals. More generally, agency managers in both career and political ranks should come to see that strategic management of personnel is the single highest point of potential leverage in the effort to strengthen government capacity to efficiently meet the needs of its citizens.

RECOMMENDATION 10

Federal agencies should modify their training policies to utilize the potential contributions of the educational community.

There is great opportunity for beneficial collaboration between the university community and the government, especially in the field of short- and medium-term intensive courses for executive-level officials. The government should commit substantial resources to such training programs and permit universities to compete in devising and implementing appropriate offerings.

RECOMMENDATION 11

Schools and faculties of public affairs must respond by vigorous efforts to build effective mid-career programs.

To accomplish this goal, they must reach out aggressively to practitioners to sharpen and refine both their program content and pedagogy to serve the needs of public officials. In so doing, they will discover the contribution that these programs make, not only to the participants, but also to the ability of their faculties to understand the actual problems and needs of those who labor in responsible jobs in public service.

RECOMMENDATION 12

University presidents, chancellors, and deans must make a commitment to improving public service.

As always, leadership is a vital ingredient of institutional progress toward important goals. Experience in several universities has already demonstrated how true this is in the vital tasks of awakening students to the challenges of government and public service and preparing able people to serve more effectively as public officials.

The American experiment in self-government faces a momentous challenge in the last decade of the 20th century. The complexity of the problems confronting society is unprecedented. The range and scope of government responsibilities have never been greater. At the same time, the political and governmental institutions on which the nation depends are fragmented, held in low esteem, and widely distrusted by the American people.

Today, the nation has the opportunity and obligation to do more to prepare young people to meet the challenges of government, both as active citizens and as committed public officials. The nation has the opportunity and obligation to capture the imagination of young people who would help build a more just, safer, and caring society through careers in public life. The nation has the opportunity and obligation to harness the imagination and capabilities of the educational system to help strengthen governmental institutions. The nation must not fail to take full advantage of these opportunities.

ENDNOTES

1. The major exception to this generalization is, of course, the U.S. Postal Service.
2. See, for example, *Deregulating the Manager: Report of the National Academy of Public Administration*, NAPA, (Washington D.C.: National Academy of Public Administration, 1983).
3. U.S. Department of Labor, *Workforce 2000* (Washington, D.C.: 1987); Hudson Institute, *Civil Service 2000* Prepared for the Office of Personnel Management (1988).
4. U.S. Representative Patricia Schroeder, Chairperson of the House Subcommittee on Civil Service, letter to Merit Systems Protection Board (Mar. 26, 1988).
5. "What You Think," *Government Executive*, 20:6 (June 1988).
6. U.S. Merit Systems Protection Board, "Attracting Quality Graduates to the Federal Government: A View of College Recruiting" (Washington, D.C., June 6, 1988).
7. *Civil Service 2000.*
8. Ibid.
9. See "NSF Recruitment of Scientists and Engineers," National Science Foundation (Mar. 1988); an analysis of federal hiring of engineers at the China Lake Naval Weapons Stations shows that most federal recruits come from schools ranked in the second tier (or below) of the nation's engineering programs. A senior federal personnel official told us that her organization no longer recruits at top engineering schools because the "returns are so low."
10. Ronald P. Sanders, "The Best and Brightest: Can the Public Service Compete?" National

Commission on Public Service, (November 1988); and Curtis Smith, Associate Director, U.S. Office of Personnel Management, personal communication, (Mar. 1988).

11. Survey response, Amherst College.

12. Roper Poll, Feb. 1987.

13. Ibid.

14. Alexander Astin et al., *The American Freshman: Twenty Year Trends* (Los Angeles, Jan. 1987). For example, from 1967 to 1982 interest in public school teaching dropped from 20 percent of freshman to less than five percent.

15. Ibid.

16. Mary A. Hepburn and John D. Napier, "Patterns of Student Attitudes toward Political Institutions and Participation," *Teaching Political Science* 10 (1983).

17. "Collegiate Community Service: the Status of Public and Community Service at Selected Colleges and Universities" (Campus Outreach Opportunity League: 1987).

18. Sanders, *op. cit.*

19. R. Freeman Butts, *The Revival of Civic Learning* (Phi Delta Kappa Educational Foundation: 1980). See also papers prepared for the Oct. 1988 conference on the future of civic education "Citizenship in the 21st Century," available through the Foundation for Teaching Economics, San Francisco, California.

20. Educational Testing Service, *College Students' Knowledge and Beliefs* (Princeton: 1987).

21. Astin, *op. cit.*

22. "What You Think," *op. cit.*

23. Butts, *op. cit.*

24. Mary A. Hepburn, "What Is Our Youth Thinking? Social-Political Attitudes of the 1980's," *Social Education,* (Nov./Dec. 1985).

25. Educational Testing Service, *op. cit.*

26. James Burry and Joan Herman, *Evaluation Report of the Constitutional Rights Foundation's Youth Community Service Program* (Los Angeles: Center for Study of Education, UCLA; May 1988).

27. Collegiate Community Service, *op. cit.*

28. U.S. Representative Leon Panetta's statement before the House Subcommittee on Employment Opportunities (May 11, 1988).

29. Stanford University Public Service Center, *Annual Report;* 1987–1988 (Palo Alto, California: 1988).

30. Response from Amherst College.

31. Harvard University Office of Career Services, *Annual Report* (1987).

32. Letter from Robert K. Weatherall, Director of the Massachusetts Institute of Technology Office of Career Services (May 1988).

33. University of Wisconsin at Madison, *Annual Report* (1988).

34. A summary of the survey results is available from Peter Zimmerman, Associate Dean, John F. Kennedy School of Government, Harvard University, Cambridge, Massachusetts 02138.

35. OPM communication. Constance Horner to Derek Bok, March, 1988.

36. Data from OPM Central Personnel Data File, personal communication from Dr. Philip A.D. Schneider, PSSB:RN dated Sep. 23, 1988; William B. Johnston *et al, Civil Service 2000.*

37. Ibid.

38. It is important to note that Table 2 refers to occupational classification in the Civil Service classification system, while Table 3 is based on entrants' academic degree. Despite

the similarity of some classifications, e.g., engineering, there is not a precise identity between the two. For example, someone with a degree in physics might be hired for a job
classified as engineering.

39. Hugh Heclo, *A Government of Strangers* (Washington, D.C.: Brookings Institution, 1977).
40. Herbert Kaufman, *The Administrative Behavior of Federal Bureau Chiefs*, (Washington, D.C.: Brookings Institution, 1981).
41. See, for example, Graham T. Allison, *Is Management in the Public and Private Sector Alike in All Unimportant Respects?*, Kennedy School of Government Discussion Paper (1979).
42. In "These Truths Are Not Self-Evident," *Government Executive*, Aug. 1988, 55–57, Andrew Feinstein, Staff Director of the House Subcommittee on the Civil Service, writes, "[T]he fact is that most federal managers do not have a clue about how Congress works, how the President staffs his administration, what motivates politicians."
43. David Swain, D.P.A., *American Undergraduate Public Administration Education: Curriculum Choices and Program Emphasis* (unpublished paper, Apr. 1987); also, Schneider, *op. cit.*, reports that in 1987, of 38,454 entrants into the federal Civil Service, only 96 had under-graduate degrees in public administration. Swain's estimate is that 76 of some 2,000 gradu-ates (3.8%) enter federal service. See also "Undergraduate Public Administration Educa-tion," by Bryan Downes, Robert Dworak, Lawrence Keller, and Eleanor Landicina (unpublished paper, July 1982).
44. Ibid.
45. National Association of Schools of Public Affairs and Administration, *NASPAA Directory* (Washington, D.C., 1988).
46. Tables 3 and 4 may seem contradictory at first glance. Table 4 shows 21% of 6,428 de-gree holders joining federal government (some 1,350 individuals) while Table 3 reports only 302 master's degrees in public administration among new entrants to the Civil Service in the same year (1987). Table 3 is drawn from OPM's Central Personnel Data file (CPDF), which has personnel records of about 1.5 million white-collar workers. Several relevant groups are excluded from the CPDF, such as Congressional staff, the Central Intelligence Agency, and political (non-career) appointees. Also, many of the NASPAA students are already government employees (75% are "in-service") and thus are not classified as "new entrants" by OPM. *NASPAA Directory*: Washington, D.C., 1988): xxii.
47. Schneider and Nenni, *op. cit.*
48. By dint of their training and exposure during their internship experience, PMIs often rise quickly through the ranks to positions of considerable responsibility at a young age. Unfortunately (perhaps as a consequence of their early prominence), many PMIs leave government at a relatively young age. One recent estimate is that the average tenure of PMIs is about five years. Exit interviews with PMIs suggest that the lack of opportunity for advancement in government is the primary cause of early departure. PMIs find them-selves on a mid-management plateau, with limited opportunities for further growth and development. See Robert Goldenhoff, "That the Best May Serve: Methods of Recruiting and Retaining Federal Entry Level Personnel," paper prepared for the National Com-mission on the Public Service, Washington, D.C. September 1988.
49. In the public sector, the general management concept has two analogues. The military has long embraced a similar concept in the idea of the general officer. And the munici-pal reform movement (which influenced the early public administration programs) con-ceptualized and encouraged the creation of the city manager form of government to professionalize municipal administration, reduce corruption, and improve performance.

50. Alfred Chandler, *The Visible Hand—The Managerial Revolution in America.* (Belknap Press, 1977). Over time, many graduates of business programs, particularly the mid-career and executive programs launched by so many business schools, have come to occupy senior leadership roles in business. It should be noted that senior leadership in the public sector usually comes from outside government through elections and political appointment.

51. *Business Week*, special issue on executive leadership (Fall 1988).

52. As part of the background to preparation of this report, staff met with a number of officials and groups, including the Interagency Advisory Group's Committee on Development and Training (IAG-CODAT) chaired by Mary Broad of the Defense Communication Agency. The IAG is a government-wide committee on which all agencies are represented. In addition, meetings and interviews were held with representatives of the General Accounting Office, OPM, several employee groups, and several informal gatherings of federal employees.

53. Members of the IAG-CODAT group pointed out the increasing need for remedial training by government agencies to ensure minimal proficiency. The combination of the declining relative salaries for federal workers, tight labor markets in many areas, and profound weaknesses in many secondary school programs (some cited undergraduate programs as well) have produced many job entrants who lack the most basic workplace skills. The Navy and Labor Departments, among others, have put new emphasis into remediation programs for recent hires.

54. Michael Beer, Paul Lawrence, D. Quinn Mills, and Richard Walton, *Managing Human Assets: The Human Resource Management Program of the Harvard Business School* (Boston: Harvard Business School, 1986).

55. Nell Eurich, *Corporate Classrooms*, Report to the Carnegie Corporation (Princeton: Princeton University Press, 1985).

56. John W. Gardner, *Leadership Development*, (The Independent Sector, 1987). Also Kotter, John, *The Leadership Factor*, (New York: The Free Press, 1988). Also, General Electric Executive Manpower System, Discussions with John Welch and Reginald Jones, Harvard Business School on Executive Succession (HBS 882–054), Boston.

57. *Federal Personnel Manual*, Chapters 315 and 410 and FPM Letter 411–1. For one department's approach, see Department of Justice order DOJ 1410.1C (Apr. 28, 1983).

58. Interview with Orion Birdsall, Deputy Associate Commissioner for Human Resources, Internal Revenue Service, Washington, D.C., April, 1988.

59. Written communication from Nancy Aldermott, Director of Personnel US.ACDA (July 8, 1988).

60. U.S. General Accounting Office, *Government Auditing Standards*, 1988 Revision: 3–2.

61. Indeed, because the federal government has little in the way of capital, plant, and equipment, and devotes little research and development to government operations, this low investment in training is all the more glaring. Many firms devote 10% to 20% of sales to investment in research, capital, and personnel. In the federal government, such investment for the future amounts to no more than a few tenths of 1%.

62. In *Training and Development of The Federal Workforce*, Brassier and Ludwig cite Ed Schroer, vice president of American Society for Training and Development as despairing that federal leadership will ever view training as a critical strategic investment, as is the case in many companies.

63. William Medina, Ph.D., *Supervisory Training and Development*, doctoral dissertation, American University, 1979.

64. U.S. General Accounting Office, "Reasons the Candidate Development Program Has Not Produced More SES Appointees" (April 1988).
65. To make one comparison, the military side of the Army has done an excellent job of developing minority leadership, numbering more than 40 minority generals (ten percent) among its top ranks. On the civilian side of the Army, minority senior executives are found less than one-third as frequently. The difference in results is testimony to the quality of the uniformed (military) Army's officer and leadership development programs and to their determination to build a leadership corps broadly representative of the Army workforce. Personal communication from Major General Charles Hines, Associate Deputy Chief of Staff (Personnel), U.S. Army, January, 1989.
66. Marver Bernstein, personal communication to Derek Bok (Oct. 11, 1988).
67. *Federal Personnel Manual*, Chapter 410, Section 5–2: "Government facilities must be selected when adequate training is reasonably available from them." Contrast the above with the basic federal policy on acquisition of goods and services expressed in OMB Circular A–76: "Government should not compete with its citizens. Whenever possible, it is the policy of the United States to rely on the private sector for the provision of goods and services."
68. This is OPM Director Constance Horner's own characterization of current training policy; personal communication to Derek Bok, (June 1988).
69. Mark Moore and Peter Zimmerman, "Report to the Association for Public Policy Analysis and Management," Kennedy School Discussion Paper (Mar. 1986).
70. Harvard's Kennedy School has six core executive programs ranging from two weeks to nine weeks in length. A 10-month long mid-career program draws many experienced government officials as well. The School conducts week-long seminars for newly elected mayors and members of Congress. Together these programs annually enroll 800 to 900 public officials. These programs engage more than half of the School's faculty teaching workload.

POLITICS AND PERFORMANCE

Strengthening the Executive Leadership System

The Report of the

Task Force on the Relations Between Political

Appointees and Career Executives

to the

National Commission on the Public Service

TASK FORCE

Elliot L. Richardson, *Chairman*

Frederic V. Malek

Robert C. McFarlane

Walter F. Mondale

Benjamin Read

Anne Wexler

Alan Wolff

WASHINGTON 1989

THE TASK FORCE ON THE RELATIONS BETWEEN POLITICAL APPOINTEES AND CAREER EXECUTIVES

CHAIRMAN

Elliot L. Richardson
Former Cabinet Member

MEMBERS

Frederic V. Malek
Former Director of Presidential Personnel

Robert C. McFarlane
Former National Security Adviser

Walter F. Mondale
Former Vice President of the United States

Benjamin Read
Former Under Secretary of State for Management

Anne Wexler
Former Assistant to the President for Public Liaison

Alan Wolff
Former Deputy Special Trade Representative

PROJECT DIRECTOR

James P. Pfiffner
Professor of Government and Politics
George Mason University

CONTENTS

PREFACE

Concerned with a growing consensus among knowledgeable observers that leadership in the executive branch has been deteriorating, the National Commission on the Public Service formed a Task Force to examine the relationship between political appointees and career executives.

Six distinguished individuals of both political parties, who had a broad range of experience in the public and private sectors over the past four decades, agreed to serve as Task Force members. In a series of meetings during 1988, the Task Force examined evidence of problems in the executive levels of political appointees and career civil servants. The Task Force examined the academic literature as well as analyses and information culled from Congressional and executive branch documents. It received feedback from regional hearings conducted by the National Commission. The Chairman and Task Force members met with White House officials, the Director of the Office of Personnel Management, and others intimately involved with Presidential personnel policy and the management of the Senior Executive Service.

After careful consideration of anecdotal, experiential, and statistical evidence, the Task Force concluded that indeed there were problems. Its recommendations are intended to improve the recruitment of political appointees and career executives and to contribute to the improvement of relationships between the two sets of officials.

In its work, the Task Force considered contributions from a number of experienced government officials who contacted the National Commission and offered their observations and advice. The Task Force's final report benefitted from input from a group of senior scholars and practioners of public administration at a conference held by the Commission at the Woodrow Wilson School at Princeton University in the fall of 1988.

The Task Force's final report draws upon studies of political and career executives by the National Academy of Public Administration, the Dual-Career Project of Harvard University, and the General Accounting Office.

Finally, this Task Force wishes to acknowledge the intellectual leadership of the late Charles Levine in the formulation of its report.

Elliot L. Richardson, Chairman
James P. Pfiffner, Project Director

Washington, D.C.
April 1988

EXECUTIVE SUMMARY

Astrong executive leadership system is essential to the effective management of the federal government and to a successful Presidency. The two components of that system, political appointees and career executives, must work together in a partnership; neither can run the executive branch alone. The President needs both the energizing force of committed political executives to lead governmental agencies, and the competence and experience of career civil servants to run programs.

But this system is not working at peak efficiency or effectiveness. A consensus is growing among informed observers of the public service that the management infrastructure of the federal government is deteriorating. This decline stems from problems involving both the political appointees and the career members of the Senior Executive Service (SES). More importantly, the decline involves the interactions between these two essential components of the executive leadership system.

Although the causes of the degeneration of the executive leadership system cannot be precisely measured or quantified, clearly a number of developments in the system are disturbing. The average tenure of Senate-confirmed Presidential appointees (PAS) is about 2.0 years. The average tenure of non-career SES members is 18 months, and every year one third of them change positions or leave the government. In contrast, 70 percent of career executives have been with their agencies for 10 years and 50 percent for 15 years.

Compounding this lack of stability at the top is the increased layering of political appointees above the career system, and the interposing of Schedule C (political) appointees between line political officials and career executives. This arrangement diffuses legitimate political authority and attenuates the link between the responsible political officials and the career implementors of policy.

The number of political appointees in the federal government steadily increased from the 1950s to the 1980s. In 1985, there were 527 Presidentially appointed, Senate-confirmed appointees, 658 non-career SES appointees, and 1,665 Schedule C appointees. (There are now more Schedule C appointees at the GS-13 to 15 levels than there were total Schedule C appointees in 1976.)

The total numbers involved are not as important as the increased numbers of political appointees at the lower level executive ranks, positions to which career employees could once aspire. If a career employee can no longer hope to become a deputy assistant secretary, it will be hard to recruit or keep the best and brightest young people for public service.

The career services have been suffering from a brain drain and decreased morale. Between 1979 and 1985, fully 52 percent of the career members of the SES left the government, many of them choosing early retirement. General Accounting Office (GAO) surveys have found that two-thirds of those leaving the SES would advise young people to pursue careers in the private rather than the public sector.

Executive compensation has eroded severely, with a drop in purchasing power of 39 percent between 1969 and 1985. This relative decline has hurt both the political and the career ranks.

As political appointees have been pushed lower into the bureaucracy, the ability of agencies to provide continuity between Presidential Administrations has been impaired. When the entire top layer of an agency leaves at the end of an Administration, often taking even secretarial staff and leaving behind career executives who have not been involved in policy deliberations, the costs of discontinuity run high.

Even though this "quiet crisis" has been growing for some time, the Task Force believes that if prompt action is taken, the deterioration of the executive infrastructure of the government can be reversed. The Task Force makes the following general recommendations to reverse the trend.

First, the President should improve the quality of political appointees and simultaneously reduce their numbers. Creating more political appointees does not necessarily improve responsiveness, and can confuse lines of legitimate authority. Presidents should make greater use of the career services in choosing leadership for their Administrations.

Second, the Office of Presidential Personnel should intensify efforts to recruit high-quality Presidential appointees, while delegating selection of non-Presidential appointments to the heads of the departments and agencies.

Third, executive salaries should be significantly increased in order to strengthen recruitment of the best and brightest for Presidential appointments, and to keep the best and brightest career executives in the government. The White House should conduct orientation seminars for all new Presidential appointees so that they can reach maximum effectiveness as soon as possible in carrying out the President's program and faithfully executing the laws. The President can increase his Administration's effectiveness by seeking commitments from his appointees to stay in office for a full term, and by periodically briefing his appointees to keep them informed of his priorities.

Despite the problems cited in this report, the combination of political and career executives that comprise the executive leadership system has served the United States well over the past two centuries. It is our hope that these proposals will restore and improve the government's leadership system in the nation's third century.

RECOMMENDATIONS

The Task Force makes the following specific recommendations (elaboration on these recommendations appears at the end of this report):

RECOMMENDATION 1

Increase the quality of political appointees while reducing their numbers, and make greater use of the career services.

A. The Office of Presidential Personnel should establish explicit criteria for the qualifications of people nominated for each Senate-confirmed position. These criteria should emphasize managerial experience and substantive expertise as well as loyalty and philosophical compatibility with the President.

B. The total number of political appointees in the departments and agencies of the executive branch should not exceed 2,000. This limit implies a moderate reduction in PAS positions (527 in 1985); a moderate reduction in non-career SES members (658 in 1986); and a significant reduction in Schedule C personnel (1,665 in 1986).

C. The President and department and agency heads should fill more positions in the mid- and upper levels of the executive branch with career civil servants rather than political appointees.

RECOMMENDATION 2

Make systematic recruitment efforts for Presidential appointments and delegate non-Presidential appointments to department and agency heads.

A. In order to facilitate the recruitment of political appointees, Presidential nominees should set up personnel planning operations immediately after the nominating conventions.

B. The Office of Presidential Personnel should be used as an active recruitment operation and not as a passive screening office.

C. The President should delegate to department heads the recruitment of noncareer SES and Schedule C appointments within the bounds of general criteria established by the White House. The President should give significant weight to the preferences of cabinet secretaries in the selection of their immediate subordinates who are Presidential appointees.

RECOMMENDATION 3

Make federal executive positions more attractive by increasing pay, and make appointees more effective by systematic orientation and longer terms in office.

A. Executive salaries should be significantly increased and financial reporting requirements should be re-examined.

B. The President should establish orientation programs for all new political appointees in the executive branch.

C. The President should seek commitments from the appointees of his Administration to remain in office for a full term.

POLITICS AND PERFORMANCE: STRENGTHENING THE EXECUTIVE LEADERSHIP SYSTEM

Astrong executive leadership system is essential to the effective management of the government and to a successful Presidency. The two components of that system, political appointees and career executives, must work together in a partnership; neither alone can run the executive branch. The President needs both the energizing force of committed political executives to lead governmental agencies and the competence and experience of career civil servants who carry out the missions of these agencies. Executive branch agencies must be responsive to Presidential direction as the President takes care that the laws are faithfully executed.

Each President brings into his Administration a substantial number of people committed to him and to his philosophy of government. These political appointees constitute an essential democratic link with the electorate. This link ensures that the permanent bureaucracies that carry out the policies of the U.S. government will be led by people who are committed to the policies and priorities of each new President. This "in-and-outer" system also brings into the government fresh ideas and new blood to try them out. It brings in people who can work at full speed on the President's program for several years and then return to their previous careers when they approach burnout.

But the huge agencies and complex programs of the government cannot be run entirely by these in-and-outers. The permanent processes and ongoing programs of the U.S. government need the continuity and expertise of specialized bureaucracies. These bureaucracies are led by the senior executives of the career services who comprise the management cadre of the permanent programs of the government.

These career executives are critical to the continuing capacity of the government to function and to the success of their political superiors in each Presidential Administration. They are highly educated, and they know the intricacies of the laws and regulations governing the programs they implement. They are the repositories of organizational memory. They have built up personal intelligence and communications networks over many years through dealing with the same organizations, people, and issues. Perhaps more importantly, career executives are the professional line managers of the programs of the federal government. They are in charge of mission accomplishment and service delivery.

But the system is not now working at peak efficiency or effectiveness. A consensus is growing among informed observers of the public service that the management infrastructure of the federal government is deteriorating. This decline stems from problems involving both the political executives each President appoints and the career members of the Senior Executive Service (SES). More importantly, the problem involves the interactions between these two essential components of the executive leadership system.

To deal with these problems in the executive leadership system, we propose several changes that we believe will improve the system and make it more responsive to Presidential direction. The following section describes the deteriorating conditions that led to our proposals. This section is followed by an analysis of the appropriate roles of political appointees and career executives in the U.S. political system. Finally, each of our proposals is explained in detail.

This report is based on the considered judgment that increasing the number of political appointees does not guarantee a more responsive government, and that career executives possess the professionalism, expertise, and motivation to enable the President to accomplish his policy goals. A change of government in the parliamentary democracies of the United Kingdom, France, or West Germany may bring in 100 new appointees, and there is little doubt that these governments are responsive to new political leadership.[1]

PROBLEMS IN THE SYSTEM

Although the degeneration of the system of executive leadership cannot be precisely measured or quantified, it is clear that there are a number of disturbing developments in the system. These developments include: rising turnover in the political ranks, an increasing number of political appointees, deteriorating relations between political and career executives, the erosion of executive compensation, and the lack of institutional memory in many executive branch agencies.

Increasing Turnover of Political Appointees

The average tenure of Senate-confirmed political appointees is relatively short and has been decreasing. The average tenure of Presidential appointees (excluding regulatory commissioners) during the Johnson Administration was 2.8 years; during the Nixon Administration it was 2.6 years; during the Carter Administration it was 2.5 years; and it was 2.0 years up to 1984 in the Reagan Administration.[2] From 1964 to 1984, the proportion of political appointees who stayed in position 1.5 years or less was 41.7 percent for cabinet secretaries, 62 percent for deputy secretaries, and 46.3 percent for under secretaries. From 1979 to 1986, noncareer members (political appointees) of the Senior Executive Service remained in office an average of 20 months. Fully 40 percent of political executives throughout the government stayed in their positions less than one year.[3] In contrast, 70 percent of career executives have been with their agencies for 10 years and 50 percent of them for 15 years.[4] Although the average tenure in office of Senate-confirmed Presidential appointees (PAS) may have increased slightly because of the two full terms of President Reagan, the tenure of these top executives is still so short as to be disruptive.

This lack of stability in the top political leadership of the federal government poses a problem for several reasons. First, on-the-job training takes time. If a new appointee needs a year to learn enough about the job to be fully effective, then on average, political appointees spend half of the time they are on the job operating at less than full effectiveness. "Appointees on the job two years have enough time to make mistakes but often not enough time to put the resulting lessons to use."[5] The effect of this turnover at the top is worse when the positions that are considered "political" are extended further down into the bureaucracy. Paul Warnke, former Chief Arms Control Negotiator, observes: "If you're going to have the kind of rapid appointee turnover, two, three, four years, you've got to have a first-rate career service. . . . I hate to see this creeping appointeeism. I think it means too many people brought in."[6] When political appointees are replaced, there is most often no overlap of tenure during which institutional memory can be passed on, even if it would be welcome.

Increasing Layers of Bureaucracy and Proliferation of Political Appointees

The increased layering of political appointees on top of the career system and the interposing of Schedule C special assistants between line political officials and career executives diffuses legitimate political authority. It attenuates the link between the responsible political official and the career implementors of policy.

There has been an increase in the number of positions at the higher level executive ranks ("administrative overbrush") as well as at lower levels. In 1976, for example, the State Department had 11 assistant secretaries; in 1986 it had 17.[7] In 1960, the Department of Health, Education, and Welfare had two assistant secretaries and 23 Schedule C appointees. In 1984, its successor, the Department of Health and Human Services, had 6 assistant secretaries and 101 Schedule C appointees; and the Department of Education, formerly a part of HEW, had 6 assistant secretaries and 98 Schedule C appointees.[8] According to Frank C. Carlucci, Secretary of Defense in the Reagan Administration, "The fact is that we have too many organizational entities, many of which are simply a collection of statutes. We do not need more organizations. If anything, we need to consolidate governmental organizations in mission-oriented departments."[9]

This increase results in confusion in the channels of communication between the President and his senior officers and their line managers. The resulting span-of-control problems lead to additional layering. The clear and coherent transmission of the President's policies through his own appointees to the career level becomes progressively more difficult as the number of Presidential appointees increases. In addition, the inflation in the number of appointees dilutes their stature and leads to a corresponding inflation in titles.

Frederic Malek, Director of the Office of Presidential Personnel in the Nixon Administration, makes the argument:

> Layering the civil service with even more political appointees would only serve to widen the gulf between the chiefs and the Indians, robbing the career executives of an opportunity to carry out many of the more demanding jobs in the government, weakening the attraction of civil service, and reducing the incentive of the best career people to remain in government. Instead, agency heads should seek to make better use of the experience that the career executives do have and should recognize that some continuity of performance can be an invaluable tool for effective management.

> Surely there is an optimum balance between the number of career and noncareer appointments in every government organization. At the federal level, that balance should be struck in favor of fewer political appointees, not more. In many cases, the effectiveness of an agency would be improved and political appointments would be reduced by roughly 25 percent if line positions beneath the assistant secretary level were reserved for career officials.[10]

These observations are even more relevant in the late 1980s than they were in the late 1970s, when Malek wrote them and when fewer political appointments were available to Presidents.

Possibly more important than the increased number of political appointees and their rapid turnover is the deteriorating relations between political appointees and career executives. This development is attributable in part to the initial attitude of suspicion that many appointees of recent administrations have brought to their jobs. They suspect that civil servants are lazy and self-serving, and they believe that the "bureaucrats" will try to undermine the policies of the Administration, drag their feet, or even sabotage Administration initiatives. They fear that the rules of the system will be used to prevent the Administration from implementing its policies.

Initial distrust leads to excluding career executives from policy discussions and to jig-saw-puzzle management, in which political executives bar career executives from the "big picture" so they will not be able to sabotage it. This attitude on the part of political appointees is self-defeating because it ignores experienced people who have potentially valuable information and advice. It also contributes to declining morale in the career ranks, which leads to early retirements and the brain drain.

Political Appointees Increasing

The number of political appointees in the federal government increased steadily from the 1950s to the 1980s. Although part of this increase is attributable to the creation of new agencies, the increase has occurred while overall civilian government employment has decreased relative to the total U.S. population. At the top levels, the number of Presidential appointments that require Senate confirmation has increased from 71 in 1933 to 152 in 1965 to 527 in 1985 (not including ambassadors, U.S. attorneys, U.S. marshals, or representatives to international organizations).[11] But PAS positions constitute only the apex of the pyramid. The total number of noncareer SES appointees has increased from 582 in 1980 to 658 in 1986 (a 13.1 percent increase) at the same time that the number of career SES personnel decreased 5.3 percent.[12] The number of Schedule C positions increased from 911 in 1976 to 1,665 in 1986. But even more striking, the number of Schedule C appointments at the GS 13 to 15 range (mid-level management) was 946 in 1986, more than the total number of Schedule C positions under President Ford.[13]

While there may be legitimate disagreements over how best to count the total number of political appointees, there is no dispute about the direction of the trend. At the same time that the number of political appointees has been increasing over the past decade, total executive branch employment has remained relatively stable. Civilian employment increased at about 0.7 percent annually, primarily in the Department of Defense, the U.S. Postal Service, and the Veterans Administration. Both the U.S. population and the total non-federal workforce grew at significantly greater rates than overall federal employment.[14]

This proliferation in the number of political appointees impairs the effective management of the government for several reasons.

The increase in political appointees undermines the capacity of the career services. Civil servants have spent their careers in the public service with the goal of rising to the top of the career ladder where their years of experience will be appreciated and put to use. When political appointees are placed in positions formerly held by career employees, the latter's long-term career opportunities are diminished. This development discourages good people from entering the public service and from staying in it when they have opportunities to leave.

The absolute size of the increase in political appointees understates this problem considerably. The increase in political appointees is not as important as the fact that the ratio is rising. The significant impact on morale is at the margins, in the positions to which career executives aspire. The more of these positions that are converted to political appointments, the more civil servants are forced to recognize that they are in dead-end career tracks. The awareness that opportunities for them are decreasing does the most harm.

The total numbers involved are not as important as the increased numbers in the lower level executive ranks. Most political positions—secretaries, deputy secretaries, most assistant secretaries, administrators, commissioners, etc.—are not in fact part of the career ladder and have never been so regarded by career people or young people contemplating public service. Thus, when jobs below these levels are converted from career to political positions, the impact on the perception of career executives is magnified. The proportion of the remaining jobs—for example, those at the deputy assistant secretary level—that have been politicized is substantially higher than the total numbers would seem to indicate.

This frustrating of hope and ambition explains why the politicization of the lower level executive ranks (noncareer SES and Schedule C), where it has been increasing at the greatest rate, is so destructive. A career executive who can no longer aspire to be a deputy assistant secretary, and who must contemplate reporting to a much younger, less experienced, less knowledgeable boss whose main qualification stems from loyal campaigning for the winning Presidential candidate, will be much less likely to stay with the government when offered a chance to leave.

Similarly, civil servants at the GS-9 to 15 levels see their promotion opportunities shrinking. When Schedule C personnel are promoted at much faster rates than career employees, the effect is doubly discouraging. They, too, may find outside opportunities irresistible. And, of course, the most skilled and talented career employees have the most opportunities to leave.

This trend is also evident at higher levels in the Foreign Service. Ronald I. Spiers, Under Secretary of State for Management in the Reagan Administration, has expressed his concern about "the often casual use of Foreign Service positions for political patronage." He continues:

> I am deeply concerned about the diminishing percent of career appointments. From a starting point in 1981, when 75 percent of our ambassadors were career Foreign Service officers, now only 60 percent of our nation's ambassadors are career officers. This is a low point for the past four decades. A net reduction of 23 senior positions filled by career personnel since 1981 makes managing the Foreign Service difficult indeed. Seeing the dubious quality of some of those judged worthy or capable of serving as ambassador, it is painful to recognize the lack of respect this implies for our profession. . . . [I]t is wasteful and demoralizing for well-qualified people to climb a 30-year career ladder, only to be preempted at the top rung by someone lacking the necessary qualifications or experience.[15]

The State Department is a special case because it has about 140 ambassadorial or chief of mission appointments that require Senate confirmation in addition to executive level positions involved with managing the department. But just as the need for professionalism in the diplomatic corps is acute, so is it also in the rest of the government.

In addition, the benefits presumed to be gained by a Presidential Administration from the increasing number of political appointees is overrated. Political appointees, especially at lower levels, may not be the best qualified, and they may be appointed because of support from Members of Congress or interest groups. Thus their loyalty may be split between the President and others. A number of Presidential appointees have even argued that political appointees, because of their divided loyalties, are less responsive than career civil servants. In a study done in the 1980s, one third of the political executives interviewed offered unsolicited critical comments about their fellow appointees. Their comments included:

> A lot of political people don't know a hill of beans about their area. Those who are confirmed by the Senate are generally good, but at the lower levels, they don't have a lot of background, and have to rely on the career people.

> To tell the truth, I have more problems working with political appointees because they are subject to political pressures. And they think they understand the political process, and most of them don't.[16]

The authors of the study conclude that the increasing number of political appointees has decreased the influence of the senior career staff at the same time that less qualified political executives are turning over so quickly that they cannot master their jobs. "The result is to weaken their ability to carry out the Administration's 'mandate' and, often, to wreak havoc in the day-to-day administration of agency programs."[17]

More Political Appointees at Lower Levels

The more positions are opened up to political appointees at lower levels, the harder it is to recruit high-quality people to fill them. Quality at the higher executive levels is not as much of a problem because of the prestige, power, and challenge of the positions. But at the lower levels, it is more difficult to recruit the best candidates, who must give up their jobs, move their families, and accept lower salaries.

This difficulty is aggravated by the increasing control over political appointments exerted by the Office of Presidential Personnel. Sub-cabinet appointees, who were often selected by cabinet secretaries in the 1960s and 1970s, have been tightly controlled by the White House in the 1980s. The positions that are of most concern here are the deputy assistant secretary positions (or deputy administrators or deputy commissioners), which in the past have been primarily filled with career executives with long experience in their agencies. According to Elliot Richardson, who has held eight Presidential appointments:

> More and more political appointees are being pushed into jobs traditionally held by career officials. In addition to reducing the number of positions at the top that remain open to a civil servant, the consequence is to place minimally qualified individuals in highly important posts. It's hard enough to get really good people to give up highly paid positions in private life and take on the demanding duties of an under secretary or assistant secretary; it's harder still to persuade an able and experienced person to accept the less prestigious title of deputy assistant secretary. Almost any job at that level, however, is more responsible and has wider impact on the national interest than most senior corporate positions. In the State Department, for example, a deputy assistant secretary is responsible for all of Southeast Asia. A deputy assistant attorney general heads the war against organized crime. Comparable responsibilities belong to every similar position throughout the government.
> Ignoring these facts, patronage offices pressed to come up with jobs for the President's loyal supporters drive the politicizing process. A White House personnel assis-

tant sees the position of deputy assistant secretary as a fourth-echelon slot. In his eyes that makes it an ideal reward for a fourth-echelon political type—a campaign advance man, or a regional political organizer. For a senior civil servant, on the other hand, it's irksome to see a position one has spent 20 or 30 years preparing for preempted by an outsider who doesn't know the difference between an audit exception and an authorizing bill. Small wonder, then, that so many members of the SES have sought other occupations.[18]

If part of what attracts the best and brightest of young people into the career services is the chance to be "in on the action," the trend of excluding career executives from policy deliberations and from the chance to become a deputy assistant secretary will discourage the best students from entering the federal service.

Brain Drain in the Career Ranks

From 1979, when the SES was created, to 1983, 2,632 SES members left the government. This exodus amounted to 40 percent of those who entered the service when it was created in 1979. By 1985, the percentage who had left had increased to 52 percent.[19] While some of those who left were at retirement age and some were undoubtedly no longer suited to the federal service, many of them chose to retire or leave government service before they had to. In 1983, 17 percent of those who were eligible to retire did. By 1985, this number had increased to 30 percent. When asked, "Is your agency experiencing a brain drain?" 73 percent of the respondents to a large survey of government executives in 1988 replied "yes."[20]

The increasing number of senior executives who are choosing to leave government service before normal retirement age is disturbing. This nation is losing some of its most experienced and qualified senior civil servants. They are not easy to replace. For instance, from 1983 to 1987, at the National Institutes of Health, 42 senior scientists (20 percent of the top scientists in the agency) left for careers in nongovernmental institutions at salary increases ranging from 50 to 300 percent.[21]

The talent hemorrhage at the top is matched by problems in recruiting at the entry levels. Surveys have shown that young people's values have changed over the past several decades; they are now much less likely to be interested in public service than in personal profit and business careers. A declining percentage of the graduates of the country's best public administration and public policy programs view the federal government as a desirable place to work. In a survey by *Government Executive* magazine, 59 percent of the respondents said that the quality of new hires at their agencies was marginally or much worse than in the past.[22] This trend has been encouraged by several political campaigns in which Presidential candidates have disparaged the career services and blamed U.S. societal and economic problems on the federal government.

Falling Morale in the Career Service

The morale of a workforce is difficult to define, much less to quantify, yet it is real and can have an important influence on the quality and productivity of work. Although the Task Force could not measure the morale of federal career executives, it found indicators that morale could be better.

In 1985, the General Accounting Office (GAO) asked those leaving the SES the most important reasons for their departure. Those who responded cited the following reasons: dissatisfaction with top management (47.3 percent), dissatisfaction with political appointees (43.1 percent), unfair distribution of bonuses (41.4 percent), dissatisfaction with agency management practices (35.1 percent), and too much political interference (33.5 percent).[23] In a 1985 Federal Executive Institute Alumni Association survey, 51 percent of the respondents felt that career-political working relations were a deterrent to effective management.[24] Perhaps more important, a GAO survey found that two-thirds of those leaving the SES in 1985 would "advise" or "strongly advise" young people to pursue careers in the private rather than the public sector.[25] In the *Government Executive* survey, only 14 percent of career civil servants rated political appointees as "well qualified" while 86 percent rated them as "marginally qualified" or "unqualified."[26] Even discounting the results for the usual amount of complaining, these figures are unsettling.

While one can quibble about some of these data, the cumulative picture is discouraging. A serious morale problem exists in the government's senior career executives, and much of it is related to the perception that less qualified appointees in the lower levels of the political ranks (noncareer SES and Schedule C) are occupying positions that in the past might have crowned the career of an experienced civil servant. This perception is not conducive to the type of teamwork that is necessary for a well managed government. To the extent that these perceived problems convince career executives to leave government service before they have to, they contribute to decreasing institutional memory and continuity.

Erosion of Executive Compensation

The Quadrennial Commission on Executive, Legislative, and Judicial Salaries has reported that between 1969 and 1985, the purchasing power of Executive Level II salaries (to which other executive salaries are tied) had decreased by 39 percent. A pay increase of 90 percent would be necessary in 1987 to achieve the same ratio of comparability (not to achieve full comparability) to private sector executive salaries that existed in 1970.[27]

The *Report of the President's Commission on Compensation of Career Federal Executives* in 1988 argued that SES pay levels present serious problems for the effective operation of the government. According to the report, "the history of broken promises and pay caps, reduced bonus provisions, the effects of inflation, the comparative pay gap with the private sector, compression within and on either end of the SES pay range" is an important component of recruitment and retention problems. The Commission concluded that, "An SES beset by retention and recruitment problems results in the will of the people, as expressed through national election, being seriously impaired. . . . Without retaining our best public servants and without the ability to recruit equally qualified personnel, our capacity as a nation to successfully respond to the domestic and international challenges we face will be severely impaired."[28]

Few would argue that public sector salaries should be fully comparable with private sector salaries, and no one argues that money should be the primary reason to choose a public sector career. But the deterioration of executive pay in the federal government has come to the point where it may be a disincentive to recruiting the best and brightest at the entry level, or retaining good people for their career. For instance, David Ruder, Chairman of the Securities and Exchange Commission in the Reagan Administration, wrote to Commission Chairman Paul A. Volcker: "We regulate an industry which has seen starting salaries for junior attorneys exceed the levels of our most experienced and outstanding attorney-managers. . . . [T]he financial sacrifice asked of our most capable attorneys and other professionals is becoming increasingly difficult to bear. Some competitive compensation relief is imperative to help slow this talent drain."[29]

The widening gap between private and federal executive pay is, of course, a problem in recruiting the best and brightest political appointees as well.

Decreasing Institutional Memory

The turnover of all political appointees when control of the White House shifts to the other party presents a problem of institutional continuity. If career civil servant positions extend to high levels and career executives have participated in the development of policy, the problem is not so severe. But this is often not the case.

While agency files contain written records, much of the nuance of policy development and of unwritten understandings with major participants does not show up in the formal records. This dimension can only be supplied by agency officials who have been privy to the policy development. The more frequently that career officials are passed over for higher level agency positions and the more consistently they are excluded from policy deliberations because of distrust, the more future political appointees—and Presidential Administrations—will suffer from the lack of that input.

Needed Improvement in Career Employee Attitudes

The need for change in political appointees is important because they are in the positions of greatest authority and power. They set the tone for their departments and agencies and for the whole Administration. But improvement in the attitudes of career civil servants is also necessary.

Career employees ought not to accept the stereotype that all new political appointees are political hacks. Most career executives have seen political hacks, just as most political appointees have seen their share of deadwood in the career ranks. The cynical attitude that "I can outlast any political appointee and thus do not have to give my full support" is destructive to our democratic system, the civil service, good management, and is unacceptable. Little will be accomplished in such a climate, and career employees displaying this attitude will give credence to the negative stereotypes of the career services.

Career executives ought to keep in mind that new political appointees join the government as the President's surrogates, and are likely to have a positive approach to their stint in the public service. New appointees may suffer from the uncertainties that result from joining a new organization and of being unfamiliar with its personnel, processes, and programs. Just as career employees want their new political bosses to give them the benefit of the doubt, so too they should extend that same good will toward new political appointees and avoid prejudging their political superiors.

Career executives should also examine their own attitudes toward Members of Congress and their staffs. The negative stereotypes of Members of Congress and Congressional staff are no more accurate than negative stereotypes of executive branch civil servants. Hostile or biased attitudes are not conducive to the cooperative efforts that are necessary to the effective management of the government.

APPROPRIATE ROLES OF POLITICAL AND CAREER EXECUTIVES

Any solutions to these problems will work only if political appointees and career executives accept their mutual responsibilities to make the system work. The legitimate role of political appointees is to represent the President, who was democratically elected to head the nation and to lead the bureaucracy. The role of civil servants is to contribute their experience and expertise in the machinery and programs of government and to help carry out the legitimate priorities of the incumbent Administration in its implementation of the laws.

The Functions of the Political Process

The function of the political process in the United States is to elect to government those who, in some general way, represent the will of the electorate. Elected officials have the right and the duty to make choices among competing claims within the society. Techniques of rational analysis can contribute to narrowing the range of choices, but ultimately the tough choices among competing priorities must be made on the basis of political values. At that point (in the executive branch), the President and his appointed officials have the duty to make choices within the legally defined boundaries of their positions.

Career civil servants do not have the legitimate right to make those choices, and they should not attempt to do so. The appropriate role of the career executive is to contribute relevant information, rational analysis, and experienced judgment as input to executive branch decisionmaking. That advice to political appointees can appropriately include judgments about politics as well as the implementation of the policy under consideration. The experience and expertise represented in this advice can be valuable, but the role is clearly advisory. Responsibility for ultimate decisions is legally, constitutionally, and morally that of the President's representatives in the departments and agencies.

If career executives are not able to support legal policy decisions made by the Administration in power, their appropriate response is to resign. They should not try to undermine or sabotage policies or programs secretly. It is the corresponding duty of the President and his political appointees to "take care that the laws be faithfully executed."

In addition to their legal duties, political appointees also are responsible for leading the executive branch. The new perspectives and fresh thinking that political appointees bring to government can contribute greatly to motivating the career services. Leadership necessarily involves not only respecting the contributions that career executives make to governing, but also bringing out the best in career officials—by convincing them that their efforts can make a difference and by challenging them to extend themselves to accomplish the goals of the Administration and the government.

The Politics/Administration Dichotomy

Some argue that a distinction exists between policy and administration. From this perspective, political leaders decide policy questions and those in the bureaucracy merely follow orders from their political superiors. Some observers have argued that such distinctions are clear and self-evident: there is no Democratic or Republican way to build a road.

But in the modern, industrialized, technocratic state these simple distinctions break down. Just as a legislature cannot specify all of the details of complex programs, neither can political appointees give precise and complete orders about how their policy decisions must be implemented. They lack the time, and, more importantly, the expertise. Career civil servants have devoted their careers to managing the details of programs, and may even have helped to draft the legislation that established those programs. They have the information upon which programmatic decisions must be made. They formulate the regulations that establish rules for applying the law to specific, individual cases. In addition, they are experts at applying the bureaucracies' own rules and regulations to the management of particular programs: they oil the budget, personnel, and paper flow parts of the bureaucratic machine.

Political appointees do legitimately get involved in the details of programs, and career executives are often involved in policy discussions because of their experience and political judgment. In the modern policy arena, where the questions are whether to build the road and where to build it, policy cannot be strictly separated from administration.

In this overlap of function, it is all the more crucial to maintain the normative distinction between the two roles. Despite the fact that career bureaucrats are involved in policy decisions, they ought not to lose sight of the democratic imperative that Presidential appointees are the legitimate locus of decisionmaking in the executive branch. The appropriate posture of the civil servant is to carry out faithfully legitimate policy decisions, despite personal preferences. Without this chain of legitimacy, the democratic linkage between the electorate and the government would become unacceptably attenuated.

To argue that career voices ought to be heard at the highest levels in the executive branch is not to argue that those views should prevail. The career executive is likely to present an institutional perspective, mindful of the longer term consequences of decisions. Short-term, political criteria are likely to be taken into account by political appointees. The point is that those political appointees at the higher levels ought to have the benefit of the best judgment of career executives about the policy in question. When political appointees are placed lower in the bureaucracy, they will put their own political spin on advice at an early stage in the process, and those at the top may never hear the straight views of career executives about policies. According to former Comptroller General Elmer Staats, President Truman would say: "Give me your best professional analysis, I'll make the political judgment."[30]

Contrasting Perspectives

In addition to these normative distinctions, differences of background and style distinguish politicians and bureaucrats. Each set of officials contributes differently to the formulation of public policy. Appointees' political skills are needed to identify goals and to mobilize support for them. The strength of civil servants, on the other hand, lies in designing programs to implement those goals. These differences reflect contrasting roles and are rooted in institutional positions. Political appointees are in-and-outers. They are recruited to serve a particular President, and rarely stay longer than that President's term, usually much less. Presidential appointees want to make their marks quickly and to move on, either to a higher position in the government or back to the private sector where salaries are much more attractive. Much of their agenda is driven by the desire to re-elect the President or to leave a good record on which the partisan heir apparent can run.

Career executives, in contrast, have longer term perspectives. They will still be operating programs and administering agencies after this season's political birds of passage have flown. This realization causes them to pay attention to the health of institutions and to the integrity of the processes that ensure nonpartisan implementation of the laws. This longer term perspective makes them less willing to upset long-established practices quickly. Bureaucrats are concerned about the institutions they manage as well as about the current policies of those institutions. Politicians tend to see organizations as convenient tools to achieve their policy objectives.

One basic dilemma that underlies government in the United States is that the permanent bureaucracy must be responsive to the incumbent President, yet it must maintain the professionalism in its career managers necessary to serve the next President equally as well. The conscientious civil servant does not want to make choices among competing political claims; that is the function of the political process and of Presidential appointees. The different strengths of political appointees and career bureaucrats must therefore be merged in an appropriate balance if government is to be both responsive and effective. A certain amount of tension, however, will always be present in that balance.

The Cycle of Accommodation

Career executives are critical to the success of their political superiors in many ways. They are highly educated, and they know the intricacies of the laws and regulations that govern programs they implement. They possess institutional memory. They know where to go for help in central management agencies or in Congress. They have built up personal intelligence and communications networks over many years through dealing with the same organizations, people, and issues. They have earned the respect of their fellow professionals through years of service.

Career executives must follow legitimate orders, but they should do more than merely carry them out passively. A "yes boss" attitude is not merely inadequate, it may be downright dangerous. True neutral competence involves "loyalty that argues back," as Hugh Heclo, author of A *Government of Strangers*, has aptly said. For the boss to have "my own person" in the job is not enough; that person must have the requisite knowledge and skills to make the bureaucratic machine work, and the good judgment to delineate the pros and cons of various options.

Some political appointees make the mistake of using an unsophisticated version of the politics-administration dichotomy to exclude career executives from policy deliberations. This attitude has negative long term consequences. Heclo puts it this way:

> When senior political appointees fail to include higher civil servants in substantive policy discussions, there is little reason for permanent career staff to acquire more than a narrowly technical, routine perspective. When careerists are denied access to an understanding of the political rationales for top-level decisionmaking, they inevitably become divorced from the "big picture" and incapable of communicating it to subordinates. . . . In short, without good faith efforts at the highest political levels, the upper reaches of the bureaucracy go to seed.[31]

Elliot Richardson argues that to be an effective political appointee one must treat career subordinates with respect:

> People in the career services need to be met with respect from a point of view that takes for granted that they would not be there if they did not care about the merits

of the public service in which they are engaged, and with a willingness to listen and to ask questions.[32]

People who have devoted a lifetime or a significant part of it to expertise in their field are entitled to be listened to with respect. . . . Many Presidential appointees make the gross mistake of not sufficiently respecting the people they are dealing with . . . and get themselves into trouble as a result.[33]

Despite initial distrust and suspicion toward career executives, political appointees usually develop trust for and confidence in the career executives who report to them. This predictable cycle of accommodation has operated in all recent Presidential Administrations, if not in all political appointees. Initial suspicion is followed by a period of learning to work together, resulting in a more sophisticated appreciation of the contribution of the career service and in mutual respect and trust.

In comparing the quality of high-level executives in the public and private sectors, Alan K. (Scotty) Campbell, who was the first Director of the Office of Personnel Management (OPM) and later executive vice president of ARA Services, Inc. said:

The quality of top managers I knew in the federal government. . . is every bit as high as we have at ARA; and on the whole, the people at ARA are paid from one and one half to three times more than their public sector counterparts.[34]

In letters to Chairman Volcker, members of the Reagan Administration voiced similar opinions. According to Secretary of State George P. Shultz: "Speaking as one who has also served in the private sector and academia, I [believe] that the Department's workforce is on a par with the best I have known in the private world." Secretary of Energy John S. Herrington wrote: "On the whole, I believe career federal employees are as capable, conscientious and effective as their counterparts in the private sector."[35]

In a survey, the National Academy of Public Administration asked all Presidential appointees between 1964 and 1984 to characterize how responsive and competent the career executives in their agencies were. Favorable responses (4 or 5 on a 5-point scale) were reported by 77 percent or more in each of the past five Administrations. The responses broken down by administration, were as follows (Table 1):

Table 1
Appointees' Perception of Career Civil Servants[36]

Administration	Competent	Responsive
Johnson	92%	89%
Nixon	88	84
Ford	80	82
Carter	81	86
Reagan	77	78

The sooner that this cycle of accommodation begins in an Administration, the sooner a President can accomplish his goals.

Reagan Administration Secretary of Agriculture Richard Lyng offered this advice from his several tours as a Presidential appointee:

> In every case, I found career people that were absolutely splendid. Their experience was absolutely invaluable. I needed them, it was essential. The career people kept me from shooting myself in the foot. . . . The way you get them with you is to treat them like equals, point out I need you to help me. These people want the job done right. I never cared if a fellow was a Democrat or a Republican, because. . . all of them are nonpartisan. . . . A Presidential appointee who doesn't work with the career people will not make it.[37]

RECOMMENDATIONS FOR IMPROVING THE SYSTEM

Even a partial acceptance of the preceding data and arguments would compel the conclusion that the executive leadership system of the federal government has problems that require attention. The combination of rapid turnover of political appointees and their increasing numbers in the lower executive ranks has created a management void in many places. Using more political appointees to achieve political control eventually reaches a point of diminishing returns, and that point has long been passed in the federal government. "Ironically. . . the politicization of government positions has tended to reduce, not increase, political leadership; we need more political leadership, less politicization."[38]

RECOMMENDATION 1

We recommend that the Office of Presidential Personnel establish explicit criteria for the qualifications of people nominated for each position, and that these criteria emphasize managerial experience and substantive expertise as well as loyalty and philosophical compatibility with the President.

A President wants to accomplish a number of things in making political appointments. He wants to entrust executive branch direction to those who are loyal to him and who share his political philosophy. He may wish to reward past political service in the government or the party. But a President also wants his policies to be carried out effectively.

In recent Administrations, Presidents have increasingly emphasized political loyalty, narrowly construed, in selecting candidates to serve in the executive branch. Commitment to the President's philosophy and programs is essential to an effective Administration, but stressing past loyalty at the expense of present competence, broadly defined, is short-sighted and self-defeating.

The characteristics that are manifest in the best political appointees include leadership abilities, managerial competence, substantive expertise, and an appreciation for the constitutional context within which the executive branch operates. "There is no such thing as management divorced from substance and there is no such thing as effective management with substance that does not address considerations of process."[39] In recruiting Presidential appointees, an appropriate balance must be struck, one in which overall managerial competence and substantive expertise are given substantial weight.

At the PAS level, we recommend that the Office of Presidential Personnel establish the qualifications, substantive and managerial, that are necessary to perform the duties of each position. Each candidate for a PAS position ought to be measured against these criteria.

At the noncareer SES level, we recommend that Qualification Review Boards (QRBs), similar to those established for filling career SES positions, be established by the Office of Personnel Management (OPM) to ensure that political appointees have at least adequate qualifications for the positions to which they will be appointed.

We recommend that the qualifications of people hired for each Schedule C position be at the same level as the qualifications of career civil servants who are at similar GS ratings and performing similar duties.

RECOMMENDATION 2

The total number of political appointees in the departments and agencies of the executive branch should not exceed 2,000.

This implies a moderate reduction in PAS positions (there were 527 in 1985); a moderate reduction in noncareer SES members (there were 658 in 1986); and a significant reduction in Schedule C personnel (there were 1,665 in 1986). Ambassadors, U.S. marshals, and U.S. attorneys should not be included in this calculation.

Some organizational positions, of course, are specified by statute and the President must work closely with Congress to streamline departmental organization. These actions may lead to some positions being abolished and some going unfilled. This examination should be conducted on a department by department basis, and we expect that it will lead to reduced layering of bureaucratic levels in the executive branch.

At the noncareer SES level, we recommend that OPM establish criteria for the continuation or creation of SES positions in the departments and agencies. In allocating these political positions among the departments and agencies, the burden of proof ought to be on agency heads to show that their proposed or continuing positions fit the criteria established by OPM. These OPM criteria ought to include the extent to which the incumbent of each position is expected to play a significant policymaking role or be involved with the advocacy of administration priorities.

Dr. Otis R. Bowen, Secretary of Health and Human Services in the Reagan Administration, wrote to Chairman Volcker:

> I see a need to really examine the practices relating to placement of noncareers. I believe these appointees should be in positions that truly require political and confidential relationships. If we politicize all top jobs, we remove an incentive for careerists to aspire to these posts. Noncareerists should fill noncareer type positions, i.e., those dealing with the highest levels of effort in legislation, public affairs, general policy and the like.[40]

Schedule C positions are filled with persons at the GS-15 level and below who will be involved in Administration policymaking or who will have confidential relationships with policymakers, such as confidential secretaries and special assistants. With the reduction of PAS and noncareer SES positions, the need for Schedule C appointees will decrease. We recommend that Schedule C appointees not be placed in line management positions, and when they are in staff positions, they should not function as barriers between the responsible political executives and career managers. We also recommend that OPM establish criteria for the continuation or establishment of Schedule C positions, and that these be reviewed periodically to determine if they are still necessary.

RECOMMENDATION 3

The President and department and agency heads should fill more positions in the mid- and upper levels of the executive branch with career civil servants rather than political appointees. Particular emphasis should be placed on taking advantage of the continuity and institutional memory that career executives can provide across Administrations.

Some of the problems we have mentioned would be greatly alleviated if the appropriate roles of political appointees and career executives were more clearly understood and accepted. Those positions that are policy determining or that involve the advocacy of administration positions should appropriately be filled with political appointees. Appointees in top line positions should be allowed to have an appropriate number of confidential staff assistants. The above recommendations imply that career civil servants should be put in all other positions, especially those demanding a working knowledge of ongoing programs and administrative procedures. For the most part, Presidents can strike this balance by their own appointments in deciding whether to fill a given position with a political appointee or a career executive. SES provisions allow career executives to accept PAS positions and return to the career service at the end of their tours of duty.

John Gardner, Secretary of Health, Education, and Welfare in the Johnson Administration, argues that a new political executive can put together a loyal management team that includes members of the career service:

> I would strongly urge any incoming top official to come in with the recognition that he has a lot of potential allies around him. . . . People who would be glad to help if they got the chance. One of the great mistakes people make in coming in is developing a we/they attitude toward their own staff. . . . Big mistake. There are a lot of potential teammates out there, and you have to find them. And the faster you do the better. . . . I fairly soon found the people who could keep me out of the beartraps and could advise me. . . . I found that immensely helpful, and I think any newcomer will.[41]

The implication of this is that many positions now filled by political appointees can be filled by career executives. But some positions should be filled only by career executives. Some of these are now specially designated as "career reserved" and can be filled by only career executives and not by political appointees. Positions demanding high levels of technical competence or the absolute impartiality of the official (for example, in tax administration) are among the career-reserved positions.

The First Hoover Commission (the Commission on the Executive Branch of the Government) recommended that the position of assistant secretary for administration (or its equivalent) be filled only by career executives, and so it was in the 1950s and 1960s. But in the 1980s most of these positions were filled by political appointees. These positions usually cover budget administration, personnel, and physical space administration and call for familiarity with bureaucratic rules, regulations, and institutional history. Of course, policy decisions (such as budget allocation priorities) are appropriately made by political officials. The presumption ought be that these administrative positions be filled by career civil servants. Personnel decisions covered by the merit system must be scrupulously free of any partisan considerations. Therefore the administration of the career personnel system should also be placed under the direction of career officials.

It is also crucial in these administrative areas to maintain continuity between administrations. It is difficult for political appointees to provide this continuity at the end of an Administration when they are looking for jobs rather than remaining available for the incoming Administration. The ongoing administrative processes of the government, such as budget, personnel, and physical space, should be conducted by those who are dedicated to serving the next as well as the incumbent President.

RECOMMENDATION 4

In order to facilitate the recruitment of political appointees, we recommend that Presidential nominees establish personnel planning operations immediately after the nominating conventions.

One of the first major tasks of a President-elect is to recruit people to fill leadership positions in his Administration. But the volume is great and the time is limited: only 11 weeks between election and inauguration. Early planning is important. But the work is so sensitive that it is difficult to compile names for specific positions because if names are leaked, the results can be damaging. The infrastructure of a computerized personnel recruitment system can be set up ready to be put on line immediately after the election.

Although each Administration has compiled lists of the positions it may fill in the executive branch, we recommend that an ongoing capacity be created to maintain these records. The capacity should be created and housed in Office of Management and Budget (OMB) or a White House secretariat and maintained by career civil servants. It should include position descriptions of each PAS position along with brief descriptions of primary duties and should be updated regularly. It should also include the names and addresses of the people who have held the positions for the previous 10 years so that new nominees for the post could consult them.

RECOMMENDATION 5

The Office of Presidential Personnel should be used as an active recruitment office and not as a passive screening office.

The major focus of the President's Personnel Office should be not on the seekers but on the sought.[42] As important as it is to stay on top of the flood of job applicants and recommendations, the President's programs and reputation will depend on the quality of the top-level managers who will administer the government. If a system to do this is not in place immediately after the election, the new Administration may find itself burdened with appointees of poor quality who will be difficult to fire.

The problem is that the best people do not always bring themselves to the attention of the White House. So the White House should aggressively reach out to locate the best and the brightest people in the country who are qualified to fill Administration positions. It should not passively screen political recommendations and self-applications that come in over the transom. A Presidential "head-hunting" operation should be initiated early and should be staffed with professionals in political and executive recruitment. It should concern itself primarily with PAS appointments and leave SES and Schedule C recruitment to department and agency heads.

RECOMMENDATION 6

The President should delegate to department heads the recruitment of noncareer SES and Schedule C appointments within the bounds of general criteria established by the White House. The President should give significant weight to the preferences of cabinet secretaries in the selection of their immediate subordinates who are Presidential appointments.

In recent years, the Office of Presidential Personnel has assumed close control over all political appointments in the government, including noncareer SES and Schedule C appointments that are technically agency head appointments. We urge the President to allow his cabinet secretaries to have an appropriate say in the appointment of their immediate subordinates and in the forming of their management team. The White House has a legitimate interest in ensuring that all Presidential appointees are loyal to the Administration, but insisting on controlling all appointments undermines the department secretaries and overextends the capacity of the Office of Presidential Personnel. According to Frederic Malek, White House Personnel Director for President Nixon, "If you try to do everything, I'm not so sure you can succeed. It's an awfully difficult job just to handle the *Presidential* appointees. I'm concerned that if you try to do too much, you may be diluted to the point where you're not as effective." [Emphasis added.][43]

The need to build a management team with a shared philosophy and good interpersonal chemistry is of direct concern to agency heads, but of less concern to the Office of Presidential Personnel. Secretary Carlucci's advice to new political appointees is:

> Spend most of your time at the outset focussing on the personnel system. Get your appointees in place, have your own political personnel person, because the first clash you will have is with the Office of Presidential Personnel. I don't care whether it is a Republican or a Democrat. If you don't get your own people in place, you are going to end up being a one-armed paper hanger.[44]

A *modus vivendi* must be worked out that establishes an appropriate balance between these two legitimate claims.

We recommend that the Office of Presidential Personnel recruit actively for PAS appointees, but that White House candidates not be forced upon department or agency heads. The President should consider seriously candidates recruited by cabinet secretaries. With respect to SES and Schedule C appointments, the agency head should have broad discretion to recruit people of their own choosing. The White House should retain veto power over any proposed nominee of a department head, but it should exercise that veto sparingly. It should also weigh heavily any objections of agency heads to White House nominees, and only in exceptional circumstances should an appointee be forced on an agency head against his or her preferences.

One way of facilitating this process during the transition is to have a person in the office of each cabinet secretary and agency head who has the trust of the Office of Presidential Personnel and the confidence of the agency head to act as liaison for Presidential appointments between the White House and the department or agency.

RECOMMENDATION 7

Executive salaries should be significantly increased and financial reporting requirements should be reexamined.

The level of compensation for political executives is a serious impediment to recruitment for new Administrations. The President should take seriously the recommendations of the Quadrennial Commission on Executive, Legislative, and Judicial, Salaries and should support significantly increased salaries for the executives of the federal government, both career and political. In reflecting on public servants, Secretary Carlucci observes, "We cannot pay them properly, and senior levels are burdened by petty harassment and the bureaucratics of the Ethics in Government Act. Indeed, it is amazing to me that our government servants are as good as they are, and they compare favorably with the private sector. But even dedication has its limits, and I now see a clear erosion of quality."[45] More specific recommendations on pay levels are included in other parts of the Commission's final report, *Leadership for America: Rebuilding the Public Service.*

The President should support legislative efforts to change the Ethics in Government Act to simplify financial reporting requirements and to ease the tax consequences of putting stock assets in blind trusts. This improvement can and should be done without undermining the ethical intent of the act. Public disclosure of financial information should be required only of candidates for very high-level positions, including PAS positions.[46]

The reporting requirements for financial disclosure for nominees for Presidential appointments (SF 278, "Executive Personnel Financial Disclosure Report") constitute a significant obstacle that Presidential nominees must overcome. The information required is difficult to reconstruct, and the form itself is complicated, often requiring professional legal and accounting advice. In a survey by the National Academy of Public Administration, more that 70 percent of Presidential appointees reported that they had difficulty in filling out the forms, and 25 percent reported that coping with the form delayed their taking office.[47]

The process could be improved by simplifying the forms and by requiring less detail. Reporting of income or holdings worth less than $1,000 could be dropped entirely. The law should be written so that a mistake in filling out a form does not incur criminal penalties.

While the requirement of divestiture of financial assets to preclude conflicts of interest serves an important purpose, individuals should not be forced to suffer undue financial hardship in order to accept a Presidential appointment. The President should support legislation that would allow the rolling over of assets into investments that provide no conflict of interest without immediate capital gains tax liability.

RECOMMENDATION 8

The President should establish orientation programs for all new political appointees in the executive branch.

When new political appointees enter the federal government, they are often thrust into their positions with little preparation or orientation. Only 20 percent of PAS appointees from 1964 to 1984 received any orientation when they joined the government. While some new appointees have had previous government experience, 60 percent of them come from outside of the government. The orientation of new appointees should be more systematic than it has been in the past.

Appointees with backgrounds in business, the law, or academia may possess impressive expertise and experience, but the federal management context is unique in many important ways. The environment of federal organizations is dominated by Congress and the White House and is affected by the central management agencies. The internal management environment is dominated by budget, personnel, and administrative procedures that are unique to the federal government. The relationship between political appointees and career executives has few parallels in the business world. Policymaking in the federal government involves much more coordination than in most other management contexts.

But even if new appointees have worked in the federal government, they still need to learn the priorities and policy development processes of their President. Department heads need to know how the President expects them to interact with the White House staff. What are the ground rules for communicating with Congress? What role will the White House play in selecting noncareer personnel in departments and agencies?

The White House should provide an orientation program for all new PAS appointees. Recent Administrations have provided some form of orientation program for new appointees, and in the Reagan Administration the Assistant for Presidential Personnel has organized White House briefing seminars for new appointees.[48] These efforts need to be institutionalized. That is, the organization of the orientation capacity should be established in a way that will ensure its continuation across Administrations. The function could be housed in the Office of Presidential Personnel or in a permanent White House secretariat.

The persons in the office should be primarily career civil servants who will know how the sessions have been conducted in previous Administrations and who will adapt the orientations to the needs of a new Administration. This office should be responsible for developing a set of materials to which appointees can refer regarding the issues covered. The materials should include selections from relevant statutes and regulations when appropriate, for example, conflict of interest rules from the Office of Government Ethics.

Although such a unit can do the legwork, the whole program will only be effective if it has high level backing in each Administration's White House staff. Whenever possible, social functions accompanying orientation programs should include spouses of Administration officials, in order to acquaint appointees' families with the responsibilities of these offices. These programs should be set up to handle large volumes at the beginning of a new Administration and should be run on a regular basis for new appointees joining the Administration later in its tenure.

Briefing programs ought to include presentations by career executives, both to take advantage of their expertise and experience and to begin the process of acquainting new appointees with career executives with whom they will be working. It should also be emphasized that political appointees are entrusted for a short time with the management of the permanent interests of the American people and the U.S. government. This trust should not be taken lightly and should be honored so that the institutions of the government can be passed on to the next Administration in sound condition.

Senior officials are so busy in the early months of a new Administration that they find it difficult to set aside time and personnel to conduct orientation programs. Yet that is when the need is the greatest. Orientation should be assigned an early and high priority in a new Administration.

Because it is so difficult to draw busy high-level officials away from their new jobs, these orientation sessions must be conducted from the White House itself, and attendance should be mandatory. The nuts and bolts substance of the orientations should include sessions on personnel rules, budget procedures, dealing with the press, relations with Congress, and legal and ethical guidelines. They should also include briefings on the policy-development processes of the Administration as well as on the priorities of the President. The sessions can be conducted most effectively by high-level members of the Administration and by former Presidential appointees.

Orientation sessions for PAS appointees that cover agency- specific and programmatic matters should be conducted in the departments and agencies. Beginning in 1988, OPM conducted orientation sessions for noncareer members of the SES and Schedule C appointees. We endorse these programs and recommend they be institutionalized in OPM so that each new Administration can take advantage of the capacity when it takes office. The substance of the courses should be similar to the programs run in the White House.

Although career senior executives are familiar with the routine processes of the federal government, they need to be oriented to certain aspects of a new Administration. Orientation sessions should acquaint them with the personnel and policy priorities of the new Administration. The sessions should give senior executives a clear picture of the direction of the new Administration, assure them that they will be included in consideration of new policies, and reiterate that they will be expected to support actively the new Administration's policy directions. The more that career employees are involved and interact with their new political superiors, the less likely it is that suspicion and distrust will grow between the two groups.

A new President should instill a team spirit in his Administration. An ongoing program of policy briefings during an Administration can help to sustain this team spirit as well as keep officials up-to-date on Administration priorities. A President should also try to include career executives as part of the team and invite them to briefing sessions when appropriate. Joint briefing and training sessions (for example, at the Federal Executive Institute) are also useful in engendering mutual trust and smooth working relationships between career and political executives.

RECOMMENDATION 9

The President should seek commitments from the appointees in his Administration to remain in office for a full term.

As a practical matter, it would be difficult to enforce this commitment, but giving one's word to the President may be weighed heavily by those he selects to run his Administration. Of course, this would not preclude the President from asking for resignations from any appointee who does not perform up to expectations.

We conclude by quoting Secretary Carlucci on the pressing need for improvements in the executive levels of the public service:

> There was a Prime Minister in the Fourth Republic who, as best I can tell, was known for nothing other than the following quote: "Politics is the art of postponing decisions until they are no longer relevant." Well, that may work on most issues, but it will not on this one. Current trends are making the situation worse, and it just will not go away. Many of us have devoted a lifetime to government service. Others are at the peak of their careers. We served because we believed in the meaning of government and a free society. Nothing has happened to change that.[49]

ENDNOTES

1. See James W. Fesler, "The Higher Civil Service in Europe and the United States," in *The Higher Civil Service in Europe and Canada* ed. by Bruce L.R. Smith (Washington, D.C.: Brookings, 1984), p. 87.
2. See Carl Brauer, "Tenure, Turnover, and Postgovernment Employment Trends of Presidential Appointees," in *The In-And-Outers*, edited by Calvin Mackenzie (Baltimore: Johns Hopkins University Press, 1987), 175; Carolyn Ban and Patricia Ingraham, "Short-Timers: Political Appointee Mobility and its Impact on Political-Career Relations in the Reagan Administration," paper presented at the National Convention of the American Society for Public Administration, Anaheim, CA, 1986.
3. Ban and Ingraham, "Short-Timers," ASPA Paper, 1986.
4. Patricia W. Ingraham, "Building Bridges or Burning Them?: The President, the Appointees, and the Bureaucracy," *Public Administration Review* (September/October 1987), p. 429.
5. Hugh Heclo, "The In-and-Outer System: A Critical Assessment," in *The In-And-Outers,* edited by G. Calvin Mackenzie (Baltimore: Johns Hopkins University Press, 1987), 208.
6. Quoted in Paul Light, "When Worlds Collide: The Political-Career Nexus," in *The In-and-Outers* edited by Calvin Mackenzie (Baltimore: Johns Hopkins University Press, 1987), p. 157.
7. Data supplied by the Office of the Under Secretary of State for Management, January 1988.
8. These data are taken from the *Plum Books* of 1960 and 1984: U.S. Government Policy and Supporting Positions, House Committee on Post Office and Civil Service (86th Congress, 2nd Session) 1960; and U.S. Government Policy and Supporting Positions, Senate Committee on Governmental Affairs (98th Congress, 2nd Session) 1984.
9. Frank Carlucci, "A Private Sector and National Perspective," in *The State of the American Public Service* (Washington: National Academy of Public Administration, 1985), p. 7.
10. Frederic V. Malek, *Washington's Hidden Tragedy* (New York: The Free Press, 1978), pp. 102–103.
11. For the first two years cited see David T. Stanley, et al. *Men Who Govern* (Washington, D.C.: Brookings, 1967), p. 4. For the 1985 data see Patricia Ingraham, "Building Bridges

or Burning Them?" *Public Administration Review* (September/October 1987), p. 427.

12. General Accounting Office, *Federal Employees: Trends in Career and Noncareer Employee Appointments in the Executive Branch* (July 1987), GAO/GGD-87-96FS, p. 11.

13. Ingraham, "Building Bridges or Burning Them?" *Public Administration Review* (September/October 1987), p. 429.

14. Congressional Budget Office, *Federal Civilian Employment*, Special Study (December 1987), p. ix.

15. National Academy of Public Administration, "Perspectives on the Public Management Challenge," Remarks by Ronald I. Spiers (March 1987), pp. 30–31.

16. Quoted in Ban and Ingraham, "Short-Timers," ASPA Paper, 1986.

17. Ban and Ingraham, "Short-Timers," ASPA Paper, 1986.

18. Elliot L. Richardson, Article for the Ripon Society (September 10, 1987). For another version of these remarks see Elliot L. Richardson "Civil Servants: Why Not the Best?" *Wall Street Journal* (November 20, 1987).

19. Patricia Ingraham, "Building Bridges or Burning Them?" *Public Administration Review* (September/October 1987), p. 431.

20. Clyde Linsley, "The Brain Drain Continues As Top Government Managers Leave for the Private Sector," *Government Executive* (June 1988), pp. 10–18.

21. *New York Times*, December 14, 1987.

22. Timothy Clark and Marjorie Wachtel, "The Quite Crisis Goes Public," *Government Executive* (June 1988), p. 28.

23. General Accounting Office, *Senior Executive Service: Reasons Why Career Members Left in Fiscal Year 1985*, GAO/GGD-87-106FS (August 1987), p. 8.

24. Patricia Ingraham, "Building Bridges or Burning Them?" *Public Administration Review* (September/October 1987), p. 431.

25. Charles H. Levine and Rosalyn Kleeman, "The Quiet Crisis of the Civil Service: The Federal Personnel System at the Crossroads," National Academy of Public Administration (1987), p. 6.

26. Timothy Clark and Marjorie Wachtel, "The Quite Crisis Goes Public," *Government Executive* (June 1988), p. 28.

27. U.S. Commission on Executive, Legislative, and Judicial Salaries. "High Quality Leadership—Our Government's Most Precious Asset." Report of the Commission (December 15, 1986), pp. 19–20.

28. *The Report of the President's Commission on Compensation of Career Federal Executives* (February 26, 1988), pp. 3–6.

29. Letter from David Ruder to Paul Volcker, dated 3 November 1987.

30. Statement at the Panel meeting of the Presidency Project of the National Academy of Public Administration, May 17, 1988. Elmer Staats was chair of the Panel.

31. Hugh Heclo, "The In-and-Outer System: A Critical Assessment," in *The In-and-Outers*, edited by G. Calvin Mackenzie (Baltimore: Johns Hopkins University Press, 1987), 202.

32. Testimony of Elliot Richardson, Hearings before the Senate Committee on Governmental Affairs on the *Presidential Transition Effectiveness Act* (100th Congress, 1st and 2nd Sessions), 1988, p. 91.

33. Quoted by James P. Pfiffner, "Political Appointees and Career Executives: The Democracy-Bureaucracy Nexus in the Third Century," *Public Administration Review* (January/February 1987), p. 61. The interview was conducted for the Presidential Appointee Project of the National Academy of Public Administration.

34. Quoted in James Fesler, "Politics, Policy, and Bureaucracy at the Top," *The Annals* 466 (March 1983), p. 33.
35. The letters are in the files of the National Commission on the Public Service.
36. National Academy of Public Administration, *Leadership in Jeopardy* (1985). See Paul Light, "When Worlds Collide: The Political-Career Nexus," in *The In-and-Outers*, edited by G. Calvin Mackenzie (Baltimore: Johns Hopkins University Press, 1987), p. 158.
37. Quoted by Pfiffner, "Political Appointees and Career Executives," p. 61.
38. Elliot L. Richardson, Testimony before the Senate Committee on Governmental Affairs. Printed in Hearings on the *Presidential Transition Effectiveness Act* (100th Congress, 1st and 2nd Sessions), 1988, p. 89.
39. Testimony of Elliot Richardson, Senate Governmental Affairs Committee Hearings on the *Presidential Transition Effectiveness Act* (1988), p. 89–90.
40. The letter is in the files of the National Commission on the Public Service.
41. Quoted in Pfiffner, "Political Appointees and Career Executives," p. 61.
42. For proposals to improve the political recruitment process see, *Leadership in Jeopardy: The Fraying of the Presidential Appointments System*, National Academy of Public Administration, 1985.
43. National Academy of Public Administration, "Recruiting Presidential Appointees: A Conference of Former Presidential Personnel Assistants," (December 13, 1984), p. 19.
44. Quoted in James P. Pfiffner, *The Strategic Presidency: Hitting the Ground Running* (Chicago: Dorsey Press, 1988), p. 81.
45. Frank Carlucci, "A Private Sector and National Perspective," (Washington: National Academy of Public Administration, 1985), p. 8.
46. See National Academy of Public Administration, *Leadership in Jeopardy* (1985). See also "Report of the Public/Private Careers Project," Center for Business and Government of the JFK School of Government, Harvard University (16 December 1987).
47. See Leadership in Jeopardy, pp. 13–15.
48. For an overview of the Reagan Administration approach and a proposal for continuing orientation sessions see, "Orienting Presidential Appointees," paper prepared by Edward Preston for the Standing Committee on the Public Service of the National Academy of Public Administration. See also, James P. Pfiffner, "Strangers in a Strange Land: Orienting New Presidential Appointees," in G. Calvin Mackenzie, *The In-and-Outers* (Baltimore: Johns Hopkins University Press, 1987), pp. 141–155.
49. Frank Carlucci, "A Private Sector and National Perspective," (Washington: National Academy of Public Administration, 1985), p. 10.

FACING THE FEDERAL COMPENSATION CRISIS

The Report of the

Task Force on Pay and Compensation

to the

National Commission on the Public 'Service

TASK FORCE

James L. Ferguson, *Chairman*

James E. Burke

Richard A. Debs

Robert S. McNamara

G.G. Michelson

Donna E. Shalala

Alexander B. Trowbridge

WASHINGTON 1989

THE TASK FORCE ON
PAY AND COMPENSATION

CHAIRMAN

James L. Ferguson
Chairman, Executive Committee
General Foods Corporation

MEMBERS

James E. Burke
Chairman and Chief Executive Officer, Johnson & Johnson

Richard A. Debs
Former President of Morgan Stanley, Inc.

Robert S. McNamara
Former Secretary of Defense

G.G. Michelson
Senior Vice President, R.H. Macy & Co.

Donna E. Shalala
Chancellor, University of Wisconsin

Alexander B. Trowbridge
President, National Association of Manufacturers

PROJECT DIRECTOR

Lyn M. Holley
Senior Staff
National Commission on the Public Service

CONTENTS

PREFACE

The Task Force on Pay and Compensation of the National Commission on the Public Service focused on the four core systems of federal compensation: pay for top-level appointed and elected executives in all three branches of government, for career executives, for the white-collar workforce, and for the blue-collar workforce.

The Task Force chose this focus to provide the broadest view of the subject for policymakers and taxpayers. Within the federal government, these four systems generally guide developments in the other three dozen or so federal pay systems. Moreover, analyses of this sort on federal pay and compensation are useful to state and local governments and independent sector organizations.

Members of the Task Force collectively brought almost two centuries of business and government experience to their work. The Task Force used studies, reports, and analyses prepared by professional associations, universities, government agencies, and other governmental and nongovernmental commissions. The Task Force was supported by a Project Director; a multidisciplinary report team of experts who served *pro bono publico*, contributed original research or analysis, and wrote source papers; many reviewers and advisers; several organizations that contributed resources and expertise; and an able production staff. The work of the Task Force was also informed by correspondence sent to the Commission and by testimony and comment offered in the Commission's regional dialogues at the University of Southern California, the Lyndon Baines Johnson School of Public Administration, the Georgia State University School of Public and Urban Affairs, the John F. Kennedy School of Government, and New York University and by a meeting at the Gerald Ford Library of the University of Michigan.

The Task Force reached consensus on the nature of the problem and a program of work at its organizing meeting on October 29, 1987.

The Project Director and the report team then developed materials describing the history of federal pay-setting from 1789, highlighting what had been tried, what had worked, what had not worked, and why. Other materials developed described how the size and composition of the federal workforce had changed in response to changing needs, provided information about results of research on pay as a motivator, summarized the federal experience with pay comparability for white-collar workers since 1962, and explained and analyzed federal pay-setting practices in relation to private-sector practices.

The Task Force decided in a teleconference that it was not practical to address directly many of the decisions fundamental to overall design of a compensation system. For example, should a system be designed to retain staff for 20 to 30 years, or to encourage more rapid turnover? Should a system be designed to attract "the best and the brightest" or the "average" candidate? Those matters are too diverse and are far beyond the mandate of the Task Force. It was decided to study the pay-setting systems now in place, analyze them to determine the assumptions of their current design, note how and where each had been successful or unsuccessful, and recommend improvements.The Task Force met in New York on February 18, 1988, and subsequently developed an action plan that included specifications for improvements needed in the federal compensation system for the large white-collar workforce and activities to support the next executive pay increase. The Commission considered the plan at its April 26, 1988, meeting. The Task Force tested the climate for acceptance of its recommendations by informally vetting a model for locality pay.

The Task Force considered the first comprehensive draft of its report at its September 15, 1988, meeting in New York. The Commission Chairman and Executive Director and the Task Force Chairman and Project Director reviewed the work of the Task Force at Princeton University on September 30, 1988, with a group of 60 national experts in public administration and political science. The Commission considered the Task Force report and recommendations at its plenary meeting on October 19, 1988.

Although geographically dispersed and diverse in background, members of the Task Force conducted an active, independent consideration of federal compensation issues and developed a consensus on how to address these issues. Task Force recommendations cover every level of federal work, and its report and source papers should inform future action on compensation issues.

Acknowledgments

Lyn Holley served as Project Director through the courtesy of the U.S. Customs Service. Each member of the report team was recruited for a particular expertise or ability, and worked many hours without compensation or reimbursement except through their love of the subject and their deep commitment to public service. Report team members were: T.J. Black, Herbert Block, Arnold Gerber, Sharon Gressle, Eugene McCarthy, Mark Musell, Howard Risher, Sue Scheig, Barbara Schwemle, Harvey Shaynes, and Lucretia Tanner.

Individuals who lent their considerable expertise to advising and informing the work of the Task Force include: Robert Mosel of the George Washington University; Rosslyn Kleeman and Robert Shelton of the General Accounting Office; Robert Wait and Sally Donner of General Foods; Barbara Fiss, Fred Hohlweg, and Phillip Schneider of the Office of Personnel Management; Fritz Wenzler and Randy Christian of Johnson & Johnson; Charles Fay of Rutgers University; Fred Pauls, Roger Walke, and Ronald Moe of the Congressional Research Service; George Stelutto, Charles O'Connor, Sandra King, and Eva Jacobs of the Bureau of Labor Statistics; Miriam Ershkowitz, Management Consultant; Fred Tingley and Wayne Coleman of the U.S. Customs Service; Frank Cippola of the Department of Defense; Howard Messner of the American Consulting Engineers Council; Lawrence Korb of the Brookings Institute; Norman Carlson, former Director of the Bureau of Prisons; John Palmer, Dean, Maxwell School at Syracuse University; James Perry, Indiana University; George Maharay and Joe Howe, consultants to the National Academy of Public Administration; John Mulholland, Robert Edgell, Peter Tchirkow, and Arne Anderson of the American Federation of Government Employees; Frank Seidl of the Office of Management and Budget; J.L. Cullen, Chair of the President's Commission on Compensation for Career Federal Executives; Fred Wertheimer and Ann McBride of Common Cause; Alan Barak of the U.S. Department of Agriculture; Sylvester Schreiber of the Wyatt Company; Bun Bray and Robert Tarr of the Council of Former Federal Executives; and Maureen Gillman of the National Treasury Employees Union. We are indebted to Catherine Tashjean, the Office of Personnel Management reference librarian, and her staff for guiding us through their unique collections.

Organizations that have been particularly helpful to the work of the Task Force include: the Classification and Compensation Society and the Federal Executive Institutes, both of which directed their programs throughout the year toward professional examination of Task Force issues; the Advisory Committee on Federal Pay and the Commission on Executive, Judicial, and Legislative Salaries, which provided excellent reports and opportunities for testimony; the American Society for Public Administration and the National Academy of Public Administration, which provided studies and hosted discussions of these issues; the Public Employees Roundtable; the Senior Executives Association; the Select Committee on Administration of the U.S. Judiciary; the Government-University-Industry Research Roundtable and its members; and the New York and the Newark Federal Executive Boards, which provided data and analysis about the impact of the current compensation situation on federal work. The other Task Forces of this Commission contributed to our work by illustrating or covering the aspects of compensation that fell most in their areas: the impact of inadequate pay and ineffective pay-setting on recruitment and retention; the requirements for financial divestiture that further reduce compensation of many politically appointed executives; and the root cause of federal pay problems—a poor public perception and understanding of the contributions and value of federal work.

Individual members of the Commission staff have been vital to the success of our work: Executive Director L. Bruce Laingen diplomatically integrated strong opposing views and bore the formidable burden of coordinating all efforts, Deputy Director Charles Levine provided our grand design and inspired us to extend our best, Senior Advisor Paul Light challenged us and broadened our thinking, Joseph Laitin and Joseph Foote guided and shaped our report, Marjorie Jones and Lillian Logan volunteered much of their time and many a long night of production and moral support, Lois Waldman and Mary Harrington coordinated and facilitated countless contacts and appointments, and Diane Yendrey made it all come together into a publication.

All of the organizations and individuals mentioned share a deep commitment to public service, and have worked together in the hope that these recommendations may help achieve the small but significant component of public administration that is fair pay for those who serve.

James L. Ferguson, Chairman
Lyn M. Holley, Project Director

New York City
April 1989

EXECUTIVE SUMMARY

The nation requires effective performance from its federal workforce in order to prosper. Effective performance depends in large part on adequate compensation. The level of federal compensation has been deteriorating for more than 10 years, but the effects are only now beginning to show. There is still time to correct this situation, but immediate and decisive action is necessary.

Federal compensation levels have fallen so much that they are now major obstacles to recruiting and retaining a quality federal workforce. While the government's open recruitment policies still produce long lines of applicants for most federal jobs, those well qualified to perform the work in many key areas and occupations are not in those lines. Current compensation levels limit recruitment for government jobs to the lower end of the labor market, to candidates who are willing to accept the below-average salaries the government offers. This limitation undermines government ability to maintain a high-quality workforce capable of providing reliable advice about tax provisions, effective inspections of food, banking practices or aviation safety, and efficient defense acquisitions. The *Workforce 2000* report forecasts a shrinking pool of suitably qualified candidates, which will make the government's recruiting problems even worse.

While the compensation crisis has been caused in part by fiscal expediency, the underlying cause is the mistaken view held by much of the American public that federal employees contribute little to the prosperity of the nation. People will not pay for what they do not value. The Task Force on Pay and Compensation urges the President and Congress to lead the American people in placing an appropriate value on the work of federal employees.

Federal compensation systems are complex. The federal workforce, military and civilian, numbers more than 5 million, and covers almost a thousand occupations in locations throughout the United States and the world. Nonetheless, government and nongovernment compensation systems are governed by the same basic principles, and the public as well as federal employees already understand these principles on the level of their personal experiences. Communicating how federal workers are paid has been neglected; and discussion of federal pay issues in the media is often greeted with vigorous expressions of public suspicion and displeasure about how federal employees are paid, or about how much they are paid. The Task Force concludes that the President and Congress must act to restore public confidence in federal pay-setting both by setting pay more effectively, and by informing the public about it.

One well-understood compensation principle is that pay is a necessary condition for attracting and retaining the workforce needed to carry out business. Most employers set their rates of pay according to what their competitors are offering, i.e., to the labor market they face. Employers try not to offer more than competitors and cannot offer less, so most employers tend to offer salaries that are about the average or median for a particular occupation or location. The government has traditionally relied on "psychic" income—the gratification of serving the nation—to supplement the low pay of the few thousand elected and appointed officials at the very top. For most federal jobs, however, pay must be about average for the market faced in order to support recruitment and retention. *In a general sense, the nation is now spending only enough to recruit in the lowest quartile of the labor market,[1] far below the average or median level required. Executive pay levels have dropped below levels needed to recruit or retain fully qualified persons who depend on their salaries for their livelihood.* The Task Force believes that rates of pay for jobs below the executive rank must be brought up to comparability with relevant labor markets, and that executive pay must be increased. This could be accomplished over time without undue increases in the amount spent on the federal payroll.

In times of fiscal austerity it is especially important that federal dollars be well spent. The trade-off for phasing in better levels of compensation and better pay-setting practices is not only quality of government performance, but also at this point, perhaps, even the viability of some federal operations. Savings to offset costs of improving compensation could be achieved through among other things, reducing overhead and increasing organizational effectiveness; for example:

- Improved organization and job design by reducing "layers" of supervision and middle management levels of organization, and reversing the trend of designing the job to get the highest possible grade (a practice sometimes used to counteract poor market position).

- Improved accountability, e.g., by making agency personnel, payroll, and performance information systems compatible, accessible, and accurate so that use of resources can be monitored efficiently.

- Improved organization performance through more effective recruitment and retention.

Psychic income is a significant part of compensation that requires no cash outlays. It can be much enhanced by increasing respect for government employees at all levels and by improving working conditions. Top-level managers can be held accountable for communicating that employees are doing something important, worthwhile, and difficult and for insisting on a quality job.

The quality of the direction of the workforce is the key to effective government performance of any activity—including containing payroll costs. If recommended improvements in respect for federal work, flexibility in managing it, and in compensation are realized, the government can recruit and retain the executives it needs. Such executives would be effective in recruiting and retaining qualify staff, even attracting staff who are competitive at the top of their labor market, while offering salaries that are only average—along with the opportunity to serve a great nation.

RECOMMENDATIONS

Federal pay systems themselves are flawed or in disarray. The Task Force studied four major pay systems that cover directly or indirectly most of the federal workforce: the top executive levels in all three branches of government; and, in the executive branch, the career executive levels, white-collar work, and blue-collar work. All systems studied had different histories, traditions and problems. The recommendations that follow are designed to stop the erosion and turbulence that currently characterize levels of federal pay and benefits, and to rebuild federal pay systems so that they are perceived by federal employees at all levels and by the public to be reasonable and fair.

Top-level appointed and elected executives in all three branches of government since the founding of the Republic have been paid salaries that are low when compared with their private-sector counterparts. It has been expected that leaders will serve, accepting lower pay in part in consideration of the gratifications of serving at these levels. However, the purchasing power of judges, Members of Congress, and top federal executives has decreased by 35 percent from its already relatively lower level in 1969, retention is becoming a problem and recruitment risks becoming limited to the wealthy or the inexperienced. The Task Force recommends immediate moves toward restoring lost purchasing power of executive pay in all three branches as a preferred option, but offers an alternative in the event that immediate increases for Congress are not feasible. The Task Force also recommends actions necessary to address public concerns about and problems with Congressional pay-setting from both an historic and a current perspective—most particularly the absence of an objective frame of reference for evaluating adequacy of Congressional pay.

Top-level career executive (Senior Executive Service) pay is compressed between pay of top appointed and elected executives, who are always paid below the market, and pay of white-collar (General Schedule) managers who are supposed to be paid "comparably" with the labor market. The Task Force recommends that career executives' pay rates be increased in concert with increases for top level executives.

Option A.
RECOMMENDATION 1

The 101st Congress should enact legislation to increase pay of Members, judges, and elected and appointed executive branch officials to half of the amount recommended by President Reagan, to increase pay again by the same amount effective in 1991, and to act promptly to terminate honoraria.

RECOMMENDATION 2

President Bush should issue an executive order to increase the Senior Executive Service (SES) pay rates to the amounts last recommended by President Reagan (except that the top rate would be adjusted to not exceed the salary of Members of Congress).

RECOMMENDATION 3

The 101st Congress should enact legislation to establish a bipartisan Temporary (3 years) Citizens Advisory Panel of 50 members that is broadly representative of the United States—geographically, economically, ethnically, and in gender; with members to be nominated by state Governors, and the members and chair to be selected by the President. Each Governor would be asked to designate at least three nominees in order to help the President balance representation. In view of public objection expressed about the current process for setting Congressional pay, and the lack of focus or dignity in discussions of the amount of Congressional pay, the Panel should be charged with and funded to:

• Develop an objective frame of reference for evaluating the adequacy of top executive pay that is widely accepted as appropriate and fair;

• Develop a process for measuring and implementing the levels implied by the frame of reference, and

• Develop and recommend legislation to establish the frame of reference and the process, and to adjust Congressional pay to the acceptable level.

RECOMMENDATION 4

President Bush should mandate arrangements to improve the SES pay-setting process including: charging the Office of Personnel Management with providing a biennial report to the President that evaluates SES compensation practices; and, following completion of the work of the Temporary Citizens Advisory Panel, with developing a framework for evaluating the adequacy of SES pay and for establishing appropriate pay-level distinctions within the SES and among special occupations associated with the SES or with supergrade positions (e.g., Administrative Law and Contract Law Judges).

If the Congress does not find this approach acceptable:

Option B.
RECOMMENDATION 1

The 101st Congress should pass legislation to immediately increase pay of Judges and elected and appointed executive branch officials 12½ percent, and to phase in equal increases over the next three years until the full amount of increases recommended by President Reagan has been reached.

RECOMMENDATION 2

President Bush should issue an Executive Order to provide a similar schedule of increases for the Senior Executive Service (SES), up to the amounts last recommended by President Reagan.

RECOMMENDATION 3-a

The 101st Congress should enact legislation to create a bipartisan Temporary (three-year) Citizens Advisory Panel that is broadly representative of the United States—geographically, economically, ethnically, and in gender, as described in Option A above, to develop an acceptable frame of reference and process for setting the pay of Congress, and to recommend levels of pay for Congress that are broadly accepted as appropriate and fair.

RECOMMENDATION 3-b

The Citizens Advisory Panel, as soon as possible after being established, should consider and recommend to Congress some means for adjusting Congressional pay in the interim to prevent further erosion of pay until the frame of reference, process and level of pay established on the basis of Panel recommendations has been accomplished, also to facilitate prompt termination of honoraria. Some regular performance measure, e.g., the Employment Cost Index, might provide annual adjustments, and some special increases of pay might be considered as honoraria are phased out.

RECOMMENDATION 4

President Bush should act to improve the SES pay-setting process by requiring reports and guidelines be developed as described in Option A.

White-collar (General Schedule) workers' pay in 1989 is 22 percent behind the labor market. Although the established system for setting General Schedule pay was intended to provide for market comparability, the political will to resist short-term expedient cuts in the increases needed to maintain pay at market levels has not been strong enough. The pay-setting system itself is flawed by a requirement for uniform, nationwide rates of pay that do not represent the real labor market, which varies by geographic area and occupation.

RECOMMENDATION 5

The 101st Congress should enact, and President Bush should approve, legislation to change the process for making comparability adjustments to pay. The legislation should require:

• Comparability adjustments based on the relevant *local* labor market, rather than one, across-the-board, across-the-nation figure;

• A decentralized, coordinated system for pay-setting modeled on the system currently in effect for blue-collar wage-setting (the Federal Wage System), and taking into account lessons learned in the history of operation of that system;

• Recruitment and retention pay rates for use as exceptions that respond to the high-priced occupational groups that distort overall salary survey findings;

• Phased implementation over a period of years to accommodate fiscal restraints and to provide for orderly phasing out of expedients taken to counteract pay erosion; and

• Modernization of systems and methods used in pay-setting.

Blue-collar (Federal Wage System) workers' pay is determined by surveys of the labor market in the areas where they are employed; the Task Force found that this pay-setting system had worked well, in the main, until rates were "capped" by Congress and limited to increases for General Schedule workers.

RECOMMENDATION 6

President Bush and the 101st Congress should phase out the ceiling on market adjustments of blue-collar prevailing rates, and simultaneously direct the Federal Prevailing Rate Advisory Committee to explore any improvements needed to improve the credibility of the blue-collar (Federal Wage System) pay structure.

All Federal Pay Systems

RECOMMENDATION 7

President Bush should direct departments and agencies, in collaboration with the Office of Personnel Management, to sponsor small-scale research and demonstration projects directed toward developing a base of knowledge to inform policy decisions about the financial terms and conditions of federal employment. The projects should especially explore linking financial incentives to performance, measuring and comparing total compensation, and adapting to a rapidly changing and nontraditional work environment and labor force (for example, public-private partnerships and appropriate compensation for employed retirees). Demonstration projects that change basic terms and conditions of compensation should be undertaken, however, only in areas where compensation is reasonably adequate.

RECOMMENDATION 8

President Bush and the 101st Congress should act to restore confidence of federal employees and of the American public in the fairness and effectiveness of the federal pay-setting process. They should, among other things, articulate and establish in law criteria for all normal federal pay-setting processes; the criteria might be that processes are:

• Easily communicated to the federal workforce and to the public, and understood to be fair, equitable, and efficient.

• Easily monitored by the President and Congress; and

• Adequate to meet the needs of the federal government in respect to recruitment and retention of qualified employees.

They should communicate what the pay-setting provisions are, how they work to provide reasonable pay, and how the provisions represent an efficient application of tax dollars.

RECOMMENDATION 9

President Bush and the 101st Congress should stabilize and carry out the terms and conditions of federal compensation and avoid expedient deviations that have characterized the past.

RECOMMENDATION 10

The President and Congress now and in the future should lead the American people in placing an appropriate value on the work of federal employees. Through leadership and personal example, they can direct the workforce toward maximizing the intrinsic rewards and satisfactions potentially available from working directly for the United States of America.

FACING THE FEDERAL COMPENSATION CRISIS

Effective performance as a nation requires high-quality government support, but federal compensation systems in disarray have been undermining that support for more than 10 years. Although several factors have masked the effect of this deterioration on the quality and effectiveness of the federal workforce, the effects of the breakdown are now becoming increasingly noticeable.

Men and women who become and remain federal employees do not expect to accumulate great financial wealth. Their rewards include the gratification of serving a great nation and gaining a reasonable measure of job security. It is dangerous for the nation, however, when compensation is not adequate to recruit and retain a high-quality workforce.

The Task Force recommends restoring both adequacy of pay and confidence in federal pay-setting processes. This reform is urgently needed to prepare the Civil Service for the 21st century.

The Value of Federal Compensation Has Declined

The purchasing power of salaries of top executives of all three branches of the federal government has decreased more than 30 percent over the past 20 years, while private-sector executives have enjoyed substantial increases in purchasing power that was higher than federal compensation to begin with.[2]

The effects of low and decreasing purchasing power include an alarming number of resignations of federal judges, a dysfunctionally brief tenure among Presidentially appointed executives who direct operations of the government, and dissatisfaction with the practice of private payment of honoraria to Members of Congress. More and more, recruitment for the top executive group must focus on the wealthy, the economically unsuccessful, or the untried.[3]

Compensation for the Senior Executive Service (SES), consisting mainly of career executives who report to political appointees, has less purchasing power now than when the SES was established in 1979. One study found a 58 percent gap in 1984 between the SES level 6 salary and salaries of private-sector counterparts; by 1987, the gap was 65 percent.[4]

General Schedule (GS) employees, who are the white-collar workers, receive pay that is on average 22 percent below rates paid for similar types of work in the private sector.[5] Each year for the past 10 years, pay increases needed to bring federal pay rates even with the labor market were computed by the President's Pay Agent as required by law and published. Each year for the past 10 years, however, the President has reduced the increases and the Congress has accepted the reductions to accommodate "national emergency or economic conditions affecting the general welfare," usually with little explanation to the employees affected.[6]

From 1970 to 1987, the cost of living as measured by the consumer price index increased 183 percentage points; pay for white-collar workers in the private sector increased 165 points, and pay rates for federal white-collar work increased 124 points.[7] *For 10 years, increases needed to keep pace with increases in nongovernment salaries have not been granted. The nation now faces the twin realities of pressure for immediate spending cuts to reduce the federal deficit,* *and a shortfall in accumulated raises in pay for 1.4 million GS employees, an aggregate shortfall of more than $12 billion.*[8]

Pay increases for federal blue-collar workers have been limited to the increases for white-collar workers. As a result, pay for blue-collar workers is even with the labor market in some areas, and as much as 24 percent below the labor market in other areas.

The entire nonpostal civilian federal workforce receives substantially similar noncash benefits. Available studies show that the federal benefits package, once considered to be generous, is now at best only about 3 percentage points (as a percent of cash salary or wage) "ahead" of the average private-sector benefits package, and for employees hired since 1984 who are covered by a different retirement system, the benefits package is even less favorable.[9]

Effects Are Beginning to Show

The effects of the decline and breakdown of federal pay-setting have been masked over the years by factors such as the gradual nature of the decline of federal pay rates relative to those of other employers; measures that have permitted pay increases for particular groups (for example, special rates, demonstration projects, or legislated exceptions); lack of comprehensive or adequate measures of government performance; and lack of comprehensive, valid measures of federal workforce quality.

As the years have passed, problems have begun to surface. Some studies, conducted in response to requests for increases in compensation, have documented operational problems in key areas and occupations.[10] Studies also show declining trends in quality of candidates as measured by scores of recruits on tests such as the Scholastic Aptitude Test (SAT), the certifying examination for accountants, or the clerical verbal skills test.[11]

Unless compensation and other terms and conditions of federal work improve, the outlook for federal workforce quality and performance is not good. An already bad situation could become worse as employee experience becomes thinner and the labor market becomes tighter.

Experienced employees are now held by retirement benefits they will lose or have diminished if they leave government service. About 30 percent of federal employees were hired after 1983 and are covered by a different retirement system with benefits that can be retained when they leave government service. Average length of service and years of federal experience are expected to decrease as employees in the older system retire and employees in the newer system find themselves free to leave government service without financial penalty.

The study *Civil Service 2000*[12] forecasts an entry-level workforce that is generally inadequate in size and mismatched in skills to meet national labor force requirements. The federal government is hard-pressed to compete in the labor market now; it will face even greater difficulty in competing in the tighter labor market of the future. About 5 million men and women work for the federal government, including the uniformed services. They are skilled in more than 900 occupations and work in more than 100 departments and agencies.

The costs of raising compensation of the greatest number of federal employees to an appropriate level are significant. The effects of inadequate compensation on operations, however, are being felt now. *At the minimum, there is an immediate need to halt and reverse erosion of the value of pay in relation to the labor market, and to establish an improved pay-setting process that employees and the public can trust.*

The President and Congress should formulate policy based on a commitment to fair pay and to a reliable pay-setting process that will reverse the destructive effects of the federal compensation crisis and attract and hold a hard-working and productive Civil Service.

UNDERLYING CAUSES OF FEDERAL PAY PROBLEMS

Three basic causes underlie most federal pay problems, and must be addressed if any lasting remedy is to be effected.

Public Perceptions and Values

The President and Congress set the pay of the federal workforce. As elected officials, they make decisions on behalf of the voters. The electorate weighs the pay of its federal workforce against the perceived contribution of that workforce to the security and quality of life in America.

People will not pay for what they do not value. Studies suggest that the President strongly influences media attention to the federal workforce. The President chooses the metaphor, such as, "Is the federal workforce mainly composed of high-performance model, hard workers, or lazy timeservers who can't be fired?"

The Task Force believes that the President and Congress must lead the American people in placing a positive value on the work of federal employees. The discussion of psychic income in the following section underscores the significant impact of public perception and values on the ability of the federal government to attract and retain the high-quality workforce needed, even while in the best of times it offers only average levels of pay.

Education and Information

Voters tend to view the nominal amounts of federal salaries in reference to their own salary experiences, yet the federal workforce is not a mirror of the electorate.

Federal jobs require professional, administrative, or technical education or training in almost double the proportion of that for the general working population (more than 57 percent of federal jobs require this preparation, while 30 percent of private-sector jobs require it).[13]

The electorate seems largely unaware of the daily contribution of the federal workforce; the most readily identified federal worker is the letter carrier. Federal work is spotlighted during moments of high drama (such as the Three Mile Island nuclear accident or the landing of the first man on the Moon), but quickly fades from view. No level of society exhibits an abiding awareness of the nature and necessity of the federal contribution to business and everyday life in the United States. A long-range, multifaceted education and information effort is needed to prepare the public to protect its own interests with respect to management of its federal workforce.

Unique Pay-setting Mechanisms

Federal pay-setting processes have evolved in the absence of key performance data, flexibility, and confidentiality (for example, the bottom line of profitability, the use of stock options, and restricted access to information about salaries and bonuses) that have defined private-sector pay-setting. Federal requirements also include rigid rules to ensure equal pay for equal work, and to insulate career employees from partisan bias in setting their pay and directing their work. Nonetheless, the federal government faces a labor market that is predominantly shaped by pay practices of private-sector employers.

LESSONS OF HISTORY[14]

Federal pay-setting practices have been evolving since 1789. Periods of *ad hoc* Congressional pay-setting in lump sums (giving each department head a total amount of money for salaries) once alternated with statutory rates (specifying the pay rate for each job). Today's more systematic approach is based on description and classification of work, identification of jobs with grades representing levels of work, and surveys of the private sector to determine comparable rates of pay. But the Civil Service reform movement has a long history, one that is not yet finished.

Struggle for Control

Congress and the executive branch have contended for control of the great majority of federal jobs. In the first hundred years of the Republic, Congress used its control over pay and appropriations to place relatives, friends, and political supporters in the executive branch, job by job—a practice known as the "spoils system." As the federal workforce increased in size and complexity, and as a commitment to merit staffing became law, Congressional control evolved from job-by-job actions to legislated systems and procedures (the job classification system, the performance appraisal system, or various pay-setting systems).[15] Congress still exercises some controls, such as those over staffing ceilings or floors, and continues to specify some particular job actions (for example, specifying that appropriated funds may not be used to pay the salary of a particular position).

Another factor complicating Congressional control is that the national portion of the labor market is diffusing into markets that differ for different areas or occupations, a trend that is expected to continue.[16] Congressional approval of every adjustment, area, or occupation takes too much time. The lack of such adjustments has placed the federal government at a tremendous competitive disadvantage in many key labor markets.

In its most recent step in pay-setting, Congress removed itself from approving pay for each job, and decided instead to exercise control through approving pay-setting and annual adjustments for Executive Levels and the General Schedule (GS). *The Task Force recommendations, aimed at permitting varied comparability adjustments for different areas or occupations, urge Congress to remove itself from approving each comparability adjustment for the GS, and to exercise control by approving the system for making adjustments and by monitoring and evaluating compensation practices.* Pay adjustments for the blue-collar Federal Wage System workforce are now controlled in that way.

Proliferation of Kinds and Levels of Work[17]

Few kinds and levels of work have become many as the federal government has added services (the Post Office in 1792), responded to economic interests (by 1918, the Departments of Agriculture, Commerce, and Labor had been added), regulated its expanding economy (beginning in 1887, with the Interstate Commerce Commission), and made commitments as a nation (World War I, the New Deal, and World War II).

After World War II, America's position as world leader required agencies to administer programs for foreign aid and development, intelligence networks, and information dissemination as well as programs serving war veterans. The emergence of science and technology as the new engines of economic growth required agencies to explore space and develop new communications or military hardware, while social concerns of the 1960s and 1970s brought new domestic programs.[18]

The 1789 generic white-collar career job title of government clerk and a handful of different annual pay rates have multiplied into more than 900 occupations, thousands of titles, and hundreds of rates of pay. Systems for setting pay and for classifying jobs have evolved to respond to changes in the workforce. The most recent fundamental step taken in pay was the adoption of comparability in 1962 and 1970; and the most recent in job classification was the Job Classification and Pay Act of 1949, which identified common grade levels of difficulty across groups of formerly separate occupations, and defined grade levels. Currently, both pay-setting and job-classification systems need modernization.

Declining Value of Compensation

The real value of federal compensation has tended to drift down until a national crisis or public outcry focusses attention on public servants. This trend may reflect, among other things, the political nature of pay for public servants. For the government's white-collar workers, the trend was broken for some years following the achievement of pay comparability in legislation in 1962 and 1970, but it resumed in 1978 when the President and Congress began to give smaller increases than necessary to maintain comparability.[19]

The downward drift typically triggers predictable pressure from agencies for exception from the general pay limitations, which is often followed by Congressional action, followed by a vigorous outcry about the inequalities thus occasioned and transfers of desirable staff members to the better paying agencies, followed by Congressional reaggregation of related pay systems. Meanwhile, the downward drift of the real value of pay diminishes the prestige and desirability of federal employment. When the government must respond to a crisis, such as Sputnik, prestige and compensation for government work tend to rise.[20]

This downward cycle is now in progress. During 1988, two agencies that had followed the GS pay rates have left it: the Federal Reserve Board has announced that it will pay market rates, and the Federal Deposit Insurance Corporation has begun to add area cost-of-living differentials to GS rates. The Federal Aviation Administration, the National Aeronautics and Space Administration, and many other agencies not free to leave the GS have requested that Congress exempt them from it. In 1988 Congress considered, but did not approve legislation that would remove up to 250,000 jobs from the GS to participate in demonstration projects testing a range of compensation approaches, along with expanded application of special rates exceptions (more than 140,000 jobs are already on special rates). Congress provided Federal Bureau of Investigation agents in New York City with a 25 percent salary adjustments and relocation bonuses for agents moving there. Federal Executive Boards in New York and New Jersey have documented reduced quality of applicants and unacceptably high rates of turnover; in 1988 the New York Federal Board requested a 25 percent across-the-board salary adjustment for a three-county area.[21]

Today, the time available to respond to international challenges such as Sputnik is much shorter than it once was. It takes years to recover from a period of decline in effectiveness in the federal workforce. The demands of this era require exercise of the political will necessary to counter trends such as the downward drift of pay that diminish effectiveness of the federal workforce. The Task Force recommends practical measures to halt and reverse that trend. It is urgent that they be implemented.

COMMON COMPENSATION CONCERNS

Before turning to analyses of the four major pay groups in the federal government, it is useful to review several concerns that are common to policy regarding federal compensation generally.

The Notion of Adequate Pay

Pay (salary) is one of a variety of extrinsic rewards (such as promotion, status symbols, or perquisites) available to employers. Pay itself can be designed and distributed in a number of ways; it can be based on type and level of job or on skills; keyed to performance through individual bonus awards or through gainsharing[22] within an organization; or based on an external market relationship or internal equity relationships. Employers determine adequacy of pay in terms of what is necessary to attract and retain the optimum workforce for the employing organization. In the free market economy, employers tend to set pay on the basis of what competing employers pay for the same types and levels of work. In a recent survey of private-sector pay practices by the Advisory Committee on Federal Pay, more than 95 percent of employers responding indicated that they pay managers and professionals salaries that are at least average (or above) relative to those of competitors, and most tend to follow the same strategy for all employee groups.[23]

The Davis Bacon Act of 1931 required contractors to pay certain workers on federal government contracts the wages and fringe benefits that prevail in the area. This and other legislation, along with the emergence of other advances in management, sparked improvements in techniques for surveying compensation. The efficiency and precision of survey techniques, the variety and complexity of pay packages, and theories about various aspects or effects of compensation practices are all significantly more advanced now than 40 years ago. The central theme of pay-setting, however, has not changed markedly. Private-sector pay-setting is a pragmatic process of adjusting to the market rate for the type and level of employees needed.

The federal government accepted this process and, in the Federal Salary Reform Act of 1962, espoused the concept of comparability with the private sector for its white-collar workers. The Federal Pay Comparability Act of 1970 provided guidance on methodology for surveying private-sector rates. Adoption of comparability as a reference point for adequacy of GS pay was a major improvement in pay-setting. For reasons made clear later in this report, however, white-collar pay rates have not maintained the intended comparability in recent years (see "Compensation Systems Studied" on page 217).

Historically, federal agencies tended to pay prevailing rates to blue-collar workers, a practice legally mandated by the Prevailing Rate Act of 1972 and one largely achieved except in areas affected by the cap on blue-collar pay increases. However, top federal executives have not been paid rates comparable with the private sector since the founding of the

Republic. Then, as now, an obligation of leaders to serve in the government, along with the gratification and honor of serving at these levels, has operated to balance levels of compensation that are not comparable, and indeed are considerably below private- and independent-sector positions from which top federal executives are recruited. Discussions of adequacy of top executive pay sometimes focus on pay for top positions in the private or nonprofit sectors, sometimes on general increases for occupational groups (e.g. lawyers or all white-collar workers) and sometimes on costs of maintaining homes in two places. There is no generally accepted frame of reference for these discussions of adequacy of compensation for top federal executives.

Pay and Psychic Income

Pay must be set at an adequate level to attract and retain employees. Data on private-sector employer practices suggest that the adequate level is at least average relative to competitors. Alternate pay strategies discussed in the next section may permit some insulation from the labor market, and benefits, also discussed in the next section, are a significant part of compensation. But current research suggests that another type of reward—often called psychic income—must be considered as well.

Deci's attribution (or locus of causality) theory suggests that pay can be subordinate to the employees' own perception of why they are doing the work. The attribution might be, "another day, another dollar," or it might be, "today we won one for the environment."[24]

Joseph Campbell refers to a somewhat similar aspect of self-characterization as the "metaphor." The metaphor might be, "I'm a wage slave like everybody else," or "I am responsible for sampling and evaluating groundwater pollution to keep the American people safe from toxic waste."[25]

Both reasons and both metaphors could refer to the same job with the same pay. There is some indication from Deci's research that the employee's experience and even performance on the job would differ if the attribution were different.[26]

The 1987 Wyatt *WorkAmerica* study found that, among determinants of employee commitment, compensation, which traditionally had ranked first in surveys of this type, ranked fourth, behind communication, job content, and career development.[27] In 1987, Louis Harris' *Inside America* reported that 48 percent of those surveyed were most attracted by work that "gives a feeling of real accomplishment," while "good pay" was most important to only 18 percent.[28] Private-sector employers typically pay rates that are at least the average of those of their competitors; in these circumstances, the intrinsic rewards of work—psychic income—will make the difference.[29]

There are some indications that psychic income is important for workers who accept pay levels well below market rates. Anecdotal evidence from executives who have served in appointive office at the federal level frequently refers to the exciting and satisfying nature of the work.[30] Surveys of federal workers tend to show high levels of job satisfaction, even as they show both lower satisfaction with pay and declining morale.[31] The fact that federal executive jobs can be staffed at all with qualified individuals (particularly those of judges, who are expected to serve for life) may further attest to the potency of these rewards.

Executives and other leaders exert a strong influence on employees' attributions or metaphors in relation to their work. Public pronouncements from the top are important. Who has not been moved to serve by President Kennedy's challenge: "Ask not what your country can do for you, rather, ask what you can do for your country"?

This area is a relatively new one for executives and managers, although indirectly, many post-Industrial Revolution management theorists (such as Mary Parker Follett, Henri Fayol, and Elton Mayo) have recommended management techniques and approaches that enhance attribution or intrinsic job satisfaction.

Management theories strongly suggest, therefore, that political appointees at the top can influence workforce performance by the way they characterize the work of the government and the roles and responsibilities of civil servants. This invisible bonus of intrinsic job satisfaction, which derives from the attribution or metaphors that employees apply to their work, is a powerful part of compensation. It is explicitly mentioned in public statements of former cabinet and Senior Executive Service members, judges, and Members of Congress as part of the trade-off of job satisfaction against financial sacrifice.[32] This factor has special importance for employers, such as the federal government, that offer less than top pay but require a high-quality workforce.

The Task Force recommends that the President and his appointed officials take the lead in placing a positive value on the work of the federal government, and that they consciously guide the perceptions of the federal workforce toward positive views of its own role, value, and obligations.

It is important to bear in mind that the financial trade-off at some point becomes unacceptable and unduly limits the population that can be recruited or retained. The Task Force concludes that this point has been reached in the federal government.

Insulation from the Market

Various features of federal employment have mediated the influences of the labor market on recruitment and retention. These deliberate or serendipitous strategies include:

• Offering attractive opportunities for advancement during the first 10 years of a career, plus a substantial deferred benefit to hold employees after 10 years (the benefit might be one such as the Civil Service Retirement System pension, which covers employees hired before January 1, 1984; its major benefit is lost when that individual leaves);

• Having a monopoly on a function and on training for that function, and providing training contingent on a legal or implied commitment to a number of years of service or to a career (for example, customs inspectors or astronauts); and

• Creating an internal market for groups of jobs largely specializing in systems or operations unique to federal government such as its budget process, some accounting and personnel systems.

These strategies seek to achieve stability by isolating and insulating some federal government operations and processes from the environment. These strategies are not, however, geared to respond to an environment that changes rapidly and unpredictably. It is difficult to recruit people into the middle ranges of these specialized careers; fewer opportunities exist for careerists who may want to change direction, and less informal opportunity arises for transfer of technology with organizations outside the federal government.

The labor market, on the other hand, is sensitive to the environment. It immediately registers a market consensus on the relative worth of a new occupation, and responds to supply and demand.

Over the years, the federal government has been moving toward more flexibility in employment practices. The benefits of the Federal Employees Retirement System, in effect since the beginning of 1984, are portable. Functions being performed by the federal government are increasingly being privatized. In the Federal Salary Reform Act of 1962 and the Federal Pay Comparability Act of 1970, Congress directed the federal government to participate in the non-executive labor market on the basis of comparability. All of these changes make it more possible for the federal government to exchange staff and experience with the external, non-federal environment.

Internal Equity and Accountability

Changes propelling the federal government toward more exchange of staff and experience with the non-federal environment will, at the same time, require more precise and timely information about internal management of compensation. The information will be needed to among other things ensure accountability for equitable and efficient, or at least correct spending on payroll.

A primary vehicle for providing this information is the job classification system. Job classification provides an accounting code for each type and level of work. These codes for type and level of work make it possible to monitor rates paid, for example to entry level accountants, by different agencies in different locations at different times; to compare federal rates of pay with rates paid by other employers; and to compare rates paid to different groups of employees for the same type and level of work. Almost all white-collar and blue-collar federal jobs below executive levels have job classification codes.

Internal equity is achieved by setting pay for work consistently with an accepted criterion for the relative value of work. *For the large white-collar GS workforce, the agreed values that distinguish levels of work are generally articulated for each grade level in law (5 U.S.C.5104); to the extent that they are appropriately applied, they provide for a high degree of internal equity. If appropriately applied, they insulate the government as employer from the influences of unacceptable practices on the labor market (such as gender or race discrimination).*

The Task Force recommendations assume that the GS grade level relationships will continue to be defined by law. However, overall precision and timeliness of federal job classification processes has been declining for more than 10 years, in part through lack of capital investment to maintain and develop job classification, and in part through pressure to counteract less competitive pay by moving jobs to higher grades. The Task Force recommendation to adjust pay rates by location or occupation, as necessary to participate more effectively and credibly in the labor market, will facilitate needed improvements in job classification systems and processes.

Benefits

With the exception of executive perquisites, benefits in most large public and private organizations tend to be universal, rather than distributed by job, as are salaries. If one employee receives health insurance, all do.[33] Benefits packages typically include health and life insurance, pensions, pay for time not worked (holidays, vacation days, and sick days), disability and unemployment compensation, and services such as day care, health facilities, or credit unions.

In 1920, the federal government was among the first employers to offer a pension benefit, and was a leader in offering paid time off in the 1950s. In recent years, however, federal benefits have become less competitive. One survey traces the growth in private sector benefits from 25 percent of payroll in 1950 to 41 percent in 1980.[34] A 1984-85 survey by Hay, updated to 1986, estimated that the federal fringe benefits package was at best 3 percent better than the private sector's; further, the 3 percent was predicated on full indexing of the federal retirement plan; without full indexing of the retirement benefit, federal benefits were estimated to be 6 or 7 percent lower than benefits for the private sector.[35]

The Hay comparison was based on a federal benefits package that included the Civil Service Retirement System pension plan. The same study reported the federal health insurance benefits to be dramatically behind, while paid leave still provided the federal sector "a very small advantage." Federal employees hired since 1984 are covered under a different pension plan, the Federal Employees Retirement System (FERS), which is not fully indexed and is even less competitive than the figures indicate.[36]

The perception that the federal government is a leading employer in terms of benefits is not accurate.

The old Civil Service Retirement System plan did not include Social Security coverage. It is often referred to as the "golden handcuffs," because it provided no benefit portability or disability or death benefits if employees left federal employment before retirement age. Employees could either accept a refund of only their own contributions without interest, or wait for a deferred annuity at age 62, which by then would have been diminished by inflation.

The FERS plan has three components: Social Security, a defined-benefits pension, and earnings on a voluntary tax-deferred thrift plan with limited matching employer contributions. The minimum age for retirement under FERS was increased from 55 with 30 years of service, under the old plan, to 57 with 30 years of service. Compared with the old plan, FERS is highly portable; upon leaving federal employment, Social Security coverage continues and thrift accounts can be rolled over into other deferred-income accounts. Under the FERS pension plan, nondisability retirees receive no cost-of-living adjustments until age 62, and the adjustments are set at 1 percent below the increases in the consumer price index.

Health insurance coverage for federal employees is provided under the Federal Employees Health Benefits program. Participation is voluntary. Under the program, employees are permitted to select health coverage from among a variety of plans (430 plans were offered in 1988). Employees may switch health plans during the annual open season. Both employees and the government contribute; the government contribution equals 60 percent of the average premiums of the six largest health plans, but may not exceed 75 percent of the total premium costs for any plan. Employees pay the remaining costs, including deductibles. Premium costs have increased dramatically in recent years; from 1987 to 1989, the plans covering the most workers will increase by almost 30 percent. A recent study conducted for the Office of Personnel Management (OPM) concluded that costs of health benefits were unnecessarily high in relation to the benefits provided, and that the number of plans should be reduced.[37]

Actions to improve arrangements with vendors of health benefits (including some major employee unions) are in progress, and such negotiations are an appropriate central agency concern. Still, Congress—not the agencies—determines the level and shape of federal fringe benefits, and does so largely independently from its determination of federal pay.

Benefits constitute a significant proportion of payroll expenditure, and it would be useful to study and manage benefits in coordination with pay. In time, total compensation—salary and benefits—should be surveyed and benefits as well as salary should be comparable with non-federal employers. Development of a total compensation comparison methodology for the federal government will take years, particularly because many areas of judgment and discretion must be worked out.[38] On the other hand, problems with existing processes for setting salary are severe, and should be addressed immediately.

Elsewhere, the Task Force recommends studies to develop an appropriate total compensation comparison methodology for the federal government. In the near term, the studies could provide some points for comparison of benefit programs in the federal and private sectors.

Pay for Performance

Almost all private-sector employers (90 percent) use merit pay as the basis for granting salary increases to white-collar employees; the majority of organizations grant merit increases annually. For all employee groups, organizations tend to rate about 20 percent of employees in the highest performance category, and fewer than 5 percent in the lowest performance category. The amount budgeted for merit pay is typically about 5 percent of current salaries; employees rated in the highest performance category receive increases ranging from 6 percent to 10 percent. Fewer than 10 percent of employers communicate to employees that annual salary increases are general or cost of living increases.[39]

Some recent studies indicate, however, that these increases may not motivate performance. Analysis of studies carried out during 1971–75 linking financial compensation and productivity improvement, shows that four out of five studies had either questionable or unreported statistical significance, or were questionable on other grounds.[40] Meta-analysis (that is, subsequent reevaluation of original data) of productivity interventions has shown that in 98 out of 207 productivity interventions, financial compensation programs did not produce a statistically significant impact on productivity.[41]

Psychologists such as Edward Lawler and William Rambo who have studied pay and motivation point out that several conditions are necessary for employees to believe that a performance-based pay relationship exists. The conditions include a visible connection between performance and rewards, and a climate of trust and credibility in the organization.[42] Joseph Zeidner and others go on to suggest that it is necessary to develop performance standards and to quantify productivity; simple jobs are more amenable to quantification than complex jobs.

To illustrate the importance of workers' perceptions of the path to rewards, Rambo poses the situation of someone asking a worker, "What do you have to do around here to make more money?" In many organizations, the answer to that question would not point to job performance as the path to more pay, e.g., "Do favors for the boss", or "Get a different job."

In the 1987 Wyatt *WorkAmerica* study, only 28 percent of the private-sector managers and workers surveyed said that there was a clear link between pay and performance.[43]

The literature cites frequent negative side effects of performance-based pay plans, including social ostracism of good performers, defensive behavior, and giving false reports about performance. Two grievous errors cited are: depending on completely subjective performance appraisals for the allocation of pay rewards, and rewarding top managers for short-term results at the unintended expense of long-term profitability. Other errors noted included rewards for individual effort that lessen the incentive for workers to help or train each other, or to cooperate to reach an organizational goal.[44]

Pay for performance is, however, still the almost universally preferred way to distribute annual salary increases in the private sector.

Federal experience with pay for performance has generally been less extensive than private-sector experience. Traditionally, it has been limited to granting within-grade (step) increases only to those who perform at the fully successful level or better.

The Civil Service Reform Act of 1978 eliminated within-grade increases for supervisors and managers in grades GS-13 to GS-15, and provided for salary advancement based on merit pay along with some bonuses for covered employees. Performance in these jobs however, was among the most complex and difficult to quantify.[45] In 1985, OPM, itself responsible for guiding agencies in developing performance appraisal standards, produced *Issue Analysis, Performance appraisal System*, which concluded that 45 percent of federal worker performance standards were "less than satisfactory."

The Civil Service Reform Act also created the Senior Executive Service (SES), with no pay ranges but more generous provisions for performance bonuses. A 1986 General Accounting Office survey of career SES members leaving in 1985 showed that two of the top six reasons for leaving were related to "unfair" distribution of bonus or rank awards; their top reason was "dissatisfaction with management."[46]

Federal experience with pay for performance has clearly been less than successful in regard to establishing the perception that these pay increases are connected to performance. The climate of mistrust and lack of credibility in the federal civil service is indicated among other things by the relatively high percentage of federal workers who, when surveyed, report that morale is low (70 percent) and that they would not recommend federal employment to young people (60 percent).[47]

A number of the conditions regarded as necessary for successful implementation of merit pay do not exist in the federal service. Private-sector situations in which merit pay is established and accepted are further characterized by base pay levels that are at least at the average for other employers in the labor market.

The Task Force recommends studies and experiments that would develop knowledge needed to inform decisions about terms and conditions of federal compensation, particularly in respect to linking financial incentives with performance. Experiments should be undertaken only where basic compensation is reasonably adequate and where other conditions important to success of the experiments are present.

COMPENSATION SYSTEMS STUDIED

More than 5.2 million employees work for the three branches of the federal government (Table 1). By statute or executive order, compensation for top executives of all three branches is linked together; the pay of appointed executives is linked at the rate for Executive Level II ($89,500) with the pay for Members of Congress and for district court judges. Executive Levels have 5 rates, and in 1987 included 834 Presidentially appointed officials, 535 Members of Congress, and 1,113 federal judges.[48]

Compensation for nonpostal white-collar workers in all three branches is in most cases linked or set in relation to the General Schedule (GS) of the executive branch, and pay rates

Table 1
Federal Employment
(September 30, 1988)

Branch	Employees
Judicial and Legislative Branches	59,049*
Executive Branch	5,229,710
Civilian**	2,221,760
Uniformed Military Members	2,175,936
Postal Service	832,014
Total Federal Employment	5,288,759

*The OMB analysis does not provide separate figures for the judicial and legislative branches.

| Judicial Branch | 21,502 |
| Legislative Branch | 37,547 |

From: *Federal Civilian Work Force Statistics: Employment and Trends*, as of September 1988, an Office of Personnel Management publication. Figures include full- and part-time employees.

**Excludes the Central Intelligence Agency, the Defense Intelligence Agency, and the National Security Agency.

Source, Office of Management and Budget, *OMB Special Analysis: Budget of the U.S. Government*, Analysis I, FY 1990.

are uniform nationwide. The GS covers directly 1.4 million white-collar workers in more than 400 occupations.[49]

Compensation for uniformed military personnel is based on a separate system of internal equity relationships, and increases for basic military pay are linked by law to GS increases, even though they are frequently given separate increases through the appropriation process.

Compensation for blue-collar workers in all three branches is in most cases set according to the Federal Wage System (FWS) surveys of prevailing rates. Pay rates cover more than 400 occupations and differ for 135 local labor markets.

Compensation for the Postal Service is set by collective bargaining in isolation from other federal pay systems.

Table 2 shows levels of federal pay current in January 1989 and shows pay linkages at executive levels in the three branches of government, and with the GS. Chart 1 shows distribution of jobs in the different pay categories of the executive branch.

Table 2
Compensation Relationships: Current Salary Rates—January 1989

Executive Branch	Legislative Branch	Judicial Branch
Vice President $115,000	Speaker of the House . . $115,000	Chief Justice $115,000

Executive Level I 99,500
Executive Level II . . . . . 89,500——Members of Congress . . 89,500*——District Court Judges . . . 89,500
Executive Level III 82,500
Executive Level IV . . . . . 80,700┐
Executive Level V 75,500

*May earn additional outside income: Senators up to 40%—$125,300; Representatives up to 30%—$116,350.

Senior Executive Service

Executive Schedule 6 . .$ 80,700┘
Executive Schedule 5 . . 78,600
Executive Schedule 4 . . 76,400
Executive Schedule 3 . . 74,900
Executive Schedule 2 . . 71,800
Executive Schedule 1 . . 68,700*

*Must exceed rate for GS–16 step 1, $67,038.

FEDERAL WHITE COLLAR PAY SCALE 1989

	STEP 1	2	3	4	5	6	7	8	9	10
GS-1	$10,213	$10,555	$10,894	$11,233	$11,573	$11,773	$12,108	$12,445	$12,461	$12,780
GS-2	$11,484	$11,757	$12,137	$12,461	$12,601	$12,972	$13,343	$13,714	$14,085	$14,456
GS-3	$12,531	$12,949	$13,367	$13,785	$14,203	$14,621	$15,039	$15,457	$15,875	$16,293
GS-4	$14,067	$14,536	$15,005	$15,474	$15,943	$16,412	$16,881	$17,350	$17,819	$18,288
GS-5	$15,738	$16,263	$16,788	$17,313	$17,838	$18,363	$18,888	$19,413	$19,938	$20,463
GS-6	$17,542	$18,127	$18,712	$19,297	$19,882	$20,467	$21,052	$21,637	$22,222	$22,807
GS-7	$19,493	$20,143	$20,793	$21,443	$22,093	$22,743	$23,393	$24,043	$24,693	$25,343
GS-8	$21,590	$22,310	$23,030	$23,750	$24,470	$25,190	$25,910	$26,630	$27,350	$28,070
GS-9	$23,846	$24,641	$25,436	$26,231	$27,026	$27,821	$28,616	$29,411	$30,206	$31,001
GS-10	$26,261	$27,136	$28,011	$28,886	$29,761	$30,636	$31,511	$32,386	$33,261	$34,136
GS-11	$28,852	$29,814	$30,776	$31,738	$32,700	$33,662	$34,624	$35,586	$36,548	$37,510
GS-12	$34,580	$35,733	$36,886	$38,039	$39,192	$40,435	$41,498	$42,651	$43,804	$44,957
GS-13	$41,121	$42,492	$43,863	$45,234	$46,605	$47,976	$49,347	$50,718	$52,089	$53,460
GS-14	$48,592	$50,212	$51,832	$53,452	$55,072	$56,692	$58,312	$59,932	$61,552	$63,172
GS-15	$57,158	$59,063	$60,968	$62,873	$64,778	$66,683	$68,588	$70,493	$72,398	$74,303
GS-16	$67,038	$69,273	$71,058	$73,743	$75,473	$76,678*	$78,869*	$81,060*	$82,500*	
GS-17	$76,990*	$79,556*	$82,122*	$82,500*	$83,818*					
GS-18	$86,682*									

*The rate of basic pay payable to employees at these rates is limited to the rate for level V of the Executive Schedule, which would be $75,500.

Chart courtesy of the Advisory Committee on Federal Pay, updated

Chart 1
Structure of the Executive Branch,
nonpostal civilian workforce, full-time employees
March 1987*

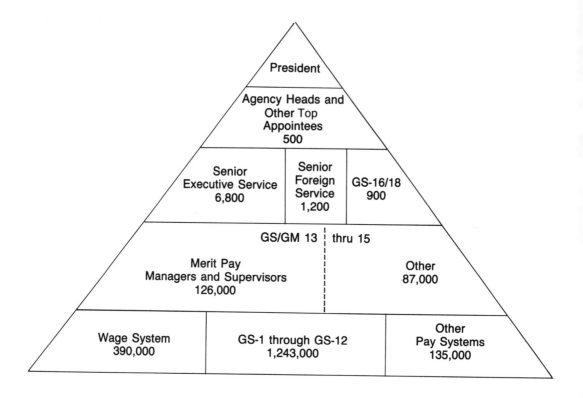

Note 1: Excludes the Central Intelligence Agency and the National Security Agency.

Note 2: As of September 1987, the distribution of Senior Executive Service members (career, non-career, and limited appointment) among the six SES salary rates was: ES-1, 6.0%; ES-2, 8.1%; ES-3, 15.3%; ES-4, 51.6%; ES-5, 13.8%; ES-6, 5.3%.

Source: *The Report of the President's Commission on Compensation of Career Federal Executives* (the Cullen Commission), Feb. 1988, Chart 1.

Executive Levels

These officials occupy the very top levels of government. Executives paid at these levels include federal judges, cabinet Secretaries, directors of biomedical and other research programs, the Director of the Internal Revenue Service, and the Administrator of the Federal Aviation Administration.

The pay for Members of Congress has been treated as an upper limit for pay of judges and subcabinet level appointed executives. The rationale for this cap has been the desire to maintain parity among the three branches of government. Raising pay for Members of Congress, however, has been less acceptable to the public than raising pay for judges or chief scientists and other executives. Public opposition to raising Congressional pay has tended to hold back pay increases in the other branches as well.

Pay-Setting Process[50]

Article I, Section 6, of the Constitution requires that the pay of Members of Congress will be set "by Law." This provision has been taken to mean that, because only the Congress can enact a law, only Congress can set its own pay.

In 1967, Congress instituted an additional pay-setting procedure intended to distance Members from the politically sensitive act of increasing their own pay by statute. Congress established the Commission on Executive, Legislative, and Judicial Salaries, the so-called "Quadrennial" Commission, to be appointed every four years to recommend to the President pay rates for Members of Congress, judges, and appointed officials in top executive levels. The President would then consider and propose to Congress pay rates that would become effective unless Congress disapproved them. The enabling legislation provided that a resolution of disapproval passed by either House would nullify the President's recommendations.

In 1969, Congress received its first increase under the procedure (from $30,000 to $42,500). In 1974, the Senate disapproved the recommended increase, and between 1969 and 1975, Congressional salaries stagnated while the cost of living increased 47.5 percent.

In 1975, Congress passed the Executive Salary Cost-of-Living Adjustment Act, which automatically provided federal executives the same percentage annual increase as that approved for the General Schedule (white-collar workers), unless Congress disapproved it. It was thought that more frequent adjustments would be smaller, and would be more likely to be accepted than the large adjustments needed to "catch up" after a long period without increases. In 1975, Members received the increase (salaries went to $44,600). Congress disapproved increases in 9 of 13 years subsequently.

In 1977, Congress accepted its second pay increase under the Quadrennial Commission procedure—from $42,500 to $57,500—but went on to amend the Quadrennial process to require a recorded vote. In 1981, both Houses nullified the President's recommendations.

In 1984, Congress again moved away from the requirement for a recorded vote, and accepted recommendations of the Quadrennial Commission, endorsed by the President, which provided that the President's pay recommendations would take effect unless both Houses disapproved them. The joint disapproval mechanism also responded to a Supreme Court decision (*INS v. Chada*, 462 U.S. 919 (1983)) that declared the legislative, one-House veto unconstitutional. Only procedural changes were made by that Quadrennial Commission, and a Special Quadrennial Commission was convened in 1986 to recommend salary increases. In accordance with the new procedures, Congressional salaries were increased to $89,500 in 1987 as recommended by the President. The $89,500 figure was considerably less, however, than the figure needed to restore purchasing power of salaries and recommended by the 1986 Special Quadrennial Commission.

The 1988 Quadrennial Commission also recommended an increase intended to restore lost purchasing power of salaries. President Reagan accepted the recommendations and proposed that Congress increase the salary of Members to $135,000. At the same time, it was proposed that Members should pass legislation that would preclude them from supplementing their salaries by accepting honoraria (speaking fees). Members of the House may currently accept honoraria up to 30 percent of base pay, and Members of the Senate 40 percent.

The recommended increase was greeted by a storm of public criticism nationwide, particularly in the daily press and on radio talk shows. The Senate voted to disapprove the increase and, although the House came within days of permitting the increase to take effect, it finally voted to disapprove.

Congress had again denied itself the fiscal year 1989 increase permitted under the Cost of Living Act, so Congressional salaries and the cap on salaries for judges and top executive branch directors and scientists remained at $89,500.

Growing Discrepancies

Pay-setting for top level federal executives follows an historic pattern of lengthy periods of stagnation and relative decline of the purchasing power of salaries. Even with three mechanisms for increasing Congressional pay—by statute, Quadrennial Commission process, and annual increase—the purchasing power of pay for federal elected and appointed executives decreased by 35 percent from 1969 to 1988. During this same period, total cash compensation of private-sector executives has increased substantially (see Chart 2).[51]

Setting levels of executive pay is an important decision typically made to achieve the overall results intended in the context of the organization and the existing labor market. If the result intended is to research and develop a cure for AIDS, to regulate currency expansion and debt to maximize economic growth, to legislate effective national energy or pollution policies, or to dispense even-handed justice in a court of law, compensation should be set to permit recruitment of top talent.

In government, psychic income, or the satisfaction of contributing to the country and the prestige of these high positions, has traditionally been a major factor in balancing sala-

Chart 2
Salary Comparisons
Level II Executive Pay Versus Private Sector Corporate Executives
1969 to 1988

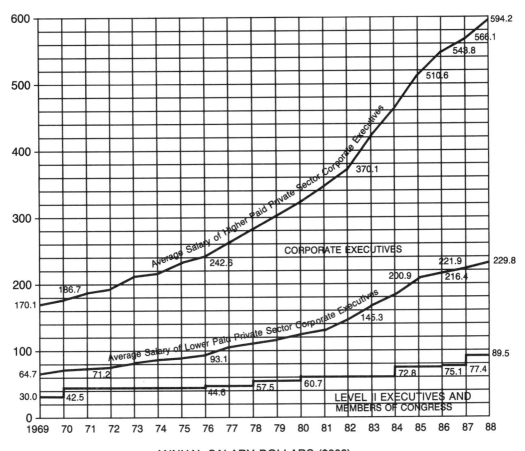

ANNUAL SALARY DOLLARS ($000)

Source: HayGroup

ries that are low relative to the qualifications required. Salaries for these positions have drifted down, however, to a point well below what is sufficient to provide a standard of living expected by most of those who are well qualified, even taking psychic income into account. In fact, many state governments, municipalities, universities, and nonprofit organizations offer opportunities for "psychic" income, and far higher salaries as well (see Chart 3).

Consequences of these salary discrepancies may include limitation of candidates for top federal executive positions to those who do not depend on their income for their livelihood, those who have not achieved the measure of economic success usual for their qualifications, or the inexperienced and untried. These discrepancies have already precipitated resignations of a number of federal judges. Some top executive branch positions (especially in research) have gone vacant for years as salaries at universities and other nonprofit organizations outdistance top federal salaries, often by whole multiples.

Chart 3
Salaries of Non-Profit Executives Compared to Level II

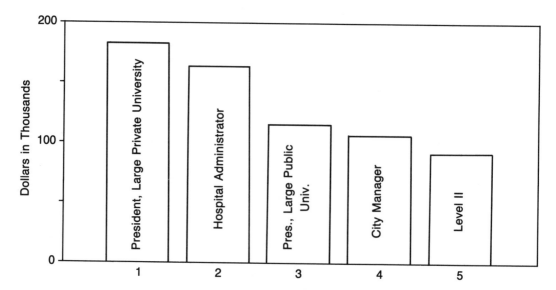

Sources: 1. College and University Personnel Association; "Administrative Compensation Survey," March 1988; For private universities with budgets over $83.1 mil.
2. "Modern Health Care," Oct. 28, 1988, Vol. 18, No. 44; For nonprofit hospitals with over $80 mil. in revenues.
3. College and University Personnel Association; "Administrative Compensation Survey," March 1988; For public universities with budgets over $169.1 mil.
4. International City Managers Association; Municipal Yearbook, 1987–1988. For cities with populations over 500,000.

Source: The Report of The 1989 Commission on Executive, Legislative and Judicial Salaries: Fairness for Our Public Servants.

The situation also invites some back-door approaches to increasing income, such as allowing Members of Congress to accept honoraria. Former Senator Howard Baker testified before the 1988 Quadrennial Commission, "I . . . know how impolitic it is to appear to be in the clutches of special interests, to rely on their financial favor—in the form of honoraria— for a substantial portion of a public servant's livelihood, and then to try to be a disinterested party when one of those special interests comes calling." Common Cause, an independent citizens organization, testified that acceptance of honoraria by these prominent public figures has undermined public confidence in government.

This Task Force observes that these indirect means to supplement pay contribute to the public's reluctance to increase federal salaries.

Measuring Adequacy of Compensation[52]

In 1789, a tradition of serving in Congress without substantial remuneration was begun. Attempts to raise Congressional pay have been met typically with strong public resistance. Public discussion of pay increases has been unfocused and subjective, frequently devolving into attacks on the Congress as a whole (even while most critics have exempted their own representatives). The debate accompanying the increase proposed by the 1988-89 Quadrennial Commission was virulent, and recalled discussions of pay increases proposed for the General Schedule (GS) prior to the Federal Salary Reform Act of 1962.

Prior to 1962, discussions of GS pay increases often featured speculative comparisons of standards and circumstances of work and life of various income groups or individuals, with the supposed circumstances of government workers. Discussions of pay increases became occasions for venting of populist distaste for disparities in income levels and living circumstances in the population. Similarly, recent discussions of the pay increase proposed for Congress frequently mentioned raising the minimum wage as a possible *quid pro quo* for the increase, made reference to the disparity in income between the "rulers and the ruled", and included many suggestions to Congress about how they might "make do" on $89,500 a year. For the GS, the commonly accepted objective frame of reference (the market) established by the Federal Salary Reform Act of 1962, moved the weight of discussion away from speculation about the needs of government employees as individuals, and toward improvement of the process for measuring the market (the annual Professional Administrative Technical and Clerical (PATC) survey). The objective frame of reference lent dignity to the debate and facilitated resolution of differences.The Task Force believes that some objective frame of reference for adequacy of Congressional pay is needed.

Public Criticisms

Public criticisms of Congress as a whole reported and expressed in the media included doubts about objectivity and quality of Congressional performance in view of payments Members may accept from special interests while they are serving and after they leave office, and dissatisfaction with Congressional performance in respect to some persistent problems such as the deficit. To the extent that these criticisms represent a lack of confidence in that institution beyond scapegoating, they are cause for concern and should be addressed.

A Vulnerable Proposal

Particular features of the increase proposed in 1988 made it vulnerable to media criticism: the size of the increase (51 percent of base pay) was a headline-grabbing figure; coverage of Congressional benefits provoked speculation that benefits made up for any deficiencies in pay; the Quadrennial Commission appeared to some to be a group of wealthy, distinguished men recommending pay increases for their peers; and the method of approving the increases without a recorded vote was often described as somehow underhanded. Any future mechanism or proposal for raising Congressional pay must take into account these vulnerabilities.

There is an obvious need for the dignity and order in discussions of pay for top federal executives that a well-accepted objective frame of reference can provide, and features of the pay setting-process that make it vulnerable to criticism should be changed. However, the need to raise pay to broaden recruitment and support retention at these levels is urgent.

The most desirable course of action would be to raise pay to restore lost purchasing power in support of recruitment and retention and to terminate honoraria, even while proceeding to develop an accepted frame of reference for adequacy of pay and an improved pay-setting process. An accepted frame of reference and an appropriate process could be developed in two to three years by a broadly based, temporary Citizens Advisory Panel. An example of a frame of reference for pay that the Panel might consider is comparability with executive compensation in the nonprofit sector. The Panel, assisted by compensation professionals, would identify the frame of reference most acceptable to the public and to all three branches of government as fair and equitable.

If Congress is unable to raise pay for all three branches however, they should immediately begin to phase in higher pay for judges and chief scientists and other top executives up to the full amount recommended. Polls indicate that other executives, especially judges, are more popular with the electorate,[53] and presumably wage increases for them would be more acceptable. At the same time, Congress could establish a Panel as above to develop a frame of reference for Congressional pay within three years. To prevent further erosion of Congressional pay during those years, the Panel might first recommend some interim adjustment, such as some performance measure, perhaps the Employment Cost Index. The Employment Cost Index is an indicator of the overall increases in wages of Americans. The Panel might also consider and recommend special increases as needed to facilitate prompt termination of honoraria.

Senior Executive Service

If Executive Level leaders translate the President's political program into general goals, the next level down—the Senior Executive Service (SES)—translates those general goals into plans that the federal bureaucracy can understand and implement. In corporate terms, the Executive Level provides the executive leadership and the SES fills the top management function. The SES was designed to be responsive to executive direction. The President sets SES pay rates, performance bonuses may be awarded by management, and SES members may be subject to frequent transfers (with only a few protections).

A typical day for a member of the SES involves long hours under intense pressure. The men and women in the SES are pressured from above to show positive results in carrying out the President's program, and they are pressured from below to make major decisions that can affect the future of millions of people and involve the expenditure of tens of millions of dollars.

For all the importance of their work, however, members of the SES are compensated far below their counterparts in industry, the nonprofit sector, and—in many cases—academe. Salary levels are set by the President within an upper boundary that cannot exceed Executive Level IV ($80,700) and a lower boundary that does not fall below General Schedule (GS) level 16, step 1 ($68,700). There are about 7,000 members of the SES. Another 900 workers in grades 16, 17, and 18, whose salaries cannot exceed $75,500, comprise the so-called "supergrade" group who carry on work similar to that of the SES but who are senior scientists or experts with no significant management role, or managers who opted not to join the SES when it was formed in 1979. (Political appointees may encumber up to 10 percent of all SES positions.)

Thus, SES personnel are caught in the jaws of an unforgiving vise: the President cannot raise their salaries until Executive Level IV is raised, yet they must daily lead a federal workforce that slowly erodes in skill and motivation. Although it is admittedly hard to measure morale, available surveys indicate morale within the SES is low, especially following Congressional rejection in February 1989 of the proposed pay raise for Members of Congress that would have included Executive Level IV. According to the Senior Executive Association, which pushed for that pay raise, as many as half of the career executives in the federal government could retire at this time, and many may do so unless salaries are increased.

Solution: Raise SES Salaries

The Task Force believes that SES personnel operate in an untenable environment and that the performance of the SES is bound to suffer. The government will find it increasingly difficult to retain the experienced and capable senior executives who will be needed to carry out the large and complicated programs of the Departments of Health and Human Services, Housing and Urban Development, Veterans Affairs, and the National Aeronautics and Space Administration, to name only four multi-billion-dollar agencies. The government will find it increasingly difficult to convince senior executives to remain at the helm in agencies such as the National Institutes of Health, where the attractions of high private-sector salaries (often double those in the SES) are strong.

Performance bonuses, for which career SES personnel are eligible, offer some additional incentives for these executives. In fiscal year 1987, fully 33 percent of career SES members received bonuses, at an average level of $5,894 or 8 percent of average SES pay.[54] The Task Force believes that the idea of performance bonuses for SES members is a good one, but that current implementation of the idea amounts to little more than use of bonuses to increase the salaries of deserving executives. That end result is laudable, but use of the back door of performance bonuses is no way to achieve it.

The 1988 *Report of the President's Commission on Compensation of Career Federal Executives* (Cullen Commission) found that average SES real pay in 1987 was slightly below its 1979 value, that available data indicated SES compensation was up to 65 percent lower than compensation for similar jobs in the private sector, and that compression of pay levels within the SES was detrimental and had persisted over many years because of the pay cap. The Cullen Commission surveyed federal agencies with 86 percent of the total SES career population, and found that their two highest ranking concerns were difficulty in attracting high-quality candidates for SES vacancies and lack of a federal compensation package competitive with comparable academic or private-sector positions. The report recommended raising SES pay levels and relieving compression.

A 1987 study, *The Government's Managers: Report of the Twentieth Century Fund Task Force On The Senior Executive Service*, pointed out that centralized collection and analysis of data about the SES are not really adequate for evaluation of SES workforce trends. The Cullen Commission corroborated that observation. A complicating factor is the absence of an established frame of reference for evaluating adequacy of SES pay; both reports considered comparability with university or private sector counterparts, but did not propose it as the appropriate measure.

Problems

Two major problems afflict the SES. First, since the SES was formed in 1979, SES pay rates have been compressed because of the modest increases in Executive Levels pay rates. This problem continues today.

Second, the SES is experiencing undesirable turnover. Studies suggest morale problems that are related to, among other things, the inadequacy of various features of SES compensation.

The key problem with SES pay has been compression beneath depressed levels of federal executive pay. The compression problem cannot be addressed without raising Executive Level rates; this Task Force recommends that those rates be raised immediately.

Evaluation of adequacy of SES pay should be improved. This Task Force recommends that the Office of Personnel Management continuously monitor and analyze SES compensation, and provide the President with a biennial report on SES compensation practices. Following completion of the term of the Citizen's Advising Panel on Executive Pay, OPM should develop and establish a framework for evaluating adequacy of SES compensation, and for establishing appropriate pay level distinctions within the SES and among special occupations associated with these levels.

General Schedule

The federal government is losing its competitive position in the hiring of highly qualified men and women for its white-collar workforce, known as the General Schedule (GS). The government must regain that position, especially because the pool of people qualified for many high-skill jobs will be so heavily recruited by the private sector in coming years and because the pool itself is shrinking. If the government fails to regain its position in the open marketplace, it can look forward to inevitable declines in white-collar productivity and in the effectiveness and efficiency of delivery of services. The stakes in a high-quality white-collar workforce are extremely high. The government's GS workers form the bulk of administrative muscle in federal programs. These men and women operate the computers in the Internal Revenue Service, protect national parks and forests, conduct sting operations to uncover corruption and apprehend drug dealers, inspect meat and poultry, patrol the borders, perform research on disease and control epidemics, protect the civil rights of individuals, design communications equipment for the space shuttle, and conduct the tedious experiments in genetics and crop management that have made American agriculture the wonder of the world.

Increasingly, however, the federal government cannot compete with the private sector in attracting people who can take on these kinds of jobs. Many white-collar assignments in the federal government are highly demanding and can be entrusted only to trained and experienced people. When the government wants to audit the books of a large division of General Dynamics, whom should it send to do the job? A young man or woman fresh out of business or accounting school? (The Task Force heard one anecdote in which a government "expert" sent to inspect a toxic waste dump turned out to be 22 years old.)

General Schedule workers also include the thousands of valuable support personnel who operate the word processors, maintain filing systems, answer citizen and taxpayer requests for information and assistance, and otherwise keep the government functioning. Skill levels needed for these functions are rising steadily as office administration shifts rapidly from paper-based to electronic-based operations. Enlightened managers in private business, financial institutions, and the nonprofit sector are paying much attention to the quality of their support staffs, and the government should as well.

The answer to this troubling situation, the Task Force believes, is to improve the government's position as an attractive employer, through more realistic salary structures, a salary system based on local or regional comparability with the private sector, and other elements of compensation that will attract highly qualified workers.

Pay-Setting Process[55]

Workers in grades GS-1 through GS-15 are paid according to the type and level of work that they do, and are selected competitively. At least since 1923, the GS has provided for internal equity and cost control by applying uniform guidance for evaluating jobs and for computing individual pay rates. The system also provides for external equity with the labor market based on nationwide adjustments proposed by the President and accepted by the Congress; localization of that external equity with labor markets is not provided for, however.

The annual Professional, Administrative, Technical, and Clerical (PATC) Survey of private-sector rates matches types and levels of work that are similar in both the private and federal sectors. Calculations based on survey data compare average pay for types and levels of work that are similar in both the private and federal sectors, and establish the adjustment needed to make federal rates comparable with the private sector. The result is a federal salary structure that has one uniform pay range for each grade level nationwide.

Chart 4
Comparison of Selected Salaries by Geographic Area

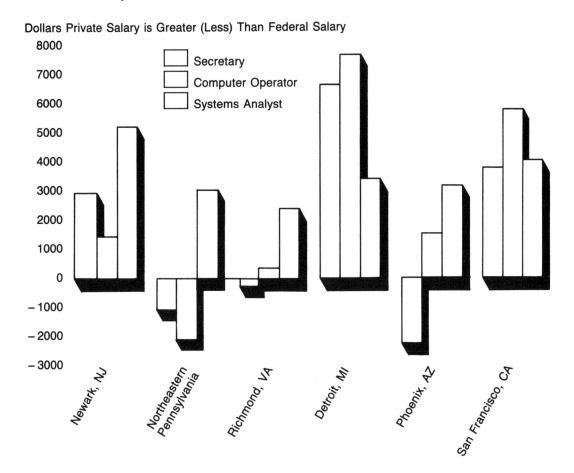

Dollars Private Salary is Greater (Less) Than Federal Salary

Source: Bureau of Labor Statistics

This approach sets federal pay based on an artificial national market. The private sector tends to survey rates paid by competing employers in a particular location or setting, and may assign a different salary rate range to the same level of job content in different locations or settings. Because federal salary grades for particular job content are the same nationwide while private-sector rates may not be, comparisons of private-sector with federal-sector rates place federal pay above private pay in some locations, and below it in some others. (See Chart 4)

Basic pay rates are one matter; raises are another. Federal employees receive salary raises through annual comparability increases that adjust pay to the external "labor market" and by "within-grade" or "step" increases that permit employees to advance through the rate range of their grade. Within-grade increases are 3 percent of the rate for the first step of each grade and go to employees whose performance is at least fully satisfactory; they are given annually to employees in the lowest third of the rate range, biennially in the middle third, and triennially in the top third of the rate range until the top of the rate range is reached.

Middle-management federal workers, project leaders, and most others at grade levels GS-13, 14, and 15 receive merit increases in lieu of annual step increases within the pay ranges for their grades. Employees covered by these provisions are called General Merit (GM).

Private-sector employees, on the other hand, progress on the basis of an annual merit increase. Large, private-sector firms typically budget for one annual merit increase to staff of 5 percent of payroll. Marginal workers receive 0 to 2 percent of pay, and the top-rated (about 20 percent) workers receive increases ranging up to 10 percent of pay.[56] The merit increase recognizes performance and indirectly accommodates advancement of the salary structure in the labor market and increases in the cost of living.

Trend Starts Down

For years following the Federal Pay Comparability Act of 1970, federal pay rates as measured by the annual nationwide PATC survey kept pace with private-sector pay rates for similar types and levels of work. In 1978, however, a trend of giving smaller increases than needed to maintain comparability began.

As pay rates drifted down, the federal government turned to expedients to make up for the pay gap,[57] including:

- Adjusting job classifications upward, that is, structuring work to produce more high-grade (higher paying) jobs;

- Paying special rates in areas able to demonstrate recruiting and retention problems, where affected federal agencies have existing budget money to cover the special rates (about 10 percent of all GS employees are covered so far);[58]

- Hiring at progressively lower levels of competitiveness;[59]

- Cutting back on employee time in training; and

- Relying on employees who are "locked in" to take up more and more of the slack.

Other measures taken have involved distorting administrative systems, rules, or laws by, misclassifying jobs,[60] for example, or deferring maintenance of and capital investment in technology needed to carry out pay-setting (deferring modernization of job classification standards and process).

*While expedients may be useful over a short time, long-term use erodes accountability, manage-
ment information, organization performance, perceived equity of pay, and employee confidence in
management.*

Federal Pay is Losing Ground

Because comparability increases have not kept up with the labor market, the federal
salary structure is currently 22 percent lower than the *average* rate that private-sector employers pay for similar types and levels of work. *The real value of GS pay rates has declined in
respect to increases in both the cost of living and private-sector pay rates. From 1970 to 1987, the consumer price index increased 183 percentage points, private-sector white collar pay increased 165, and
federal white-collar pay increased 124.*[61]
Although GS pay may be competitive in some labor markets, the annual announcement of the pay increase determined by the established pay-setting process, calling for a significantly larger increase than the increase actually given, has had a negative effect on the
morale of the workforce as a whole. There is growing evidence of a problem in recruiting
and retaining federal white-collar workers, and some evidence of a decline in quality of applicants, particularly in urban areas.[62]

Need for New Concept of Comparability

The federal government needs a new concept of comparable pay for GS employees
if it is going to participate in the labor market and attract and retain competent workers.
It also needs a new process. The Task Force has determined that the President and Congress
may have diminished the annual comparability adjustments needed to maintain the current
concept of nationwide comparability at least in part because of the way in which increases
are presented for approval, and because of problems with the credibility of the figures.
Each year, comparability increases are presented all at once—expressed as a single,
nationwide percentage figure, priced at billions of dollars (the 4.1 percent increase effective
in 1989 translates into more than $3 billion for both civilian and military), and made sub-
ject to a much-publicized process of approvals by the President and Congress. The media
frequently report the story as "billions for bureaucrats."
This manner of presentation treats pay out of the context of what is needed to get
work done, and invites trimming of pay increases in order to find money for federal programs. Each year, diminishing the increase needed to keep pace with comparability seems
to the President and Congress to be a small sacrifice to ask of each employee, especially
when the alternative may be cutting federal programs. Over the years, however, the amount
needed to bring the General Schedule alone up to comparability has reached more than
$12 billion, a large "sacrifice" to ask of federal employees even collectively.
The comparability figures of the annual PATC nationwide survey can surprise and
confuse the public because they apply nationwide the same rate for the same work. Bureau
of Labor Statistics Area Wage Surveys have shown that geographic wage differences can exceed 30 percent for similar jobs. Personally observed private-sector/federal-sector comparisons made by the public and other employees may place federal pay above private sector
pay for similar work in some locations, and below it in others. This difference damages the
credibility of the pay-setting process with employees and with the public.[63]
Another problem involves grouping different types of work into the same grade lev-

el, when private-sector pay for that work may be considerably above the rate range for that grade. When higher pay rates for auditors, for example, are included with the average for all occupations at that grade, they distort pay for the grade, but still may not pay enough to recruit and retain auditors.

Special rates provisions help alleviate this situation somewhat by permitting payment of higher rates in localities or for occupations with demonstrated recruitment and retention difficulties. The special rates feature, however, was designed for an environment of full-pay comparability with the private-sector average, and its rate enhancements are too limited to be of benefit in many situations.

Reforms are Needed

The current process for computing comparability on the basis of an annual nationwide survey needs to be refined to reflect private-sector practice more effectively: adjustments to GS rates to respond to labor market differences in locations or occupations should be made a normal part of pay-setting.

Presentation of annual adjustments to the GS for approval should be changed to continue meaningful control by Congress, but to allow specific adjustments to be made without Congressional approval.

Another federal pay system, the Federal Wage System, provides a useful precedent for this approach. The Task Force has produced a staff paper describing in greater detail a model of an improved GS pay-setting process and how it might work. The paper is a Commission source document and can be made available on request.

Federal Wage System

Federal blue-collar workers are paid under the Federal Wage System (FWS). The FWS workforce of about 400,000 employees includes government truck drivers, mechanics, and printers who help to keep the federal establishment going; about 85 percent of them work for the Department of Defense.

The FWS bases wages on comparable levels in the locality for the same skill. This system was introduced some years ago and has been refined to a considerable degree. The Task Force believes that the system works well, so well, in fact, that it can serve as a model for locality-based mechanisms for GS workers. Some further refinements in the FWS are desirable, but they are few and are modest compared with the improvements needed in other quarters of federal employment.

Prevailing Rate Approach

Workers in the FWS are paid on an hourly basis according to the type and level of work that they do. They compete for jobs on the basis of merit. Their pay is set on the basis of what employers in their wage area pay ("prevailing rate"), not on a uniform nationwide scale as is the case with the General Schedule. The FWS includes 135 wage areas.

Each wage area has an appointed local wage area committee that monitors prevailing private-sector rates and participates in survey design and implementation; at least one member of each committee is designated by an employee union. The OPM administers the program with assistance on survey matters from the Bureau of Labor Statistics.

Blue-collar jobs are evaluated on the basis of national job classification standards for

kind and level of work. Rates are adjusted after surveys and approvals at lead agency headquarters and at OPM. The Federal Prevailing Rate Advisory Committee (PRAC) recommends
to the Director of OPM needed changes to the system (for example, boundaries of wage areas).
Adjustments are not made on a fixed annual schedule. Beginning in 1989, the PRAC rather
than the Bureau of Labor Statistics will provide assistance with the survey.

Although the prevailing-rate wage mechanism works well for the FWS, some changes
would be useful. For example, survey adjustments for wage areas have been "capped" since
1978 and not allowed to exceed GS increases. Consequently, even while many areas still pay
the prevailing rate, there is an average of a 12 percent lag nationwide; and in Seattle, for
instance, the lag is 24 percent.[64] The lag has caused recruitment problems in key areas. Also,
some refinements in data collection and comparability of salary structure are still needed.

FWS Is A Useful Model

The FWS is the most successful of the pay-setting systems studied. It covers more than 400 occu-
pations in 135 wage areas, and could provide a model for improvements needed in the GS pay-setting
process.

The Task Force has one major exception to this conclusion: The capping of prevailing-
rate increases should be phased out. The Task Force would also note that minor improvements in the FWS process itself could be made.

RECOMMENDATIONS FOR ACTION

In summary, federal pay systems are flawed or in disarray. The four major pay systems studied had different histories, traditions and problems. Implementation of the recommendations would stop the erosion and turbulence that currently characterizes levels of federal pay and benefits, and lay the foundation needed to rebuild federal pay systems so that
they are reasonable and fair.

Top-level appointed and elected executives in all three branches of government since the
founding of the Republic have been paid salaries that are low when compared with their
private-sector counterparts. It has been expected that leaders will serve, accepting lower pay
in part in consideration of the gratifications of serving at these levels. However, the purchasing power of judges, Members of Congress, and top federal executives has decreased
by 35 percent from its already relatively lower level in 1969, retention is becoming a problem and recruitment risks becoming limited to the wealthy or the inexperienced. The Task
Force recommends immediate moves toward restoring lost purchasing power of executive
pay in all three branches as a preferred option, but offers an alternative in the event that
immediate increases for Congress are not feasible. The Task Force also recommends actions
necessary to address public concerns about and problems with Congressional pay-setting
from both an historic and a current perspective—most particularly the absence of an objective frame of reference for evaluating adequacy of Congressional pay.

Top-level career executive (Senior Executive Service) pay is compressed between pay of top
appointed and elected executives, who are always paid below the market, and pay of white-
collar (General Schedule) managers who are supposed to be paid "comparably" with the
labor market. The Task Force recommends that career executives' pay rates be increased
in concert with increases for top level executives.

Option A.
RECOMMENDATION 1

The 101st Congress should enact legislation to increase pay of Members, judges, and elected and appointed executive branch officials to half of the amount recommended by President Reagan, to increase pay again by the same amount effective in 1991, and to act promptly to terminate honoraria.

RECOMMENDATION 2

President Bush should issue an executive order to increase the Senior Executive Service (SES) pay rates to the amounts last recommended by President Reagan (except that the top rate would be adjusted to not exceed the salary of Members of Congress).

RECOMMENDATION 3

The 101st Congress should enact legislation to establish a bipartisan Temporary (3 years) Citizens Advisory Panel of 50 members that is broadly representative of the United States—geographically, economically, ethnically, and in gender; with members to be nominated by state Governors, and the members and chair to be selected by the President. Each Governor would be asked to designate at least three nominees in order to help the President balance representation. In view of public objection expressed about the current process for setting Congressional pay, and the lack of focus or dignity in discussions of the amount of Congressional pay, the Panel should be charged with and funded to:

• Develop an objective frame of reference for evaluating the adequacy of top executive pay that is widely accepted as appropriate and fair;

• Develop a process for measuring and implementing the levels implied by the frame of reference, and

• Develop and recommend legislation to establish the frame of reference and the process, and to adjust Congressional pay to the acceptable level.

RECOMMENDATION 4

President Bush should mandate arrangements to improve the SES pay-setting process including: charging the Office of Personnel Management with providing a biennial report to the President that evaluates SES compensation practices; and, following completion of the work of the Temporary Citizens Advisory Panel, with developing a framework for evaluating the adequacy of SES pay and for establishing appropriate pay-level distinctions within the SES and among special occupations associated with the SES or with supergrade positions (e.g., Administrative Law and Contract Law Judges).

If the Congress does not find this approach acceptable:

Option B.
RECOMMENDATION 1

The 101st Congress should pass legislation to immediately increase pay of Judges and elected and appointed executive branch officials 12½ percent, and to phase in equal increases over the next three years until the full amount of increases recommended by President Reagan has been reached.

RECOMMENDATION 2

President Bush should issue an Executive Order to provide a similar schedule of increases for the Senior Executive Service (SES), up to the amounts last recommended by President Reagan.

RECOMMENDATION 3-a

The 101st Congress should enact legislation to create a bipartisan Temporary (three-year) Citizens Advisory Panel that is broadly representative of the United States— geographically, economically, ethnically, and in gender, as described in Option A above, to develop an acceptable frame of reference and process for setting the pay of Congress, and to recommend levels of pay for Congress that are broadly accepted as appropriate and fair.

RECOMMENDATION 3-b

The Citizens Advisory Panel, as soon as possible after being established should consider and recommend to Congress some means for adjusting Congressional pay in the interim to prevent further erosion of pay until the frame of reference, process and level of pay established on the basis of Panel recommendations has been accomplished, also to facilitate prompt termination of honoraria. Some regular performance measure, e.g., the Employment Cost Index, might provide annual adjustments, and some special increases of pay might be considered as honoraria are phased out.

RECOMMENDATION 4

President Bush should act to improve the SES pay-setting process by requiring reports and guidelines be developed as described in Option A.

White-collar (General Schedule) workers' pay in 1989 is 22 percent behind the labor market. Although the established system for setting General Schedule pay was intended to provide for market comparability, the political will to resist short-term expedient cuts in the increases needed to maintain pay at market levels has not been strong enough. The pay-setting system itself is flawed by a requirement for uniform, nationwide rates of pay that do not represent the real labor market, which varies by geographic area and occupation.

RECOMMENDATION 5

The 101st Congress should enact, and President Bush should approve, legislation to change the process for making comparability adjustments to pay. The legislation should require:

• Comparability adjustments based on the relevant *local* labor market, rather than one, across-the-board, across-the-nation figure;

• A decentralized, coordinated system for pay-setting modeled on the system currently in effect for blue-collar wage-setting (the Federal Wage System), and taking into account lessons learned in the history of operation of that system;

• Recruitment and retention pay rates for use as exceptions that respond to the high-priced occupational groups that distort overall salary survey findings;

• Phased implementation over a period of years to accommodate fiscal restraints and to provide for orderly phasing out of expedients taken to counteract pay erosion; and

• Modernization of systems and methods used in pay-setting.

Blue-collar (Federal Wage System) workers' pay is determined by surveys of the labor market in the areas where they are employed; the Task Force found that this pay-setting system had worked well, in the main, until rates were "capped" by Congress and limited to increases for General Schedule workers.

RECOMMENDATION 6

President Bush and the 101st Congress should phase out the ceiling on market adjustments of blue-collar prevailing rates, and simultaneously direct the Federal Prevailing Rate Advisory Committee to explore any improvements needed to improve the credibility of the blue-collar (Federal Wage System) pay structure.

All Federal Pay Systems

RECOMMENDATION 7

President Bush should direct departments and agencies, in collaboration with the Office of Personnel Management, to sponsor small-scale research and demonstration projects directed toward developing a base of knowledge to inform policy decisions about the financial terms and conditions of federal employment. The projects should especially explore linking financial incentives to performance, measuring and comparing total compensation, and adapting to a rapidly changing and nontraditional work environment and labor force (for example, public-private partnerships and appropriate compensation for employed retirees). Demonstration projects that change basic terms and conditions of compensation should be undertaken however, only in areas where compensation is reasonably adequate.

RECOMMENDATION 8

President Bush and the 101st Congress should act to restore confidence of federal employees and of the American public in the fairness and effectiveness of the federal pay-setting process. They should, among other things, articulate and establish in law criteria for all normal federal pay-setting processes; the criteria might be that processes are:

• Easily communicated to the federal workforce and to the public, and understood to be fair, equitable, and efficient.

• Easily monitored by the President and Congress; and

• Adequate to meet the needs of the federal government in respect to recruitment and retention of qualified employees.

They should communicate what the pay-setting provisions are, how they work to provide reasonable pay, and how the provisions represent an efficient application of tax dollars.

RECOMMENDATION 9

President Bush and the 101st Congress should stabilize and carry out the terms and conditions of federal compensation and avoid expedient deviations that have characterized the past.

RECOMMENDATION 10

The President and Congress now and in the future should lead the American people in placing an appropriate value on the work of federal employees. Through leadership and personal example, they can direct the workforce toward maximizing the intrinsic rewards and satisfactions potentially available from working directly for the United States of America.

APPENDIX

Other Options Considered for the General Schedule

Cost-of-living Differentials[65]

Cost-of-living differentials might compensate for some of the large disparity in comparability of federal salaries among different geographic locations.

Cost-of-living differentials raise problems in many respects. Difficult and controversial choices must be made in the course of computing area-to-area cost-of-living differences; for example within each area, costs typically vary more by neighborhood than by area. In selecting neighborhoods within an area as a basis for computing the area cost of living, sen-

290/REBUILDING THE PUBLIC SERVICE

sitive issues must be considered in regard to the standard of living acceptable or desirable for public servants—issues such as the public's expectations and civil servant's freedom of choice. If the cost-of-living levels in too many neighborhoods are averaged together, the resulting cost-of-living figure will not be adequate for some groups of employees and may be above expectations for other groups in the same area. This over-averaging undermines the credibility of surveys.

The relationship of cost-of-living adjustments to pay for work performed can be unclear. Cost-of-living differentials are sometimes viewed, for example, as an entitlement.

Area-to-area cost-of-living differences may not be the same as area-to-area cost-of-labor differences. For example, the cost of clerical labor in New York City may not be the highest in the country, but the cost of living there is among the highest in the country. Tying increases in salaries to increases in cost of living is a form of indexing and is not viewed as a progressive business practice. It is not typically used in the private sector to make area-to-area distinctions except in compensation related to relocation.

Pay-banding[66]

Pay-banding in the federal government has come to mean reducing the number of grade levels of work and establishing an extended salary range for each grade level. An example of pay-banding would be the combining of grade levels GS-11 and GS-12, and merging of the 30 percent ranges of these two grade levels into one extended range of approximately 60 percent. The pay given individuals for different levels of work within the range is decided on the basis of individual performance, rather than in relation to the objective content of a level of work. Demonstration projects implementing pay-banding systems have been established in two Navy laboratories. Evaluation of the success of the demonstrations has not produced clear results, although anecdotal evidence has been positive in the main.

Private-sector application of pay-banding is largely limited to laboratories. Universities often use a pay-banding type of compensation system.

The literature supports the use of pay-banding only in situations where performance criteria are well established and accepted and consistently applied.

Performance appraisal has not been sufficiently successful to support expansion of pay-banding beyond its current applications in the private sector. Performance-appraisal systems tried throughout the federal sector have proven too weak to provide a basis for making financial distinctions among employees. This finding indicates that pay-banding, which requires performance-appraisal systems sufficient to support major distinctions in pay, would not be useful for all or most federal jobs.

Large private-sector companies and many states currently have more grade levels of work than does the federal General Schedule. Because pay-banding reduces the number of grade levels of work, it would further reduce the precision of compensation surveys, and could reduce the credibility of the surveys.

Agency-specific Systems

It has been suggested that each federal department and agency might be better off establishing its own salary structure and compensation practice. It is expected that agencies could use this flexibility to good advantage. For example, they could set their own priorities in regard to which occupations should receive the more competitive rates.

The private-sector model is useful. Centralized, aggregated systems and decentralized, disaggregated systems both exist in the private sector. The private sector tends to decentralize and disaggregate compensation systems when corporate entities do not compete for the same skills and are not parts of an integrated enterprize. Where there is a need for interchange of employees between entities, or when activities of entities are interrelated, the private-sector systems are centralized and aggregated[67].

The federal practice is somewhat similar to private-sector practice. There are several indications that changing to permit each agency its own unique systems would hinder, rather than improve, federal operations. With some exceptions (such as Customs Inspectors), the executive branch generally experiences considerable interchangeability of skills and personnel. This cross fertilization has been valued in the past as a means for sharing of ideas and experience among agencies, and as a means for making government responsive.

The agencies and departments of federal government are often charged with interrelated objectives. For example, drug enforcement involves the Drug Enforcement Administration, the Customs Service, the Coast Guard, and the Federal Bureau of Investigation, among others.

Past federal experience with agencies and departments creating their own compensation systems has not been positive. That experience includes the two periods of "lump sum" appropriation in the 1800s,[68] and the period prior to 1972 with the agency blue-collar wage system. The earlier federal experiences were characterized by pay scales below market rates, and were affected by inequities brought about by competition among federal agencies; particularly when the overall pay scales were inadequate. When they could not compete in the larger labor market, federal agencies competed with each other. Better funded agencies drained agencies less well funded, with no overall gain to the government or the taxpayer. These periods were characterized by distracting and somewhat disruptive employee protest of inequities.

Collective Bargaining

Collective bargaining is an expected feature of pay-setting for nonsupervisory and nonmanagerial workers in the more traditional sectors of American enterprise (for example, the automobile and steel industries). It is also a prevalent form of wage-setting in state and local governments.

Discussions about collective bargaining in the federal sector tend to focus on the pay-setting requirements that are unique to that sector, such as its sovereign status, the absence of external economic constraints, and national security requirements. These unique federal requirements suggest that federal experiences with collective bargaining would be a better indication of how collective bargaining might work in the federal service than would be the experiences of state governments or industry.

The largest current federal application of collective bargaining is in the U.S. Postal Service, with approximately 800,000 employees. Conditions in the Postal Service that are considered critical to collective bargaining capability[69] include:

• Together, the four major nonexempt employee unions represent about 90 percent of the workforce. The unions are the Mail Handlers Union, the American Postal Workers Union, the Letter Carriers Union, and the Rural Letter Carriers Union.

- Together, the unions negotiate a single national pay scale and benefits package for all the employees they represent. For example, all letter carriers in the same pay grade are paid the same throughout the country.

- Disputes about wage increases are resolved through binding arbitration.

- Management has clear authority to set the pay for positions, exempt and nonexempt, not otherwise covered by collective-bargaining agreements.

- Management has clear authority to consummate agreements with unions in full faith and confidence that its agreements will be executed. Management prepares and administers its own revenue and expense budget and financial plan. It does not require congressional or Office of Management and Budget approval of expenditures.

Postal Service pay scales compare much more favorably with consumer price index growth from the inception of collective bargaining in 1970 to 1987 (+ 270) than does private-sector white-collar pay (+ 165), or federal-sector blue-collar (+ 181) or federal-sector white-collar pay (+ 124).[70]

It is doubtful, however, that conditions considered important to collective bargaining in the Postal Service could be generalized to the rest of the executive branch.

Employee participation is essential to credibility of any pay-setting process. Even without collective bargaining, unions should be included in the process. Employee participation is key in developing pay for performance plans, particularly those currently viewed as most effective, such as group or unit performance awards.

ENDNOTES

1. This figure is based on unpublished data collected from the private sector during the nationwide, annual Professional, Administrative, Technical and Clerical (PATC) survey for calendar years 1987 and 1988, and on federal figures for average pay available through the OPM Central Personnel Data File. It was computed by comparing federal mean and median pay for occupations and grade levels covered with the wage distributions of private employees. Calculations made against occupational groupings reported in the Current Population Survey confirmed the results of PATC analysis.

2. For current purchasing power of salaries of Members of Congress (which are linked to federal executive salaries) see *Rate of Increase of Selected Public and Private Wages, Public Pensions, and Social Security Compared with Change in Consumer Price Index, 1969–1988*, (Washington: Congressional Research Service, #8-231 GOV), Mar. 22, 1988; for purchasing power as of 1986 and some private sector salaries, see Commission on Executive, Legislative, and Judicial Salaries, *Quality Leadership: Our Government's Most Precious Asset*, the Report of the Dec. 15, 1986; for an index of private sector-salaries, see the Wyatt Company (and American Management Association) *Executive Compensation Surveys*, Annual Series.

3. Testimony before the Commission on Executive, Legislative, and Judicial Salaries, Nov. 1988.

4. Hay Huggins Company and Hay Management Consultants, *Study of Total Compensation in the Federal, State, and Private Sectors,* (Washington: U.S. Government Printing Office, 1984). prepared for the Committee on Post Office and Civil Service, U.S. House of Representatives, as quoted in *The Report of The President's Commission on Compensation of Career Federal Executives,* Feb. 1988.

5. Advisory Committee On Federal Pay, *Report on the Fiscal Year 1989 Pay Adjustment Under the Federal Statutory Pay Systems,* Aug. 1988. A pay increase of 4.1 percent went into effect for the General Schedule and uniformed military workforce in January 1989, bringing the pay gap down from 26 percent to 22 percent.

6. *Ibid.*

7. Advisory Committee on Federal Pay, *Report on the Fiscal Year 1988 Pay Adjustment Under the Federal Statutory Pay Systems,* Aug. 19, 1987.

8. Pay Agent's estimate given in August 1988 of cost of closing the "gap" using the General Schedule pay-setting process now established, for the General Schedule, Foreign Service and Department of Medicine and Surgery was $13.0766 billion; the General Schedule alone was reported at $12.4 billion. These amounts would be reduced by the 4.1 percent increase given in Jan. 1989, and increased by wage advances in the private sector during 1989.

9. Testimony of Gregori Lebedev, Hay Group, and Edwin C. Hustead, Hay-Huggins, before the House Committee on Post Office and Civil Service on *Pay Comparability System and Related Matters,* (99th Cong., Second Sess.), 1986, p. 31–32.

10. New York Federal Executive Board, *New York's "Not So Quiet' Federal Employment Crisis,* a special study, Apr. 1988, and Newark Federal Executive Board, *The New Jersey Crisis: A Report on the Decline of Federal Service in New Jersey,* Aug. 1988.

11. *Ibid.* Unpublished studies of SAT scores of scientist and engineer recruits done by Department of Defense Manpower Data Center; Certified Public Accountant scores from unpublished studies of Internal Revenue Service (IRS) recruits done by the IRS; clerical test scores from published studies by New York and New Jersey Federal Executive Boards.

12. Hudson Institute, *Civil Service 2000,* (U.S. Office of Personnel Management, June 1988), 17–20.

13. Congressional Budget Office, *Federal Civilian Employment,* Dec. 1987, and U.S. Bureau of Labor Statistics Jan. 1986 data; for corroborating data see *Civil Service 2000,* 10–15.

14. Eugene M. McCarthy, *The Congress and the Civil Service: A History of Federal Compensation and Classification,* a source paper for the National Commission on the Public Service. This section rests on original research reported in that paper, unless otherwise noted.

15. *Ibid.*

16. *Civil Service 2000,* 17–18.

17. Sue Scheig, *Size and Composition of the General Schedule WorkForce,* a source paper prepared for the National Commission on the Public Service. Observations discussed were drawn from that analysis.

18. *Ibid.*

19. The Postal Service Act of 1970 separated the approximately 800,000 employees of the Postal Service from the General Schedule (now at approximately 1.4 million employees), and provided for pay-setting by means of collective bargaining. Pay increases for the Postal Service have been larger than for the General Schedule.

20. Eugene M. McCarthy; see also, Arnold J. Gerber, *Historical Background: Classification and Compensation in the Federal Service,* source paper for the National Commission on the Pub-

lic Service, 1987.

21. Op.cit., Advisory Committee On Federal Pay, *Report on the Fiscal Year 1989 Pay Adjustment Under the Federal Statutory Pay Systems.*

22. The government or nonprofit sector version of profit-sharing, in which savings realized by the workforce are shared with the workforce.

23. Wyatt Company, *Salary Management Practices in the Private Sector*, a survey conducted for the Advisory Committee on Federal Pay with the cooperation of the American Compensation Association, Sept. 1987, 27–29.

24. William W. Rambo, *Work and Organizational Behavior*, (New York: Harcourt, 1982), Chapter 7, "The Rewards of Work: Financial Incentives," 188–191.

25. Joseph Campbell, *Myths to Live By* (New York: Bantam Books, 1972).

26. William Rambo on Deci, 190.

27. Reported in "Rise and Shine," *The Wyatt Communicator*, second and third quarter 1988, 6.

28. Louis Harris, *Inside America*, (New York: Vintage Original, 1987): 53–55.

29. William W. Rambo, 207.

30. Elliot L. Richardson, "Civil Servants: Why Not the Best?" *Wall Street Journal* (Nov. 20, 1987).

31. *The Government Executive* survey, June 1988, discussed in National Academy of Public Administration report, *The Executive Presidency: Federal Management for the 1990s*, Sept. 1988, 20.

32. Commission On Executive, Legislative, and Judicial Salaries, *Quality Leadership: Our Government's Most Precious Asset*, Dec. 15, 1986; also transcribed testimony to the 1988 Commission.

33. Mark J. Wallace, Jr., and Charles H. Fay, *Compensation Theory and Practice*, 2nd Edition (Boston: PWS-KENT Publishing Company, 1988): 268.

34. *Ibid.*, 266.

35. Lebedev and Husted testimony, 31–32.

36. For more extensive descriptions of provisions of both plans, see *Federal Employees' Almanac, 1988* edited by Dawn Mace and Joseph Young, Federal Employee News Digest, Inc.; analysis of issues involved in designing and structuring the plans is presented in House of Representatives Post Office and Civil Service Committee documents, "Background of the Civil Service Retirement System," Committee Print 98–5, Apr. 20, 1983, starting on page 43, and "Designing Retirement Systems for Federal Workers Covered by Social Security," Committee Print 98–17, Dec. 1984.

37. Towers, Perrin, Forster, and Crosby, *Study of Federal Employee Health Benefits Program* for the Office of Personnel Management, 1988, 137.

38. Consultation with Charles H. Fay, Institute of Management and Labor Relations at Rutgers University; Howard Risher, Principal of the Wyatt Company; and federal government and federal employee union officials.

39. *Salary Management Practices in the Private Sector*, 14–19.

40. Katzell, Beinstock, and Foerstein, *A Guide to Worker Productivity Experiments in the United States, 1971–1975*, (New York: New York University Press, 1977).

41. Joseph Zeidner, ed., *Human Productivity Enhancement Series, Vol. II: Organizations, Personnel and Decision Making*, Chapter 2, by Pavett, Broedling and Huff, "Productivity in Organizations," (New York: Praeger, 1987).

42. Edward E. Lawler, III, *The Design of Effective Reward Systems*, a study completed under contract to the U.S. Navy, Apr. 1983.

43. *Wyatt Communicator*, 12.

44. Edward E. Lawler, III, 26.

45. Harvey Shaynes, "The Misapplication of Merit Pay in the Executive Branch," unpublished

paper, Dec. 1987; see also, General Accounting Office study, "Implementation of the Performance Management and Recognition System," Jan. 1987 (GGD 87–29).

46. Charles H. Levine and Rosslyn S. Kleeman, *The Quiet Crisis of the Civil Service: the Federal Personnel System at the Crossroads*, for the National Academy of Public Administration, Dec. 1986, 11.

47. *Government Executive* survey, June 1988.

48. Commission on Executive, Legislative, and Judicial Salaries, *Quality Leadership: Our Government's Most Important Asset*, Dec. 15, 1986.

49. Some localities or occupations or agencies are excepted temporarily from the General Schedule and paid "Special Rates" based on documented recruitment and retention problems where funds are available. More than 140,000 employees are paid Special Rates (September 1988 OPM figure).

50. Descriptions of pay changes, dates, and salary amounts in this section were drawn from Paul E. Dwyer and Frederick H. Pauls, *A Brief History of Congressional Pay Legislation*, a Congressional Research Service report for Congress, Aug. 12, 1987 (87–685 GOV); dates and salary amounts are listed chronologically in Paul Dwyer, *Salaries of Members of Congress: A Chronology of Votes and Other Actions*, CRS report for Congress, Dec. 16, 1987 (87–972 GOV).

51. Wyatt Company (and American Management Association) *Executive Compensation Surveys*, annual series.

52. For brief, definitive discussion of issues surrounding this process, see reports of the Commission on Executive, Legislative, and Judicial Salaries, 1984–1985, *The Quiet Crisis*, and Dec. 15, 1986, *Quality Leadership: Our Government's Most Precious Asset*.

53. Gregory D. Foster and Sharon Koval Snyder, *Public Attitudes Toward Government: Contradiction, Ambivalence, and the Dilemmas of Response*, a report prepared for the National Commission on the Public Service, Feb. 1988, 23.

54. *Report of The President's Commission on Compensation of Career Federal Executives*, Feb. 1988.

55. See Robert W. Hartman, *Pay and Pensions for Federal Workers*, (Washington: Brookings Institution, 1983) for an excellent discussion of the survey process and related issues, particularly Chapter 2, "Pay," 21–49; see also, Advisory Committee on Federal Pay, *A Decade of Federal White-Collar Pay Comparability, 1970–1980*, for a brief, excellent description of the Pay Comparability Act, problems it was intended to address, and evolution of its implementing mechanisms.

56. *Salary Management Practices in the Private Sector*, 14–19.

57. Based on testimony and correspondence to the Commission and as otherwise noted.

58. Office of Personnel Management figure quoted Sept. 1988.

59. New York and New Jersey FEB Studies; unpublished IRS studies of its accountants; and, to the extent that the "gap" is as wide as indicated by the PATC survey, it is *prima facie* evidence.

60. Office of Personnel Management, *A Report on Federal White Collar Position Classification Accuracy*, March 1983. The report was based on an audit of a stratified random cluster sample of positions in the 48 continental United States. At that time overall 14.3 percent of positions were found to be overgraded; positions in grades GS-1-11 were more likely to be overgraded than positions in GS-12-15; and those in the Washington, D.C. area were more likely to be overgraded than those in other areas.

61. *Op. cit., Report on the Fiscal Year 1988 Pay Adjustment Under the Federal Statutory Pay Systems*, Table 4.

62. *The Not So Quiet Crisis*, a special study by the New York Federal Executive Board, special study by the New Jersey Federal Executive Board, and unpublished Department of Defense studies of Scientist and Engineer recruits.

63. Supported by anecdotal data, bolstered by results of annual Bureau of Labor Statistics (BLS) Area Wage Surveys. While the BLS surveys focus on office clerical, skilled maintenance, and unskilled plant jobs, wide area-to-area differences characterize results (as much as 40 percent range in 1986, reported in BLS June 1987 Summary 87–3). Studies published in 1988 by the Federal Executive Boards of New York and New Jersey provide statistics that support the idea that area-to-area wage differences are significant for all occupations. Private consultations with compensation managers in major corporations supports the notion that, although salary "structures" for professionals and managers are nationwide, area adjustments to accommodate for area differences are normal. This notion is further borne out by consultation with private sector compensation consultants.

64. Figures provided upon request by the Prevailing Rate Advisory Committee and the Department of the Army, Sept. 1988.

65. Based on a special analysis prepared for the Commission by Howard Risher, Principle, the Wyatt Company, and consultation with experts in the Bureau of Labor Statistics.

66. This discussion is based on advance information from a forthcoming Congressional Research Service report on this subject.

67. Based on a summary of Conference Board discussions provided by Harvey Shaynes.

68. Eugene M. McCarthy: *The Congress and the Civil Service: A History of Federal Compensation and Classification.*

69. The analysis of conditions follows from a paper by Herb Block, former Director of Compensation, U.S. Postal Service, for the National Commission on the Public Service.

70. *Report on the Fiscal Year 1988 Pay Adjustment Under the Federal Statutory Pay Systems*, Table 4.

Biographies of Commission Members

Anne Armstrong is Chairman of the President's Foreign Intelligence Advisory Board. She has a long history of public service, including serving as Counsellor to Presidents Nixon and Ford, a member of Cabinet and Ambassador to Great Britain. She is a Director of General Motors, American Express, Boise Cascade, and Halliburton. She is also Chairman of the Board of the Center for Strategic and International Studies and a Regent of the Smithsonian. Ms. Armstrong graduated Phi Beta Kappa from Vassar College.

Derek Bok is President of Harvard University. He has also served as Dean and Professor of Law at Harvard Law School. He is currently a member, fellow, or on the Board of Directors of the Institute of Medicine, the American Philosophical Society, the American Academy of Arts and Sciences, the National Association of Independent Colleges and Universities, and the Business-Higher Education Forum Human Capital Task Force. Mr. Bok received an A.B. from Stanford University, a J.D. from Harvard Law School, and an A.M. in economics from George Washington University. He was also a Fulbright Scholar in the Institute of Political Science at the University of Paris.

John Brademas is President of New York University. He served as United States Representative in Congress from Indiana for 22 years. He serves on the Boards of Directors of Columbia Pictures Entertainment, Inc., Loews, Scholastic, Inc., Texaco, Inc., Alexander S. Onassis Public Benefit Foundation, Rockefeller Foundation, Wheatland Foundation, and the American Council for the Arts and the University of Notre Dame. He is Chairman of the New York State Council on Fiscal and Economic Priorities; member, Carnegie Commission on Science, Technology and Government; and member, the Consultant Panel of the Comptroller General of the United States. Dr. Brademas graduated with a B.A., *magna cum laude*, from Harvard University. He studied as a Rhodes Scholar at Oxford University, from which he received a Ph.D. in Social Studies in 1954.

James E. Burke has been Chairman of the Board and Chief Executive Officer of Johnson & Johnson since 1976. Active in civic affairs, Mr. Burke among other things is a member of the President's Commission on Executive Exchange, the Advisory Committee for Trade Negotiations, and the Board of Directors of the United Negro College Fund and Vice Chairman of the Corporate Fund of the John F. Kennedy Center for Performing Arts. He serves on the Boards of Directors of the International Business Machines Corporation and Prudential Insurance Company and is a member of the Planning and Policy Committees and Chairman of the Human Resource Task Force of the Business Roundtable. He is also a member of the Business Council. Mr. Burke graduated from Holy Cross College in 1947 and received an M.B.A. from Harvard Business School in 1949.

Yvonne Brathwaite Burke is a partner in the law firm of Jones, Day, Reavis & Pogue. She also currently serves as a member of the Board of Regents of the University of California, the Board of Trustees of the Amateur Athletic Foundation (formerly the Los Angeles Olympic Organizing Committee), the Board of Trustees for The Ford Foundation, and the Educational Testing Service. She was elected by the Board of Governors as Director of the Los Angeles Branch of the Federal Reserve Bank of San Francisco. She served six years as California Assemblywoman and six years in the U.S. House of Representatives. Mrs. Burke received a B.A. degree in political science from the University of California at Los Angeles and a J.D. degree from the University of Southern California School of Law.

Dr. Robert A. Charpie served as Chief Executive Officer of Cabot Corporation from 1969 to 1988. He is now a Special Partner of Ampersand Ventures. He serves on the Board of Directors of Champion International Corporations, Northwest Airlines, Inc., and Ashland Coal, Inc. He is a Trustee of Carnegie-Mellon University and a member of the Massachusetts Institute of Technology Corporation. He is a member of the National Academy of Engineering and a Fellow of the American Physical Society, the American Nuclear Society, and the American Academy of Arts and Sciences. He has served on the National Science Board, the Commerce Technical Advisory Board, and a variety of panels of the National Academy of Engineering and the National Research Council. Dr. Charpie, a graduate of Carnegie Institute of Technology, received a B.S. in 1948, an M.S. in 1949, and a D.Sc. in Theoretical Physics in 1950.

William T. Coleman, Jr., is senior partner in the law firm of O'Melveny & Meyers. He served as Secretary of the U.S. Department of Transportation in the Ford Administration and has served in advisory or consultant positions to five other Presidents. Mr. Coleman is a graduate of the University of Pennsylvania and the Harvard Law School.

Richard A. Debs is Chairman of R.A. Debs & Co., an advisory firm founded following his retirement as President of Morgan Stanley International Incorporated in 1987. He became President in 1976, after having been First Vice President and Chief Administrative Officer of the Federal Reserve Bank of New York, where he served for 16 years. He is a Director or Trustee of several corporate and non-profit boards. He received a B.A., *summa cum laude*, from Colgate, an M.A. and Ph.D. from Princeton, and an LL.B. from Harvard Law School and is a graduate of the A.M.P. program at the Harvard Business School.

James L. Ferguson is Chairman of the Executive Committee of General Foods Corporation. He has been Chairman and Chief Executive Officer of General Foods Corporation as well as past Chairman of Council for Aid to Education, a member of the Business Roundtable, the Business Council, International Councillor, Center for Strategic and International Studies and a member of the Council on Foreign Relations. Mr. Ferguson received an A.B. from Hamilton College and an M.B.A. from the Harvard Business School.

Gerald R. Ford served as President of the United States from 1974 to 1977. He is currently a member, Trustee, or on the Board of Directors of several national firms, associations, and councils. Prior to becoming President, he represented Michigan in the U.S. House of Representatives for 25 years. President Ford graduated from the University of Michigan and went on to Yale to earn a degree in law. He has received Honorary Doctor of Law Degrees from 27 colleges and universities.

Douglas A. Fraser is a Professor of Labor Studies at Wayne State University. He is a past President of the United Auto Workers. He served on many governmental commissions, including the Arms Control and Disarmament Advisory Committee from 1978–81.

John W. Gardner is involved in a five-year program of leadership studies under the sponsorship of Independent Sector. He served as Secretary of Health, Education, and Welfare from 1965 to 1968. He has been Chairman of the National Urban Coalition and he founded Common Cause in 1970. He is the author of *Self-Renewal* (Rev. Ed. 1981) and *Excellence* (Rev. Ed. 1984) and was the editor of President Kennedy's book, *To Turn the Tide*.

General Andrew J. Goodpaster, U.S. Army (Ret.) is a former NATO Supreme Commander in Europe and Superintendent of the U.S. Military Academy at West Point. He served as White House Staff Secretary under President Eisenhower and as Assistant to the Chairman of the Joint Chiefs of Staff, in addition to a wide range of military command and staff assignments. A 1939 graduate of West Point, he later received an M.A., an M.S.E. and a Ph.D. in International Relations from Princeton University.

Walter A. Haas, Jr., is Honorary Chairman of the Board of Levi Strauss & Co. He is a former member of the Executive Committee and past Regional Chairman for the National Alliance of Businessmen. He was a member of the Trilateral Commission and the Presidential Task Force on International Development. He co-chaired the Business Steering Committee for the National Cambodia Crisis Committee and was a member of the Citizens Commission on Private Philanthropy. Mr. Haas is a 1937 graduate of the University of California, Berkeley, and received an M.B.A. from Harvard Business School in 1939.

Rev. Theodore M. Hesburgh, C.S.C., is President Emeritus of the University of Notre Dame. He has served 6 Presidents on 12 Presidential Commissions and has been Chairman of the Commission on Civil Rights as well as the Select Commission for Immigration and Refugee Reform. President Carter named him Ambassador for the U.N. Conference on Science and Technology for Development. Father Hesburgh studied philosophy at the Gregorian University in Rome and theology there and at the Catholic University of America, where he received the doctor's degree in 1945.

Vernon E. Jordan, Jr. is a partner in the law firm of Akin, Gump, Strauss, Hauer and Feld. His public service career includes serving as President of the National Urban League, Inc., Executive Director of the United Negro College Fund, and Director of the Voter Education

Project, Southern Regional Council. Mr. Jordan received a B.A. degree from DePauw University and a J.D. from Howard University Law School, and was a Fellow in the Institute of Politics at the John F. Kennedy School of Government, Harvard University.

Donald Kennedy is President of Stanford University. He has been a senior consultant to the Office of Science and Technology Policy, Executive Office of the President, Commissioner of the United States Food and Drug Administration, and a founding director of Health Effects Institute and of Clean Sites, Inc. He is a member of the California Commission on Campaign Financing and the Carnegie Commission on Science, Technology and Government. Mr. Kennedy received a Ph.D in Biology from Harvard in 1956.

Leonard H. Marks is Chairman of the Executive Committee of the Foreign Policy Association. Mr. Marks was formerly Director of the USIA and has served as Ambassador to the International Telecommunications Union. He has also served as Chairman of the Reform Observation Panel for UNESCO and is currently Chairman of the Advisory Committee on International Communications and Information Policy at the Department of State. Mr. Marks received a B.A. and LL.B. from the University of Pittsburgh. He was a member of the faculty at the University of Pittsburgh Law School and at the National University Law School of Washington, D.C.

Charles McC. Mathias, Jr., is a partner in the international law firm of Jones, Day, Reavis & Pogue. He is also the Milton S. Eisenhower Distinguished Visiting Professor of Public Policy at Johns Hopkins University. He served as U.S. Senator from Maryland from 1969 to 1987. During his last Senate term, Sen. Mathias was Chairman of the International Economic Policy Subcommittee of the Senate Foreign Relations Committee, of the Rules and Administration Committee, and of the Subcommittee on Patents, Copyrights, and Trademarks of the Judiciary Committee. Sen. Mathias attended Yale University and received a B.A. degree from Haverford College and a law degree from the University of Maryland Law School.

Robert S. McNamara is the former Secretary of Defense (under Presidents Kennedy and Johnson) and the former President of the World Bank, having retired in June 1981. In addition, Mr. McNamara has served in the United States Army, taught as a Professor at Harvard University, and served as an executive, and ultimately President, of the Ford Motor Company. Mr. McNamara graduated from the University of California, where he was elected to Phi Beta Kappa, and received an M.B.A. degree from the Harvard Graduate School of Business Administration.

G. G. Michelson is Senior Vice President of External Affairs for R.H. Macy & Co., Inc. She served on the National Manpower Commission, New York Financial Control Board, and the Mayor's Committee on Appointments. Mrs. Michelson is a graduate of Pennsylvania State University and recipient of an LL.B. from Columbia Law School.

Walter F. Mondale is a partner at the law firm of Dorsey and Whitney in Minneapolis. He was the Democratic Nominee for President in 1984. He served as Vice President of the United States with President Carter from 1977 to 1981 and as Senator from Minnesota from 1964 to 1976. He chairs the National Democratic Institute. Mr. Mondale graduated from the University of Minnesota Law School in 1956.

Edmund Sixtus Muskie is a senior partner with Chadbourne & Parke, an international law firm. He served in the United States Senate for 22 years and as Secretary of State under President Carter. Prior to his election to the Senate he served as Governor of Maine. He is the Chairman of the Institute for the Study of Diplomacy at Georgetown University and Chairman of the Center for National Policy. He serves on the Board of Directors of the American Academy of Diplomacy and the Committee for a Responsible Federal Budget. Mr. Muskie graduated *cum laude* from Bates College, where he was a Phi Beta Kappa, and from the Cornell University Law School.

Nancy M. Neuman is President of the League of Women Voters. She was recently appointed to the Judicial Review and Inquiry Board of Pennsylvania. She has served on a number of Boards of Directors, including the Pennsylvania Housing Finance Agency, Federal Home Loan Bank of Pittsburgh, and Disciplinary Board of the Supreme Court of Pennsylvania. Ms. Neuman received a B.A. from Pomona College and an M.A. from the University of California at Berkeley.

Paul H. O'Neill is Chairman and Chief Executive Officer of the Aluminum Company of America, Pittsburgh. Mr. O'Neill's career includes 16 years of public service that began in 1961 with the Veterans Administration and concluded in 1977 at the Office of Management and Budget, where in 1974 he was appointed Deputy Director. He has spent the past 12 years in the private sector. He serves as a Director or Trustee of numerous organizations involved in governmental, educational, business, health care, and charitable affairs. Mr. O'Neill received a B.A. degree in economics from Fresno State College and a masters degree in public administration from Indiana University. He also participated in graduate studies at Claremont Graduate School and George Washington University.

Norman J. Ornstein is a Resident Scholar at the American Enterprise Institute for Public Policy Research; political contributor to the MacNeil/Lehrer NewsHour; and election analyst for CBS News. In addition, Dr. Ornstein is co-director, with Andrew Kohut, President of the Gallup Organization, of *The People, Press & Politics,* a Times-Mirror Company study of the American electorate. He is one of the founders of the National Commission on the Public Service and serves on its Board of Directors. Dr. Ornstein received a B.A., *magna cum laude,* from the University of Minnesota, and an M.A. and Ph.D. from the University of Michigan.

Elliot L. Richardson is a senior partner in the Washington office of Milbank, Tweed, Hadley & McCloy. His extensive public service career includes serving as Secretary of Commerce, Secretary of Defense, Secretary of Health, Education, and Welfare, and Attorney General of the United States. A founder and Director of the National Commission on the Public Service, his other activities include the United Nations Association of the USA, the Council on Ocean Law, the Citizens Network for Foreign Affairs, and the Inter-American Dialogue. Mr. Richardson received an A.B. from Harvard College and an LL.B. from Harvard Law School.

Charles S. Robb is a U.S. Senator from Virginia and served previously as Governor of Virginia. His extensive public service record includes chairing: the Southern Governors' Association, the Democratic Governors' Association, the Education Commission on the States, the Democratic Leadership Council, the Twentieth Century Fund's Task Force on the Senior Executive Service, and Jobs for America's Graduates, Inc.; co-chairing the Committee on Federalism and the National Purpose; and serving as President of the Council of State Governments. Senator Robb received a B.B.A. from the University of Wisconsin and a law degree from the University of Virginia.

Donald Rumsfeld is an Advisor to Mason Best Company, a merchant banking firm, and a Senior Advisor to William Blair & Co. He is a member of the Boards of Directors of Kellogg Co. and Sears, Roebuck & Co. A former four-term Congressman, he served as U.S. Ambassador to NATO, White House Chief of Staff, Secretary of Defense, and Presidential Envoy for the Middle East. He also served as Chief Executive Officer of G.D. Searle & Co. He currently is Chairman of the Eisenhower Exchange Program. Mr. Rumsfeld received a B.A. from Princeton University.

J. Robert Schaetzel is President of the American Council for Jean Monnet Studies, Inc. and of the Council on U.S. International Trade Policy, as well as being a writer and consultant. He was a career officer in the federal government. He has served in the Budget Bureau, the State Department, and as Ambassador to the European Community. Mr. Schaetzel received a B.A. and LL.B. from Pomona College and did graduate work at the University of Mexico and Harvard University.

Donna E. Shalala is the first woman to serve as Chancellor of the University of Wisconsin-Madison, the nation's fourth-largest university. In her first year at her post, she and colleagues have launched the Madison Plan, an ambitious agenda for strengthening opportunities for women and minorities at the university. She spent two years in the Peace Corps in Iran, teaching English and working in community development and, while a professor at Columbia University, served as Director and Treasurer of the Municipal Assistance Corporation for the City of New York. She is Vice President of the Children's Defense Fund and, as a trustee of the Committee for Economic Development, was Vice Chair of the committee that, in late 1987, issued the report *Children In Need: Investment Strategies for the Educationally Disadvantaged.* Dr. Shalala received a B.A. from Western College for Women and a Ph.D. from Syracuse University, and has been awarded more than a dozen honorary degrees.

Rocco C. Siciliano is retired Chairman and Chief Executive of Ticor, a national concern in the field of financial services. His government posts include Under Secretary, U.S. Department of Commerce, Assistant Secretary, U.S. Department of Labor, and Special Assistant to President Eisenhower for Personnel Management. He served on the Federal Pay Board, and also chaired the Committee for Economic Development's report, *Improving Management of the Public Workforce.* Mr. Siciliano is an honors graduate from the University of Utah and received a law degree from Georgetown University Law School.

Elmer B. Staats, retired, served more than 20 years in the Bureau of the Budget (now Office of Management and Budget), 11 of them as Deputy Director under Presidents Truman, Eisenhower, Kennedy, and Johnson. From 1953 to 1958, he served as Executive Officer of the Operations Coordinating Board of the National Security Council. He was appointed Comptroller General of the United States by President Johnson and completed his 15-year term in 1981. Since then he has served on a number of corporate boards and commissions as well as several non-profit organizations. He is a founding member of the National Academy of Public Administration and the American Society for Public Administration. Mr. Staats received a B.A. from McPherson College, an M.A. from the University of Kansas, and a Ph.D. in political science, economics, and business administration from the University of Minnesota.

Alexander B. Trowbridge, President, National Association of Manufacturers, served as Vice Chairman of Allied Chemical Corporation and as President of the Conference Board. In 1967 and 1968, Mr. Trowbridge was Secretary of Commerce, having served as Assistant Secretary of Commerce for Domestic and International Business from 1965 to 1967. He was appointed by President Reagan to the White House Task Force on Private Sector Initiatives, the National Commission on Social Security Reform in 1982–83, the Commission on Executive, Legislative and Judicial Salaries in 1985, and the President's Board of Advisors on Private Sector Initiatives in 1986. Mr. Trowbridge graduated *cum laude* from Princeton University's School of Public and International Affairs.

Carolyn Warner is a nationally recognized lecturer and educational leader. Her firm, Carolyn Warner and Associates, serves as consultant to numerous public and private partnerships. Warner was elected to three consecutive terms as Arizona State Superintendent of Public Instruction and was her party's nominee for Governor in 1986. She serves on the Executive Committee of the Arizona Economic Council, as well as a number of other corporate and public-service boards. Ms. Warner attended the University of Oklahoma and holds a degree in communications from Stephens College.

Paul A. Volcker is the Chairman of the National Commission on the Public Service. He is also the Chairman of James D. Wolfensohn, Inc., and the Frederick H. Schultz Professor of International Economic Policy at Princeton University. From 1979 to 1987, he was the Chairman of the Board of Governors of the Federal Reserve System. He has served five Presidents and his responsibilities have included Under Secretary of the Treasury for Monetary Affairs. Previous to becoming Chairman of the Federal Reserve, he served as President of the Federal Reserve Bank of New York. Mr. Volcker is associated as a Trustee, member of the Board of Directors, or on the Executive Committee of the Trilateral Commission, the Council on Foreign Relations, the Japan Society, the American Council on Germany, and the Mayo Foundation. He is Chairman of the Advisory Board of the Center of Strategic and International Studies. Mr. Volcker earned a B.A. at Princeton University, and an M.A. in political economy and government at the Harvard University Graduate School of Public Administration, and attended the London School of Economics as a postgraduate student.